SPITFIRE

Other books by John Nichol

NON-FICTION

Return Of The Dambusters
The Red Line
Arnhem
Medic
Home Run
Tail-End Charlies
The Last Escape

AUTOBIOGRAPHY

Tornado Down
Team Tornado

FICTION

Point of Impact
Vanishing Point
Exclusion Zone
Stinger
Decisive Measures

SPITFIRE

A Very British Love Story

JOHN NICHOL

SIMON &
SCHUSTER

London · New York · Sydney · Toronto · New Delhi

A CBS COMPANY

First published in Great Britain by Simon & Schuster UK Ltd, 2018
A CBS COMPANY

1 3 5 7 9 10 8 6 4 2

Simon & Schuster UK Ltd
1st Floor
222 Gray's Inn Road
London WC1X 8HB

www.simonandschuster.co.uk
www.simonandschuster.com.au
www.simonandschuster.co.in

Simon & Schuster Australia, Sydney
Simon & Schuster India, New Delhi

A CIP catalogue record for this book is available from the British Library

Hardback ISBN: 978-1-4711-5920-6
Trade Paperback ISBN: 978-1-4711-7688-3
eBook ISBN: 978-1-4711-5922-0

Typeset in the UK by M Rules
Printed and bound by CPI Group (UK) Ltd, Croydon, CR0 4YY

For Sophie

CONTENTS

This book is dedicated to all those
men and women who designed, built,
serviced, flew and loved the Spitfire

ACKNOWLEDGEMENTS

Many people willingly offered their valuable time and considerable expertise while I researched and wrote this book. Without their input, my task would have been almost impossible. I cannot mention every person individually but I am eternally grateful to you all. My sincere thanks also go to:

Andy Saunders, editor of *Britain at War* magazine, who provided much background information, many contacts and photos, and proofread the manuscript.

Author Mark Hillier, who arranged and hosted my visit, with Joe Roddis, to Goodwood, provided me with a number of other veterans' accounts and pictures, and proofread the manuscript.

Dave Homewood and Larry Hill from New Zealand spent many hours searching for stories and putting me in touch with veterans on the other side of the world.

Steve Brew, 41 Squadron historian and author, and Erik Mannings, 72 Squadron historian, helped with countless pictures and archive accounts.

Peter Devitt and Gordon Leith from the RAF Museum in Hendon searched the museum's archives and provided some valuable accounts and contacts.

Graham Cowie from 'Project Propeller', who organises reunions for WWII veterans, provided many introductions and invited me to attend his events and meet the veterans.

Harry Tangye spent many hours searching both the family and Imperial War Museum archives for his father's letters, diaries and pictures. Andy Perkins introduced me to Spitfire pilot Allan Scott, copied his memoirs and photographs and liaised over countless phone calls and meetings.

Squadron Leader Clive Rowley, a former Commanding Officer of the RAF Battle of Britain Memorial Flight, provided veterans' accounts and offered expert advice on the draft manuscript.

Air Marshal Cliff Spink and everyone at the Aircraft Restoration Company at Duxford for facilitating my visit with WWII veteran Brian Bird and fulfilling his dream of getting airborne again in a Spitfire. And Gerry Jones at the Boultbee Flight Academy, Goodwood, for organising a tour of a Spitfire.

Squadron Leader Andy Millikin, Commanding Officer of the Battle of Britain Memorial Flight, and Flight Lieutenant Tony Parkinson, BBMF Operations Officer, offered much appreciated knowledge on both the Spitfire and the wartime veterans who flew it.

Nigel Price, Group Editor at Key Publishing for giving me access to their incredible photograph archive.

The team at my publisher Simon & Schuster for their expertise, and to Thomas Harding for his time and assistance.

My friend and agent of twenty-five years, Mark Lucas, who has always been there to offer guidance, advice and support.

My wife Suzannah and daughter Sophie for their ever-present and hugely important love and support.

Finally, I am truly grateful to the countless veterans and their relatives who told me their Spitfire stories; this incredible group of men and women are ageing rapidly and, sadly, many of those I met and interviewed died as I was writing this book. I could use only a fraction of the extraordinary accounts I heard, but I hope I have done all of them justice.

* * *

Many other authors, historians, Spitfire enthusiasts and researchers offered invaluable information and contacts. It is impossible to name them all, but the following provided important leads, accounts, pictures or advice:

Bob Alford, Peter Arnold, Paul Beaver, John Bendixsen, Chris Bird, Scott Blyth, Jacque Boyd, Eugenie Brooks, Sarah Byrn Rickman, Chris Cannon, Max Collett, Jonny Cracknell, Ken Delve, Thomas Docherty, Gerard Drake-Feary, Jamie Dundas, Joe Farish, Jon Fellows, Norman Franks, W. Peter Fydenchuk, Ilya Grinberg, David Hamilton, Claire Hartley, Richard Henriquez, John Hurst, Jacky Hyams, Jamie Ivers, David Jones, Tinus Le Roux, Darren Lewington, Tom Lewis, David Lloyd, Group Captain Nicky Loveday, Angus Mansfield, Steve McLean, Tom Moulson, Tony Murray, Nick Oram, Alan Paisey, Mo Patz, Heather Peart, Andy Perkins, Barry Perks, Ian Phythian, Group Captain Ron Powell, Sarah Quill, Wilhelm Ratuszynski, Sarah Rickman, Daniel Scott-Davies, Ady Shaw, Geoff Simpson, Craig Sluman, Georgina Thynne, Group Captain Patrick Tootal, Kurt Turchan, Ron van de Put, Stephen Vizard, Keith Webb, Johnny Wheeler, Group Captain Tim Willbond, Geoff Zuber, Owen Zupp.

PROLOGUE

June 2016

Mornings were a struggle for Ken Farlow; the cocktail of drugs softened but did not kill his pain. But the Yorkshireman was made of sterner stuff and a night of broken sleep wasn't going to stop him relishing every last detail of the sight that he had travelled so far to enjoy. He had lost many good friends to a different battle many years before and he knew life was precious. The cancer had been discovered a few months earlier and he had given his daughter a wish list of things he wanted to achieve before the end. Crucially, he wanted to see his beloved Spitfire one last time.[1]

The young Ken Farlow had left his Yorkshire roots seventy-six years before, in 1940. Life had been tough in the poverty-riven mining community he'd been brought up in, where a mere apple core could be an item of trade. He had left school at fourteen because money was needed to sustain his family. Still, he'd enjoyed a loving upbringing with his parents and sister Renée, in a house that had been full of fun and laughter. Until 1939, when the world around him changed forever and it became time to grow up and to give something back. His beloved country and very way of life were under threat and it would be up to teenagers like Ken to fight back. He joined the Royal Air Force as a mechanic and served around the world for the entire war.

It had been both the best, and the worst of times. He had dodged

U-boats in the North Atlantic, and had lived in trenches in the baking heat of day then the freezing cold of the desert night. Fresh drinking water was rare because of the dead bodies, animal and human, the enemy dumped in the wells.

He had formed lifelong friendships forged in the teeth of conflict that only those who had been there could understand. He had been strafed by low-flying Messerschmitts and watched his mates die next to him, blown apart by Nazi bombs. He had seen their shattered bodies wrapped in canvas ready for burial. He had helped to rescue stricken aircrew from burning aircraft and recovered their mangled bodies from catastrophic crashes. Of course, like most of his generation, he didn't talk about the horrors he'd witnessed or how they had affected him. Not until the end was near. Then the long-buried memories would easily bring a tear to his tired eyes. But he had loved his time in the RAF, working on the likes of Wellington bombers and Hurricane fighters. And, of course, the Spitfire.

Now, at ninety-five, he was reliving the happier days of the war that had been the making of him. He sat silently in his wheelchair, gazing through the chain-link fence at Gloucester airport. Here she was, the iconic Spitfire, sunlight glinting on her long, slender nose and distinctive wings. He marvelled once more at the sleek, elemental beauty of the machine which, perhaps more than any other, had secured our enduring freedom.[2]

His ground-crew friends no longer swarmed around the airfield working on her, ensuring she was ready for battle. Her engine cowling was screwed shut, her cockpit canopy secured, her ammunition long ago removed and stowed elsewhere. Yet he could still hear the beat of her propeller blades, the throb of the Rolls-Royce Merlin engine at her formidable heart. Some described it as Wagnerian; others, a roar of defiance.

He could feel her accelerating giddily down the runway, lifting off, the gentle clunk of the wheels tucking themselves away beneath her leaf-shaped wings as she reached again for the sky. It didn't take long to fall in love with the Spitfire. Pilots, mechanics, land girls, civvies – they all fell under her spell. Ken certainly loved her. And once you were smitten, she never let you go. It was different for her enemies, of course. For them, she was beautiful but unobtainable. And deadly.

As Ken stared through the fence, he gave a sigh of happiness tinged with melancholy. It was also a sigh of satisfaction. He had done his bit; though he always denied he'd been a hero, he was an honourable man who'd led a good life and fought for his country.

Now he had fulfilled his final wish to see his beloved Spitfire one last time before he died. He was ninety-five; it wouldn't be long now. The tears and sadness turned to a smile.

Ken Farlow died in November 2016.

Ken Farlow

INTRODUCTION

What is it about the Spitfire? Why do people stop and gaze in awe at her sleek lines? Why do eyes turn skywards when the distinctive growl of her engine is heard? Why, over eighty years after she first flew, is the Spitfire regarded as the very symbol of Britishness; of tenacity, courage, dedication, faithfulness? Why is this *particular* aircraft loved so much?

To be honest, I hadn't thought about these questions until I had a chance meeting with an elderly Second World War Spitfire pilot. My background in the Royal Air Force had been on more modern aircraft: the Tornado Ground Attack and Air Defence jets. My post-RAF writing career had concentrated on the aircraft of Bomber Command during WWII – the legendary Lancasters and Halifaxes, and the staggering bravery of the men who flew them. The Spitfire had never been on my radar. This all changed during a visit to the Imperial War Museum at RAF Duxford, where my eyes were opened to the legendary status of an aircraft that had first flown in March 1936.

Children and adults alike were experiencing the awe of the mighty warplanes close up. The mammoth B52 bomber, the menacing outline of the Stealth bomber, the hedgehog spikes of machine guns covering the B17 Flying Fortress, the power of an F15 fighter and that great British warplane, the Vulcan bomber. The visitors to RAF Duxford were gripped by the aviation giants, eager to absorb as much detail as possible in the limited time they had available.

As I stood on the airfield, away from the public areas on grass that had once seen scores of Spitfires take to the skies during WWII, I watched in amazement as an astonishing phenomenon unfolded. For a moment, the cough and splutter of an engine went unnoticed – like the preliminary chords of an orchestra – and people carried on their conversations. Then the stammer turned into a roar as soothing as anything philharmonic. Chatter stopped, cameras pointed away from the domineering aircraft – even from the majestic Concorde – and towards the sound humming from the runway. People began to pour out of the exhibition halls and move, some even running, struggling to release cameras from their bags, towards the barriers at the edge of the airfield. The aircraft they sought out was small, one of the smallest on the Duxford track. They had recognised the distinctive notes of a Merlin engine and, yet to actually see the aircraft itself, they still knew what was to come. A few heads nodded in recognition; enthusiasts squinted, trying to identify the variant. Parents pointed and whispered to children: *Spitfire*.

The hum turned to the glorious crescendo of the Merlin engine at full power as the fighter streaked down the grass runway mere yards away from the admiring crowd. In seconds its curved, leaf-like wings were outlined above as the wheels tucked neatly into its lean belly. Cameras tracked skywards. It was a wonderful treat to see a Spitfire in flight. Something to show those back home. As the fighter disappeared into the Cambridgeshire sky, the visitors turned back to the other displays with broad grins, happy that they had seen a legend, no, *the* legend, take to the air. Some had frowned at a slight deviation in the Spitfire's usual elegance. A second canopy sat behind the first, for this was one of the few two-seat versions which carried passengers. What they couldn't have known – the reason I was there, the reason this book came about – was that a ninety-year-old veteran, who had not flown a Spitfire for nearly seventy years, sat in the rear cockpit, grinning like a schoolboy.

* * *

After a frantic last few months fighting the Germans in Italy, Brian Bird had eventually landed after his final operational flight and jumped down from his trusty Spitfire on 28 June 1945. It was a sad moment, turning his back on the finest aircraft he had ever flown. As the postwar years went by, the sound of a single-engine aircraft would often turn his head, just in case the distinctive shape of the 'Spit' could be seen overhead. But the years passed and memories of his beloved fighter seemed to fade.

Then one day in August 2014 the phone was brought to him at his British Legion veterans' home in East Sussex. Brian was recovering from a hip operation and was on enforced bed rest.[1]

The caller was a television producer I was working with on an aviation documentary. When she told me she'd found a Spitfire veteran we might be able to take airborne again I was delighted. Knowing little about the incredible history of the aircraft, I presumed it would be a veteran of the Battle of Britain. No, she told me, Brian had flown Spitfires in Italy during WWII in 1945. I was confused – Spitfires? In Italy? In 1945? I asked her to check the facts again. They were correct and it transpired I had much to learn about the war record of the Spitfire.

Initially, Brian was doubtful about the reality of taking his beloved aircraft into the skies again. He was ninety, relied on a wheelchair and walking frame, was on a cocktail of drugs and fitted with a catheter – how could he possibly fly again? But his wartime spirit shone through and a few days later his GP had passed him fit to fly once again. The no-nonsense matron from his care home, understandably concerned about the risks involved and the number of disclaimers that had to be signed, took it on herself to supervise the whole trip. So it was she who had the honour of wheeling Brian across the hallowed Duxford airfield to stare again at the fighter he had loved so much.

Scrambling out of his wheelchair, he grabbed his walking frame and slowly, painfully, made his way around his beloved Spitfire. The joy, and perhaps a little sadness, on Brian's face were clear to see, and those of us gathered around were more than aware of the significance of this reunion. We stood back and allowed them both some time together.

While ageing had marked Brian's face, the Spitfire's perfect lines remained smooth, polished and unchanged since their last meeting in 1945. He recorded his memories of the day in a letter he later sent to me; they are a testament to both him and the Spitfire. 'The sight of a Spitfire gracefully sitting there – no one will ever experience the degree of thrill I felt at that moment; it boosted my resolve to overcome my disabilities and get airborne.'

He marvelled at the deadly beauty of the aircraft he had loved and flown so many years before. He was twenty again, smitten by her curves and allure. She too was a veteran of WWII, having been delivered to the RAF in 1944 and flown on many operational sorties towards the end of the war.[2] Refurbished, maintained and loved by an endless array of engineers and enthusiasts, she had been converted into a two-seat aircraft and, at the tender age of seventy, was still flying regularly, now worth many millions of pounds. She is one of just a handful of WWII Spitfires still flying today.

Brian was a fount of information about the Spitfire; it was he who educated me about its incredible history and set me on a path to discover more about its fabled status. He was among some of the few surviving Spitfire pilots to have fought in the war, flying during the conflict's closing weeks, hitting the Germans on the ground as they retreated from Italy. He had flown a Mark IX; in his opinion, the greatest of all Spitfire models. It could fly high, fast and turn on a wingtip. The Mark IX had evolved from the original Spitfire Mark I which, at the outbreak of war, had seen off raiders over the North Sea, helped protect troops over Dunkirk then established itself as a national icon by fighting alongside the sturdy Hurricane to keep the Luftwaffe at bay during the Battle of Britain.

The aircraft was constantly improved, getting stronger, faster and more deadly as the war progressed. Every time the Germans fielded a competitor or developed a new threat, our scientists and engineers came up with a new mark to counter the Nazi challenge.

It evolved, grew and adapted during the war; the final version of the near-23,000 Spitfires, and its naval counterpart the Seafire, built would be the Seafire Mark 47.[3] The Spitfire had fired its first shots in combat in October 1939 when 603 Squadron brought down a German bomber off the Scottish coast near Edinburgh. The last time a Spitfire fired its guns in anger was during the Malayan conflict in 1951.

By the time Brian was flying a Spitfire, it had long evolved from its legendary status as a fighter in the skies during the Battle of Britain, and he was tasked to use it to strike targets on the ground, increasing the danger to pilots, bringing them well within reach of the Germans' anti-aircraft guns and small-arms fire. This fact had been made brutally clear to him in the briefing before his first operational flight in April 1945. Hence his nerves as he waited for the pre-dawn take-off, the Spitfire's engine ticking over.

'I can still remember the collywobbles I had at the end of the runway at 5am, and I tell my family this – sometimes, if you get nervous, just switch off; ignore the fears and you will become lethal. And that is exactly what happened when I got to the end of the runway, I turned the fear off and I became lethal.'

On the Duxford airfield Brian was surrounded by former and current RAF fliers, including myself, who had experienced similar dangers in later conflicts. Air Marshal Cliff Spink had volunteered to take Brian flying again. Cliff had been my Station Commander at RAF Coningsby and had commanded part of the Tornado Air Defence force during the first Gulf War in 1991 when I'd been shot down over Iraq. He had also amassed huge experience on countless aircraft – Spitfires, Hurricanes, Mustangs, Hunters, Lightnings, Phantoms and Tornados, to name but a few. A renowned aviator himself, he was keen to ask a WWII pilot what it had really been like to fly the Spitfire in action.

'Did you take any hits?' he asked.

'Oh yes, one or two during strafing runs,' Bird replied, shrugging his shoulders as if seeing bullet holes appearing in your aircraft was as common as ice on the car windscreen. 'But generally only in the wings,' he added, almost apologetically. Having taken a 'few hits' myself when I was shot down, I couldn't help laughing at his nonchalance. And, in a further nod towards just how much times had changed, he added, 'When you came down with holes in your wings, you just went off to breakfast and by the time you came back the mechanics had mended them and you were airborne again.' Sticky tape and filler; with such meagre items battles had been fought for our nation's survival.

It was time for the next part of Brian's adventure as Cliff asked him, 'How would you like to fly a Spitfire again?' His smile of unbridled delight said it all. 'I'd love to! Absolutely love to. Yes, yes I'm game. I have not lived this long not to have another go!' Despite his ailments Brian was already trying to clamber back on the wing as Matron carefully moved to restrain his enthusiasm.

Getting Brian, who could not stand unaided, into the cockpit was something of a battle itself but six of us managed to lift, carry and push him up some hastily found steps and lower him over the side of the fuselage and down into the cockpit where he was securely strapped in. Although Matron wisely wondered how he might get out in an emergency, Brian wasn't about to wait for the answer.

Brian knew the drill from here. As Cliff went through start-up checks, he secured the hood, then his eyes roved over the instrument panel and settled on the oil temperature gauge.

'Cliff,' he spoke into the microphone to the former senior RAF officer piloting the plane. 'Should it be showing fifty degrees before engine warm-up is complete?'

'Not bad for a ninety-year-old memory!' the retired air marshal replied as he opened up the throttle.

As the remarkable song of the Merlin engine, that spoke of power, endurance and consistency, filled the cockpit, Brian instinctively checked left and right, above and behind. He was back in April 1945, on that early morning in northern Italy, a line of Spitfires assembled in front of him, propellers blurring amid the collective sound of their Merlins' dominant roar.

'I had two 250lb bombs under me and guns full of ammunition. At the age of nineteen I was flushed with nerves as I sat at the end of the runway awaiting instruction to take off.'

It was Brian's first operation against an enemy who had developed a canny skill in using anti-aircraft fire to bring down ground-attacking Spitfires. He looked down the dusty runway and up to the brightening sky. He was struck by the sudden anxiety of going into the unknown, where the law was kill or be killed. His grip tightened on the stick. *Bloody collywobbles.* He opened the throttle and he felt his nerves calm as the plane gracefully lifted into the air. His instructor's words came back to him: become absolutely lethal.

'Immediately I was airborne those nerves had evaporated, never to return. Thus it was no surprise to me at Duxford that, once the Spit was in the air, I felt no nervous emotion at all.'

He felt a bump as Cliff let the Spitfire rise from the grass runway and into the friendly skies above Cambridgeshire. Seventy years on, the fighter was still as doughty and reliable as it had been during the war. For twenty glorious minutes the present became the past as Brian swooped and roared around the airfield. The aching bones, the painful hips, the failing body were all forgotten. He had waited for this moment since 1945. Sergeant Brian Bird, Spitfire pilot, was back.

For those of us on the ground it was a magical experience; we had managed to give something back, a tiny reminder of a glorious past, to a man who had given so much to his country. As time went on we began to search the skies in readiness for Brian and Cliff to appear. Matron, who had gone to enjoy a well-earned cup of tea, returned and asked, 'Where's Brian now?' As the words left her lips, we all ducked as the Spitfire roared over our heads at around 50ft, waggling its wings in salute. I pointed to the sky at the retreating shape of a Spitfire: 'He's up there!'

As the Spitfire taxied back towards us, Brian pushed back the hood and undid his harness, just as he had done during his wartime sorties. His enthusiasm was contagious. 'It's a dream come true! It brought back so many memories. It was great, terrific. Really terrific! Everything came back to me!'

'Do you think you could take her up on your own?' I asked. There was no hesitation as Brian replied: 'Yes, yes.' And I believed him. His face suddenly lit up, perhaps thinking it wasn't in jest. 'Do you want me to do it now?'

His hands hovered over the throttle as he glanced towards Matron, who gently shook her head. There were a few more chuckles.

The Spitfire had acted like an elixir on Brian, as if the short flight had restored something from his youth, not quite a spring in his step, but certainly a revitalisation of the spirits. The freedom and delight of flying a Spitfire had never left him, and to step back into the aircraft in his nineties was a tonic he thought he'd never take again. I could see a mental and physical change in his demeanour; it had been a privilege to see how one of the last of those who had flown the Spitfire in its fierce wartime role could now revel in the pleasure it gave in peace.

Sadly, it was to be Brian's final flight, as he died just a few months afterwards. In his last letter to me he wrote: 'After a gap of seventy years since my last operational sortie in a Spitfire, the opportunity to sit in a Spit cockpit and to get airborne was an unimaginable thrill and made me wish for a return to my youth!'

In a way, though, he truly had recaptured a sense of his youth on that last flight.

So here was the very essence, the magic of this aircraft; the Spitfire was more than a plane; it was an aircraft like no other, it was an icon loved, worshipped by all those – apart from her enemies – whose lives she touched.

I was determined to find out more about her and subsequently discovered many hundreds of books that already recount the technical development and wartime record of the Spitfire. This is not one of those books. I wanted more; I wanted to hear that 'human' story of the Spitfire, the story of the men – and women – who flew, serviced and built her. People like Brian Bird and Ken

Farlow – why were they so desperate to have one last glimpse, one final flight in their beloved Spitfire, before they died? I wanted to understand the personal story of the Spitfire and why those connected with her seemed to fall in love with this iconic lady of the skies . . .

John Nichol, April 2018

CHAPTER ONE

BIRTH OF A FIGHTER

SPRING 1932

Half-a-crown was all eleven-year-old Allan Scott needed for the ten-minute flight circling above Southport's landmarks with the flying circus which had come to town. It was 1932 and many people were still wary of entering the strange machines that left the safety of the ground, with a mere engine to keep them aloft. It was less than thirty years since Orville and Wilbur Wright had tossed a coin to see who would be first to try out their new invention: the *Wright Flyer*, a skeletal flying machine constructed out of wood, string and muslin. That very first, twelve-second, 120ft flight over the sands of Kill Devil Hills, Kitty Hawk in North Carolina changed the world forever and gave mankind a tool that would revolutionise both peace and warfare.

The science of flight was still in its relative infancy as Allan headed alone to the Fox Moth biplane. He was gripped by the excitement of taking to the air. 'I could not believe that it was me, that it was really *me* following the attendant towards the Moth. My heart thumped all the way.' Allan was helped up the ladder into the small passenger cabin, similar to a train carriage with bench seats facing each other. He sat facing forwards, glancing out of the window at Southport's flat, sandy beach, anxiously anticipating the moment of take-off. 'Hello, this is the pilot.' A voice called from the cockpit above him. 'We're just about to take off.' The aircraft rolled forwards, moving faster and faster across the ground. 'I found myself staring at the sand whizzing by in a long strip at what seemed like a dizzying speed until it came to that incredible, magical feeling of lift. We were in the air, we were *flying*.'[1]

As the left wing dipped and they headed out to sea at 100mph, Allan marvelled at the tiny dots of cars and people disappearing below. 'It was the most wonderful, most exciting sight to behold, but I had only a few moments to take it in before the sand was whizzing by again and I felt a bump.' They had landed.

'The whole trip took ten minutes but what could I expect for only half-a-crown [12½ pence]? As far as I was concerned, it was worth every single penny. The seeds of my future were sown the minute I had stepped into that Moth.'

A few years later, as the storm clouds of war spread over Europe, Allan found himself drawing precise lines and reading mighty tomes as an architect's apprentice. He was bored and his mind drifted both to flying and to duty. His thoughts went back to the empty seats in the Fox Moth and to his twin sister, Lena. They had both been caught by the tail end of the influenza epidemic that had followed the Great War. Allan, being the stronger of the two, had survived. Lena, aged four, had not. Somewhere in his heart he felt that she had died so that he could live. He would make something of himself, something of which she would have been proud.

He now knew precisely what that was.

He was going to be a fighter pilot.

* * *

It was perfect timing. Flying was no longer the exclusive preserve of the rich or the military. The sleek, streamlined aircraft competing in the Schneider Trophy heralded a new era of speed that seemed fully in tune with the decade of Art Deco, Hemingway, champagne

Jeffrey Quill in prototype K5054, 18 June 1936, before the first demonstration to the press

and jazz. Crowds of 200,000 or more would clamour to watch the race for the world's fastest seaplane.

The trophy had largely been won by Italians and Americans, until a Staffordshire-born engineer stepped into the arena. Hard-working, plain-speaking and brilliant, R. J. Mitchell built the swift and elegant S5 and S6 racing seaplanes which from 1927 won three Schneider competitions in a row, thus securing the trophy permanently for Britain. The S6B was the first to break the 400mph barrier, setting a new world record in 1931.

Other nations took note. None more so than the Germans. They were beginning to take their flying – and everything else – very seriously indeed.

April 1935

Two years into power, Adolf Hitler had openly established his 'air weapon', in direct violation of the Treaty of Versailles. The time of secretly training pilots in glider clubs or the Soviet Union was over. The Luftwaffe began its first fighter pilot training sorties in February 1935.

Winston Churchill warned of Nazi belligerence. 'A terrible process is astir,' he wrote in the *Daily Mail*. 'Germany is arming.' But he was virtually a lone voice. Britain and the rest of the world still chose to avoid confrontation.

The Nazi threat was seen first-hand by RAF pilot Jeffrey Quill when he flew a grand tour of Europe soon after. Quill was a cool, astute observer of people and places, and not readily fazed by confrontation.

His skills had been quickly recognised by the RAF. He had first flown solo after just five hours and twenty minutes of instruction, when the average was over ten hours. He achieved an 'exceptional' rating out of the four possible categories for trainee pilots. And he took one particular piece of wisdom from his instructor very much to heart: 'Aeroplanes are not inherently dangerous, but they are very unforgiving.'

His fortitude had been further examined in the hazardous Meteorological Flight. Taking temperature and humidity readings at 20,000ft in an open-cockpit Siskin biplane was a challenging occupation. Foul weather sometimes made it impossible. But for every calendar day of 1935, bar Sundays, Quill and a fellow pilot flew through storms, hail, fog and blizzards, earning the Air Force Cross, awarded for valour while flying not on combat operations.

He was a good man to examine the calibre of the new enemy at close quarters. On his flying tour of Germany, Quill landed first in Saarbrücken, which Hitler had recently managed to get returned to German sovereignty by plebiscite. No 'booted and strutting Nazis' appeared at the small airfield before Quill refuelled and continued to Munich.[2]

A visit to a *bierkeller* further calmed his fears. The mood was jovial and boisterous. Buxom waitresses carried five massive steins of Bavarian beer in each hand, and slender women polished them off as if they were cups of tea.

Then he began to notice aerodromes packed with paramilitary aircraft and flying clubs full of purposeful-looking air and ground crew. The atmosphere of vigour and menace made Quill uneasy.

There was only one conclusion: *Britain was being left behind in a race that had no rules.*

The RAF had been basking in the glow of bygone days. Small, agile biplanes with a couple of Vickers machine guns were the norm. But some members of Britain's defence establishment had begun to share Churchill and Quill's concern. As the Luftwaffe sprang into life, the Air Ministry issued Specification F10/35 in the search for a new fighter.[3]

The RAF had woken up to the demands of modern air warfare. They needed a single-engine, single-seat fighter armed with eight machine guns that could produce the greatest destructive power possible in one quick attack.

Building on his success in the Schneider Trophy, R. J. Mitchell seized upon F10/35 and assembled a team at Supermarine's headquarters at Eastleigh, Hampshire, to come up with the best possible design for a fast, manoeuvrable aircraft. Its planform wing, a leaf-like elliptic or oval shape, was close to perfection aerodynamically, and allowed the thinnest possible structure to accommodate four machine guns.

Using the technical skills evolved from the successful seaplane designs, the prototype took shape in an erecting shop at Supermarine's aircraft manufacturing plant in Southampton. Hitches were overcome. Rolls-Royce's magnificent Merlin engine had originally been developed for the Wellington bomber, not for a high-altitude fighter, and lost efficiency the higher it went. Rolls-Royce's engineers resolved this by using a coolant of pure ethylene glycol, which boiled at 160°C at sea level and 120°C at 27,000ft.[4] Mitchell had more difficulty with the aircraft's name. He had hoped to call it the Shrew. Sir Robert McLean, chairman of Vickers engineering company, who now owned Supermarine, wanted it named after his daughter Ann, 'a little spitfire'. On such a minor whim, a legend was born.[5]

Willy Messerschmitt did not need a name for his deadly efficient fighter. A number was enough. Three years younger than Mitchell, aged thirty-six, the brilliant German aircraft engineer designed the prototype of the 109 that took to the air in May 1935 and moved swiftly towards mass production.

Spitfire prototype K5054 made an eight-minute maiden flight over Southampton ten months later.

It had cost £20,765 to develop, looked good and flew well. Everyone at Vickers Supermarine was delighted.

But it was not headline news.

The very next day, 7 March 1936, Hitler's Stormtroopers marched into the Rhineland demilitarised zone.

Summer 1936

There was a certain élan about the members of White's Club, the exclusive gentlemen's club in Mayfair, London. Blue stock and Tory, many had time on their hands, and most had a sense of duty and a nose for danger. Some were restless, some eccentric. And some had the prescience to realise that defending the skies would be vital in any future conflict.

Lord Edward Grosvenor, son of the Duke of Westminster, an habitué of White's and a former naval flier, had set up 601 as one of the five new squadrons in the Royal Auxiliary Air Force. The Auxiliaries were formed as an elite corps of civilian pilots who would fly for the RAF in time of war. The initial batch of pilots for 601 was almost exclusively recruited from the distinguished drinking clientele of White's. It seemed only sensible that their summer camps should be held at Lympne airport in Kent, close to Goldenhurst Farm, owned by Noël Coward, and Port Lympne, seaside home of Sir Philip Sassoon, the urbane politician and art collector.[6]

It was to prove a most satisfactory way of balancing the intensity of flight with the more indulgent demands of their lifestyle. And there was much that was indulgent about Port Lympne. Gilt-edged chairs with jade-green cushions stood in the dining room; nude statues disported themselves among the greenery of the splendid landscaped garden. Its guest list was as notable as the roses and juniper trees: Hollywood's Charlie Chaplin, Winston Churchill, the backbench MP, and T. E. Lawrence, of Arabia fame.

The men of 601 Squadron were welcome any time. Port Lympne was their unofficial mess, where officers came to swim, sunbathe and play tennis.

Wealth counted for something in Lord Grosvenor's selection criteria, but not everything. One recruit who turned up for interview wearing a shiny suit and scuffed shoes refused to accept his rejection and soon embraced the Auxiliary ethos: 'Be a good pilot and a good comrade, but don't take anything other than flying too seriously.'[7]

* * *

Jeffrey Quill certainly took flying seriously. Despite some misgivings, Quill had resigned his RAF commission and joined Vickers as Assistant to the Chief Test Pilot.

When he saw the Supermarine fighter take to the air, he knew he had made the right choice. Three weeks after the maiden test flight he climbed into the Spitfire cockpit for the first time.

He was immediately struck by 'a very long nose' that completely blocked the forward view. Zigzagging to ensure all was clear ahead, he opened the throttle for take-off. The acceleration was 'sluggish'. Strangely, he needed to apply full right rudder to maintain a straight line.

When the wheels of the Spitfire finally left the ground Quill was immediately impressed. It was in a class of its own.

'It began to slip along as if on skates with the speed mounting steadily. An immediate impression of effortless performance was accentuated by the relatively low propeller RPM at that low altitude. The aeroplane just seemed to chunter along at a very much higher cruising speed than I have ever experienced before, with the engine turning over very easily. In this respect it was somewhat reminiscent of my old Bentley cruising in top gear. I climbed up to a few thousand feet and carried out some steep turns and gentle rolls. The aeroplane was light and lively, but with a tendency to shear about a bit directionally. I put it into a gentle dive and it accelerated with effortless ease; then it was time to rejoin the circuit for landing . . . As I chopped the throttle on passing over the boundary hedge, the deceleration was hardly discernible and the aeroplane showed no desire to touch down – it evidently enjoyed flying. I noticed how the stick hardly moved during the flare-out for landing, and in fact the aircraft seemed almost to land itself. "Here," I thought to myself, "is a real lady."'[8]

Despite its smoothness the plane was struggling to find the speed required of a true fighter. Quill recorded a disappointing 335mph on his first outing, in the same league as the Hawker Hurricane, the other new single-seat monoplane fighter. There would be no room for two fighters of the same ilk. And no production order.

The Spitfire's two-bladed propeller was taken off and worked on by Mitchell's team of engineers to make it produce more speed by refining the tips, making them more aerodynamic. It was also given an ultra-smooth paint finish. 'I think we have something here,' Quill said on landing in May 1936. Its top speed was now 348mph – close enough to Mitchell's 350mph objective for it to be sent to the RAF for official trials just three months after its maiden flight.

On 26 May 1936, Humphrey Edwardes-Jones, commander of A Flight at the RAF testing airfield in Martlesham, became the first air force pilot to fly the Spitfire.

On landing he had been instructed to immediately call the Air Ministry.

'I don't want to know everything and obviously you can't tell me,' the Air Ministry man said. 'All I want to know now is whether you think the young pilot officers and others we are getting in the Air Force will be able to cope with such an advanced aircraft?'[9]

His answer was affirmative. Edwardes-Jones shared Quill's sentiments.

'The aeroplane is simple and easy to fly and has no vices,' the official report said. 'The controls are well harmonised and appear to give an excellent compromise between manoeuvrability and steadiness for shooting. Take-off and landing are straight-forward and easy.'

The Ministry immediately put in an order for 310 of them. On the same day, 6 June 1936, it signed a contract for 600 Hurricanes. Finally, the RAF would have a force of modern fighters.

* * *

The Germans flew the V1 prototype Me109 proudly over the audience for the Berlin Olympics in August 1936.[10]

Willy Messerschmitt had focused on combining the most powerful engine with the lightest possible body. He built an advanced, all-metal airframe with closed canopy and retractable landing gear. German test pilots were impressed with its speed and agility.

When it went up against the Luftwaffe's He51 biplane in a mock dogfight in front of the *Reichsminister* of Aviation, Air Marshal Hermann Goering, he too was impressed. With news of the major Spitfire and Hurricane commitment, Goering ordered it into production at the Regensburg factory in Bavaria in November 1936.

It was also going to have one significant advantage over its British rivals. The 109 was going to war. By February 1937 the first models were delivered to the front line in Spain to help prop up Franco's Nationalist government.

As the Germans trialled their aircraft in combat, the British were using dried split peas to improve performance.

The prototype Spitfire, serial number K5054, had employed flush riveting to create a smooth, aerodynamic surface. Cheaper dome-headed rivets would be required for mass production. Supermarine glued hundreds of split peas to the flush rivets in various key locations and then removed them progressively, in order to identify the most effective balance of cost and performance.

The Spitfire's pilots quickly discovered that its slender wings produced turns so tight that the resulting G-force induced blackouts. The classic elliptical wings also allowed for an excellent climb rate and lower stall speed. More importantly, and unlike the Me109, the elliptical wings also produced an alarming wobble if a turn was about to lead to a stall, giving the pilot a chance to pull out. Being able to out-turn an opponent in a dogfight and pre-warning of a stall could prove decisive in the fast-evolving world of aerial combat.

New exhaust pipes boosted the top speed to 362mph. Engine heat was diverted to the wings to prevent the eight machine guns freezing at high altitude.

The first Spitfire Mark I was soon ready to take to the sky. Sadly, it would not be witnessed by its creator. R. J. Mitchell finally succumbed to cancer aged forty-two in June 1937. 'His work,' wrote one admirer 'is his memorial.'[11]

Seeing the Spitfire in the skies gave some succour to a British public worried by an increasingly bellicose Germany. Jimmy Taylor, a schoolboy at Eton, the renowned English public school, was on manoeuvres with the Officer Training Corps when one streaked low over Aldershot's bracken. It was a wonderful moment for the fifteen-year-old aeroplane enthusiast who always had a camera to hand. The sight encouraged his belief that he might one day be alone with his thoughts in a flying machine that responded instantly to his every wish.

His father, the Reverend Harold Taylor, had administered to the dying and led the burial service far too often as a chaplain in the First World War. Such conflict, he concluded, was obscene. So he had taken his son to Portsmouth a few years earlier to see first-hand what life was like aboard a submarine.

The exercise worked. Much to his delight, when young Jimmy clambered out of the cramped, oily and nausea-inducing vessel, he had vowed never to join the navy.

He would join the RAF instead.[12]

* * *

Jimmy Taylor had seen just a single Spitfire. Delivery dates for the batch of 310 were badly adrift. A desire to rapidly rearm was one thing; the practicalities were altogether different. British industry simply wasn't equipped to deal with the demands that it now faced. Large-scale, specialised expansion with skilled labour could not happen overnight. Supermarine had to subcontract the work, which led to further delays. Delivery of its wings was held up for months. Manufacturing fell at least six months behind schedule.[13]

The Southampton plant managed to roll out its first production Spitfire in May 1938. At the same time Me109s were coming off the Bavaria assembly lines in their hundreds and the Luftwaffe had 20,000 airmen with operational experience from the Spanish Civil War. In just five years it had become the best-equipped, most technologically advanced and battle-hardened air force in the world.

Many hoped that it would not be put to further use. Foremost among them was Prime Minister Neville Chamberlain, who flew to Munich in September that year to head off Hitler's threat to seize the Sudetenland. A chunk of Czechoslovakia was the price for appeasement. Chamberlain returned to Heston airport, waving his piece of paper and declaring 'peace for our time'. Then his car got stuck in the mud.

Jimmy Taylor was on hand with his Eton pals to help push him out of the quagmire.[14] He had survived the bullying and beatings at Eton by closeting himself in his study-bedroom and building an armada of 1:72 scale models. Hawker Furies, Wellingtons and a Spitfire were carefully constructed and painted. He also lost himself in the tales of dashing pilots like Biggles in his Sopwith Camel.

Reverend Taylor had first taken his family on a tour of Nazi Germany, along the fast and impressive *autobahnen*, in their Ford V-8 in 1935. Then, the only sign of military activity on that first trip had been a labour battalion carrying polished spades.

Three years later, during the Taylors' most recent visit, the shadows had lengthened, though Jimmy had found some kindness among the swastikas and massed ranks of Stormtroopers. One helped him find a space to photograph Hungary's Admiral Horthy driving through Berlin to meet Hitler in August 1938. Jimmy retained a 'warm spot for that soldier, whatever his future role . . .'

While Goering's boasts of Luftwaffe supremacy were widely reported, Vickers remained an old-fashioned institution that saw publicity as vulgar and undesirable. So when Jeffrey Quill flew the Spitfire from London to Paris in a record-breaking forty-two minutes and thirty seconds in November 1938, virtually nothing appeared in the press.[15]

1939

While Messerschmitt employees were hard at work in Regensburg, the gentlemen of 601 Squadron were not far away, enjoying fresh snow in the Bavarian mountains. With poor weather in January and February and a scarcity of Spitfires or Hurricanes to practise in, downhill skiing seemed a good alternative.[16]

Germany might have been considered a curious choice of venue in early 1939. The remilitarised Rhineland was churning out arms, the Condor Legion had subdued the Spanish Republicans, Czechoslovakia had been eviscerated and Hitler was making noises about Poland. However, Chamberlain's 'peace' still held.

Although the snow was glorious, the edge of their enjoyment was taken off somewhat when they skied alongside a detachment of German alpine troops. There was something in their swagger that suggested both confidence and menace.

Something was afoot.

* * *

The Germans could build three Me109s in the time it took to construct one Spitfire. With its revolutionary wings and complex engineering, the British fighter was a tricky machine to assemble.

Under the muddled leadership of motoring magnate Lord Nuffield, the Castle Bromwich factory set up in 1936 to turn out

100 Spitfires a month was experiencing major delays. The First World War plant in Eastleigh, near Southampton, Hampshire, had to step up to the plate. But, as the American millionaire flier Charles Lindbergh, famous for his solo non-stop transatlantic flight in 1927, could not fail to notice on a visit in 1939, it lacked the chromium-plated modernity of Germany's Regensburg production line.[17]

Lindbergh had been invited to Europe by Goering for a red-carpet tour of the ultra-modern Messerschmitt factories, where 2,000 fighters had already been assembled. He was invited to Supermarine's Eastleigh works afterwards. As the aviator's eye roved over the old wooden roof trusses and factory floor, Jeffrey Quill detected only a passing interest in the Spitfire. 'I was suddenly aware of a burning anger and resentment which I hope I managed to disguise. As he taxied out I felt like shouting after him in the American idiom, "OK, wise guy, just you wait."'

Sadly, it was the RAF that would have to wait. Things at Eastleigh were not about to improve, and progress at the Castle Bromwich factory verged on the non-existent. Then, in June 1939, a government memorandum appeared. It suggested that on completion of the order for 310 Spitfires, Eastleigh should concentrate on building Beaufighters, the heavily armed, twin-engine night-fighter.[18]

There were no plans for continuing with the Spitfire beyond the Mark I.

* * *

Ken French's love of trout fishing should have kept him casting into the lakes and rivers that flowed through the green hills of West Cork for the rest of his life. But a well-off Protestant family was always going to be a target in post-independence Ireland. His uncle had been taken hostage by the IRA and his father only just avoided summary execution.

In the end, it was the economy that lured Ken French abroad, as it did for thousands of his compatriots. For an educated young man, England offered opportunity. It was his brother's suggestion that the number of pretty girls there were worth more than a boatload of trout that finally made up his mind. In July 1939, aged eighteen, he landed the princely sum of £83 a year as a clerk for North British and Mercantile Insurance in London.[19]

He arrived in Southend in time for the carnival. Everyone was happy and carefree and his brother's promise was not unfounded. Ken's love of dogs, and slight limp – from a knee injury sustained at Portora Royal School, which had counted Oscar Wilde and Samuel Beckett among its past pupils – provided frequent openings for conversation that he rarely passed up.

* * *

Hugh Dundas joined the part-time pilots of the Auxiliary Air Force too late for the Bavarian alpine jaunt. But the 6ft 4in redhead was made of the right stuff. He wanted the kind of excitement that wasn't on offer in a solicitor's chambers. For reasons never given, he failed his medical three times, despite being at peak fitness, so found a rugby-playing Irish doctor to sign him off, fit for duty.[20]

By June 1939 Dundas was a 'Pupil Pilot' flying Avro Tutor biplanes with 616 Squadron. The thrill of flight swept aside everything else going on in the world. Nicknamed 'Cocky' by one of the veterans who thought he resembled a Rhode Island Red rooster, he was a quietly popular source of advice. But during annual camp among the orchards of east Kent, he also showed an eighteen-year-old's eagerness for the new and the magical.

He learned the joy of taking off into the dawn sky, of crossing the Channel when the air was crisp, of glimpsing the luxurious Pullman coaches that waited at Calais and Boulogne to transport travellers to far-off places.

Afternoons were reserved either for drinking gin in the mess tent or dozing in the sunshine, or both. There was little to trouble them beyond their imminent inspection by Air Vice-Marshal Trafford Leigh-Mallory, brother of George Mallory, the Everest mountaineer who died in 1924.

Formalities over, Leigh-Mallory took a snifter of gin and accepted the popular mess-game challenge to shimmy up one marquee pole, through the ventilation hole, along the spine then back down the other. Despite some middle-age 'thickening', Leigh-Mallory achieved the first phase of the mission, but became stuck when he attempted the descent. A climber was sent up to pull No.12 Fighter Group's commander through the hole. He popped out like a champagne cork and descended the last 10ft in freefall.

Restored with a stiff whisky, he promptly left.

Two days later, the squadron was enjoying its postprandial nap when the mess tent received news that a Nazi–Soviet Pact had been signed.

'Well that's fucked it,' one pilot, a former Guards officer, said. 'That's the start of the fucking war.'

In less colourful language, Jimmy Taylor's father told his family to pack their bags in readiness to flee France. The family were holidaying in the Pyrenees as Hitler's forces massed on the Polish border. The Reverend's hopes and prayers that his three boys would avoid war had proved forlorn.[21]

The Taylors were forced to leave the blue skies and tranquillity of the mountains when their hotel shut down. They headed north to the nearest port for passage to England, threading through mobilised French reservists. When they got to St Malo it was crammed with their fellow countrymen fighting to return home.

They boarded the ferry to Portsmouth on the morning of 1 September, after a final sightseeing trip to celebrate the 'splendid defiance' of Mont St Michel, as the Luftwaffe bombed the Polish town of Wieluń, killing 1,200 civilians.

* * *

Flames lit the night sky to the north of their Kent home the night Brian Bird's half-brother was born in 1936. Brian rushed downstairs to tell his stepfather the news that the Crystal Palace, the glory of Victorian Britain, was burning down after an accident.[22]

Three years later, on Sunday, 3 September 1939, fifteen-year-old Brian prepared to bring him an even more momentous bulletin. He crouched by the wireless, waiting for the Prime Minister's 11am announcement. His stepfather had gone to church, having left him with strict instructions to be kept informed.

'This is London . . .'

It was 11.15.

Brian felt the tension crackle in the air as Chamberlain began speaking. 'It is therefore with regret that I have to tell you we are at war with Germany . . .'

His address had barely ended when Brian was pedalling hard through the deserted streets of Sittingbourne.

Somewhat self-consciously, he marched up the aisle of St Paul's Church and delivered the note his mother had written just as his stepfather began the sermon.

Air-raid sirens wailed as he cycled home. Brian stopped and raised his eyes to the sky with a deep sense of foreboding. Even at the tender age of fifteen, the young Brian Bird was shaken by the sound. He contemplated what the future might hold for both him, and his country. He could never have imagined.

* * *

The shows still went on in London's West End. Ann Todd was treading the boards on her way to becoming a Hollywood star, winning praise for her poignant performance in *The Man in Half Moon Street*, the story of a man who retains his youth and cannot die.[23] The morning's sirens had disturbed the city's Sunday peace. She counted ten people dotted about the stalls. They were ushered to the front and the show began with blackout curtains in place. The performance was completed in half its usual running time, and audience and actors gratefully left the building.

Ann Todd took a taxi and drove through the night to Shropshire to be reunited with her small son David from her first marriage and her budding fighter pilot boyfriend, soon to be husband, Nigel

Tangye. They made an intriguing couple. Todd was a diminutive and beautiful blonde, nicknamed 'the Pocket Garbo'. Tangye was a tall, good-looking Cornishman with a colourful history. He had combined journalism with clandestine work for MI5 during the Spanish Civil War, and had joined the Auxiliary Air Force a few months earlier. He had just been called up by the RAF.

Ann Todd experienced the same moment of introspection that couples all around the country were feeling: uncertainty and fear.

'During that long drive I realised how important it is to belong to someone who cares, when one is in danger and to a woman, how necessary it is to have a man around. It was interesting when the raids were on and there was fear for survival. Couples who weren't getting on or even disliked each other rushed into each other's arms and clung together rather than be alone.'

* * *

The Vickers Supermarine workforce in Eastleigh looked at each other in resignation and dismay. They had known for some time that their precious fighter would be tested in combat, and were working their hardest to assemble as many as they could. But resources and capacity were still limited. As the bungling at Castle Bromwich continued, all Eastleigh could manage in September 1939 was thirty-three Spitfires.[24] The Messerschmitt factory built more than 120 Me109s. At the outbreak of war little over 300 Spitfires had been built, with less than a dozen squadrons operational.

They did not have to wait long for the first Spitfire action. Sadly, it was an engagement all concerned wanted to forget. At 6.15am on 6 September, Spitfires from 74 Squadron were scrambled by ground control to vector on an enemy presence over the River Medway in Kent. Two aircraft were shot down. But they were Hurricanes, not Messerschmitts.

The scientists had to come up with a solution fast to prevent further 'friendly fire' tragedies: the first 'Identification Friend or Foe' system that could spot friendly aircraft was introduced.

A transponder that was fitted onto RAF aircraft amplified and returned the incoming radar signal. It gave a distorted 'blip' on the radar operator's screen, which made it easily identifiable as non-hostile on the ground controller's screen.

German bomber crews were not new to combat. Nor were they particularly nervous. Most had seen action in Spain or Poland. They had confidence in themselves and their aircraft.

The Junkers 88 crews had more right to be confident than most. Their *Schnellbomber* – fast bomber – was designed to outrun fighters. Twin Jumo engines could power it to 320mph, roughly the same speed as a Hurricane. They had been briefed about the Spitfire. They knew it was dangerous and fast, that it could top 350mph, possibly 364mph. But they also knew its eighty-five-gallon fuel tank limited its range to 425 miles.

Thus when *Leutnant* Horst von Riesen was ordered to bomb the Royal Navy at their Scottish base in the Firth of Forth on 16 October 1939, he was content.[25] There was enough speed in the V12 Jumos to get them out of trouble, and they had a 1,400-mile range.

After the two-hour trip across the North Sea he watched with satisfaction as his boss, *Hauptmann* Helmut Pohle, straddled the cruiser HMS *Southampton* with 3,000lb of bombs.

Moments later his face fell. Pohle's aircraft ditched into the chilly Firth of Forth, riddled with bullets.

Seconds later von Riesen saw the sleek outline of a Spitfire for the first time, over his right shoulder. He acted swiftly and instinctively. The procedure was to drop to 50ft above the water, protecting their vulnerable underbelly from enemy fire.

As von Riesen streaked across the wave tops, raindrops peppered the surface. Except there was no rain.

The clatter of metal on metal a split second later confirmed his fears.

Then came the unmistakable churn and screech of mechanical failure. The starboard engine cut out. Von Riesen shut it down, reducing the fire risk, and held the Ju88 steady. There was little else he could do. He risked another glance over his shoulder. *Thank God*. The Spitfires had broken off.

Some 375 miles of open sea separated them from Germany, and they were limping along at barely 100mph.

He consulted the three other crew members. 'Turn back and ditch in the Firth of Forth or carry on?'

'No, no, never,' one rasped over the intercom. 'If we go back, the Spitfires will certainly get us.'

He was right. *Better take our chances swimming in the North Sea rather than face the ferocious fighters again.*

Von Riesen kept the Ju88 aloft for the next four hours, until the seaside lights of Westerland, lying off the Danish peninsula, twinkled on the horizon. They were home.

* * *

German bomber crews were not going to be put off by a few losses. And they were out to prove a point to the RAF: *We're not scared, and we're coming for you.*

Despite growing rumours about the Spitfire, the *Staffel* – squadron – of He111s that left Germany early on 8 December 1939 were confident of catching the Royal Navy in port.

If they came from far to the north, there was little chance of detection by whatever paltry defences the British might muster, and thus a greater chance of surprise. The squadron was cruising south of Aberdeen when the gunner-radio operator in the lead aircraft received a three-letter code. '*Careful. You have been detected by the defence.*'[26]

He repeated it to the *Staffel Kapitän*. 'Rubbish,' the officer replied. 'The English defences are no good.'

But he took the precaution of gaining height on his way down to the Firth of Forth.

It was a wise decision.

Flying directly towards them and a few thousand feet above were five Spitfires from 72 Squadron.

They had been scrambled just after midday when radar picked up seven enemy aircraft flying towards the warships moored in the Firth of Forth.

For the first three months of the war, Flying Officer Desmond Sheen, twenty-two, had spent hours searching the skies for his first enemy targets. He had come over from Sydney, Australia, two years earlier to join the RAF and by December 1939 he was impatient for action. When he spotted the bomber formation he felt his heartbeat quicken.[27]

'Blue Flight strike!' he ordered over the radio, not caring whether he used the right terminology.

The lead Heinkel's gunner saw them coming. 'Behind us. Fighters!'

'All right, turn away to the North Sea,' the *Staffel Kapitän* calmly replied. 'We can fly for a long time, they cannot. We'll have to shake them off.'

The Heinkels dropped to sea level then closed in tight formation as the Spitfires dived near vertically down onto them.

The fighters were met with a curtain of defensive gunfire. Sheen ignored the streaks of tracer and fired on the rear bomber, scoring multiple hits. The Heinkel quickly lost height.

The Australian turned his attention elsewhere. He pulled a tight turn, swept past a lighthouse fifteen miles out to sea, and zeroed in on a Heinkel on the extreme right that had already been hit. The other Germans fought hard to protect their comrade, but to no avail. The bomber's guns went silent and it began to drop away.

The lead German gunner was not going to let the British fighter claim another victim. He was a veteran and excellent shot. But this was his first close combat with a Spitfire and he knew their weapons would be deadly at close quarters. He waited patiently for the British pilot to close in then let go burst after burst of 7.92mm fire.

Sheen was caught in the crossfire of three Heinkels' rear-facing machine guns. A bullet smashed through his canopy and sliced through his earphones, cutting his ear as it skimmed past his head. Another speared through the cockpit and into his thigh. The damage to his body he could deal with, but not the damage to the aircraft. A round had blown a hole in its fuel tank. Petrol streamed into the cockpit, stinging his skin, blurring his vision.

Sheen tried to pull round for another attack but he felt light-headed, dizzy, verging on blackout. He manoeuvred back to the coast.

The battle was far from over. Seeing Sheen hit put his 72 Squadron comrades in vengeful mood. The Spitfires went for the Germans, diving and firing in fury. The Heinkel gunner looked left and right. Only one other rear gunner remained in action. But he was inexperienced and slow, engaging the enemy only after they turned away from his tail.

The 72 Squadron pilots were quick to spot an easy prey. They dived on him relentlessly.

The Heinkel gunner fired a long salvo in his comrade's defence. There was a metallic click. He'd finished his last drum of ammunition. He turned and shouted at the *Staffel Kapitän*: 'All the ammo you have, back to me at once!'

The *Staffel Kapitän* didn't need to hear it twice. He made his way on his hands and knees along the catwalk between the bomb racks, dragging the much-needed ammunition behind him.

The gunner whipped on a drum and fired. As he pulled the trigger he shouted: 'More. Quick!'

The *Staffel Kapitän* crawled back as quickly as he could. For what seemed like an age the gunner aimed, fired and changed drums while the officer frantically fed him ammunition. Another Spitfire was hit and began smoking. The fight had taken them far out to sea.

Finally the British broke off and headed home.

The Heinkel gunner sat back, wiping the sweat from his brow. He looked over at the *Staffel Kapitän*. They both grinned and shook their heads. The officer pointed to his trousers. He had donned his best uniform that morning. Now they were threadbare at the knees.

The Heinkel's interior was a mess, its aluminium fuselage torn apart by .303 Browning rounds. Brass casings and empty ammo drums were strewn everywhere. The gunner wiggled his toes then pulled off his flying boot, emptying a cascade of shell casings. The plane lurched and he looked out of the window in time to see one of their fellow bombers gently ditch onto the water.

They could do no more than wave at the survivors before setting their own mauled Heinkel on a south-easterly course for home. But they had a problem. The wireless had been shot to pieces and after the long-running battle no one had any idea where they were. At that moment one of the two engines stopped.

The Heinkel lost height.

Five hundred metres. Two hundred metres.

We're going to join our comrades in the sea.

One hundred metres. Fifty metres.

Slowly, the pilot managed to get the nose up.

Thirty metres.

Their position held just above the waves. At any moment they expected the machine to give out and plummet into the sea.

Then they had a stroke of luck. The direction-finding instrument suddenly sprang into life, giving their position and course.

The nearest airfield was Westerland, on the island of Sylt, just off the Denmark peninsula. They headed straight for it, making a belly-landing.

They had survived. Just. It was a testament to the He111's durability.

It had been estimated that bombers needed to be hit a maximum of 300 times to be sure of destruction.

'Counted holes in aircraft,' the gunner recorded. 'Three hundred and fifty.'

The bomber's resilience and the Spitfire's inability to bring it down only strengthened German confidence.

72 Squadron's encounter did not go unnoticed. RAF Fighter Command pored over every scrap of after-action report. How could seven Spitfires fire 2,400 rounds each – their full complement – and only account for two out of seven He111s in such favourable circumstances?

An inquiry was ordered. It found that the bullet groupings of the eight Browning machine guns was too far apart, lacking the concentration needed to fatally damage a plane. It recommended that the muzzles be refocused to concentrate the spread of bullets at 300 yards rather than 400 yards.[28]

Fighter Command was learning some valuable lessons.

ATA pilot Diana Barnato Walker

1940

Diana Barnato Walker joined the British Red Cross in the belief that there would be mass casualties on declaration of war.[29] By early 1940, they hadn't materialised and her services were not required.

For the granddaughter of Barney Barnato, joint founder of De Beers mining, and the daughter of the multimillionaire racing driver Woolf 'Babe' Barnato, there was only one thing left to do. Socialise.

After a long night dancing at the Embassy Club on Bond Street, Diana decided to go skiing in France. It was mid-January 1940. Bar the odd sandbag, the war had barely touched London, and she'd heard the Scots Guards were on manoeuvres in Chamonix. Diana came from a hugely enterprising and fearless Jewish family; she was not going to let a war put her off. And the opportunity of skiing with the Guards was too good to miss.

Driving off the ferry in Calais, she discovered that France offered a number of immediate benefits. With no rationing she could fill her thirsty Bentley as often as she liked. She motored south, via an overnight château stop, to the slopes of Mont Blanc.

She couldn't pass Paris on her return without dropping in on her friend Gogo's *atelier* studio. During Diana's five-day stay, the House of Schiaparelli created a collection for her that included a pink satin evening dress and silk afternoon outfit in duck-egg blue with fine red and blue stripes.

Before finally heading back to Calais, Diana lunched with Count Henri de la Falaise in Amiens, where he was acting liaison officer to the 12th Lancers. As the two friends shared an excellent duck pâté at the Café Godebert, the German General Staff were finalising their plans for the invasion of France.

* * *

Joe Roddis felt the same joy when he tinkered with a motorcycle as he'd had assembling his red Meccano steam traction engine. He understood it, cared for it and could fix it.[30]

Joe passed the RAF recruiting office every day as he fetched the sandwiches for his mates at their Sheffield motorcycle workshop. His desire to service fighters that could fly at five times the speed of a Royal Enfield Bullet motorbike increased each time he saw the Spitfire and Hurricane posters. As did his determination to provide his impoverished family with a steady income.

When the eighteen-year-old Yorkshireman's application to join up was accepted, he was overjoyed. His sandwich delivery duties were cut short, as was his mechanics course when he was put on a wartime footing. Joe was posted to 234 Squadron at RAF Leconfield in Yorkshire to await delivery of their Spitfires.

When the red Very flare went up over the airfield signalling a scramble for another squadron, Joe sprinted across to see his first ever Spitfire in flight. 'It was magical and elegant. The tail was just coming off the ground. It looked like it was doing 400mph. It was a beautiful war machine, especially to have on our side.'

But the thrill quickly evaporated as a Miles Magister training aircraft taxied onto the runway. The Spitfire pilot could not avoid a collision. His whirling propeller cut through the open cockpit of the monoplane trainer, which disintegrated in a shower of plywood and fabric. The Magister's pilot was killed instantly.

'There was nothing we could do. It was just a mass of human flesh scattered around which had to be cleared up. I picked up a flying boot with a foot in it. The seagulls had been feeding on it for a while. A terrible sight.' It was 21 February 1940, and Joe's first view of death close up.[31]

The gloom lifted considerably a fortnight later with the arrival of eighteen brand-new Spitfire Mark Is. 'We crawled all over them, taking the cowling off and drooling over the Merlins. It really felt we were becoming part of the war, part of the fight. You could also see the change in the pilots. They were drooling over the aircraft too, desperate to get airborne.'

He and his fellow mechanics learned the intricacies of the Rolls-Royce engine and could soon feed the gun belts all 2,400 rounds and fill the eighty-five-gallon tank in twenty minutes. The pilots learned to fly and fight the plane, whose value was so high that they were dispersed to fields a few miles away every night, to protect them from marauding German bombers.

With his RAF pay packets, Joe made regular visits to the local pubs and, when he felt really flush, took a bus to the pictures in Hull. But at that point there was little social mixing between what he described as the different classes. 'Ground crew would never dare initiate a conversation with a pilot. The aircrew then were from rich backgrounds. They were only used to telling a garage mechanic to fill up their Bentley or wipe the windscreen. They were not rude, but we rarely spoke to them other than about the aircraft.'

But the distinctive lines of the British class system, which had survived relatively unscathed from the Great War, were about to become severely blurred. The divide between mechanic and pilot would quickly close, as neither the Spitfire, nor the war, would be any respecter of class.

CHAPTER TWO

The Fall of France

Hugh 'Cocky' Dundas

The incursions across the North Sea proved useful continuation training for the Luftwaffe bomber force. In April 1940, following the pattern set in Spain and Poland, they started bombing civilians in Norway.

Britain's hapless participation in the Norway campaign led to Chamberlain being replaced by Churchill on 10 May 1940. Hours later, the German *blitzkrieg* – lightning war – was launched on the Low Countries.

The British Expeditionary Force (BEF) had been sent to France on the outbreak of war to bolster the French army, as it had done in the previous war. But it was ill-equipped to fight the *blitzkrieg*.

German paratroopers swept through Belgium's defences, rendering France's fabled Maginot Line an irrelevance. And the campaign came to an irreversible conclusion when General Erwin Rommel's 7th Panzer Division ghosted through the Ardennes.

The French rustled up a mixed bunch of 826 combat-ready fighters and 250 bombers. Their command and control systems were chaotic at best, and at times non-existent. More than 4,000 Luftwaffe aircraft were released to bomb them into submission.[1]

As the French lines collapsed, the BEF called for Spitfires to cover its headlong retreat. Churchill had fought in the trenches alongside the French army, and felt compelled to assist. But Air Chief Marshal Dowding had other ideas.

Sir Hugh 'Stuffy' Dowding, head of Fighter Command, was not widely loved. Socially awkward and abidingly obstinate, he appeared to deserve his nickname. However, he was also focused, clear-sighted and iron-willed – essential qualities for the times.

It was Dowding who had the foresight to ensure the RAF had a modern fighter, and to make radar integral to home defence. He had overseen the introduction of the Fighter Control System, which used a combination of radars, direction finders and the Observer Corps. It gave Fighter Command headquarters the direction, height and time of incoming raids, allowing them to 'vector' fighter squadrons for the intercept. This saved on fuel, engine use and perhaps most importantly pilots' energy, as they were not required for airborne patrols. It also sapped German morale. The Luftwaffe had underestimated Britain's complex home defence system which left its pilots bemused how nearly every raid was met with RAF fighters waiting to pounce.

But Dowding now had to answer the most burning question of the conflict thus far: would his Spitfires be able to blunt the Luftwaffe's efforts long enough for the French army to regroup?

In a two-page memorandum to the Air Ministry on 18 May 1940, he set out his arguments.

While the Allies might still prove victorious, defeat had to be contemplated. If this happened, he 'presumed' Britain would fight on – and therefore required a minimum fighter strength. 'I would remind the Air Council that the last estimate which they made as to the force necessary to defend this country was fifty-two squadrons, and my strength has now been reduced to the equivalent of thirty-six . . .'[2]

The Air Ministry needed to decide as 'a matter of paramount urgency' what numbers should be left to defend Britain. Once they had done so, he wanted reassurance that 'not one fighter will be sent across the Channel, however urgent and insistent the appeals for help may be'.

Then came the final, career-risking but visionary paragraph. 'If the Home Defence Force is drained away in desperate attempts to remedy the situation in France, defeat in France will involve the final, complete and irremediable defeat of this country.'

Dowding was listened to.

Not one Spitfire would be deployed in the defence of France. The force of 452 Hurricanes, joined by the woefully inadequate Bristol Blenheims, Fairey Battles and Lysanders, would have to make do.

May 1940

RAF pilots who made it home after crash-landing in northern France in late May reported chaos on the ground. Former portrait painter Hugh Riddle, twenty-eight, of 601 Squadron, was among them. 'Refugees block main roads and there is a sense of complete confusion. Soldiers without rifles roam aimlessly about the countryside, all making their way westwards.'[3]

Bombed to near-madness, French soldiers would run panic-stricken at the merest sound of an aircraft engine. For an orderly withdrawal to have any hope of success, the skies had to be protected from the marauding Luftwaffe.

Twelve squadrons of Hurricanes had been in France since the outset of the *blitzkrieg*, and Dowding had been powerless to prevent another eight going in mid-May, although he cannily ensured they were half-squadrons.

Churchill had done his best to keep his closest allies in the fight, but it was not enough. He finally conceded that the attempt to hold off the Germans was a 'colossal military disaster'. To retrieve anything from the impending defeat, the 400,000 men of the BEF – 'the whole root and core and brain of the British Army'– *had* to be saved.

It was vital, therefore, to protect the northern evacuation ports. Dowding could not argue against using the most modern aircraft available to cover the troops streaming towards the beaches of Dunkirk.

The Spitfire was about to be pitched into battle against an undefeated foe. All the toil that had gone into its creation would count for nothing if it proved a failure.

* * *

'I saw another Messerschmitt curving round. It had a bright yellow nose. Again I saw the ripples of grey smoke ... Red blobs arced lazily through the air between us, accelerating dramatically as they approached and streaked close by, across my wing.'[4]

It was 28 May, day two of the Dunkirk evacuation. Hugh Dundas had left the Garden of England for the Dunkirk beaches. He was about to confirm the adage that the fighter pilot's first fight was his most dangerous.

'I pulled my Spitfire round hard, so that the blood was forced down from my head. The thick curtain of blackout blinded me for a moment and I felt the aircraft juddering on the brink of a stall.'

He straightened out and his vision cleared – to reveal the twisting confusion of fighters locked in combat. Another Me109 took a shot at him. Dundas threw his Spitfire into a turn so tight it led to another blackout. For a split second, a Messerschmitt filled his windscreen. Dundas pressed the Dunlop firing button for the first time in anger. His deflection shot – estimating his foe's flight path and shooting ahead of the moving target so the bullets would intersect with it – was wide of the mark.

The enemy were all around him. 'I was close to panic in

bewilderment and hot fear. Instinct drove me to keep turning and turning, twisting my neck all the time to look for the enemy behind. The consideration uppermost in my mind was the desire to stay alive.'

Suddenly he was all alone, far out to sea and uncertain in which direction safety lay. 'It was then that panic took hold of me for the second time that day. Finding myself alone over the sea, a few miles north of Dunkirk, my training as well as my nerve deserted me.'

He set off blindly in what he thought was the right direction, directly north into a wilderness of sea, then came to his senses and turned back. Perhaps he could crash-land and get a boat home? Spotting two destroyers below restored some calm. Then he saw the French coastline. He forced himself to work out the simple navigation problem which panic had blinded him to.

Soaked in sweat, he took a few deep breaths then set on a north-westerly course. He soon picked up Essex, then Southend Pier, and landed at Rochford, where 616 Squadron had arrived the previous night to assist the evacuation.

He recalled the unimpressed looks the 72 Squadron pilots – fatigued and scarred by the loss of comrades – had given them the day before after 616, then yet to be bloodied in battle, had demonstrated a perfect formation landing.

As he taxied to the dispersal point, knowing the ground crew could see he had fired his guns in anger, he felt himself transformed, Walter Mitty-like, from frightened child into debonair young pilot.

His barrack-room mirror demanded a more honest appraisal. 'Well, Hughie, you couldn't insure your life now, for love nor money,' he told his reflection. He was nineteen, and felt far from immortal.

* * *

The whistle of artillery fire punctuated the screech of Stukas as the Germans closed in on Dunkirk. The beaches, crammed with soldiers, became, as one German pilot saw it, a place of 'unadulterated killing'.

Discipline was just holding in the long lines waiting to board the boats. Signaller Sidney Leach had queued for ten hours when a naval officer told him a ship was waiting at a pier several miles away. As shells dropped around them the soldiers trudged through the sand, fighting exhaustion and the scars of battle.[5]

At 4am, just as Leach reached the jetty, a shell burst in front of him. He was thrown backwards along the pier, just managing to avoid a plunge into the sea. Painfully, he got up and dusted himself down, then saw the piles of French dead stacked on the pier. He stared at the pale, blank faces for a moment then quickly walked past. Finally, at 6am, he boarded a minesweeper and put out to sea.

They did not get far. Whether it was a bomb from above or a shell from shore-based artillery made no difference. The ship began to sink by the stern. Leach scrambled onto a lifeboat that rowed them to another minesweeper headed for home.

But that still did not mean safety. The Luftwaffe did not want a single British soldier surviving long enough to fight their Wehrmacht comrades on the English beaches. Leach and his companions were attacked every nautical mile until they were halfway across the Channel. 'Planes followed us, continually bombing and machine-gunning us until about halfway across.' The Luftwaffe appeared to have freedom of the skies.

Many a Tommy had looked skywards at the black crosses of the German planes during the crossing and cursed the scarcity of RAF roundels.

A bitter feeling took hold. *Where the bloody hell are the RAF?*

The vast black smoke cloud that now stretched for seventy miles across the beaches might have helped as a navigation aid for the British rescuers, but it was working more in the enemy's favour. The thick, oily plume from burning equipment was used by the Germans as cover for their bombing and strafing runs.

At least two if not three RAF squadrons were patrolling constantly overhead in daylight, but intercepting the enemy far from the English coast, and their radar cover, was tricky and they could manage little more than forty minutes at a time over Dunkirk.

The Germans also had far more planes to throw into the fight.

Pilot Officer Johnny Allen of 54 Squadron had been patrolling up high without success, so took his Spitfire down to 4,000ft. When he got there, he instantly regretted it. Immediately overhead was a formation of twenty enemy bombers escorted by forty fighters – and he'd given up the precious advantage of height.[6]

Allen rammed the throttle forward, pulled back the stick and soared upwards, speeding towards his first dogfight against an Me110. Happily, he found that the Spitfire's manoeuvrability far outclassed the twin-engine fighter. In a matter of seconds the enemy's rear sat nicely at the centre of his sights.

He thumbed the trigger button once then twice. The smell of cordite fumes blowing back from the Brownings' 153 'squirts' a second filled the cockpit. Flame spurted from the enemy aircraft as rounds hammered home. For a fraction of a second, Allen saw the pilot's head half-slewed round to see what was attacking him. Then the 110 plummeted downwards.

Wow, that was bloody dangerous, Allen thought, as the exhilaration of the dogfight wore off.

The Messerschmitt pilot was almost certainly experienced, but he was not prepared for the ferocity and agility of their new foe. 'The British attack with the fury of maniacs,' a surviving comrade wrote in his diary.[7]

The RAF pilots faced two certainties: the Nazis were ominously close to their home shores, and they had to do everything possible to save the troops below.

This was not immediately apparent to those on the ground, bruised by defeat and retreat. One army officer made the mistake of confronting the high-class amateur boxer-turned-pilot Ken Manger after he had just bailed out onto the beach and queued patiently for a destroyer. 'All boats are for the Army and not the RAF.'[8]

Manger responded with a punch that sent the officer sprawling into the sea, then calmly stepped on board. He was back in the fray, flying over the beaches, the very next day.

* * *

Jack Bell, a former solicitor and now with 616 Squadron, sampled similar chagrin in more trying circumstances. He had dived after a flight of Messerschmitts machine-gunning ships, downed one, then had to bail out himself. He spent some time in the water, until an open boat crewed by navy ratings came alongside. Instead of bringing the shivering airman on board, the sailors used their oars to push him away. When Bell finally persuaded them he was an RAF pilot he was sarcastically told they thought all airmen in the area were German.[9]

A diminished RAF presence was not the Luftwaffe's experience over Dunkirk. 'Our bombers pressed home their attacks but were constantly harassed by the RAF who inflicted substantial losses,' wrote the Luftwaffe ace Ulrich Steinhilper.[10] 'I understand that it is a complaint of many British and French soldiers who were on the beaches that the RAF were nowhere to be seen. Believe me, they flew to their limit.'

23 May 1940

Squadron Leader Francis White, of 74 Squadron, had got into a tangle with some Me109s and a two-seat Henschel 126 reconnaissance plane whose rear gunner scored a lucky hit. With glycol pouring out of his cooling system, White was forced to crash-land his damaged Spitfire at Calais Marck airfield. Germans were driving past the main gate as he landed and Calais was encircled. There was no way back to the beaches.

His friend Squadron Leader James 'Prof' Leathart, of 54 Squadron, had seen White go down, and was determined not to let him fall into enemy hands. He dashed back to Kent and grabbed the squadron's two-seat Miles Master trainer. The Master had the advantage of a Kestrel engine that gave it 142mph, but as a trainer its underside was painted bright yellow. Not ideal camouflage for a combat zone. It was decided to fly very low level, escorted by two Spitfires flown by the New Zealander Al Deere and Johnny Allen, twenty-four, and already credited with 54 Squadron's first kill, shooting down a Ju88 the previous day.[11]

The plan was for Leathart to land on the airfield and taxi with engine running in the hope that White would show himself and they'd take off. Leathart began his approach to land unobserved by the German trucks and motorcycles driving past, but not by those in the skies above.

Deere had sent Allen 'upstairs' to provide top cover while he shepherded the Master. Allen abruptly ran into a dozen 109s, all streaking towards Calais Marck airfield. 'I'm going to have a go at them,' he brusquely told his wingman below and thrust his throttle to maximum power.

No one could alert Leathart in the Miles Master. He had no radio.

Deere was contemplating waggling his wings as a warning when he spotted a Messerschmitt tearing down onto Leathart's Master. He squeezed off a burst that was enough to divert the German's attention.

'Red One – I'm surrounded, can you help me?' Allen pleaded as he tore into the fighters above.

'Try and hang on, Johnny,' Deere replied, 'till I kill this bastard in front of me and I'll be right up.'

He stayed doggedly on the 109's tail, waiting for him to make a mistake. The German was desperate to get away. In a final attempt to avoid Deere's fire, he straightened out of a turn and, perhaps overestimating the Me109's rate of climb, pulled vertically upwards.

For Deere the pilot had written his own death warrant. He'd presented the Kiwi with a perfect point-blank shot from dead below. 'I made no mistake.'

Scores of rounds raked the 109. The fighter slowly heeled over then plunged vertically into the water's edge from 3,000ft.

Leathart had just managed to avoid the attentions of the 109 as he came in to land. 'I pulled around in a tight turn, observing as I did so the Messerschmitt shoot straight past me. I literally banged the aircraft onto the ground and evacuated the cockpit with all possible speed, diving into a ditch that ran around the airfield's perimeter.

Just as I did so, I saw an Me109 come hurtling out of the clouds and crash with a tremendous explosion a few hundred yards away.'

Leathart watched the drama unfold from the ditch that happily contained another occupant – Squadron Leader White, the friend he had come to rescue. Both looked on anxiously as 109s continued to swoop out of the clouds, usually with a Spitfire on their tail. After watching three German planes plummet to earth, the officers leapt out of the ditch and raced to their plane. But there was a problem. The Master had no electric starter.

One turned the crank handle to start the engine while the other jumped into the cockpit. As German vehicles continued to trundle past, the engine spluttered then roared. 'When it seemed safe we made a hasty take-off and a rather frightening trip back to England and safety,' Leathart said. Throughout the rescue, German troops failed to spot the drama that had unfolded under their noses.[12]

Despite his bravery, Deere was beginning to feel the psychological effect of being outnumbered. 'Odds of 20–1 and 12–1 in consecutive engagements were too much for one's nerves.'[13] Deere received the Distinguished Flying Cross for his actions.

* * *

Deere was resilient. Others were not. Unable to contemplate a duel to the death in the skies, a fellow pilot had broken down in tears as he went to climb into his plane. The medical officer was quickly summoned. He was clearly of the old school. 'The doc gave him a terrific punch and a few well-chosen words,' a 616 officer observed. 'And we had no further trouble.'[14]

There were some who relished the thought of closing with a force they increasingly viewed as downright evil. 'I felt no mercy must be shown to a people who are a disgrace to humanity,'[15] said Brian Lane, the twenty-three-year-old commander of 19 Squadron, after a Stuka became his first kill. 'I had wondered what it would be like to shoot down an aircraft . . . Now I knew, and it was exhilarating.'

Duelling in the air was an intimate affair. The most successful pilots were those who got in close before opening fire, sometimes seeing pieces fly off the pilot as well as his plane. They were experiencing the full spectrum of emotions that came from fighting a fellow human being to the death. For some it was a killing rage, for others cold, clinical and remote.

Nineteen-year-old Tim Vigors' first success over Dunkirk felt similar to bagging a pigeon. The Anglo-Irish Old Etonian of 222 Squadron said: 'I was aware that I had killed a fellow human being and was surprised not to feel remorse. Of course, Hitler's atrocities had been well-publicised and we had got into the way of identifying all Germans with their leader.'[16]

Late May 1940

Bernard Brown

With Dowding limiting Spitfire numbers, the RAF threw whatever they could into the fight. This included the Hawker Hector, a 187mph biplane whose only previous action had been on India's North-West Frontier, keeping musket-toting insurgents at bay.

The situation in France was desperate. The BEF needed some

relief from the German onslaught closing around Calais. 613 Squadron were in the process of converting from Hectors to slightly more modern Lysanders when the call to action came. They were to bomb a German artillery battery in a chalk pit outside Calais.

Bernie Brown was among those assembled who looked at their CO with a mixture of dismay and astonishment when he was allocated an older Hector. Even if the Hectors did get past the modern German fighters and vicious anti-aircraft fire, *what difference would our two paltry 112lb bombs make?*[17]

It was not what Brown, twenty-two, had signed up for when he'd left his job as a postman in New Zealand in 1938 and followed his boyhood desire to join the RAF and fly. But *desperate times require desperate measures*, he consoled himself, as he puttered across the Channel.

With Calais looming, Brown decided to test the Hector's single Vickers machine gun. As he pulled the trigger there was an almighty bang. Something wet splashed over his face. His skin stung. He smelt fuel and experienced the darkest terror of every pilot. Fire.

Damn it!

His goggles were smeared in fuel. He pulled them off and looked over the nose. There was a gaping hole in the main fuel tank and bits missing from the Vickers. A piece of the machine gun had flown off and gouged the tank. Behind him, he could still see the English coast. He glanced below and released the two bombs into the sea.

He ate up the miles back to Kent, spotted a strip of green and finally managed to put the battered Hector down on Herne Bay golf course. Bernie Brown was forthright in his view. 'It was damn dangerous. Most of my fellow crews were captured or killed. There were nine of us on the squadron and only two survived. I thought, "To hell with this job." I knew that if I stayed on Hectors I'd be dead.' He was convinced his future would be more secure if he could transfer onto a faster, lighter aircraft, one with more punch. A fighter.

* * *

Despite his reservations at committing precious aircraft to the doomed mission, Dowding conceded that some invaluable lessons had been learned over France.

The early skirmishes over the North Sea had already suggested that focusing the Spitfire's cone of bullets to meet a 'kill spread' for the eight Browning machine guns at 400 yards was too cautious. Without the heavy calibre 20mm cannon, the .303 rounds were not causing enough damage. The most effective pilots in France were those who got in close and had their guns refocused to within 250 yards. It soon became the standard.

The 'ring-and-bead' circular, iron gunsight of the First World War had been replaced by a system of lenses set behind the windscreen. Its illuminated amber circle with a dot at the centre gave much greater accuracy, and the ability to fire in poor light.

It was not only good shooting that was making the Luftwaffe's aces begin to twitch, but the fighter's agility. 'The bastards make such infernally tight turns, there seems no way of nailing them,' was an observation many German pilots were making about their new adversary.

Despite this, the Luftwaffe knew the Me109 was far superior to any other fighter aircraft. It could climb quicker, dive faster and, with its two 20mm cannon and twin nose-mounted 7.92mm machine guns, could deliver far superior firepower. The problem was, in a dogfight it couldn't grab the Spitfire by the tail.

Other lessons were absorbed and improvements quickly made. A rear-view mirror was installed, along with a two-inch-thick slab of laminated glass on the windscreen against head-on attacks. An alloy cover was fitted over the main fuel tank and 73lb of armour plating behind the pilot's seat.[18]

But nothing was done as quickly or as efficiently as the replacement of the Spitfire's propeller. The original 'two-speed' propeller did not give the performance it deserved. An improved 'constant speed' version that had been developed for the new Spitfire Mark II (initial plans not to develop the aircraft beyond the Mark I version had already been dropped) offered even greater manoeuvrability, better climb and a higher ceiling.

Dowding understood the implications. He ordered it to be retro-fitted on the Mark Is as 'a matter of supreme urgency'.[19]

On 24 June 1940, De Havilland began producing twenty airscrew conversion kits per day. The conversions began at a dozen squadrons at the very moment the French army formally surrendered to the Germans. Working fifteen-hour shifts, 'supreme urgency' was clearly fixed in their minds.

The new prop reduced the take-off run by more than a quarter – from 320 yards to 225. More importantly, the climb rate to 20,000ft reduced from eleven minutes to less than eight.

The speed of these improvements reflected the realisation in the RAF establishment that they had a world-class fighter on their books. The decision was made to build as many as possible, as quickly as possible. By 15 August, 1,051 Spitfires and Hurricanes had been retro-fitted with the new airscrew. Eventually, 1,567 Spitfire Mark Is were built along with 920 Mark IIs.[20]

June 1940

It was crucial to the RAF to find out the weaknesses and strengths of the leading German fighter before the coming battle. Fortunately, an Me109 captured by the French had arrived in England before France's defeat. It was decided to stage a mock dogfight between a Spitfire Mark II and the Messerschmitt at Farnborough airfield.[21]

The British plane dived from 4,000ft and stuck relentlessly to the German aircraft's tail. Despite the Messerschmitt's efforts to shake him off, the Spitfire remained within effective range. The Spitfire pilot then allowed the 109 to manoeuvre behind him. It didn't last for long. With a few manoeuvres the Spitfire was free, and by executing a steep turn, was back on the enemy's tail.

The Spitfire was also now faster in straight and level flight. The first supplies of 100-octane fuel had arrived from America a few months earlier, replacing the less powerful 87 octane and producing the capability for emergency boost. If in trouble, the pilot could push a red thumb-lever to override the engine's boost control, activating fuel injection for an extra 34mph. To preserve the engine it had to be used sparingly.

The trial made the RAF confident that the Spitfire could outfly, outclimb and outfight the Messerschmitt. But it was misplaced confidence. The 109E model used in the test probably had engine-cooling problems. Its two-stage supercharger normally gave it far superior climbing and diving capabilities than both Spitfire and Hurricane. And the Germans never intended to fight in the way the RAF wanted them to. Their tactic was to climb high, dive fast, strike, then race back up to safety.

As well as packing more punch with their cannons, the 109s had self-sealing petrol tanks, which reduced the chances of fire. Better still, the 109E had fuel injection at negative gravity, allowing the pilot to push his stick forward into a steep dive confident the engine wouldn't cut out.

No fuel could get to the Spitfire's Merlin engine in a vertical dive, as there was no fuel injection to feed back up to the engine. The only solution was to flip it onto its back, turning the engine upside down and getting the fuel running back. It was an awkward way to fight a plane.

The Luftwaffe was also learning things about the Spitfire that gave them confidence. They were quick to test one captured in Dunkirk when the pilot failed to destroy it after a forced landing.

The German ace Werner Mölders was less than complimentary. 'As a fighting aircraft it is miserable. A sudden push forward on the stick will cause the motor to cut and, because the propeller has only two pitch settings [take-off and cruise], in a rapidly changing air combat situation the motor is either over-speeding or else is not being used to the full.'

But they were only testing the early Mark I version and had yet to capture a Mark II. Both sets of trials had flaws and the harsh reality of combat would prove a very different testing ground for the aircraft and their pilots.

If the Germans had greater numbers, more experience and better aircraft than their RAF counterparts, why weren't they making it count?

It was a question both sides asked themselves soon after a lone yacht slipped off the northern French beaches on 4 June and carried the last handful of Dunkirk evacuees home.

As Europe fell under Nazi domination, the escape of a third of a million professional soldiers was a victory of sorts. 'Wars,' Churchill reminded the nation, 'are not won by evacuations.'

The Luftwaffe lost 132 aircraft at Dunkirk to the RAF's 99 (which included 38 Spitfires and a total of 80 pilots). But numbers, especially for the well-supplied German war machine, were not everything.

On 4 June, the day the week-long evacuation ended, Fighter Command was left with 331 Spitfires and Hurricanes, despite Dowding's parsimony. The RAF needed fliers and aircraft.

The heroics over Dunkirk meant the Spitfire was establishing itself in the public eye, but ready cash was needed to build it in its hundreds. Each production Spitfire cost just under £9,000. Lord Beaverbrook, the press baron turned manufacturer, decided to publish a price list to give it some meaning. The £2,000 engine, the £2,000 wings and the £800 Brownings were contrasted with the more affordable compass (£5), clock (£2), spark plugs (eight shillings) and rivets (sixpence).[22] The average civilian worker's pay was about £3.10s. a week, with fighter pilots getting around £5. The Spitfire Fund was launched by Beaverbrook through the media in the early summer of 1940. The public duly chipped in. In fact, they did more than that. The £1 cheques grew into thousands, and ultimately the fund reached £13 million.

The money came from all corners. The people of Basutoland in southern Africa stumped up enough for an entire squadron; a South Wales village raised £5,000 following the death of a son flying for the RAF. In Manchester, prostitutes arrested for soliciting were given the option of 'donating' a princely £3 rather than facing prosecution.

The shape and size of the aircraft also drew people in. 'There is something irresistibly endearing about a very small thing that fights like hell,' a *Daily Telegraph* columnist observed.

The fundraising drew even more attention to the Spitfire. It was becoming a national symbol of defiance as well as a tool for retribution.

* * *

The British had been quick to recognise and capitalise on the Spitfire's global appeal. Colourful images showing a Spitfire flying over the White Cliffs of Dover with titles of 'Wings for Victory' or 'Back them Up' appeared in publications around the world.

As a teenager John Blyth was enthralled by stories of the great heroes of aviation, often daydreaming in class about being in a Spitfire cockpit and taking on the 'Hun'.

There was one small snag. Although his parents were English, he was an American citizen from Oregon on the West Coast and, although he talked little about it, his father had been gassed on the Western Front while serving in the British Army during the Great War. After the war, he emigrated with his wife to America where they managed to scratch out a rural living among the giant redwoods of Oregon until the 1930s Great Depression struck. At one point John's father resorted to foraging cascara bark, used as a laxative, to pay for his son's school uniform.

John had excelled at school, reading books voraciously and aviation ones in particular. One day he opened a magazine to find flights advertised for 'a penny a pound'. As he weighed only 90lb, John managed to persuade his father to part with ninety cents and found himself trundling over a bumpy field in a vintage biplane. Then he was in the air. 'I couldn't see much over the edge of the cockpit so I had to open the little side door for a better view. I loved it, I really loved it, but never imagined I'd one day take these machines into battle.'

Blyth learned to fly by joining the nascent Oregon Air National Guard. But he told his parents he felt it was his duty to go to England

and join the war effort. 'I knew about the dangers but thought that was something that had to be faced. I remember saying goodbye to my parents. They understood the dangers too but also knew this was something I needed to do. Flying was the most important thing to me, then fighting the war.'[23]

* * *

If Castle Bromwich had been better managed, there should have been 1,000 Spitfires ready for the front in summer 1940 – enough to equip all of Fighter Command's squadrons in the south of England. But despite Nuffield's promise of sixty per month by April 1940, the plant had yet to build its first Spitfire four years after its foundations had been laid.

Churchill recognised in Beaverbrook a man who got things done, and duly appointed him Minister of Aircraft Production. It did not take his lordship long to see things were greatly amiss at the £7 million factory. Not only was the production line chaotic, the unions seemed unaware of the very real danger Britain faced. There were sit-down strikes over petty pay disputes. Workers came in late and left early. There was fraud. 'In the meantime, we manage to build the odd Spitfire or two . . .' wrote one exasperated manager.

The Spitfire was a complex aircraft to build. It required precision engineering and techniques outside the experience of the Midlands automobile builders.

Beaverbrook happily accepted Nuffield's half-hearted threat of resignation on 17 May and sent in managers from the Vickers defence company, who owned Supermarine, to take over. Sackings of workforce and management followed.

Things changed rapidly. But not in time. While Hitler easily replenished his stocks after the losses sustained in France to the tune of 155 Me109s a month, just twenty-three Spitfires came off Castle Bromwich's production line in July. The Germans could also now use French factories to replace the 1,667 aircraft lost or damaged during the spring offensive.

Fortunately, employees at Supermarine's factory in Southampton were clocking up seventy-two-hour weeks. Ninety-four Spitfires were built in June, and 134 in July.

And the Luftwaffe had not only suffered physical losses at Dunkirk. Their experience of the Spitfire's venom and its pilots' tenacity had asked difficult questions of the 'master race'. 'The days of easy victory were over,' Major Werner Kreipe recorded in his diary. 'We had met the RAF head on.'[24]

It was time to pause and restock before the British could be battered into submission.

* * *

To reinforce the fact that he meant business after France's surrender, Churchill ordered the navy to prepare for the destruction of the French fleet in the Algerian port of Oran to prevent it falling into Nazi hands. The same day, 18 June, he stood up in the Commons and left no doubt as to his intentions. 'The Battle of France is over. I expect the Battle of Britain is about to begin. Upon this battle depends the survival of Christian civilisation. Upon it depends our own British life, and the long continuity of our institutions and our Empire. The whole fury and might of the enemy must very soon be turned on us. Hitler knows that he will have to break us in this Island or lose the war. If we can stand up to him, all Europe may be free and the life of the world may move forward into broad, sunlit uplands. But if we fail, then the whole world, including the United States, including all that we have known and cared for, will sink into the abyss of a new Dark Age made more sinister, and perhaps more protracted, by the lights of perverted science. Let us therefore brace ourselves to our duties, and so bear ourselves that, if the British Empire and its Commonwealth last for a thousand years, men will still say, "This was their finest hour."'[25]

Hitler was riled. Churchill would feel the wrath of *blitzkrieg*. War Directive No. 16 was drafted. German High Command was ordered to prepare for invasion. 'The aim of this operation is to eliminate the English motherland as a base from which war can be continued and, if necessary, to occupy completely.'

The key requirement was the defeat of the RAF. 'The English Air Force must be eliminated to such an extent that it will be incapable of putting up any substantial opposition to the invading troops.'

Churchill was only too aware of the threat. In the early part of his 'finest hour' speech he had asked: 'The great question is: can we break Hitler's air weapon?'

It was time to find out.

CHAPTER THREE

The Battle for Britain

19 Squadron Spitfires at RAF Duxford, May 1939

Answering Fighter Command's call for volunteers, Bernard Brown swept through the gates of Biggin Hill in his maroon J-type MG. Not one to draw attention to himself, Brown had been seduced by the advert for the sporty two-seater which promised 'The Car with the Racing Pedigree'. It was certainly an improvement on the plodding Hawker Hector biplane he had disastrously flown to Calais.

The Luftwaffe had arrived a few minutes before Brown and sulphurous smoke now billowed from a random pattern of craters. Ground crew dashed around, planting red flags next to every unexploded bomb. Above the warning shouts and cries for help, Brown could just make out the retreating throb of German bombers.

He weaved between the unexploded ordnance and parked his MG outside the Officers' Mess. Throwing a kit bag over his shoulder, he walked past the broken windows into the building. He was greeted by a mess orderly removing the names of those who had been killed in recent air battles from their pigeon-holes in the post rack. He wondered how long his name would stay up there.

'You're already an experienced pilot, Brown,' the conversion training officer had told him a few weeks earlier. 'There's a Spitfire over there. Get yourself airborne and do what you like with her.'[1]

Brown's soft eyes could quickly harden in a fight. They had gone through the full spectrum as the Mark II swept him through the air. It was unlike any aircraft he had experienced. As he put the Spitfire through its paces, soaring over the southern English countryside, he realised he had a battle-winning aircraft at his disposal. He had spent a joyful half-hour in experiencing the freedom of the skies.

Now he took in Biggin Hill's cracked windows and smouldering runway.

The Battle of Britain was underway. Churchill had asked whether the RAF could break Hitler's air weapon. If this was the answer, it was not an answer he or the free world wanted to hear.

* * *

America's support for Britain, vital in terms of materiel, was being openly questioned by Joseph Kennedy, the US Ambassador to London. If it continued, would it not be harmful to Washington's future relationship with Germany?

His views were gaining support. They were certainly backed by Charles Lindbergh, the millionaire American aviator whose caustic views on Spitfire production had already been expressed.

It had been foolish to think the RAF, with little over 300 frontline fighters, could hold off the mighty Luftwaffe.

Britain's show of defiance was coming to a humiliating end. Hundreds were dying needlessly. It was far from being the nation's finest hour. At the height of the rout in France, Lord Halifax, the Foreign Secretary, had hotly argued with Churchill to seek peace with Germany.

Churchill smote aside all dissenters with characteristic determination. 'If this long island story of ours is to end at last, let it end only when each one of us lies choking in his own blood upon the ground.'

Good as strong words were, they could not shoot down a Messerschmitt or stop a Heinkel's payload. And the French had gifted them airfields little more than twenty miles from the British coast. Now the 410-mile range of the 109s was not such an issue. They could escort their bombers some distance into England.

No one really questioned the Luftwaffe chief of staff's assertion that it would take 'between a fortnight and a month to smash the enemy air force'.

July 1940

In the build-up to their main assault, the Luftwaffe made probing attacks, seeking weaknesses in the British defences.

When a *Schnellbomber* was spotted on 7 July 1940, rapidly closing on shipping in the Humber, Green Section of 616 Squadron scrambled. Climbing hard through the overcast, they broke through into blue skies close to the distinctive pencil shape of a Dornier 17.

Hugh 'Cocky' Dundas managed a quick burst before the German pilot dived, frantically trying to hide in the broken cloud.[2] Dundas stayed relentlessly on his tail.

'There followed an exciting chase as the German pilot tried frantically to elude us. But nowhere was the cloud solid, he was bound to come out into gaps and by good fortune we maintained contact with him, worrying at his heels like spaniels hunting in cover. He fought back gallantly – desperately would perhaps be a more appropriate word – and for a time his rear-gunner returned our fire, though it was an unequal exchange, which must have been utterly terrifying for him. His tracer bullets streamed past and I received a hit on the outer part of my port wing. But the advantage was all in our favour. The rear-gunner was silenced and the dying Dornier descended in its shroud of black smoke, to crash into the sea.'

The Dornier had no answer to the Spitfire's bank of Brownings, dispatched by Dundas, a 'part-time' flier. Of the forty-two operational squadrons available to Dowding, twelve were Auxiliary Air Force. The fate of Britain rested largely in the hands of solicitors, landowners, artisans and millionaire playboys.

* * *

The fact that there was one more bomber lying at the bottom of the North Sea made little difference to German preparations. The Luftwaffe was gathering a fleet so powerful that it would sweep aside any resistance – a force of 2,460 warplanes: 1,200 bombers, 280 Stuka dive-bombers and 980 frontline fighters.

Despite the frantic efforts at Southampton, and finally Castle Bromwich, in early July Dowding could muster only 226 Spitfires and 344 Hurricanes serviceable with crew.[3] And he still had only 1,000 pilots.[4] This was simply not enough to defend Britain's coastline. Despite the best efforts of Fighter Command, Heinkels, Dorniers and Junkers were getting through the defences.

Nearby explosions were the only warning mechanic Joe Roddis of 234 Squadron had when a flight of Dornier 17s arrived at dawn over St Eval in north Cornwall. He dashed outside with the other mechanics. Incendiaries were flaring dangerously close to the row of eight wooden huts. Then some landed on the roofs. The airmen scrambled up and kicked them off. Roddis felt both terrified and excited. The screaming bombs and flying shrapnel flew through the air. Finally he was in the war.[5]

A final stick of bombs came in, throwing up soil, flames and debris as they arced across the airfield towards their accommodation. The final bomb struck the last hut along the line. This time they started an inferno that was impossible to escape. Joe looked at his fellow airmen in horror. They all knew who slept in the end hut – the young women who served them tea and sandwiches, always with a smile. Joe felt a sense of nausea creep up through his guts. *The NAAFI girls*. There was nothing that could be done. Joe watched with both horror and mounting rage as the screams subsided.

* * *

The home defences were doing their best to stop these attackers getting through. The Spitfires were often flown by men like Bernard Brown, who had barely spent a dozen hours in a fighter, or novices with ten hours' training on fighters. Luftwaffe pilots had an average of thirteen months under instruction, and 200 flying hours. As one German air ace put it, they were 'an invincible war machine that had swept previous opponents away'.[6]

Fighter Command had other weaknesses. They stuck to the rigid 'Vee' formation. The 'Vee' was formed of three aircraft, with two behind the leader, covering the rear. It was designed to take on a bomber force, in the belief that, flying all the way from Germany, they would have no escort. Following the fall of France, that was no longer a safe assumption. And those at the rear of the Vee had little opportunity to avoid a 'bounce' by enemy fighters. The best they could do was follow one veteran's advice: 'Always keep your head turning. It takes about four seconds to shoot down a fighter, so look around every three!'[7]

And silk scarves became obligatory. Constant turns of the head quickly brought on a rash when wearing a cotton shirt.

In July, 115 RAF aircraft were lost. Defending the south-east, 11 Group were stretched to the limit and beyond. They flew more than 500 sorties a day to keep the intruders at bay.

Everyone knew this was just the beginning. The intelligence was overwhelming. It was only a matter of days before the main attack would be launched.

13 August 1940

Joe Roddis was one of twenty ground crew packed onto the wooden benches of the Handley Page Harrow. Most of them could not conceal their excitement at their first flight. 234 Squadron had been ordered to Middle Wallop, Hampshire, at the core of Britain's air defences.

The 200mph converted bomber began a gentle descent over Salisbury Plain. Suddenly it lurched into a steep dive. Joe looked at his fellow mechanics. *Was this normal?*[8]

Word came back from the cockpit. *Air raid. Middle Wallop.*

The Handley Page roared towards the ground then levelled out just feet above the trees and farmsteads. Roddis found himself grinning idiotically. They finally touched down on the grass, rolled past a line of Spitfires and came to a halt. It seemed the airstrip had come through relatively unscathed.

Joe and his mates joined the other 'erks' in the mess and grabbed a turnip jam sandwich. The siren started wailing as he moved to the tea urn. Another raid was coming in. The newly arrived 234 Squadron boys sat tight, thinking, *what a shower*, as the more experienced lads from 609 Squadron scrambled for the exit. Then they heard the wail of the Jericho Trumpet that had struck terror across Europe.

Stukas!

Roddis jumped up and ran outside. Bombs were falling heavily now. Not just the 250kg Junkers 87 ordnance – 50kg stick bombs from Heinkel 111s were slamming into the ground.

Where the hell are the shelters?

He dived to the ground, hands over his ears. A building erupted. Then another and another. Hangar doors smashed open. Glass shattered from office buildings, showering the grass strip in lethal shards. The explosions went on and on.

It stopped as abruptly as it had begun.

Joe hauled himself to his feet. Smoke choked his lungs. Around him, shadowy figures staggered through the billowing dust. He heard shouts and cries for help. He stumbled forward over the fallen debris. Cries of 'stretcher bearer' pierced the clouds of dust; figures darted before him, some limping, some running. His ears rang with a constant, high-pitched whine that echoed the scream of bombs a few seconds earlier, tears streamed from his eyes as he rubbed them clear of debris. His foot caught on something mushy. He dared not look down. A forlorn cry pierced the dust cloud then abruptly stopped.

It was 13 August 1940. The Germans had finally launched *Adlertag*, 'Eagle Day', precisely ten weeks after the last BEF boot had lifted from the sands of Dunkirk. RAF fighters were being destroyed on the ground and in the air as all three *Luftflotte* – air fleets – launched simultaneously from France and Scandinavia, flying 1,485 sorties on the day.

There was no time to mourn the three airmen killed in the Middle Wallop raid. Joe Roddis was ordered to don his tin hat, get to the dispersal area and ready 234 Squadron's Spitfires. Another wave was coming in and they were needed in the air.

Fitters and riggers were each assigned their own aircraft. The 500-gallon petrol bowser pulled alongside it as the pilot left the cockpit. Ground crew swarmed over the machinery, topping up oil, glycol coolant, oxygen and ammunition. Within just twenty-six minutes the starter battery was plugged in, chock ropes stretched, ready for quick removal. The flight sergeant checked everything was in order and applied his signature beneath theirs to the paperwork, clearing the aircraft for flight.[9]

The Spitfire was ready to fly.

* * *

At 4pm that day, 609 Squadron's thirteen Spitfires were ordered to patrol at precisely 15,000ft over Weymouth and to expect a large formation of enemy aircraft. The next thing they heard was the voice of a German commander shepherding his sixty-strong fleet of Ju87 Stukas, escorted by Me109 and Me110 fighters. Not for nothing was the twin-engine 110 known as 'the destroyer'. Capable of 350mph, it carried a potent mix of two 20mm cannons, four 7.92mm machine guns and a single rear-firing machine gun. It was not something you wanted on your tail.

The Spitfires climbed to 20,000ft while a squadron of Hurricanes took care of the 110s. 609 Squadron were now behind and above the Germans. More critically, they were coming out of the sun. Some lessons from France had been well learned. With the enemy in their sights, it was time to close for the kill.

Just as the squadron leader shouted 'Tally-ho', Pilot Officer David Crook, twenty-five, saw five Me109s pass directly beneath him. Crook, a Cambridge graduate from Huddersfield who had joined the Auxiliary Air Force two years earlier, had already claimed a Stuka in the previous month. He saw an opportunity to double his tally. He immediately broke formation and dived on the trailing fighter, sending a hail of bullets from very close range. The Messerschmitt caught fire and corkscrewed down thousands of feet, leaving an endless trail of black smoke behind him. Crook followed the burning machine down through the clouds.[10]

Moments later the tangled wreckage of the 109 lay in a field, the black crosses on its wings visible through the flames. The pilot was still inside. He had made no attempt to get out while the aircraft was diving.

Crook decided he must have been killed by his first burst. He pulled back on his stick but was too late to take part in the unfolding drama above. 'Just after I broke away to attack my Messerschmitt, the whole squadron had dived right into the centre of the German formation and the massacre started. One pilot looked round in the middle of the action and in one small patch of sky he saw five German dive-bombers going down in flames, still more or less in formation.[11]

'We all heard the German commander saying desperately, time after time, "*Achtung, Achtung*, Spitfire . . ."'

It had been a complete rout. Thirteen Luftwaffe planes were destroyed in the space of four minutes. One member of 609 remarked afterwards that he might have missed the Glorious Twelfth the day before, 'but the glorious thirteenth was the best day's shooting I ever had'.

Owing to bad weather, poor intelligence and Fighter Command's resistance, the Germans failed to achieve their objective of knocking out 11 Group's airfields.

On Eagle Day the RAF bagged seventy-one aircraft and lost twenty-nine.

* * *

It was not just the machines that were having an effect. There was a tacit understanding among their pilots that they were all that stood between freedom and occupation. They were the housecarls of the skies, the men who looked the enemy in the eye and gave them a taste of Anglo-Saxon steel.

They were not all from British shores, of course. Some of the toughest came from South Africa, New Zealand, Canada, Australia, and there were also a handful of American volunteers. The fiercest came from those countries already under Nazi thrall: Poles, Czechs, French and Belgians – men with little to lose and a point to prove.

This international brotherhood did not flinch from danger. Some favoured charging directly at the enemy, spreading panic through formations. 'A head-on attack does far more to destroy the morale of the approaching bombers than anything else,' one bullish pilot advised. 'It upsets the driver so much, the poor old pilot. He was the chap who turned tail . . . go straight through the formation, turn round when you get through. And try and have another go from the rear.'[12]

For most pilots, fear was left behind as they rapidly climbed to meet the enemy. Back on the ground it was never far away, everyone knowing that this day might be their last. Friendships could be fleeting. 'See you for a drink down The Ship later,' pilots would banter on their way to a scramble, knowing that 'later' was an open-ended affair. They had seen pilots come and go. Like Arthur Rose-Price, brother of the film actor Dennis Price, a twenty-one-year-old who arrived at Gravesend to join 501 Squadron and was shot down and killed over Dungeness, Kent, the same day, leaving the luggage in the back of his car unpacked.[13]

While death was ever-present it was a subject rarely raised, until a comrade died. Even then it was often buried in the amnesia of binge drinking. Most of the young pilots dealt with it by blithely telling themselves 'it won't happen to me', but not all. It played on the minds of those who survived and lost close friends. For David Crook, who had just shot down his second German, the loss of his schoolboy friend Peter Drummond-Hay, with whom he had joined up then fought alongside, was almost unbearable. 'I could not get out of my head the thought of Peter, with whom we had been talking and laughing that day, now lying in the cockpit of his wrecked Spitfire at the bottom of the English Channel'.[14]

Although few talked of death, it stalked the dispersal room as pilots slouched, slept, joked, talked, ate, smoked and drank, while waiting for the phone to signal the next sortie. When the call came, they all, hardly more than boys, stopped talking. All eyes were riveted on the receiver.

Geoffrey Wellum, aged just nineteen, was among those who found respite through writing in the summer of 1940.[15] 'Moisture collects on my flying boots from last night's heavy dew. It's going to be a lovely day . . .

'Dispersal pen and my Spitfire. I pause and look at her. A long shapely nose, not exactly arrogant but nevertheless daring anyone to take a swing at it. Lines beautifully proportioned, the aircraft sitting there, engine turning easily and smoothly with subdued power. The slipstream blows the moisture over the top of the wings in thin streamlets. Flashes of blue flame from the exhausts are easily seen in the half-light, an occasional backfire and the whole aeroplane trembling like a thoroughbred at the start of the Derby.'

He was ready for when the order came.

'Bound to come sometime. It'll be a miracle if we get through to midday without one.

'Waiting. Thoughts race through the mind. Some read. Some sleep, such as Butch Bryson. He's out to the wide, or is he? Could be after the amount of Scotch he put away last night. I must say I enjoyed that little party a lot. You get a good pint in the White Hart. Pleasant crowd in there as well. Had a letter from a girl called Grace yesterday, sister of a schoolfriend. She seemed interested, shall have to give a bit of thought to her sometime.

'I must have nodded off into an uneasy doze. How long, I wonder. I find myself sitting bolt upright. The phone must have rung. Yes, that's it, the bloody phone again. I swear that if ever I own a house I shall never install a telephone, so help me. All heads and eyes are turned toward the telephone orderly. He seems to be listening for an agonisingly long time.'

False alarm. The NAAFI van had broken down. A flat battery.

'Relax, try to relax, I suppose that's the answer. Don't know the meaning of the word. Nevertheless, let's make a real effort. Hard work, relaxing . . .'

The phone went again. A lone German fighter had been spotted on the radar, coming over Gris Nez, most likely a dawn sortie to check on the weather over Britain.

Two aircraft were dispatched to chase him off. Five minutes later the same thing happened again.

'Black Section, scramble!'

August 1940

In the year since he had dashed to church to tell his stepfather war had been declared, Brian Bird had turned from schoolboy to farmhand.

The sixteen-year-old was cycling to work through the Kent countryside when, 'Something made me turn my head . . . As I did so, I heard with frightening clarity the familiar drone of a German aircraft and without a doubt it was very low. Turning my head skywards I immediately saw a German Dornier. It was so low I could see the crew in its cockpit.[16]

'The thought flashed through my mind that at any moment the road ahead would be peppered with cannon shells and bombs and that would be my end. I threw myself into a nearby ditch with my head firmly pressed to the ground and my heart pumping with utter fear. In a moment some degree of courage returned and it was with immense relief that I saw the Dornier had passed overhead.'

The bomber was on its way to hit an anti-aircraft battery outside the village of Iwade, as part of the plan to level the air defences prior to invasion.

It was an exceptionally dry August. German bomber formations appeared on the horizon immediately after dawn. Teenagers like Brian could only look up and stare with a mixture of awe and envy as the plucky RAF fighters tore up to meet them. 'This was followed by the sound of machine-gun fire, and one knew that the Spitfires and Hurricanes were doing their best to repel the attacks. At other times the anti-aircraft guns would open fire and we watched black balls of smoke near the invading aircraft as the shells burst many thousands of feet above.

'This was a particularly dangerous moment to be in the open fields because of falling shrapnel. On numerous occasions I found myself lying in a ditch with the female farm workers. We were far too scared of falling shrapnel to have any ideas of a quick romance, although when the all clear sounded there were a few hugs and kisses of relief.

'During a particularly heavy barrage of anti-aircraft fire I was sheltering at the doorway of a barn when I heard a whistling noise growing louder and louder. Suddenly, within a few inches of my feet there was a loud thud and upon looking down I saw a jagged eighteen-inch piece of shrapnel embedded in the ground.'

On another occasion Bird came even closer to death during a night-time bombing when he decided to dash from the vicarage's air-raid shelter to retrieve his wristwatch from his room. 'There was a long burst of machine-gun fire and the sound of an aircraft flying very low overhead.' Bird sprinted in the dark back downstairs just in time. 'There was the most horrendous explosion, the house was shaken to its foundations, glass blown out of every window and clouds of dust everywhere.' Fortunately, the family remained unscathed but Brian was determined he was going to do his bit for King and Country to defeat the 'terrible Hun' roaming freely over *his* homeland.

Bird's desire to fly had been piqued with the Air Training Corps when they visited an RAF base and he was taken up in an Anson aircraft. 'I can vividly remember the thrill of being deputed by the pilot to wind up the undercarriage just after take-off and wind it down again as we came in to land.' Brian's future was decided. He was going to become an RAF pilot and take the fight directly to the Germans in the skies.

* * *

But it was not just farm boys who suffered from the indiscriminate bombing. The Germans were intrigued by the English public school system and its ability to produce leaders. They did not want to leave it unscathed.

A shower of incendiary bombs threatened Jimmy Taylor's carefully assembled collection of model aeroplanes at Eton College in Windsor.[17] 'One incendiary fell through the roof of my house and landed on the armchair in a boy's room, burning his Eton tails and trousers. Walking to lessons next morning I saw a finned tail protruding above the surface of a piece of wasteland.'

A follow-up attack a few days later suggested that the school was indeed being deliberately targeted. A 500lb bomb demolished the music precentor's house. Fortunately, the teacher and his wife and seventy boys escaped unscathed.

The next morning, the school clerk entered his office and almost fell down a hole in the floor. At the bottom lay a delayed-action bomb, too awkwardly placed and too delicate to be defused. The area around Upper School was evacuated.

Taylor and his schoolmates continued with their schooling, although 'it was difficult to concentrate on lessons when the wretched thing was liable to explode at any moment'.

Taylor had completed his evening homework and was about to apply the finishing touches to a model Me109 when there was a tremendous roar. 'Damn the Hun,' he cursed as a yellow smudge smeared the cockpit.

A great lump of masonry had flown over the four-storey Lupton's Tower and onto the opposite side of the Yard, but the 500-year-old College Wing adjacent to Upper School remained sturdily in place.

For Taylor, the German belligerence provided further incentive to turn his model aircraft hobby into something real.

Late August 1940

The first phase of the German plan to pummel England into submission seemed relatively straightforward. Destroy the RAF on the ground and in the air; target harbours and storage facilities and level the ground defences around London.

The Heinkels, Dorniers and Junkers 88s could bomb from height, while the feared Stukas would be used for precision attacks. All would be protected by fighters.

Pilots like Helmut Wick quickly learned to use the 109's supreme climbing and diving power, along with its cannon, to great effect. Starting combat operations late in 1939, he did not have the experience of the Spanish Civil War, but already had more than a score of kills to his name. He was certainly not going to be outdone by a Spitfire, especially when he found himself suddenly outnumbered. 'To the right there is nothing, but I cannot believe my eyes when I look the other way. The sky is full of Spitfires and just a few 109s. I go straight into a dogfight but at once get a Spitfire on my back. At full speed I try to lose him. Now I have one Spitfire in front and another behind me.[18]

'Damn it! I dive vertically away to lose him then climb again. Suddenly I see white trails shooting past. I look back. Yet another is behind me, sending his tracers past my ear like the "fingers of the dead". I will thank God if my mother's son can get out of this fight! I manage to outclimb the Spitfires and try again to help my outnumbered comrades but each time the Tommies come down behind me. Suddenly a 109 comes past very fast with a Spitfire behind it. This is my chance. I get behind the Spitfire and centre it in my gunsight. After a few shots it goes down.'

The Me109 was proving a formidable adversary for the Spitfire, even for those experienced pilots like Hugh Dundas who had survived the opening salvoes of the battle. On 22 August 1940 he was 'jumped' by a Messerschmitt. The first thing he felt was the explosion of cannon shells along the fuselage.

'Smoke filled the cockpit, thick and hot, and I could see neither the sky above nor the Channel coast 12,000ft below. Centrifugal force pressed me against the side of the cockpit and I knew my aircraft was spinning. Panic and terror consumed me and I thought, "Christ, this is the end." Then I thought, "Get out, you bloody fool; open the hood and get out."

'With both hands I tugged the handle where the hood locked onto the top of the windscreen. It moved back an inch then jammed. Smoke poured out through the gap and I could see again. I could see the earth and the sea and the sky spinning round in tumbled confusion as I cursed and blasphemed and pulled with all my strength to open the imprisoning hood.

'If I could not get out I had at all costs to stop the spin. I pushed the stick hard forward, kicked on full rudder, opened the throttle. Nothing happened. The earth went spinning on, came spinning up to meet me. Grabbing the hood toggle again, I pulled with all my might, pulled for my life, pulled at last with success. I stood up on the seat and pushed the top half of my body out of the cockpit. Pressed hard against the fuselage, half in, half out, I struggled in a nightmare of fear and confusion to drop clear, but could not do so.

'I managed to get back into the cockpit, aware now that the ground was very close. Try again, try the other side. Up, over – and out. I slithered along the fuselage and felt myself falling free. Seconds after my parachute opened I saw the Spitfire hit and explode in a field below.'[19]

Dundas had been shot down in a classic Messerschmitt tactic. The Luftwaffe pilots perfected a hit-and-run: diving fast to hit their prey, usually from below, then using their superior rate of climb to get away from retaliatory attacks. It was vital to staying alive. There was growing unease that if you got into a dogfight with a Spitfire, your chances of survival were vastly reduced. While Dunkirk had given some a foretaste of the fighter's abilities, they were only beginning to sink in.

In short, the Spitfire was bad for morale.

'Spitfire *auf meinem Schwanz!*' – 'Spitfire on my tail!' – was gaining wide currency in German radio chatter. 'From then it sometimes doesn't last long until that voice doesn't exist any more.'

Ulrich Steinhilper was one pilot who'd heard the phrase too often. '"Spitfire on my tail" was usually a very bad surprise. And sometimes you panicked.'

Others shared his view. 'I know my fellow 109 pilots were very fearful of the Spitfire,' said Hans-Ekkehard Bob. 'When the message "*Achtung!* Spitfire!" came, everyone shuddered.

'The Spitfire was extremely manoeuvrable, albeit the 109 being still a bit faster, but you had to bring to bear all your skill and all of your feeling in order to be able to cope with the opponent in situations like that.'[20]

The 109 was being out-turned by R. J. Mitchell's unique wing structure, and did not have the Spitfire's ability to warn of an impending stall if it went into a spin. Messerschmitt pilots also struggled to open the narrow cockpit canopy in the panic of bailing out, and visibility was an issue. The 109 did not have the British fighter's sophisticated gunsights, so the pilots had to do their own deflection-shot adjustment mid-battle, calculating how far in front of the moving target they had to fire to hit it.

But the differences were marginal. It was now becoming a question of attrition. Who had the numbers of aircraft and airmen?

The RAF might have plucky pilots and clever aircraft, but German might was overwhelming. It was time to throttle Fighter Command into submission.

From 24 August, the Germans went for the knockout blow. For the next two weeks there were glorious blue, cloudless skies. Airfields were struck day after day, telephone lines destroyed and radar stations blasted off-line. Spitfires and Hurricanes were hit before they could take to the skies. Pilots flying four or more sorties a day were lost to battle fatigue. Some squadrons all but ceased to exist in a single day. The London Blitz had begun and the German attacks were relentless. For the next fifty-six out of fifty-seven days the Luftwaffe bombed London, with 400 civilians killed in the first attack. Throughout the war, 43,000 British civilians were to perish from Luftwaffe bombings.

Joe Roddis

At Middle Wallop the pilots of Joe Roddis' squadron were taking a mauling. Of the twenty-one experienced fliers who had arrived on Eagle Day, only three remained. 'It worried us when so many pilots were shot down. It's hard to explain but we looked up to them, were proud of them and we were doing all we could to get them airborne.'[21]

For those at the forefront of the conflict it was a desperate time to keep the fighters in the skies. The last flight of the day would usually land by 10pm, then had to be ready for action five hours later. The mechanics would often sleep under the wings.

An experienced crew using two hoses from a bowser could get refuelling times down to three minutes. Roddis immediately quizzed the pilots on where they might have been hit, then combed the fuselage for holes. 'We tracked the course of the bullets to see where they had gone and if they had caused any other damage. If they had gone through the propeller it didn't really matter as we would just use a rat-tail file to file it out and clean it up. It might whistle a bit after but that didn't matter. We had to have the aircraft ready to fly again in twenty minutes. If that couldn't be done it would be pushed aside and we would help someone else get their aircraft ready.'

Ziggy Klein and Jan Zurakowski, two Poles whose aircraft he serviced, 'were only really happy in the air shooting Germans down, and they were good at it'.[22] They and their fellow countrymen made up 5 per cent of the pilots, but their hatred of the Nazis was such that they were accounting for 15 per cent of Luftwaffe losses.[23]

The nearest protection mechanics had was a slit trench. Joe Roddis had now been bombed enough to know they had to dig deep into the solid chalk beneath Middle Wallop. The hard-won experience saved his life when the Germans used a new ruse. 'We'd been brought to full readiness but not scrambled. Pilots were in cockpits, ground crews ready for a quick start and still they held us on the ground! Directly above us, pretty high up, were hordes of 109s just circling round and round but doing nothing threatening. Everyone was watching the show above us when they suddenly stopped circling and headed off for Southampton.

'*Scramble!*

'Red Very flares flew skywards and off our squadron went, closely followed by 609 Squadron, the whole lot climbing up to get the 109s. We watched for a short while in the silence that followed. Then we became aware why they had enticed our Spitfires away. Ju87s that had been out of sight above the 109s were diving down. We didn't stop to count them, just headed at top speed for the slit trench. I dived in and crouched there, listening to the diving Stukas and the crash of their bombs flattening our buildings.

'You could see the bombs leave the Stuka at the end of its dive.'

Their speed in getting to the shelter and its depth meant the shrapnel from exploding ordnance whizzed harmlessly overhead.

'When Jerry came we got our pilots airborne then dived for the slit trench. The pilots went out to take them on and often paid the ultimate price. To us, our pilots earned everything we could do for them.'

* * *

Fighter Command was losing dozens of pilots a day – killed, wounded or missing in action. Squadrons were rotated in from around Britain to replace the dead, the lame and the exhausted.

The strain was beginning to show, with pilots noticeably more short-tempered. Some wondered aloud how much longer they could carry on.

At Biggin Hill, intolerance reached new levels. There were occasions when, if a chink of light showed from a window, the offending bulb was shot out by rifle fire.

The focus of pilots' attention remained the jangling of the dispersal phone. Nerves were frayed to the extreme.

Figures came and went. Veterans could see the look of death on the faces of some young pilots who they knew would soon become notches on Luftwaffe tally boards. And it was not just the young and inexperienced who were being claimed.

Michael Doulton had served in the RAF for almost a decade, having joined the Auxiliary Air Force in 1931. He had not gone into his family's famous ceramic business, Royal Doulton, and instead became a mechanical engineer. Standing at 6ft 8in, Doulton was not difficult to pick out in a crowd. Which was probably why the young American, Carol Christie, spotted him while skiing in Davos in 1938. Their romance swiftly led to marriage the following year then, a few days before war broke out, Doulton was called up to the RAF.

Both knew that as a fighter pilot his life was at risk every day. In mid-August he just made it back to Tangmere after his aircraft was damaged in a dogfight. That evening he went back to the cottage near the airfield that he shared with Carol, who was pregnant. He confessed his fears. She knew the dangers he faced daily; his tussles with the Germans had left him with three confirmed kills. Then, on 31 August, she waited all night for the sound of his footsteps approaching the door of their cottage. But none came. Michael had perished during a melee over the Thames.

Carol met his death with astonishing stoicism. They had discussed it in private and agreed only to dwell on the happiness they had shared. But Carol needed an outlet for her emotions and wrote a long letter to her father in Rhode Island the following day.[24] 'I pray that he came down into the sea and that he will just vanish. I have no desire for the horror of bodies or funerals to come between me and my last happy memories of Michael, young and strong and confident. To have him just disappear suddenly and cleanly in the midst of life and never return broken and dead is how it should be. You see, ever since the war started and I expected to lose Michael, I have wanted a child. So that if Michael were lost something of our love would live on and so it wouldn't be the end of everything for me . . .

'Now what is behind me is all happiness, and no two people were ever so happy right up to the last minute as we were, and I don't look forward to complete emptiness. I have his child to think of, and even if I felt hysterical I wouldn't be, because of the baby . . .

'How many times Michael and I have said: "If we died tomorrow, how much more happiness we have had than most people." I am now finding that I meant it. I keep looking at his things – everything reminds me of some happy time together. The little bear he pulled out of his cap at the station when he left Davos. The bluebird pin he gave me to keep me happy while I was at home. The five tins of his favourite oxtail soup sitting in the cupboard. His brushes. I don't want to put them out of sight. I want to have them around and relive every glorious moment . . .

'Michael was so happy about the baby – thank God he knew before he died. He made me promise I would go home to you if he were killed. But don't waste grief on me. Remember that I have a child to look forward to and that I have had eighteen months of wonderful happiness.'

Doulton's body was later found inside his aircraft, the gun button still set to 'Fire', the throttle fully open.[25]

* * *

The Battle of Britain heroics were witnessed by thousands on the ground, including boys who yearned to join the knights of the skies unashamedly glamourised in the press. Among them was sixteen-year-old John Wilkinson, who watched the aerial duels from his school in Horsham, West Sussex. 'Standing outside I witnessed the fighters perform their deadly ballet, painting condensation trails and machines falling from the sky. It filled me with awe.'[26]

When the Germans switched to the Blitz on London, Wilkinson experienced the fear and devastation of war first-hand and it made him determined to fight back. 'The noise of anti-aircraft guns firing and the bombs exploding throughout the night was horrendous. One night the house two doors from us was bombed and destroyed. Our windows were shattered, walls cracked and all our heavy plaster ceilings fell down. In the morning the streets and lawns were littered with small, very sharp shell fragments from the anti-aircraft shells.'

Getting to work as a junior clerk in the City near St Paul's Cathedral, Wilkinson had to scramble over rubble not knowing if his office would still be standing. The streets around the famous church were laced with fire brigade hoses. 'I passed buildings with flames pouring from their windows. There simply wasn't enough water to put them out. The firemen had to move to areas where they could be more effective.'

The kernel of an idea that had been forming in Wilkinson's mind began to take a grip. *I can get up there and take on the bastards who've done this.*

Three years earlier his mother had paid seven shillings and sixpence for him to go on a brief flight in a biplane. Wilkinson had been instantly hooked.

He looked up from the flames and rubble around St Paul's into the dirty smoke obscuring the blue skies. He was eighteen and could make his own choices. *I'm going to join the RAF and become a fighter pilot.*

He also had a point to prove to his mother and the wider world. Eight years earlier, his father had taken his own life after their business in the US went bust during the Great Depression. Wilkinson would prove to everyone that he was a man worthy to lead his family.

His ears caught a familiar sound. He looked up and saw a flight of Spitfires pierce the smoke to meet the enemy threat. *I have to fly.*

* * *

But the battle's losses were building and the time for someone who had more flying hours in Spitfires than anyone else in the RAF remaining a spectator was over. Civilian test pilot Jeffrey Quill knew there would be no point testing new Spitfires if there was no country left from which to fly them.

He had to do his bit. He knew Vickers Supermarine would put up a stiff fight to stop its top test pilot going to war, so he told them something close to the truth. 'In order to do my job properly I must gain first-hand experience of fighting in a Spitfire.'[27]

In August 1940, Quill joined 65 Squadron at RAF Manston and in a matter of days he began operations for real. Quill's squadron was sent to Dover, where 109s were shooting down barrage balloons. He spotted a fighter and went for him, getting close before opening fire. 'I saw my tracers going right through his fuselage. I expected him to swerve or half-roll or something, so was all keyed-up to follow but he just went straight on down so I gave him another burst and another and still he went on downwards and not very fast.

'I thought I had been spending too long on him and turned quickly to see if anyone was behind me and found all clear but a lot of aircraft swirling around some way away. Thinking about it on the way back I came to the conclusion that I must have hit the pilot in the head or the back with the first burst because of his complete indifference to my fire.' Quill had killed the German outright.

He was soon to find out that RAF Manston was high on the list of Luftwaffe target bases. On 12 August he was sitting in his Spitfire, engine running, ready to taxi out for take-off, when there was a tremendous bang behind him.

Quill looked over his right shoulder in time to see one of the hangar roofs ascending heavenwards. 'This was followed by showers of earth and black smoke, then more and louder "crumps". I caught a glimpse through the smoke of what looked like an Me110 pulling sharply out of a dive and concluded it was high time for Quill to be airborne. We were being dive-bombed.

'I put my head down, slammed the throttle wide open, wondering what chance I had of getting airborne before a bomb dropped immediately ahead of me or even on me . . . As I became airborne I glanced in the mirror and saw nothing but bomb-bursts and showers of earth and smoke immediately behind.'

Seconds after his wheels left the ground a 109 swooped overhead. Quill went to ground level, weaving furiously. In the following seconds he knew he would be cold meat for any swooping Messerschmitt. He looked around, saw no Germans and pulled the nose up into a steep spiral turn. 'We had of course been extremely lucky. But our best bit of good fortune was that the Me109s who came boring down at us just as we were getting airborne hopelessly overshot because they were going much too fast. They should have slaughtered us.'[28]

They had indeed been lucky. One part of Goering's plan had worked to perfection – to lure the fighters into the air, where his 109s would destroy them. However, the agile Spitfires eluded them.

In terms of accuracy, the attack was a resounding success. The Germans dropped 148 bombs on the airfield, but Manston was open for business the very next day. The only near-casualty had been a Spitfire whose propeller had been bent out of kilter from the blast of a bomb exploding immediately behind. The unfortunate pilot was left stranded in the middle of the target area surrounded by incoming explosions but survived physically unscathed. The British were showing an unexpected resilience that incensed Hitler and his cronies.

But their fortitude was being tested to its limits. The clear skies continued into September. The raids on air defences went on unabated. For the first time, Fighter Command's losses outstripped those of the Germans.

In a two-week period from 24 August to 4 September, 295 British fighters had been destroyed and 171 damaged, with the Luftwaffe losing barely half this number of 109s.[29] Despite Beaverbrook's improvements, the factories produced 269 new and repaired fighters. In the same period, 103 pilots were killed and 128 wounded.

Air Vice-Marshal Keith Park, the brilliant tactician in charge of 11 Group, warned of the seriousness of the losses. In desperation, the RAF returned units that had taken a battering in Dunkirk to the arena.

Among them was 222 Squadron, where Hilary Edridge, twenty-one, and Tim Vigors, nineteen, had formed a close bond on the ground and a formidable partnership in the air. Theirs was a friendship that would have been unlikely outside war. Edridge was a gentle, church-going Catholic who had a deep love of literature and music. Vigors was a proud Protestant Anglo-Irishman with the Tricolour painted on his Spitfire's nose. His grandfather, from Co. Carlow, was also something of a 'player'. When caught in bed with a maid, his excuse to his wife was: 'If one is going to appreciate Château Lafite, my dear, one must occasionally have a glass of *vin ordinaire*.' Vigors had been hooked on aircraft ever since his godmother had taken him on a flight just before the war.

Both Vigors and Edridge had been in the thick of action since Dunkirk, when they were ordered into combat for the first time. Vigors had been scared: 'My mouth was dry and for the first time in my life I understood the meaning of the expression "taste of fear". I suddenly realised that the moment had arrived . . . Within an hour I would be battling for my life . . . Up until now it had all somehow been a game, like a Biggles book where the heroes always survived the battles and it was generally only the baddies who got the chop. I knew I had somehow to control this fear and not show it to my fellow pilots.'[30]

Flying out of Hornchurch, they were quickly into the action in late August to meet another incursion. Vigors had made a tight left-hand diving turn to evade a fighter when a Dornier 17 appeared right in front of him, just 200 yards away. 'As I prepared to fire, the Dornier exploded, and a Spitfire, with guns still blazing, followed it down. I saw the registration letters of Hilary's aircraft on the side of the fuselage. I yelled with delight!'

But Edridge took no pride in killing his fellow man. During dinner, his girlfriend recounted her father's excitement at the sight of two Spitfires taking out a Dornier.[31] His face reddened, and he asked her where and at what time the fight had taken place. Then he spoke very quietly. 'One of those pilots was me.'

She asked him several more questions, but the loss of life, and what had happened to him on a sortie later the same day, had darkened his mood.

Edridge had been confronted with the terrifying prospect of burning to death in his cockpit. His Spitfire had been hit in the petrol tank and immediately caught fire. The flames licked his ankles then moved up his legs. His first reaction had been gratitude that the daily struggle to stay alive was finally over. He put up his hand to make the sign of the cross but his arm was constrained by his parachute harness.

He paused.

At the very least, he had to try to bail out. He had a duty to fight for his life.

Thankfully, the canopy flew back and he made a good getaway. He allowed himself to fall closer to earth before pulling the D-ring of his parachute. Some Germans, aware that RAF pilots who bailed out were quickly returning to the fray, had taken to machine-gunning them that day.

Edridge landed safely between the trees, albeit on the back of a sheep, at Broome Park in Kent. He peered skywards, made the sign of the cross, then looked down at his burnt legs. It was nothing, really, compared to some of the things he'd seen. He'd recover soon enough to fight again.

* * *

Unlike Edridge, who had at least had some combat experience over Dunkirk, some pilots arrived on operations having barely fired the Spitfire's guns.

After just three weeks of Spitfire training, and a few patrols from Biggin Hill devoid of any action, Bernard Brown decided to go on a foray. He drove his J-type MG up to London, parking it outside the Wagon and Horses on Regent Street, near Piccadilly Circus. Independent-minded and generally underwhelmed by authority, Brown had not bothered to register the car. Emerging from the pub he spotted a policeman standing next to the MG.

'Where's your registration?' the officer asked.

'In the pocket of the car,' Brown bluffed, hoping his RAF fighter pilot uniform might buy him some leeway. It did.

'OK, then, I shan't look,' the policeman said. 'But where are you heading to?'

'Biggin Hill.'

Spotting the glint of alcohol in Brown's eyes, the officer offered to drive him back, perhaps in the knowledge that the mess had decent beer, including Scotch Ale.

Brown was not wrong. 'Sure enough, that's what he was angling for. I invited him in for a drink. He had to borrow my sports jacket as he still had a police uniform on. I supplied him with plenty of free beer.' The hours passed and Brown wondered what to do. He did not have to worry for long. A few minutes later, a police car rolled up to the mess to collect the inebriated officer.

A few days later Brown was back at the Officers' Mess bar and looking forward to a break. At 2am, he was still taking advantage of the fact that he would not be flying that day when his Flight Commander approached him. 'Pity it's meant to be your day off,' he said. 'You're on at six.'

Brown gave a laconic shrug of the shoulders, finished his drink and headed to bed. He was fast asleep in the dispersal room when the phone shrieked its warning, and he'd barely had time to wipe the sleep from his eyes when he was tearing down the airstrip. On the squadron leader's command of 'Buster' he engaged the emergency boost, giving himself another 34mph to gain height.

Within minutes he found himself under attack.

'They were all over me. I didn't have any time for fear but it was a brutal introduction to the battle. They came down on me all guns blazing. Bullets, shells all over the place. Then there was a 109 below me. I was turning madly at the time. He must have pulled his nose up and let fly. A cannon shell came through the side of my aircraft and hit me in the left leg, exploding on the throttle box underneath my left arm. There was no control of the aeroplane whatsoever; the engine was roaring its life out and I couldn't steer, I couldn't do anything. I just thought, "Right, Brown, this is the time."

'I had to remember what had now become the most important lesson of all – bailing out! I hadn't had any official instructions but a friend had told me what to do if I ever had to jump out. Funnily enough, I remembered the drill exactly. "Take your helmet off, because it's connected to the aeroplane by the cables and you'll probably get hung." So I took my helmet off and remember hanging it on the hook in the cockpit. "Right, now undo the straps." We always went into action with the hood open because if a bullet went through the mechanism it might not slide back. I just undid the straps and thought: "Right, here we go." I turned the aircraft on its back and that was that.

'I don't remember much but the next moment I knew I was out and I could feel air rushing past my face. Then no air. I was turning over and over, spinning as I fell. I thought I'd better find that D-ring which was tucked underneath my left arm. I gave it a quick pull and then it all went dead quiet.

'I felt quite happy to be honest, I was free. I landed in the marsh, just out from Eastchurch airfield. Although I'd been blasted by the exploding shell, I couldn't feel any pain. But when I landed I just collapsed and folded up. That's when I discovered I had a big hole in my left leg.

'I looked up and saw a bloke from the Home Guard coming towards me. He got about ten yards away and stopped. He didn't say a word. Just covered me with his .303 rifle.

'Fortunately, an RAF truck came across the field. The blokes lifted me on but the Home Guard chap still didn't say a word and was still covering me with his rifle. I was more frightened about him than anything else.'

Brown joined the growing number of wounded. The 109's bullet had put a hole in his knee, destroying the tendons. Another Spitfire pilot – along with his aircraft – had been blasted from the fray. Casualties like Brown, and his Spitfire, were not easily replaced.

Speaking from their home in New Zealand, Bernard's wife had warned me her husband remembered little about the war, but once he began to reminisce during our interview the cobwebs of time fell away and it was as though he was back in the cockpit of his beloved Spitfire that day. Sadly, Bernard died a few months after I spoke to him and would not live to see this book published.

September 1940

Despite the fortitude of its airmen, the RAF was losing control of the skies over south-east England. And that was all the Germans needed.

Surely, some in the Luftwaffe asked, they had established sufficient air superiority to cover amphibious landings along the south coast before the autumn storms set in? It was early September and the seas were calm.

Fighter Command's boss, Keith Park, understood the gravity of the situation. He issued an order to 11 Group that in the event of invasion they should prepare to fly eight sorties a day, landing only to refuel and rearm.

German pride had just taken a battering when ninety-five RAF bombers penetrated Berlin's defences, causing some damage and killing ten civilians. Infuriated, Hitler acceded to Goering's request to blitz London. The RAF, Goering argued, would throw up their last fighter reserves to protect the capital. These would be dealt with, London flattened and Britain's morale destroyed.

The battle for Britain's existence was about to enter its decisive phase. It was a desperate time, and it called for desperate measures.

* * *

Rugger, rock-climbing, cricket and camping holidays had been uppermost in the minds of the young sergeant pilots who had joined the RAF Volunteer Reserve in the mid-1930s. War for the likes of Ray Holmes had seemed a distant possibility when, on the recommendation of the acclaimed racing driver E. B. Ware, he joined the reserves. At that point Holmes, from Liverpool, was a cub reporter on the *Birkenhead Advertiser*, so the idea of an intensive ten-week course learning to fly followed by weekends in aircraft was appealing. And the £25 annual bonus helped too, for it could buy a young reserve pilot a good second-hand car. The only other demand was that if war broke out the Volunteer Reserves would be mobilised immediately into the regular RAF.

So in 1939 Holmes had been rapidly drafted but then found himself kicking his heels in Scotland while all the action was going on down south. Then in late summer 1940, the Hurricanes of 504 Squadron were suddenly sent south to protect London.

Thus, on 15 September 1940, Sergeant Holmes was over central London among a swarm of Dornier bombers. After making one attack Holmes banked away then, when he came in again, found the sky seemingly empty but for a lone Dornier that appeared to be making a bomb run on Buckingham Palace.[32] Holmes had expended most of his ammunition helping to break up the thirty-strong bomber formation heading for the city. As he went to engage the Dornier in a head-on attack, his guns spluttered to a halt.

The story is picked up in an account Holmes later gave to a newspaper reporter:[33]

'He was hurtling straight for the Dornier. In a moment he must break away. But the German pilot had not deviated an inch from his course. There was only one way to stop him now. Hit him for six. In the heat of battle, with his own machine crippled and in a desperate bid to smash the invader before it broke through to his target, he shunned the instinct to turn away. How flimsy the Dornier tail-plane looked as it filled his windscreen. The tough little Hurricane would shatter it like balsa wood. As he aimed his port wing at the nearside fin of the Dornier's twin tail, he was sweating. He felt only the slightest jar as the wing of the Hurricane sliced through. Incredibly, he was getting away with it. The Hurricane was turning slightly to the left and diving a little. Suddenly the dive turned vertical, Holmes was heading down to the ground at 500mph. After a struggle Holmes managed to bail out. The scene of the Dornier, Hurricane and parachute coming to earth was watched by hundreds of grateful Londoners. The Dornier that seemed intent on bombing Buckingham Palace had been brought to earth. It was one of the many acts of heroism seen during the battle.'[34]

The 'Buckingham Palace Dornier' was among the fifty-six German aircraft shot down that day. The RAF lost half that number. It was a decisive victory.

The Blitz over London would continue for many months, but, thanks to the bravery of Ray Holmes and his colleagues, the tide was beginning to turn as German attacks were repelled. There would finally be some respite from the relentless barrages on the home defences, giving the airfields, aircraft and airmen a chance to reform and reorganise. Despite the devastation, London could take the hits.

The use of Spitfires to tackle the fighters, and Hurricanes to take on the bombers, had proved highly effective. Their success sapped German morale.

'The Spitfires showed themselves wonderfully manoeuvrable,' Max-Hellmuth Ostermann recounted. 'Their aerobatics display – looping and rolling, opening fire in a climbing roll – filled us with amazement.'[35]

Some Germans had simply had enough and reluctance to cross the Channel in the teeth of British resistance increased. The Germans called it *Kanalkrankheit* – Channel sickness.

Goering was having none of it. He strode into the forward headquarters in Pas-de-Calais, berating senior officers and seasoned pilots for failing to protect the bombers.

Meeting stony silence, Goering became more emollient and asked what they needed. One pilot replied that more powerful engines were required. The request was granted.

Then the *Reichsmarschall* turned to the distinguished ace, Adolf Galland. 'And you?'

'A squadron of Spitfires,' Galland boldly replied.[36]

Goering turned on his heels, speechless in rage.

October 1940

The shift from attempting to eliminate the RAF to unleashing the Blitz on London and other cities provided a respite for the air force, but the civilian population needed its pilots more than ever to protect them. Supermarine in Southampton had already been bombed, with the loss of more than 100 skilled workers.

Life for those living under German bombardment was as terrifying as for those fighting in the skies. At times there was typical British stoicism. The rising star of film Ann Todd was acting in *Peter Pan* when a particularly bad raid came in and the play was stopped. Todd went on stage to address the audience: 'Mummies and daddies, aunts, uncles and friends and children, there is a lot of fighting and noise going on outside, so I, Peter, suggest you stay safe and cosy underground with the Lost Boys and me till it's over.'[37]

Sometime later, Todd found herself in rather different circumstances, in a corridor in Gerrards Cross nursing home giving birth to her daughter by her fighter pilot husband, Nigel Tangye. 'The nursing home was packed with pregnant women and when the Germans bombed a wartime engineering factory nearby, this was the moment my Pippin decided to arrive.

'The lights had all gone out. Nigel was away on duty and I was alone. She was delivered by candlelight to a background of bombs falling out of the sky and the doctor's voice saying severely to me: "Please concentrate on creation, Mrs Tangye, and ignore the destruction around us."'

* * *

Hilary Edridge

After a month spent trying to recover from the wounds he suffered in late August after being shot down, Hilary Edridge left hospital in October intent on fighting, despite his barely healed burns. His friend Tim Vigors was there to welcome him back to the squadron, albeit with some reservation. 'He shouldn't have come back so quickly, but he realised we were very short of pilots and he insisted on flying again. I tried to talk him out of it but he was an obstinate devil.'[38]

Edridge thought better of telling Vigors about the vivid premonition of death he had experienced in hospital. He could not explain why, it had just come to him that he was entering his final days on earth. On one level it gave him an inner peace, a chance to say his goodbyes.

He took to the skies, attacking Germans whenever he could. He helped destroy a 110 and then survived a crash-landing after engine failure.

It was getting late in October. With the threat of autumn gales increasing, the chances of a German invasion were receding. Edridge was sent home to Bath on leave, but a strange mood overtook him. Mournful violin tunes could be heard in his bedroom, alongside the jovial sounds of Gilbert and Sullivan. He said farewell to a schoolfriend. Then, on the last day of his leave, he attended Holy Communion. Afterwards, he asked the priest for confession. Body and soul were now in harmony for what he felt was to come.

On 30 October, 222 Squadron was sent towards a vicious scrap that had spiralled westwards over East Sussex. Edridge was at the back, covering the squadron's vulnerable tail. Just before they entered the fight, Tim Vigors checked over his shoulder. A sick feeling swept through him. An ugly black cloud had engulfed Edridge's Spitfire, sending it earthwards.

Edridge was stricken but not dead. He had been shot in the head and the Spitfire's engine was disintegrating. He regained some control and brought the aircraft down fast over the neatly cropped fields of the Weald. He fought hard to keep it aloft, managing to circle the countryside around the village of Northiam, searching for a flat stretch to land. The altimeter showed he had little time in which to act. He spotted a small valley just beyond the magnificent Lutyens-designed Great Dixter House.

His plane roared towards the building, but at the last moment he managed to lift it clear, crashing into the little valley behind. Staff from Great Dixter ran to the site and found Edridge trapped in the crumpled cockpit. A knife was used to cut him out of the parachute straps then many pairs of caring hands lifted him free. Within minutes an ambulance was rushing him to a field hospital.

But it was not enough. He died two hours later.

On hearing of his great friend's death, Tim Vigors was stricken. He sat outside the dispersal hut and wept. 'A wave of misery swept over me. I just couldn't get my mind to accept it.

'I went berserk, making myself a thorough nuisance to the enemy. Once I had got it out of my system I was absolutely calm again but I still missed Hilary.'

Hilary Edridge was the 536th pilot to die in the Battle of Britain. Its last but one fatality.

'Never was so much owed by so many to so few . . .' Churchill once again captured the nation's mood.

And alongside his fellow countrymen, he had found a place in his heart for 'the very small thing that fights like hell'.

The German losses were considerable and near-irrecoverable. The Luftwaffe had more than 2,500 aircrew killed or missing plus nearly 1,000 taken prisoner. The great cohort of combat experience gained in Spain, Norway and France had been severely diminished. The material losses were also high – nearly 2,000 fighters and bombers destroyed. Fighter Command suffered too, with 544 dead, and the RAF losing 1,744 aircraft.

The human and machine losses were high, but that was not everything. For the first time the Nazi war machine had been defeated. And defeated decisively. The Spitfire had been blooded and successful in its early battles. But the war was only just beginning.

CHAPTER FOUR

Rhubarbs, Ramrods and Circuses

When Robbie Robertson picked up a newspaper and read about the capitulation of Sudetenland to Hitler he understood conflict was coming. It was September 1938. His mind raced over the possibilities and the desire to escape the tedium of life as a poorly paid London insurance broker.[1]

He saw the smooth lines of a Spitfire in a recruiting poster. *That has to be the most beautiful aircraft in the world*, he thought. Robertson's future was decided. He would become a fighter pilot and get as far as possible from the dreariness of the Ocean Accident and Guarantee Company.

He applied for the RAF Volunteer Reserve in April 1939, was accepted then told to await a medical. And he waited. War came in September and, despite recruitment offices springing up across the country, still he waited.

It was the Conscription Act that rescued him from the Ocean Accident and Guarantee Company. In June 1940, Robertson was called up for interview with several other pilot hopefuls.

'What are thirteen thirteens?' the interviewing officer asked seconds after he'd sat down.

'One hundred and sixty-nine,' Robbie immediately replied.

The man looked staggered. 'That's jolly good – did you just work it out?'

'No,' he replied. 'I just asked the last chap who came in.'

The officer chuckled and ran through a list of questions. Could he drive a car, handle a yacht, ride a horse? *Yes*, Robbie replied to all, wondering if he'd be believed. He even agreed to become an air-gunner if he couldn't be a pilot.

As Britain fought for its life during 1940, Robbie joined other potential pilots training in the Devon countryside, where they had a brief glimpse of the reality of war. During a route march, a Ju88 flew at 100ft over the column of men, smoke streaming from its starboard engine. Despite their corporal's blasphemous tirades that they'd all be massacred, the men stood staring. Seconds later two Hurricanes streaked overhead, ensuring the Ju88's destruction.

Two years after he'd first applied for the RAF, Robbie Robertson began to fly. And he was good at it. After eight hours and fifty minutes he went solo.

'Right, Robbie, the next time I see you I want to see that top button undone,' his instructor said, as Robertson stood grinning at the postings board. The hallmark of Fighter Command pilots was for their uniform to be left open at the neck.

Out of the five people on his course, only two had been chosen to go on fighters.

* * *

For those actually in the fight there was little room for mirth. Hugh Dundas had fretted at the idea of returning to action after he had been shot down in August 1940. 'I view the prospect of combat with real inner fear. The memory of what had happened last time crowded back in on me. The juvenile desire for glory which had been uppermost in my mind had been driven out altogether by the fear of death and the personal knowledge of the unpleasant form in which it was likely to come.'[2]

Cocky Dundas (right) with brother John

Dundas was not alone in warriors undone by what they had seen and experienced. The RAF's finest were beginning to wobble. It was a time for leaders in the mould of Drake, Nelson and Wellington.

It was a man with tin legs who steeled Dundas' nerves towards the end of the Battle of Britain. Douglas Bader was a man of deep resilience. He had lost both legs in an air crash when training to become an RAF pilot in 1931. First he relearned to walk then got back in a plane and passed all his flying tests. But the RAF administrators decided against having a double amputee in the air force. On the outbreak of war Bader presented himself ready for action. Desperate for pilots, the RAF took him on. They did not regret their decision. From Dunkirk onwards, he bludgeoned his way through melees, scoring victory after victory. His strong nerve, resilience, bitter humour and pure bloody-mindedness set him apart as a leader. 'Douglas showed the way a man should behave in war,' Dundas wrote.

Sometimes this was through something so fantastically calm and obscure that it could salve an entire squadron's fears. Dundas and the other sixty-odd pilots were turning butterflies in their stomachs as they waited over London for an armada of German aircraft that was surging towards them in September 1940.

Suddenly, Bader's voice came on the radio, breaking the silence they strictly followed. He radioed base asking them to locate a friend he wanted to play squash with on his return.

Dundas grinned at Bader's terse order. 'That conversation had a decidedly calming effect on my nerves and the butterflies were somewhat subdued. It was extraordinary enough that a man with tin legs should have been thinking about squash in any circumstances. That he should be doing so while leading three squadrons of Hurricanes and two of Spitfires into battle against the Luftwaffe was even more extraordinary. Here, quite clearly, was a man made in the mould of Francis Drake – a man to be followed, a man who would win.'

A few months later, in November 1940, Dundas suffered a devastating blow. His older brother John was killed in his Spitfire moments after downing the German air ace Helmut Wick, Germany's top-scoring fighter pilot with fifty-six kills to his name.

'So it happened at last,' Dundas wrote in his diary on 1 December 1940. 'I suppose that it had to happen. I suppose that we were inordinately lucky to have survived intact as long as we did.'

He later wrote: 'I think that hardly a day has gone by since then when I have not thought of John. Poor mummy ... I believe that even her brave heart will be broken.'

The loss made him focus on his own life choices. He committed to telling his girlfriend Diana that he loved her.

'Tonight I almost did tell her and then stopped and felt like a fool,' he wrote in his diary, on Christmas Day 1940. 'But of course she knows and I think she could be persuaded to love me. But then I am back full circle at the unanswerable argument that in my present occupation I can't make girls like Diana love me.'

He was in a generation where, aged twenty, you confronted the existential questions of love, death and life.

* * *

In what many considered a disgraceful coup, the architects and victors of the Battle of Britain, Air Chief Marshal Dowding and his excellent tactician Keith Park, 11 Group's commander, were removed from command. They were considered too parsimonious and too cautious in their use of fighters. A more offensive spirit was needed to take the fight to the Nazis.

'We have stopped licking our wounds,' decreed Trafford Leigh-Mallory, the new commander of 11 Group. 'We are going over on the offensive. Last year our fighting was desperate but now we are entitled to be cockier.'

That cockiness or aggressive intent was given several playful names that underplayed their danger. 'Rhubarbs' were low-level strafing runs; 'Circus' was a bombing raid intended to lure fighters into the air; and 'Ramrod' a bombing mission with Spitfires as escorts.

* * *

Like Robbie Robertson, David Denchfield had concluded that the Munich Agreement of September 1938 was a sham and war was going to be the reality. He was also in a decidedly dull clerk's job that failed to fulfil the expectations of his grammar school education. He had been seduced by the dash of a diving Spitfire on the RAF Auxiliaries' recruiting posters that went up in early 1939 and applied. His weekends had been filled with glorious days of flying and weeknights he applied himself to study. On the outbreak of war he had been called up then pushed on through advanced pilot training, forever craning his neck to the action overhead during 1940. By early 1941 his time had arrived. He was a pilot sergeant and he was in a Spitfire in the renowned 610 Squadron.

A Derbyshire lad from Eckington, Denchfield felt overawed as he was driven through ancient trees and dense fields of the

Duke of Richmond's 12,000-acre estate in West Sussex, base for the Tangmere Wing. Sergeant Denchfield's awe quickly diminished when he arrived at the satellite airfield of Westhampnett, where the divide between the comfort of the gentry and the rest became apparent.

The ground crew, or 'erks', mostly slept anywhere they could put their heads down. Goodwood had been built as a premier horse-racing grandstand in 1904. In peacetime it was a premium spot, but during the war the racecourse's two-tier open grandstand, close to the airfield, was dossers' corner for mechanics snoring under their blankets.

The 'erks' boasted to Denchfield how they had fashioned 'the cookhouse out of a shithouse', using the large circle of five-foot-high brickwork that had formerly been the 'midden' or dung heap. The airmen had cleaned out the cow dung and stinking straw then filled it with trestle tables for soup cauldrons and other kitchen equipment. A form of luxury came when a roof was fashioned from corrugated iron.

The mess was ten yards away in a large open-fronted cart shed lined with more trestle tables. Generally, the food remained warm except when rain lashed through the open front, filling plates with water.

'Better waterlogged food than dead, ain't it, sarge?' the mechanics ribbed Denchfield as they pointed him towards the low thatched cottages set aside for sergeant pilots. They lay a short distance from the officers' base in a grand flint and ivy-clad farmhouse.

Still, at least in the Spitfire we're all equal, Denchfield thought as he settled into the damp thatched cottage with its single coal fire and green-tinged whitewashed walls.

As a pilot, Denchfield, twenty-one, had been given a large downstairs room. Most mornings he was awoken at 6am with the first uncertain coughs of a Merlin followed by a roar as she caught. This subsided to a rumble as the ground crew throttled back to let the engine gently warm.

One by one, all fourteen Spitfire engines came to life, leading to a crescendo far more effective than any alarm clock. This was soon followed by an airman bringing in a cup of tea with the cheerful words, 'Readiness in five minutes, sergeant.'[3]

Denchfield enjoyed a few delicious minutes drinking the tea, exchanging the odd monosyllabic comment with the other sergeant pilots. 'Then the shocking plunge out into the freezing atmosphere beyond the blankets. A quick wash and shave, dress in the "working blue", throw on the Irvin leather jacket and then the crunching walk across the iron-hard field to B Flight dispersal.'

Sleep was quickly forgotten under the harsh glare of the Nissen briefing hut's light bulbs. With a grunted 'what-ho' to fellow pilots, Denchfield picked up his brolly and slung the parachute over his shoulder.

After slipping on the iced-over port wing, Denchfield got in his Spitfire and switched on the cockpit light for pre-flight checks.

'Check the reflector gunsight is set for 250-yard range and 60ft span – 60ft was about right for heavy stuff but I made sure that for 109s I'd be a lot closer than 250 yards. Helmet placed over gunsight, with the oxygen tube plugged into the socket. Check mixture lever right back, levers up to "off" and tail and rudder trims set for take-off. Align compass gridlines with needle, ensuring "red on red" so as not to fly in the opposite direction to that desired. Check fuel tanks full, oxygen full and "on", air and brake pressures at recommended level, radiator control lever at fully open.

'Place the four harness straps to be instantly available and not snagged on anything and then switch off the light, get out, shut the door and hood and wander back to dispersal to slump into a wicker armchair and catnap gently away with flying boots up on the cast-iron stove along with those of the other hopefuls.'

At 9am they were given a briefing by the squadron leader for the upcoming operation. 'The intention was to "wake up" the Luftwaffe in France, who were apparently having an easy life after their attacks over southern England had diminished. Specifically, it was to be the 109s we were to upset.' At this point one of the pilots, who had notched up several kills in the Battle of Britain, interjected. Why bother, it was nice and peaceful as it was? The CO ignored him.

The men rested in the dispersal room until mid-morning, when the CO popped in. 'Right, chaps, you're to be released at 1pm and off duty until tomorrow morning.' Before any further thoughts of carousing could be had, he quickly added: 'That's after we get back from St Omer. Take-off 12:00.'

Denchfield listened carefully as they were told to form up with other squadrons over Rye then escort a dozen Blenheims to cause 'great alarm and despondency with their 250lb bombs'.

On his way to lunch Denchfield asked for his aircraft to be topped up with fuel after the pre-op engine run. He had been designated 'rear-end Charlie' in the Vee formation, so he'd be doing a lot of weaving and catching up on the other dozen Spitfires.

He was also in a Spitfire Mark I, from one of the earliest batches made at Supermarine's works in Woolston, Southampton, in 1939. It had flown in action over Dunkirk.

At this stage of the war, early 1941, all pilots flying over occupied France were well aware of the risks they faced if shot down on these offensive operations. They were given a last-minute briefing then ordered to empty their pockets of any compromising documents. They had just been issued with tunics with a silk escape map and a compass needle sewn into the seams. 'Naturally we had to check them ourselves! Consequently, our re-stitching was nowhere near as neatly done and my shoulders were lumpy!'

The three fighter squadrons assembled over Rye. 'The Channel to the east looked ridiculously narrow and the skies over the snow-clad French landscape were broodingly ominous. As usual the sun glare blinding out of the clear blue made looking to the south-east difficult. God only knew what nasties were moving into their hidey-hole. As we circled over Rye for a good five minutes we certainly gave them plenty of time to get ready for us. I guess, like me, that the others had their gunsights switched to "on", their gun-firing buttons turned to "fire" and their hoods slid back for better visibility. And I bet they were sweating cobs too.'

Just after they crossed the French coast, Denchfield, weaving at the rear, spotted contrails behind and above but they quickly disappeared. The condensation trails generally formed above 25,000ft, when warm water vapour from the engine exhaust froze in cold air. Pilots frequently checked their rear-view mirrors to ensure they were not emitting a long finger of cloud pinpointing their position.

Denchfield tried to ignore the growing fear that the enemy was close. But a minute later he saw a flash far up behind. He searched the skies. *Nothing*. He looked ahead. A distance of 800 yards had opened up between him and the rest of the squadron. *Damn it*. It wasn't safe to be alone in enemy skies. He did a couple of left and right turns then pushed the throttle open to catch up.

'I was about halfway back when there was a sudden staccato vibration and sparks seemed to erupt out of my port wingtip. *Bloody hell!*'

More rounds hit the front. The rudder pedals became useless. 'As the nose fell away the cockpit filled with a white mist accompanied by the foul smell of glycol and 100-octane fuel.'

The mist cleared and he was able to assess the damage. He was at 9,000ft and still flying. Then the oil and radiator temperature began to rise, followed by a strong smell of petrol. 'Nearly twenty gallons of fuel were sloshing about in the belly of the fuselage under my feet. I now knew why my lower legs were so cold. Inside my flying boots and my trouser legs were saturated with the damn stuff.

'Some six minutes after being hit I was down to maybe 6,000ft with the radiator temperature almost in the red. I could see the Channel and the Blenheims pass about 1,000ft above me on their way home, going like the Devil.'

He was never going to make it over the Channel. With petrol sloshing at his feet he undid the Sutton harness straps. Smoke followed by jets of flame came out of the engine. The nose dipped down violently. It was time to get out. *Fast*. He shot out like a cork from a bottle.

Denchfield landed in a snow-covered field minus one boot which had been wedged in the aircraft. He 'hid' in some bushes 'even a mouse would have laughed at' and was having a pee when two German soldiers entered the field.

'They walked straight up to me and as I stood up one said: "For you the war is over." *And I thought they only said that in* The Hotspur *boys' comic!*'

He was taken to St Omer airfield where twelve Luftwaffe pilots came out of a hut and one by one came to attention and saluted. 'Of course I had to reciprocate. There was a fair degree of mutual respect between us.'

He was then introduced to Major Walter Oesau, the German ace who had shot him down. Denchfield sportingly agreed to sign his cigarette case in pencil for him to have engraved over. On closer inspection, he saw another six English signatures. *So much for causing alarm and despondency.*

* * *

Stung by reports of the Spitfire's effectiveness over Dunkirk, Willy Messerschmitt had worked hard to find a response. The Spitfire's agility had to be matched. In late 1940, the Bavaria factories rolled out the Me109 'F', which, with wings and rudder adjustments, was by far the most aerodynamically efficient of the 109 models, potentially out-turning the Spitfire. It was also more fuel-efficient; with light-alloy 300-litre drop tanks, it more than doubled the 109 'E' variant's range from 410 miles to 1,060 miles. It also came with a bullet-resistant windscreen and light-alloy armour fitted behind the pilot and fuel tanks. Generally, Luftwaffe pilots agreed that the 'F' was the best-handling of all 109s.[4]

The developments down in Bavaria did not go unnoticed by the hard-pressed Supermarine boffins working out of their sheds at the Woolston works. Under the guidance of chief designer Joe Smith, who had led the Spitfire's development after Mitchell's death in 1937, they grafted to find a design that gave the fighter speed at altitude and greater firepower while retaining its agility. Fighter Command could not continue sending up pilots like Denchfield in Mark Is for much longer. Something was urgently needed as a stop-gap measure.

In February 1941 Castle Bromwich began mass-producing a new version of the Spitfire, the Mark V, which had punch and power. Now carrying two 20mm Hispano cannons as well as four Browning .303 machine guns, it had true firepower.

With the Merlin tuned to give 1,407hp, it had a maximum speed of 371mph[5] and could reach 38,000ft at twice the rate of climb as the first Mark I.[6] Later variants were equipped to carry two 250lb bombs, giving the Spitfire the potential to become a dive-bomber. With nearly 6,500 built, it was the most produced of any mark.[7]

Jeffrey Quill, Supermarine's test pilot, had returned from active service in the RAF during the Battle of Britain with ideas for improvement. In particular, he had advocated changing the canvas ailerons – the flaps on the wings used to roll the aircraft left or right – for metal ones, which made a huge difference to high-speed turns, greatly improving manoeuvrability. These were standard by the time the MkV entered service, with one pilot describing the old ailerons thus: 'When you were diving at speed with fabric ailerons, the aircraft used to try to turn to the left and I hadn't the physical strength to straighten up.'[8]

While Hugh Dundas churned gloomy thoughts of life, death and love, fortune favoured him. In May 1941, Douglas Bader became his immediate boss and his unconquerable spirit buoyed up Dundas through the dark days.

Fighter Command sent Bader down to RAF Tangmere, on the West Sussex coast, to become a 'wing leader' with three Spitfire squadrons under his command. He chose to fly with the Auxiliaries – or what was left of the originals – of 616 Squadron. Better still, he put himself in charge of 'A' Flight, where Dundas was second-in-command.

The new strategy of grouping squadrons together required new tactics. As Denchfield's plight and others had consistently shown, the RAF's three-ship Vee formation was dangerously outdated. Bader, Dundas and others put their heads together and came up with the 'finger four' formation – roughly similar to the German tactic developed in Spain. Four aircraft would fly in line abreast, fifty yards apart, with those on the left covering the tails of those on the right and vice versa. This did away with the exposed position of rear-end Charlie at the back of the Vee formation, who regularly got bounced.

Like the Germans the previous summer, and as Denchfield had already found to his cost, Fighter Command was now experiencing the dangers of battling over enemy territory: anti-aircraft fire, a waiting enemy, running out of fuel, and bail-outs becoming POWs.

Dowding's parsimony and shepherding of his force had been replaced by a view that one-for-one losses, like sacrificial chess, were acceptable. In fact, if it had been chess, Fighter Command was heading towards checkmate. Between mid-June and September 1941, it lost 194 pilots and planes, the Germans 128.

Dundas, in mourning his brother's death, was not alone. Wilfrid Duncan Smith, an outstanding pilot with 611 Squadron, was among those who grieved over the summer after his successful fighting partnership with 'Polly' Pollard ended abruptly when his wingman was killed over France.

'The loss of a close friend in war stirs a deeper feeling of personal sorrow because of its abrupt and harsh reality. Though there is no reason to brood on the tragedy, the chances are that if his name is mentioned it will recall the happy moments of laughter shared, and never any of darkness. Though it makes one aware of the uncertainty of life, it also hardens the will to survive and in a strange way the thought of death as the final enemy transforms it instead into an honourable escape.'[9]

The losses were taking a toll on everyone and pilots took small pleasures when they could. Most resorted to drink and relied on their youth to see them through the consequences. However, to get from one pub to another required transport and more importantly petrol, so pilots topped up their cars with precious aviation fuel.

Someone tipped off the military police and they began testing fuel tanks. Sgt Alan Smith, Bader's wingman, was stopped in a 1932

MG Midget brimful of aviation gas and arrested along with several other offenders.

Before they could be dragged off, Bader pulled up in his car and stomped towards the military police on his tin legs. 'What the hell's going on here?' he demanded.

The senior policeman stood his ground, insisting the pilots had broken all the rules. He didn't get to the end of his explanation before Bader cut in. 'Get your buggers out of here and fast or *I* will sort *you* out.'[10]

The policemen did not hang around to discuss the point.

* * *

Johnnie Johnson had fought hard to fly. A qualified engineer from the East Midlands, he initially failed to get into the RAF as a pilot partly on grounds of snobbery. He was finally accepted a month before the war's outbreak, but then had had to overcome a collar-bone break sustained playing rugby in order to fly again. He proved his worth against the Luftwaffe, although by 1941 the twenty-six-year-old Spitfire pilot expressed a distaste for the current tactics.

'I loathed those Rhubarbs with a deep, dark hatred,' he wrote.[11]

Something was required to take the edge off the stresses daily endured in combat. A keen sportsman, Johnson had been quick to notice the opportunities presented by the Duke of Richmond's estate near Tangmere. Within the many acres lay the eighteen holes of the excellent Downs Course at Goodwood. Designed in 1914 by James Braid, the legendary architect of Gleneagles and Carnoustie, it provided a refuge from thoughts of mortality after a morning hunting Germans.[12]

But to remain operational while playing eighteen holes presented a challenge. Johnson developed a system whereby, if they were to be called to thirty minutes' readiness, the squadron Miles Magister would go up, find the golfers then fire off a red Very light telling them to return to dispersal.

Aside from the odd weekly casualty, all seemed to be well at

Tangmere. Then on 9 August the wing was ordered to provide cover for a mid-morning Ramrod raid on Béthune.

There was the odd bit of cumulus lingering in the blue skies as 610 Squadron took off. As they gained height, Dundas saw Bader waggle his wings vigorously and fly within 2ft of his wingtip.

'Airspeed indicator,' Bader mouthed, pointing to his instrument panel. His vital flying instrument had broken. Bader pointed ahead and Dundas took the lead to the start line precisely on time at 28,000ft. As they arrived over the French coastline someone spotted a gaggle of 109s below. Both Bader and Dundas watched them for several seconds. Something seemed odd. The bait was too easy. They smelled a rat.

With another squadron covering the sky above them, Bader gave the 'tally-ho' order. The Messerschmitts flew on, straight and steady as the flight speared towards them. Dundas fixed on a target and dived. But he was still uneasy.

'I had the strongest instinctive urge to look round behind me. We closed fast, a little too fast. With half an eye I watched Bader and the second he opened fire I did the same.'

'Break!'

At the warning of imminent danger Dundas instinctively flipped the plane hard over while searching the sky above and behind. He hunched his shoulders and his grip on the control stick tightened, expecting the canopy to shatter any second at the impact of cannon rounds. The sky behind him was full of 109s and winking guns. The Luftwaffe had executed a near-perfect ambush.

Dundas found himself in the middle of a 'hot and furious' dogfight. 'Several times I fired my guns; several times I was under hard pressure of attack. No time to worry about results, no time for anything except taut, insistent, concentrated effort to avoid getting in front of an enemy's guns. The penalty for getting caught in that game of tag was death and destruction. And everyone sooner or later got caught.'[13]

Again Dundas won through.

'Dogsbody, do you receive?' There was no reply.

'Dogsbody, come in please.' Again Dundas used Bader's call sign and got no response. Dripping in sweat, he pushed the nose down and dived back for home, hearing others try to call up the wing leader.

They returned to Tangmere in ones and twos. Bader was not in their number. There was an atmosphere of quiet desolation. Dundas immediately ordered a sweep. Four of the most experienced pilots set off to search the Channel to see if Bader had ditched. When they returned without success, Dundas knew he now had to break the news to Bader's wife, Thelma. He grabbed a bottle of sherry and some flowers. He told Thelma that Douglas was missing in action then cried all the way on the drive back. 'The thought of Douglas Bader dead was utterly shattering to me.'

The Germans quickly informed the British of Bader's capture. With some difficulty he had managed to exit his crippled Spitfire, but with one tin leg left behind, jammed in the cockpit.

A German doctor examined Bader and looked relieved to see that the missing limb was an old injury.

'Now, we look at the other leg,' he ordered Bader. Relishing the moment, Bader watched the shock register on the doctor's face when he realised the fighter pilot had no legs.

While Bader's loss was keenly felt on one level, his job had already been done. Like every effective war leader he left behind a fighting legacy.

Although Dundas and many others now felt little enthusiasm for the fight, Bader's spirit demanded they carry on. 'To pass onto the new pilots the experience and knowledge I had gained, as well as the spirit of aggression with which Douglas had imbued us,' wrote Dundas. He needed to hold on to that spirit more than most. He was the last surviving original member from 616 Auxiliary Squadron left flying. And the realisation of death's proximity was intruding on his ability to fight.

'I subconsciously shrank from battle. The instinct for survival, the urge to rest on my laurels, was very strong. During the weeks which followed there were a couple of occasions I shirked the clash of combat at the critical moment. This was a time of extreme danger for me and also to some extent the men I was leading. It was the stage of fatigue when many experienced fighter pilots have fallen as a result of misjudgement or a momentary holding back from combat.' Dundas found some solace in the brandy bottle.

Then a new menace emerged. In August 1941 the outline of a fighter appeared that was very different to the Me109. The Focke-Wulf 190 was, at 389mph, fast. It could also outmanoeuvre the newly arriving Spitfire Mark Vs and carried a bigger punch. Four 20mm cannons and two 13mm machine guns gave it unsurpassed potency.[14] The Fw190 presented a real threat to the Spitfire's future, usurping its position as the premier fighter. A riposte was urgently required and Supermarine's designers went back to work, this time frequently toiling through the night to retain the Spitfire's superiority.

As the Rhubarb, Ramrod and Circus operations over France continued, pilots reported less enemy activity than usual. There was a simple explanation: on 22 June 1941 Hitler used an army of four million, including 2,700 aircraft, to invade Russia, committing men, materiel and reputation to conquering the Bolsheviks.

A new cause was found for the RAF's Rhubarb raids on occupied Europe: they were to tie up German fighters in the west.

* * *

Those still in training and yet to combat the lethal Fw190s or suffer the mourning of lost comrades were living in a blissful world of new experiences and high jinks. The former insurance clerk Robbie Robertson, who had waited more than two years to get into the RAF after applying in late 1938, had now passed his first stage of fighter pilot training and found the biggest challenge was leading his pals to find a well-stocked pub near RAF Kidlington, Oxford. After long treks down muddy lanes they'd often reach a country inn only to find the sign: *Sorry, no beer this week.*[15]

The course ended in July 1941 and Robertson's desire to fly fighters had not diminished.

'What do you want to fly?' his Flight Commander asked.

'Day fighters!'

'How old are you?'

'Twenty-three.'

'Twenty-three! That's far too old to fly fighters. I'll put you down for instructor.'

A long argument ensued and Robertson was sent for an interview with the Station Commander. The officer was amazed, disgusted and infuriated that a trainee had questioned his authority. *Never has anyone been so audacious as to say they didn't want to be an instructor – you should consider it a damned honour!*

Undeterred, Robertson coolly replied he'd take it up at the next station. But he was in luck. A trainee who'd been posted to night fighters wasn't so keen. They swapped.

His luck then doubled. He was put on Spitfires.

After practising on a Spitfire jacked up on blocks in a hangar he was told to find a fighter and go up. As many others had already discovered, he found the Spitfire was easy to fly, and he too fell in love. 'We flew once or twice a day, for an hour or so, and began to find that the Spitfire was probably the most beautiful aircraft in the world. It was a delight to be in the air in a Spitfire, when you got to know it. It was easy to fly and very quick responses on the controls.'

Robertson was posted to 111 Squadron in North Weald, Essex, in early autumn 1941 and given an abrupt introduction to war.

'We've got a funeral tomorrow morning, you can be part of the escort,' the squadron leader told him with a smile.

After a fortnight of bedding in, Robertson was sent on his first Rhubarb operational sortie over Dunkirk. Outwardly he looked calm climbing into his Spitfire but he grabbed the cockpit rim tightly to steady his shaking hands. He was given a Czech pilot as a wingman and told to stay close. As they approached the enemy coast Robertson felt a surge of fear. 'I felt vulnerable being on the other side of Dunkirk, actually over France. It wasn't so bad when you're over the Channel because you think, "Well, if I'm shot down I've got a very fair chance of being picked up and brought back." But over France it wasn't so funny. Your stomach turns over and your nerves are still twitching just flying over there.'

But his flying log entry on 20 October 1941 omitted any reflection of feelings. It read: 'No flak, no 109s'.

Nerves got the better of the most experienced pilots during Rhubarbs. On one occasion, two of Robertson's fellow 111 Squadron pilots flew over the Channel up into cloud then came down and slipped over the coast. They spotted a train and shot it up before heading back home.

They were surprised on return to be called into the Station Commander's office.

What had they been shooting at?

A train.

Did they damage it?

Yes, quite a bit.

Did they realise the train they'd shot up was heading to Margate?[16]

* * *

Robbie Robertson meeting King Haakon of Norway

The veteran pilots soon warmed to Robertson's humour and after a few sorties he was accepted as one of their own. During one later operation his squadron was returning from escorting bombers over Le Havre, where they'd experienced heavy flak, when Robertson's engine made a churning noise and glycol came pouring out.

It was now winter, and the enemy landscape was cold and very bleak. Below was a churning sea with a couple of coasters ploughing through white-capped waves.

'Get out, get out!' Robertson's wingman shouted.[17]

The prospect of being lost in big seas and freezing to death did not appeal, especially as landfall was not far away.

'No, I'll put down on the beach.'

As he limped towards Brighton, Robertson suddenly remembered that the beach was mined. *I'll put down in a field.*

Smoke was now coming from the engine into the cockpit. *I'd better get out*. He undid his Sutton straps then paused and called up his wingman.

'Is it right you get a week's leave if you bail out?'

'Get the bloody hell out!' his wingman shouted.

Robertson pushed back the hood, trimmed the aircraft fully forward, stood up and next thing he knew he was flying through the air.

'I looked round and found I hadn't pulled the ripcord, which I did a bit smartly, and a second later there was a satisfying thump and the parachute opened. It was a very soothing experience. The only thing was that the aircraft was still on fire and flying round and round on its own. I had visions of it colliding with me.'

He landed in a tree, undid his harness, climbed down and crawled through a hedge.

'Would you like a cup of tea?' an old lady asked him on the other side.

'No, thank you very much.' He was driven to a nearby barracks. It was a Canadian dental centre, which assumed, with the second Spitfire in attendance, that he was a shot-down German pilot. The commanding officer had armed everyone with rifles, revolvers and anything they could lay their hands on.

After a whisky, cigar and good meal, Robertson was taken to overnight at Shoreham airport. 'I wasn't too popular with the lads there either. They had an air-sea rescue base with a Walrus seaplane. They'd watched me coming across the Channel with smoke and everything else billowing out and they were looking forward to doing a bit of air-sea rescue. They were most upset when I chugged across Shoreham still emitting smoke and bailed out farther on.'

On returning to base his commanding officer at first congratulated Robertson on his escape then added: 'There is one point, Robbie. You don't have to tell all the bloody German air force you're going to bail out!'

* * *

Other fresh-faced pilots were now entering the fray. Ever since his childhood flight in a Fox Moth over Southport, Allan Scott had not let go of his dream to become a pilot. He threw out plans to be an architect and presented himself before an RAF recruitment office in early 1940. On interview for pilot training he stumbled over the answer to 136 multiplied by 365. It was fortunate. A swift answer and he would have been allocated to 'observer' training.[18]

A year later he found himself behind the controls of a Spitfire. He was full of admiration. 'To fly a Spitfire you became a part of it. Sitting on the seat, it fitted like a glove, the side walls conforming to your shoulders, the controls at your fingertips and obeying every command at a touch. In combat, with a turn of the head and the eyes, it would follow that direction without deviation; upside down and you were held in your seat, as though glued to it. All these qualities proved to be so valuable in combat, especially in a dogfight when the easy flow of vital manoeuvres meant the difference between life and death.'

Scott was soon on Rhubarbs with 124 Squadron, arriving at Biggin Hill in November 1941. Like most of the pilots, he was entirely reliant on the combat experience of the squadron leader. 'If you had no battle experience you didn't see anything; the leader could be heard reporting, "Twenty-plus to your right, three o'clock coming out of the sun . . ." But no matter how much you strained, your eyeballs out like chapel hatpegs, you could not see them. This was when we relied upon our leader's experience and sight to get us through, weaving all the harder and following him blindly. We flew in sheer terror half the time and obviously there were losses.'

In just one week they lost nine pilots. 'War, sadly, cannot stop for its casualties, we just had to get on with the job,' Scott recalled. He was soon in the heart of the fighting.

'At nineteen I suddenly found myself, adrenaline flowing, coming up on the tail of a Luftwaffe twin-engine Ju88, firing at it and wondering how the hell I had got there. That was my first kill and there was no doubt about it, it was thrilling to down an enemy aircraft. This feeling increased with my catching sight that the German crew had bailed out. I hoped the pilot would be able to bail out as I hoped that's how someone would think of me.'

* * *

By now Spitfire production had fully recovered from the Battle of Britain and was running at pace, with Castle Bromwich able to churn out squadrons of Spitfire Vs by the fortnight. In the three months to 1 July 1941 the number of Mark V operational squadrons went from one to seven, with a total of thirty-two squadrons now of all types. If the war looked grim elsewhere, at least by the end of 1941 the skies over Britain were well defended.

Robbie Robertson had to wait eight months until he fired his guns in anger. The squadron had just completed a Circus sweep over Gris Nez, close to Calais, on 14 April 1942 when they were jumped by a group of Fw190s.[19]

'We were flung around in all directions. I managed to find a 190, which seemed to be a bit lost, so I fired like mad at it. Being overkeen, anxious and a rotten shot, I didn't allow enough deflection and all I did was waste a lot of ammunition. But it was quite exciting to get chased round and round.'

Ten days later he was in action again after the squadron was jumped over France and Robertson, along with his American wingman, got split up from the rest. And they were up against two formidable Fw190s. 'The Focke-Wulf is some aircraft. To start with, it's a lot faster than the Spitfire V; it seems to have all the ammunition in the world and they can start firing their cannons from miles out of range which was frightening, especially when you can see all the flashes coming from the gunports.'

The American dived after the first 190 despite Robertson yelling at him to come back as the second German was closing on his rear. 'The second 190 overhauled him like mad and although I tried to chase down after him I couldn't get within range and my number two was shot down.'

Fighting back the surging panic and distress at seeing his comrade taken out, Robertson decided to stay and fight the remaining 190.

'We went round and round in circles for a while, which was fine as the Spitfire could out-turn anything and eventually I managed to get a few hits on him. He decided to call it a day and beetled off.'

But Robertson would not let him escape. 'I followed still banging away and he started to smoke and eventually was going down almost vertically at a hell of a lick.'

Robertson also discovered that all was not lost if you did parachute into the Channel. A call went out that a bomber crew had ditched off the Dutch coast and were bobbing around in a dinghy. Five airmen were spotted drifting off German-occupied Ostend.

Robertson's flight took off to give them cover at the same time as a rescue launch shot out of Dover. With the Spitfires overhead they quickly located the crew. 'The launch got to the dinghy, swung round, grabbed the chaps aboard, all without stopping, then belted for home.'

A few weeks later they received a letter of thanks from the bomber crew enclosing a £1 note 'for a drink on us'.

* * *

What stood out most about Terry Kearins was the dark thatch of hair that sat like a bird's nest atop his head. Otherwise he was a quiet man from hardy farming folk in New Zealand. Kearins and his two siblings had been brought up in a house without central heating or electricity. It was a spartan life, where he constantly found ways to make the uncomfortable comfortable. Kearins knew the long, hard hours of labouring on the farm in Woodville, North Island. His mother showed him how the monumental tasks of running a farm and bringing up children could be done. She made the most of her wood-fired range, producing cakes, pastries and main meals. With no refrigeration she was adept at preserving all kinds of meat, fruit and vegetables. It was a rugged but wholesome upbringing, where people knew their worth and pulled their weight.

Kearins did well at school. His headmaster described him as 'of sound character, courteous in manner and of a healthy physique'. In the end Kearins gave up full-time education for his first love and became a farming apprentice.

In 1939 Kearins turned eighteen and war was looming. Realising that conscription was inevitable, he decided to volunteer to join the service of his choice. He had seen the posters, magazines and cigarette cards of the Royal Air Force's modern fighters. Boys at school had talked excitedly about Spitfires and Hurricanes. Kearins had often mused, when watching the occasional biplane buzz over his family farm, on what the ground would look like from the air and the freedom pilots had. He chose the air force and ticked 'Airman Pilot' as the number one choice on his application form. Then he answered the 'flying experience' question, writing: 'Flown once as passenger with Middle Districts Aero Club – in rough weather.'

It was perhaps the weather reference, and his list of sporting interests, that led the RAF to put him onto flying training when he arrived in Britain. But only as a glider pilot. For two years Kearins learned the fundamentals of flying, including on the Miles Master monoplane. He excelled as a glider pilot and went on to instruct. But on a posting to RAF Llandow in Wales, Kearins was given the opportunity to join a Spitfire unit. He did not say much when his flying officer instructor pointed to the aircraft and told him to go up and fly the fighter. But Kearins felt a deep sense of pride in the achievement. Here he was, a farmboy from rural New Zealand, flying the world's most modern aircraft. On entering the cockpit he placed a hand over his face to hide his grin. Then he took to the skies in a faultless take-off, flying for an hour and five minutes of pure delight.

He qualified as a fighter pilot and was ready for operations. He looked forward to the change. He'd been in Britain, training, for two years. It was time for something different.

* * *

Harry Strawn, August 1942, just after Dieppe raid

The Battle of Britain had put the RAF fighter squadrons on their knees and they'd only just recovered to be knocked down again by the Rhubarb, Ramrod and Circus raids over France. But 1941 had seen two major milestone events. While Russia drew away some of the Luftwaffe's best fighters and pilots, the Japanese attack on the American naval base at Pearl Harbor on 7 December proved a much greater boon. Previously, a handful of American fliers had risked losing their citizenship to fight for Britain at the height of its peril in 1940. A few more had trickled over to form Eagle Squadrons in 1941, but now they started coming over in numbers. And they only wanted to fly one plane: the Spitfire.

Finding that he didn't know, or particularly like, one end of a cow from another, Harry Strawn had turned his back on a career in animal husbandry and opted for a degree in advertising at the University of Pittsburgh.[20] That didn't appeal much either. In desperation, the tall young man with the classic good looks of a strong-jawed American took a job in Detroit at the Steel Office Furniture Company. At weekends he increasingly found himself drawn to the local airfield, watching P-40 fighters take off and land. He fell in love with the idea of flying and in June 1941 he joined the air force and was in training when the Japanese attacked.

A year later the American was among 12,000 troops on the former luxury liner *Queen Elizabeth* surging across the Atlantic to Scotland. Strawn recorded in his diary the welcome they received after landing in the Firth of Clyde and boarding a train south. 'The people were waving to us from every window with flags. It made chills go down my spine. The hillsides were covered in flowers and green trees and it was hard to realise we were in a war-torn country. We threw oranges to the people for which they were very grateful.'

The 309th Squadron soon received delivery of twenty-five new Spitfires courtesy of the Air Transport Auxiliary, the pilots based at High Ercall, near Shrewsbury, Shropshire, who ferried brand-new aircraft from factories and maintenance units to frontline squadrons. Strawn now found his prejudices challenged. 'One pilot came in and I went up to check him out. This pilot takes the helmet off, and this beautiful blonde hair starts falling down in cascades. Women didn't fly aeroplanes! It shocked me so badly that I said to one of my other buddies: "My God, if a woman can fly that aeroplane, I know I can."'

He also warmed to the modesty of RAF fighter pilots sent to help train the three American Spitfire squadrons of the 31st Fighter Group. 'One thing about the British, they do the shooting first and the bragging afterwards.'

Strawn and his fellow pilots adored their new fighter. 'I really fell in love with the Spitfire. It was the most fascinating aircraft and the easiest I ever flew. These Spitfire Vs are new and really fast planes – faster than our P-39s. I had a great time diving through the clouds and slow rolling, doing about every manoeuvre in the book. It made you feel like a king. It was the most gentle acrobatic thing that I ever had my hands on. It was so forgiving, you could make all kinds of mistakes.'

The biggest problem the Americans had was that the engine rotated in a different direction to the US Allison engines, causing it to swing in the opposite direction on the application of power during take-off. It caused a degree of confusion and led to some accidents.

By comparison, Strawn and other US pilots in Britain were critical of their own fighters, the P-39 Airacobra and P-40 Warhawk. 'As yet the US has no fighter plane that can touch anything the British Spit can, much less the Me109F or the Fw190,' Strawn wrote. 'We as pilots know what a good plane is, but the people at home will never know that the P-40 and the P-39 would be death traps in this war. I hope to God that we will never get them here for we wouldn't have a chance against the Germans.'[21]

A few days later the men of the 309th Squadron were banned from talking to the press. An article had appeared in *Life* magazine complaining that the US fighters 'weren't worth a damn'.

* * *

John Blyth arrived from America and celebrated his twenty-first birthday in the best possible way. When the US went to war he volunteered for the US Air Force operations in Britain.

In late 1942 he found himself at Biggin Hill in the company of the heroes he had read about in magazines. Within minutes of arriving he was next to a Spitfire, chatting with Sailor Malan and Al Deere, Battle of Britain aces he had read about three years earlier. 'It felt quite surreal to be talking to them both and it was quite an amazing birthday present.'[22]

There was one hurdle to overcome before he could start flying. It was decided that US sergeant pilots should become officers. Blyth went before several commissioning boards, always answering the same questions. Finally, he arrived in London with 250 other candidates, all in the same room and looking bored until an air force colonel addressed them. 'I've had to go through all these boards before,' he said. 'So today I am the board and today you are all second lieutenants and I hope that by next year you're all generals! Sorry I had to get you down to London to tell you that.'

Blyth was posted to the 22nd Squadron, for reconnaissance missions as part of the American 7th Photo Group based at Mount Farm near Oxford. But each day when they got into the cockpits of their P-38 reconnaissance fighters for another mission, the American pilots looked on in envy as RAF Spitfires bounced down the airstrip and danced into the air.

Why aren't we in Spits? the pilots frequently moaned.

No one was happy with the P-38. Operating in the European climate, frequently the turbo superchargers would freeze up, with catastrophic results. The Americans also complained bitterly that the US fighters did not have the power or agility of Spitfires and were vulnerable against German fighters.

Blyth forced himself to trust his P-38 as he took off for missions, but the Spitfire was always there in the background, niggling away at them by its very presence.

Still, when he did get back to base at least as an officer he had a room to himself, half-decent food and the opportunity to go out dancing with Oxford girls. It was at one such dance that he came across a dark-haired beauty called Betty. 'She looked very different from the rest of the girls; she was a classic English lady, an English rose!' Puffing up his chest in his smartly cut officer's uniform and putting on his broadest grin, Blyth introduced himself. The pair instantly hit it off and were spending a lot of time together.

Betty fell for Blyth's easy American charm and manner, and was intrigued by his English roots. For the next few weeks they went out to pubs together, more dances and even the odd dip in the River Thames.

Betty was well-spoken and clearly well-connected. She took her beau up to London where they went to dine in the Savoy and then on to a nightclub. It was all a new and wonderful experience for the American airman.

Then one day Betty announced they were going to lunch with her uncle. As Blyth went to sit down he almost got straight up again, thinking he'd got the wrong table. Opposite him was a man in a smart blue RAF uniform with lots of gold braid. His eyes fixed on the rank insignia band on the lower arm of his sleeves. *An air vice-marshal!*

'Sir,' he responded quickly as Betty introduced him as 'uncle Richard', then added 'Air Vice-Marshal Richard Peck'. The officer was quick to put Blyth at his ease and they were soon chatting amiably. Peck, who had no children of his own, clearly approved of his favourite niece's choice of companion.

After lunch Blyth found himself being driven by Peck in his car. Here he was, a mere lieutenant, being chauffeured by *an air vice-marshal!* As they drove, Peck asked about Blyth's work.

The flying was OK, Blyth responded, but it was pretty rough-going in the P-38s.

Peck's eyebrows raised. *22nd Squadron, was it?*

Blyth nodded then listened in astonishment as Peck told him they'd all be getting Spitfires very soon.

Back in Oxford, Blyth knew he was privy to some sensational information. Everyone was itching to get onto Spitfires and if he broke the good news he might be among the first on them. He sought out his Station Commander.

'We're going to get Spitfires, sir, and I'd like the opportunity to fly them,' Blyth said.

His boss looked astonished. 'Where in the *hell* did you hear that?' he fired back.

'Air Vice-Marshal Peck, sir.'

His boss shook his head in despair, only half-believing Blyth.

Blyth had to pinch himself again when, a few days later, he sat in a Spitfire cockpit with the propeller spinning, his hand resting on the throttle lever. There was little instruction, he recalled. 'We just got in the Spitfire and went flying.' The Americans were thrilled.

Blyth, Strawn and their fellow pilots' view on American fighters appeared to be reinforced when the RAF rejected the P-39 as unsuitable for warfare in western Europe.

The Spitfire was to remain the air force's premier fighter.

CHAPTER FIVE

Spitfire Women

Mary Ellis

If ever an aircraft was built for a woman to fall in love with it was a Spitfire. Of course, the ladies could admire its fine curves and elegant nose, but actually flying the thing was surely beyond them?

Female aviation pioneers like Amelia Earhart and Amy Johnson had already proven that women could fly equally as well as men.

At the outbreak of war, pilots were needed to ferry aircraft from factories and airfields. It would have been a waste of resources if, like the French, combat pilots were used. The Air Transport Auxiliary (ATA) was introduced and it didn't take long for some influential female fliers to argue for a role in the war effort.

After a brief struggle, permission was granted for eight women to join the ATA, albeit only flying Tiger Moth trainers. They demonstrated their hardiness and skills flying to Scotland in open cockpits in winter weather.

Every day the ATA pilots would wake up not knowing what aircraft type they would fly. Fortunately, they had an invaluable aid. The little 'Blue Book' had notes on more than seventy different aircraft types. Printed on both sides of postcard-size paper, it gave helpful hints such as if a plane had a tendency to swing on landing. The pilot would find the aircraft she was piloting – often for the very first time – read its notes for thirty minutes, then take to the skies.

By summer 1941 the ATA women had proven their worth. They would be allowed to fly operational aircraft and a great prize awaited: the Spitfire.

Perhaps more so than men, women fully appreciated the graceful lines that suggested a glorious flight. 'To sit in the cockpit of a Spit, barely wider than one's shoulders, was a poetry of its own,' said Lettice Curtis,[1] one of first ATA women.

The same flying circus that had taken Allan Scott on his first flight in 1932 had done the same for Mary Ellis two years earlier. She was also aged eleven when she took off in a two-seat Gypsy Moth biplane, and she too was immediately smitten by flying. 'It was the most wonderful experience I'd ever known. I simply had to do it again.'

She was gripped by the idea of being a pilot. Aged sixteen, Mary was allowed time off from school for flying lessons in Witney, near the 1,000-acre Oxfordshire farm owned by her father, and in 1941 Mary heard a radio announcement asking for women with a flying licence to join the ATA.

Her father acquiesced on one condition: 'I don't mind the flying, but I don't want you to go to war.' After a brief test flight in a Tiger Moth, Mary, now aged twenty-two, was accepted into the ATA in October 1941.

The idea now took hold that one day, maybe not in the too distant future, *just maybe*, she might fly a Spit.

When Mary arrived at nine one morning to get her 'flying chit' she was quietly delighted and proud that it read *Spitfire*. The destination was RAF Lyneham, a short hop from South Marston, near Swindon. She'd be landing the shiny new plane in front of the RAF's finest pilots.[2]

For the last twelve months she had devoured the 'Blue Book' of flying notes, paying particular attention to those on the Spitfire in anticipation of the moment. Thus, on 13 October 1942, trying to look neither overly anxious nor overexcited, she carefully walked around the Spitfire's wings, nose and tail.

Remaining professional, she went to climb into the cockpit. As she did so an engineer tapped her on the shoulder.

'Your parachute, miss,' he said, handing up the pack. 'Hope you enjoy your flight.' She gave a brief nod, saying nothing.

'How many have you flown?' he enquired.

'This is my first Spitfire,' Mary said in a voice she hoped conveyed confidence. The engineer looked momentarily horrified. Mary jumped in the cockpit and quickly waved the chocks away with a hand signal to the ground crew.

She fired up the engine and taxied over to take-off point. 'My little heart was beating very fast but . . . I was off. And somehow I managed an excellent take-off. Once I was in the air I did a few manoeuvres to make sure I knew what I was doing. And then I set off for RAF Lyneham, a thirty-minute flight. Thankfully it was a very nice day. The Spit handled beautifully. It was thrilling.'

Mary did a few laps round the aerodrome looking for a space between other aircraft coming in.

'I made a perfect landing. All my anxiety disappeared completely. From that day on I fell in love with flying fast and furious aeroplanes.'

She returned to South Marston via the transport aircraft to ferry her second Spitfire. 'As for those guys on the ground who watched me take off, I think they were horrified that this little fair-haired young girl was flying a very valuable war machine twice in one day. But they seemed happy when I got back to ferry the second one. One guy even gave me some of his sweet coupons as a reward.'

* * *

Diana Barnato Walker had learned to fly before the war at Brooklands, Surrey, where as a child she watched her father, Woolf, speed round the motor-racing circuit.

Diana shared her father's skill for speed. After a mere six hours' flying, her instructor climbed out of the Tiger Moth and told her to get on with it on her own. Diana taxied to the take-off point then was abruptly waved to a standstill. A pair of gnarled, ugly hands reached into the cockpit, followed by a hideously scarred face.

'The man implored me not to fly. He had been a flier and had crashed and the burning aeroplane had seared and burnt his flesh. He didn't want this to happen to anyone else, far less a pretty young girl. I didn't take any notice of his words and took off.'

Diana turned up for her ATA flight test wearing her stepmother's leopard-skin coat and was told that she looked far too attractive to know much about flying. She flew flawlessly. It was late 1941 and, after her ski jaunts, fashion shopping and a failed attempt to become a Red Cross nurse, Diana had at last found a way to contribute to the war effort.

Her competence was such that soon she read *Spitfire* on her flying chit. It was a clear, bright day. She was delighted to discover she was to fly a photo reconnaissance, or PR, variant. The advantage of having up-to-date photographs of the battlefield and enemy deployments had been long recognised. The Spitfire was a perfect vehicle to give commanders 'near real-time' intelligence. She was small, unobtrusive, and could fly high and fast. A handful had been deployed to France in 1940 with a camera fitted to each wing.[3] Photo reconnaissance was also becoming increasingly important to assess the damage following Bomber Command strikes. Guns made way for fuel tanks to give the Spitfires greater range.

With no guns or armour, the PR Spitfire was light, agile and glorious to fly. It was also easy on the eye, with smooth lines and a pleasing azure camouflage.

Love at first sight, thought Diana as she took the controls. The flight took her forty minutes, perhaps a touch longer than it should have done. 'No one would have blamed me for those extra few minutes of familiarisation, not to mention pure pleasure, in that, my very first Spitfire.'

Being an independent-minded woman, Diana Barnato Walker was not always going to play strictly by the rules. With no instrument or navigation training and flying exclusively in daylight, most ATA pilots could only ferry planes when visibility cleared to 1,500 yards and there was 800ft cloud clearance. If the weather deteriorated they were to put down or turn back. In Diana's case, the choice usually depended on whether a date awaited back home or on the 'star rating' of accommodation at the destination aerodrome.

Monday, 6 April 1942 was a particularly gusty day, so she followed the rules and put down her Miles Magister trainer at RAF Debden in Essex and waited for the storm to pass.

During lunch in the Officers' Mess she sat next to the blue-eyed, thick-set commander of 65 Squadron, noting he had one of the worst hairstyles she'd ever seen. 'None of it seems to stay put.'[4]

Despite the unruly mane, she was soon chatting easily with Squadron Leader Humphrey Gilbert, a capable pilot who had accounted for several Luftwaffe during the Battle of Britain, flying in his blue-nosed Spitfire.

After lunch the wind dropped. Diana said her goodbyes and went to fire up the Magister. It did not start and she was forced to stay. Gathering in the mess with some old acquaintances, along with Gilbert, they made a night of it. The next morning the Magister again refused to start and, despite several attempts, failed to do so the rest of the day. Gilbert placated Diana's irate commanding officer in a phone call and she was allowed to stay another night.

Romance soon blossomed with the Spitfire commander. Diana made regular visits to Debden, with one of Gilbert's junior officers ferrying her back and forth. Within a month they were engaged. A few days later Diana dropped in for a brief visit but could not find the blue-nosed Spitfire anywhere. An ashen-faced officer took her aside.

Gilbert had been killed the previous day in a Spitfire accident. Diana was devastated. 'This was the first time that someone who really meant something to me was no longer around.' She carried on flying, letting out a *howl* whenever she flew over Debden.

It was only a few days later, when she spoke to one of Gilbert's friends, that she found out the real reason for her three-day delay at Debden. After their initial lunch Gilbert had ordered a mechanic to remove the Magister's spark plugs and sworn the ground crew to secrecy.

Diana had just presumed Humphrey Gilbert had been shot down. She was given a day off to attend his funeral and was out ferrying planes the next day. Sometime later she found out the true cause of his death. Gilbert had once flown in the single-seat Spitfire with a friend on his lap to get to a party in London after their two-seater light aircraft had broken down. It appeared he had repeated the performance, but this time with a large, heavy male RAF aircraft controller, and they crashed.

* * *

Joy Lofthouse, along with her sister Yvonne, were among a generation whose friends were not surviving beyond their teenage years. Three years into the war and eight had died. Among them was Yvonne's childhood love, Peter Comley, nineteen, shot down over the Channel in 1940.[5]

The uncertainty of life intensified relationships. When her pilot boyfriend, Tom Wheatley, proposed in late 1941 after less than a year's courtship, Yvonne readily agreed. 'Something told me, as young as I was, that I had to spend as much time as possible with Tom. The war itself made you hurry. Better to make a decision and do something because tomorrow you might be gone. It was a strange time for decision-making. In a way you didn't really think you'd be spending your life with someone. Not when all around you

Joy Lofthouse in 1944

people you knew were being killed. At one point, I'd gone to see a boy I knew at his base, only to be told he'd had an accident and been killed. The whole thing made you feel as if the ground was constantly shifting under your feet.'

Yvonne had been married for less than a year when a church minister and woman volunteer turned up at her door. She knew instantly that it was 'my turn' for bad news. Tom hadn't come back from his first mission over Germany. He was piloting a Halifax bomber when it was shot down by a German night fighter over Holland. Tom went down with the plane while the crew bailed out.

The first thing Yvonne did was call Tom's mother. 'She'd just lost her son but she'd also lost her husband six months before. He was killed at El Alamein and they never did find his body.'

When Yvonne met with his mother at York station, the widow's first words were: 'I can be brave if you can.' They went back to Tom and Yvonne's Kent home and stayed the night together, the mother sleeping in the same bed her son had slept in the night before.

'I would often go for walks in the country and just lie down, looking up at the sky, watching the planes. After Tom died I was always thinking about what had happened to him, in the last few minutes, when he knew the plane was going down. Again and again I'd think: "Did he know it was hopeless?" You can't help asking yourself those questions.'

Yvonne stayed for a while with Tom's mother. It was a difficult time, especially when she walked Tom's dog Buffy. 'If Buffy saw anyone in uniform he'd gallop up to them eagerly. Then, as soon as he saw it wasn't Tom, he'd trot back to us.'

Soon afterwards, in early 1943, Yvonne saw an advertisement for women pilots in *Aeroplane* magazine. She told her sister Joy and they both volunteered.

Joy and Yvonne knew absolutely nothing about aircraft. However, they were both bright and sporty, winning scholarships to Cirencester Grammar School. Out of 2,000 women who applied for the ATA, they were two of only seventeen accepted.

Joy left her job at a bank and entered the rigorous three-month training programme flying numerous aircraft. Six months later she was in a Spitfire.

'I went to the corner of the airfield and there was my first Spitfire. Oh, it was so powerful. After everything else you'd done before, this was like someone kicking you up the backside.

'It was so light, compact and incredibly easy to manoeuvre. You almost had to breathe on the controls and they moved.'

Yvonne agreed. 'Flying the Spitfire was a kind of freedom you never got any other way. More than anything, with the Spit it was as if you had wings sewn on your back. It was so manoeuvrable.

'Once, on a cloudy rainy day, I ran my right wing through a rain cloud: rain on the right wing, on the left there was sunshine. You could do almost anything with those planes.'

* * *

While they faced many dangers, at least the ATA did not have to confront the gnawing worries of the dispersal hut, awaiting the order to scramble.

Diana Barnato Walker described a more relaxed atmosphere as they awaited flying orders at Hamble, near Southampton.[6] 'A jumble of chairs and tables and a few well-arranged flowers first meet the eye, which scans to see "Jackie" from South Africa turning her morning somersaults at the far end of the room. A radio provides the background to a cacophony of voices.

'In the midst of these can be seen the more domesticated type cutting out a frock on hands and knees, with the material stretched beneath her on the rather uneven linoleum floor . . . a backgammon game is going on and Maureen is trying to do a jigsaw puzzle.

'Suddenly the loudspeaker blares: "Will all pilots report to the Operations Rooms for their chits!"

'Everyone immediately drops what she happens to be doing and goes to the hatchway to be briefed for her job for the day. Then follows a scurry into the lockers for maps and helmets, followed by a visit to the Met for the weather . . . If a pilot gets a type of aircraft she has not flown before she goes to the book of Pilots' Handling Notes which will tell her all she requires to know about how to fly the machine. The taxi pilots study their carefully worked-out itineraries and go out to the Anson or Fairchild [transport aircraft] to get the engines started and warmed up.

'The day's work has begun; as the pilots plod out one by one across the grass, lugging parachutes and overnight bags, none knows what the day may bring or whether she will manage to get back to base in time for that long-standing date of a lobster dinner at the Bugle Inn on the edge of the Hamble River.'

In an age when most women stayed at home, or at the most worked in the factories and fields to aid the war effort, Diana, Joy, Yvonne and the other ATA women were trailblazers of their generation. They were at the forefront of a feminist revolution, years before the term had been coined. But there were still important matters of the time to be dealt with. Like socialising.

Diana had spent a long night in the 400 Club. The Leicester Square venue was filled with its usual smoke, banter and close dancing. After all, the club was, according to the press, the 'night-time headquarters of society'. And they were probably right.

On one side of Diana was Max Aitken, fighter pilot and son of Minister of Aircraft Production, Lord Beaverbrook. On the other was Old Etonian, Oxford graduate, British international skier, stockbroker and Hurricane ace Billy Clyde. The two men were listening intently, and with a degree of jealousy, as Diana described what it was like to fly the latest Spitfire.

'What's it like for blind flying?' Aitken asked in passing. He referred to the pilot's necessary skill for poor weather, when they had to rely on a few key instruments to stay aloft: the altimeter, artificial horizon indicator, airspeed and the climb and descent indicator.

'Oh, we're not taught how to blind fly,' Diana said blithely, sipping a martini. 'We're told if we stay in sight of the ground we should be all right.'

'What?' They both looked dumbfounded.

'Oh yes,' Diana replied, warming to the often talked about theme in ATA dispersal. 'We don't have radios or any ammunition either.' She chuckled. 'They say if we should come into contact with the enemy we would normally be low enough for ground defences not only to recognise us but to engage and shoot down our enemy marauders. People in authority do come up with some wonderful theories, don't they?'

'Bloody hell!' Splashes of Clyde's whisky and soda frothed onto the tablecloth.

'But blind flying?' Aitken interjected. 'Not teaching it is damn near criminal, especially with our lousy weather.'

'Well, I have to tell you, Max,' Diana found herself laughing slightly nervously, 'I have absolutely no idea how some of the blind-flying instruments even work.' She giggled at his stunned expression.

Aitken then grabbed one the 400 Club's pink napkins and began to draw diagrams explaining blind flying, followed by a lecture on how to deal with cloud.

'Straighten up first,' advised Aitken. 'And *think*. You usually go into cloud sideways if you're trying to avoid it.'

'Watch your safety height, so climb up high enough,' interjected Clyde. 'And get back on your original course, then turn slowly round. Keep that turn ever so shallow.'

'Leave your throttle setting where it was when you went in then let down in as shallow a dive as you can,' Aitken added.

Then they lectured her on the 'safety break-off height', the minimum height to avoid high features such as hills. Aitken took Diana's hand and looked her in the eye. 'If you get to your break-off height and you're still in cloud . . . then forget it. Get up again. High. And quick. Then bail out!'

Flying in a brand-new Spitfire, Diana smiled to herself as she recalled Aitken's urging of 'if in doubt bail out'. Despite the late night she was in excellent spirits. In blue skies above the rolling Cotswolds in the 'truly frontline fighter', she relished the evening's memories. She yawned then looked down at her smart uniform skirt and jacket. Running late after her night out, she had not had time to get dressed in flying fatigues before being flown to her pick-up point.

Her thoughts turned back to Aitken's words. He was right of course. The ATA girls were told that their flying skills were far more valuable than any aircraft, even the latest Spitfire. The order was 'save yourselves and forget the plane'.

In the interests of getting pilots quickly qualified the ATA did not teach blind flying. The idea was ATA pilots only flew when visibility and cloud level were optimal.

Diana continued in beautiful weather towards Cosford in Shropshire enjoying the freedom of flight when she looked up from her map and suddenly found herself engulfed in thick cloud. She was mystified. *There was no Met forecast of a weather front.*

Although the Met reporting was a bit haphazard they would not have missed a whole front! *Well, would they?*

At first Diana thought she'd flown into a patch of cloud so she followed the advice of the night before. 'I straightened out, got back onto my course and *thought*! I didn't seem to climb up, but when I glanced at the altimeter it was at 6,000ft, with thick cloud still outside.

'I was faced with two alternatives: bail out or turn round, then let down towards lower ground behind me where I knew the sun had been shining.'

But there was a problem with bailing out. She was still in her skirt.

'My black stockings were a bit short too, leaving off just above my fat knees, so my wartime panties, being made of silk from old parachutes, didn't come down to meet the stockings, leaving a large gap of *me* in between. The parachute harness also chafed the inside of my legs anyhow so I thought that not only will it hurt when I bail out but it will really look silly floating down in a hitched-up and very tight navy serge uniform skirt. I was very modest.'

Diana simply could not accept putting her bare legs and knickers open to view.

She settled on the second alternative – to very slowly turn round and head back, setting a minimum 'safety break-off height' at which to abort. Diana put this at 800ft then began a very gentle descent. After a few minutes the altimeter showed 800ft and she was still in zero visibility. She pulled back on the stick. Skirt or no skirt, it was time to abandon the brand-new Spitfire.

'So that was it! Poor little Spitfire, that could be the end of you or me. I'll have to go up again and do some more *thinking* about bailing out. Oh, if only I wasn't wearing a skirt!'

In the back of her mind she knew she was seconds and a few feet from impact.

The Spitfire lurched in turbulence and the altimeter jerked alarmingly to 600ft. She stiffened. By her dead reckoning ground level was supposed to be 750ft. She was seconds away from death.

'At that very moment I came out of cloud at treetop height. The trees flashed by with cloud sitting on the topmost branches and rain simply pelting down. As I crabbed in and out of the stuff beside the trees, I caught a glimpse of an aircraft on a bit of grass.'

She pulled a tight turn then her spirits sank. The landing strip was flooded. Nose-heavy Spitfires had a tendency to flip over in puddles. Three days earlier a very tall ATA pilot had done just that and drowned while strapped into his open cockpit.

But Diana had no choice. 'I was thinking of all this but I knew I had to put down there no matter what because I wasn't going to be able to anywhere else.'

Mud and water spewed over her as the Spitfire slewed and dragged through pools of rain before finally coming to a halt.

She taxied over to the parked aircraft she'd seen. As she stepped out of the cockpit her legs collapsed beneath her. A tall RAF man in a rain cape came over. Still shaking, she pretended to be kneeling, looking in the cockpit for maps.

'I say, miss, you must be good on instruments!' he said, gallantly covering her with the rain cape.

'*I can't blind fly*,' she croaked.

The airman threw back his head and roared with laughter, thinking she was joking. Not wanting to disappoint by asking where she was, Diana walked with him into the base hut where she found the answer on a sign: *RAF Windrush. Navigation and Blind Flying Establishment. Altitude 560 feet.*

Windrush was somewhere between Oxford and Cheltenham and six miles from her destination of Little Rissington.

She phoned the ops room at White Waltham and was put straight through to the commanding officer.

'Stay there!' he said curtly. Then, after a pause, he quietly added: 'I'm glad you got down safely.'

He explained that there had been an unusually high 'dewpoint', the moisture content in the air, with central England swallowed by rain-cloud. Several ATA aircraft had crashed. Two pilots had been killed.

With the help of Aitken and Clyde's advice, and a large slice of luck and skill, Diana had managed to survive. But it reinforced her view of the authorities' poor decision not to train them in blind flying. 'I think the powers that be made a hash of that decision. I am certain more ATA pilots would have survived had blind flying been a requirement of training. If nothing else, we would have grown far fewer grey hairs above our worried brows.'

* * *

By coincidence Ray Holmes – who had brought down the German Dornier heading to Buckingham Palace during the Battle of Britain – found himself temporarily attached to the ATA during the harsh January of 1941. Hundreds of aircraft had been rolled out of factories but could go no further due to the weather. Packed together, they presented a perfect target for the Luftwaffe, who with a stick of bombs could wipe out a month of factory production. When the weather cleared, experienced RAF pilots were seconded to clear the backlog. Holmes, who was flying Hurricanes with 504 Squadron, reported to ATA headquarters at Whitchurch, near Bristol, on 5 February 1941.[7] 'Our duties were clear-cut. We would collect an aeroplane from A and fly it to B. That we had never even seen that type of aeroplane before, let alone flown one, did not matter. This was the challenge of the job. My first day there I climbed into an Avro Anson with twelve other pilots, clutching a chit authorising me to collect a Spitfire Mark II from Yeovilton in Somerset and deliver it to Llandow in the Vale of Glamorgan.'

It was an ideal opportunity for him to compare the two iconic British fighters.

'My forms authorising me to collect my Spitfire were in triplicate because I could have been a shot-down Luftwaffe pilot stealing an aircraft to escape back to France.

'It was my first introduction to the Spitfire. Basically, it was similar to the Hurricane and half an hour studying the Pilots' Handling Notes sorted out the differences. The Spitfire handled beautifully. It was lighter to loop than the Hurricane yet heavier to roll. This was a proud moment and would give me the laugh on the boys at 504, none of whom had ever flown a Spit.'

While men ferrying planes was regarded as perfectly normal, the ATA 'girls' came in for a degree of sexist comment, usually along the lines of 'the hand that rocked the cradle wrecked the crate', but it was rare. With the Nazis knocking on the door, gender had become an irrelevance; this was war and everyone was in it together.

The ATA women went some way to promoting equality. They were initially paid £230 a year, considerably less than the £310 enjoyed by male ATA pilots. The point was firmly made that if both sexes were flying the same planes to the same places, why were the women getting less? The authorities agreed. In 1943 the ATA women became the first in British history to receive equal pay.[8]

By flying aircraft from factories to their bases the ATA freed up pilots needed for combat, relieving the pressure on front-line squadrons.

Lord Beaverbrook, Minister of Aircraft Production, had high praise for their work: 'The ATA sustained and supported the RAF in battle. They were the soldiers fighting in the struggle, just as completely as if they had been engaged on the battlefront.'[9] And that support was vital; both Spitfires and aircrew were in high demand in ever-increasing numbers around the world.

CHAPTER SIX

MALTA

A Spitfire Mk V destined for Malta

The aircraft carrier's cavernous hangar vibrated to the roar of the Spitfires above. Michael Le Bas might have amassed 182 hours flying the fighter but nothing had prepared him for this.[1]

In a few minutes he would be raised from the gloom of the ship's bowels into the sunlight of the deck and make his first ever take-off from an aircraft carrier.

His destination was 660 miles away, at the end of the Spitfire's range. His route would require him to fly close to enemy air-bases teeming with fighters. He'd have little fuel and even less ammunition for a dogfight. And at the end of his flight he was to land on a small Mediterranean island surrounded by the enemy. Malta. It was 20 April 1942 and the island was nearing the end of its resistance to the Nazi-led onslaught. Spitfires were needed urgently.

A Merlin engine increased its revs above him. The first Spitfire was about to take off. Le Bas, twenty-five, felt his heartbeat quicken.

Already there had been one fatality: a mechanic had stepped backwards into a Spitfire's spinning propeller, which had sliced through his upper torso, removing his head and shoulders. As the remains were gathered up, the blade was simply wiped clean, checked for damage then cleared for flight. This was war. There was no time for sentiment.

Le Bas could not see what was going on behind but he could hear his boss's engine burst into life before being rolled onto the flat, square platform of the aircraft lift. Le Bas was happy to be behind Squadron Leader John Bisdee, the man he'd heard described as a 'cheerful, blond mountain of confidence'. Bisdee, twenty-five, had fought relentlessly during the previous summer, recording six kills.

Le Bas was next in line. His Spitfire Mark V, fitted with its new ninety-gallon drop tank, was heavy with all the extra fuel. Along with the other forty-six pilots, he had heartily tucked into the USS *Wasp*'s generous supply of Coca-Cola and ice-cream. He was struck by a sudden thought. *Bisdee weighs three stone more than I do. If he gets airborne, I'll be all right.*

He craned his neck round in time to see Bisdee's aircraft move backwards onto the lift. US sailors in denim trousers gathered on Le Bas' wings and pushed him to where Bisdee had been seconds earlier. They stepped back and one ordered the engine started. No sooner had the Merlin settled than the lift was on its way back down. Le Bas was pushed on and ascended towards the sunlight of the flight deck. A foot before the top he received the signal to taxi forward. The deckhand timed it perfectly. As the lift slotted into place the Spitfire's tail wheel was off and the great slab of steel was already descending. Ahead, Bisdee's aircraft was climbing.

The deck officer rotated his chequered flag. Le Bas pushed his Spitfire's throttle forward to maximum revs.

* * *

For three months, three weeks and three days, 641 Knights Hospitaller had fought off 30,000 Turks during the Great Siege of Malta. It was 1565 and the Ottoman Empire was trying to seize control of the Mediterranean. Four centuries later a similar campaign was being waged in the same place for the same reasons.

Strategically important, Malta was located in the perfect spot in the Mediterranean where Axis shipping crossed from Italy to supply Rommel's campaign in North Africa. Hitler's grand strategy of sweeping through Egypt, cutting off the eastern half of the British Empire and seizing Arabian oil fields was being held up by an island of 290,000 people and an assortment of RAF aircraft.

By the end of 1941, air and naval attacks from Malta had sunk 64 per cent of ships carrying fuel, tanks and personnel destined for Rommel's Afrika Korps.[2]

Malta was a menace and a sore and had to be eliminated. Hitler had originally entrusted the task to Mussolini and his bombers of the Regia Aeronautica. Infuriated by the island's obduracy and the Italians' inability to succeed, late in 1941 Hitler ordered Goering to do whatever necessary to take Malta.

Confident that the Luftwaffe would not be required for much longer in subduing Russia, Goering sent a frontline force of 600 fighters and bombers to Italy under the command of *Generalfeldmarschall* Albert Kesselring.

Bull-faced, determined and forceful, Kesselring was the man to get the job done. An artillery officer in the First World War, Kesselring had been entrusted with building up the Luftwaffe. He had learned to fly at the age of forty-eight. He was a general who genuinely cared for his troops, and the ranks gave him their devotion in return.

Taking Malta should have been straightforward. The early Maltese air defences had pretty much shrunk to three Gloster Gladiator biplanes nicknamed *Faith, Hope and Charity*. Somehow these obsolete biplanes flown by flying-boat pilots and others managed to shake off the first Italian attacks in 1940.

They had been reinforced by handfuls of Hurricanes either requisitioned when en route to North Africa or flown in from aircraft carriers. But the Hurricane, which had had a hard fight against the 'E' version of the Me109, was outclassed by the 'F' mark. Only the Mark V Spitfire could meet the 109F on equal, if not superior terms.

Britain was not having a good war in early 1942. Aside from the Rhubarb, Ramrod and Circus losses, there were setbacks in almost every theatre, culminating in the disastrous loss of Singapore to the Japanese in February 1942. Ominously, Erwin Rommel was beginning to make inroads towards Egypt.

Only belatedly had Britain's commanders woken up to Malta's importance, that it gave the navy a fighting chance of getting convoys through to Egypt, saving freighters 15,000 miles and forty-five days off the journey round South Africa.

Malta was also a vital, unsinkable aircraft carrier that could be used as a naval and RAF base to strike against Axis supply lines. If Malta fell, North Africa would most likely follow. Then the Middle East would be threatened and the consequences after that were unimaginable. India? Turkey? Russia's southern underbelly? It was clear – Malta had to be saved whatever the cost. And yet again, the Spitfire would be called to the forefront of the action.

* * *

The islanders' allegiance to Britain had endured since Admiral Lord Nelson ousted Napoleon's haughty French troops and made Malta part of the British Empire. That loyalty was about to be tested as Kesselring ordered his men to smash Malta's air defences as the prelude to invasion.

The Germans stuck to their well-used script, flattening homes and damaging Malta's three airfields in a wave of bombings.

The ageing Hurricanes were simply no match for the agile Me109Fs. At times, Luftwaffe pilots deliberately flew their fighters in front of the Hurricanes to demonstrate their superiority. They needed a fighter that could hold its own. A frantic signal was sent to London: *SPITFIRES NEEDED STOP MOST URGENTLY STOP.*

The call for Spitfires was heeded and the first batch of thirty-one fighters was flown off HMS *Eagle* on 7 March 1942. They immediately entered the fray, giving an instant boost to morale. But they were hopelessly outnumbered.[3]

'The most heroic sight was to see about half-a-dozen of these fighters in the air, taking on all comers,' one anti-aircraft gunner wrote. 'They were frequently shot down, but seldom without first having scored a success against their opponents.'

The enemy, used to easier pickings, were distinctly unnerved by the new arrivals. One RAF listening post on Malta reportedly heard a Luftwaffe fighter leader's dismay on spotting the fighter. 'Christ, Spitfires! We weren't told that there were Spitfires on Malta. Back we go!'[4]

Handfuls of Spitfires were not enough. Malta was approaching the point where it would have to surrender and was too weak to resist invasion. The basics of wheat, flour, oils, coal, fodder and ammunition were urgently required.[5]

Meanwhile, German paratroop commanders, in preparation for a possible invasion, were examining maps of south-east Malta, where they planned to jump in. Warships and landing vessels were readied for the main assault.

The bombing was relentless. The tonnage that fell on Malta in March and April 1942 exceeded that of the bombs dropped on London during the whole of the Blitz. One thousand civilians were killed in air raids and 10,000 homes destroyed.

More Spitfires trickled in. But they were not enough. When the Germans mounted eighty bomber raids with fighter escort, all that could be thrown at them were between four and six Spitfires. The pilots were tiring against insurmountable odds.

By the end of March a ragtag collection of between twenty and thirty British fighters was the only air defence that stood against the 600-strong German and Italian air force.

On some days the island was entirely defenceless. Undeterred, the veteran fighter controller Group Captain 'Woody' Woodhall, whose soothing voice had provided much-needed reassurance to pilots during the Battle of Britain, developed a clever ruse.

With a shortage of aircraft but an excess of airmen, 'Woody' came up with the idea to put pilots in cubicles with transmitters simulating flights of Spitfires, giving each other false targets while on the German wavelength.[6] 'Officer Humguffery', as the ploy became known, caused considerable uncertainty among Luftwaffe pilots and intelligence gatherers.

When one bomber force approached, Woodhall put a Canadian with a distinctive voice on a spare microphone and began issuing false orders. The Canadian responded convincingly and it was not long before a cry of '*Achtung!* Spitfire!' came over the radio. In the resulting chaos, two German pilots shot each other down in the mistaken belief they were firing at Spitfires.

But it was the Germans who were proving the masters of the air, if not the airwaves.

* * *

In early April 1942, Churchill was told that the navy had no carriers available to transport Spitfires for at least another month. To avoid disaster there was only one course left: *the Americans.*

Churchill wrote a long personal telegram to President Roosevelt giving details on why there were no British carriers available. He then concluded:

> *Would you be willing to allow your carrier WASP to do one of these trips? ... With her broad lifts, capacity and length, we estimate that WASP could take 50 or more Spitfires.*
>
> *Thus instead of not being able to give Malta any further Spitfires during April a powerful force could be flown into Malta at a stroke and give us a chance of inflicting a very severe and possibly decisive check on the enemy.*[7]

Roosevelt proved a worthy ally. The British could use USS *Wasp*. It would arrive in Glasgow on 10 April.

Over the next few days pilots and aircraft were assembled. The operation was almost scuppered after it was found that the streets to the Clyde were too narrow for the Spitfire's 36ft wingspan. Nerves were calmed when a mechanic suggested they remove the wingtips and eventually forty-seven fighters were moved by truck through Glasgow and stowed in the *Wasp*'s spacious hangar.

A hotchpotch of hastily gathered pilots came aboard. They were formed into four squadrons as they stood on deck, being picked like a school football team. Within four days, the *Wasp* was steaming towards the Mediterranean.

Six days later, on 20 April, she turned into the wind and came to full speed.

Michael Le Bas was grateful to the captain for giving the fliers a good headwind for take-off.[8] As his engine vibrations increased he glanced skywards. Squadron Leader Bisdee's plane was climbing despite the drop tank bulging under its belly.

Les Bas' thoughts again turned to his weight. The extra fuel meant the Spitfire was 770lb overloaded. *But Bisdee got off and he's three stone heavier than me.*

He was out of time to dwell on the possibilities. The American deck officer was rotating his chequered flag.

He pushed forward the throttle, revving the engine to a screaming 3,000rpm. The Spitfire juddered, impatient to be airborne, only the brakes holding her back.

The chequered flag dropped.

Le Bas instantly released the brakes and threw the throttle forward to emergency boost. The extra 34mph could make all the difference.

Freed from her traps, the Spitfire charged along the deck, picking up speed as she whipped past the white markings.

Le Bas saw the bows approaching and glanced down at the dials – 75mph. *Christ! Not enough airspeed.*

He was too fast to stop, too slow to take off. If he went over the bow there was little chance of survival. The nose-heavy Spitfire would quickly plunge into the depths.

Then he was over the edge.

The wave tops lapped just 60ft below his wings.

He retracted the undercarriage. Still there was not enough air-speed for flight.

He had to pick up speed. Gently he eased the stick forward. The Spitfire's nose dipped towards the wave crests.

Down the Spitfire went, now out of sight of those onboard the *Wasp*. In just a matter of seconds he would hit the water.

At 15ft Le Bas felt a slight lift in the wings.

He checked his speed. It was hovering over 85mph. He took a breath and eased the stick back towards him. For what seemed like an age the fighter just stayed level then slowly it lifted, parting with the swell below. Le Bas thanked the heavens for R. J. Mitchell's clever wings.

As he climbed away gaining height, Le Bas switched over from the main to the drop fuel tank. The engine coughed once then the fuel kicked in. At 10,000ft he joined the rest of his squadron of twelve and they set off for their new home, throttling back to 1,800rpm to cruise at an economical 200mph.

The extra fuel in the ninety-gallon external slipper tank gave them a 940-mile range. It was 660 miles to Malta so there was some margin, allowing for headwinds and enemy aircraft that might launch from Pantelleria, the island 150 miles north-west of Malta. It would have to be a brief dogfight. Just two of the four 20mm cannon were armed with sixty rounds, enough for a short squirt.

The sky was cloud-free and to the south he could make out the intriguing reddish-brown peaks of the mountain range that ran along the Algerian coast.

Le Bas reflected on the peaceful lives of the people below. How different would it be to the cauldron he was approaching? He recalled the response of Wing Commander 'Jumbo' Gracie when asked what the odds were in Malta. 'Forty or fifty to one,' he replied. Gracie also mentioned that when he had left the island the previous month there were only three serviceable Spitfires left.[9]

Le Bas swept the skies behind, below and above. His mind drifted. He had to concentrate for every second of the three-and-a-half-hour flight. The sun climbed, the haze swallowing the mountain view. Cloud built up below, hiding the sea and the important navigational point of Cap Bon, north-eastern Tunisia.

Then he spotted a pall of smoke on the horizon. *Malta!*

* * *

Le Bas' squadron made a perfect formation landing at Takali airfield in the centre of the island, stopping just short of several smoking bomb craters.[10]

'You've just missed the nine o'clock raid,' a fitter told Le Bas as his precious Spitfire was pushed into a blast pen, made from local stones. Airmen scrambled onto the wings to begin laboriously refuelling by hand using twenty-one four-gallon petrol tins, while cursing the Germans for blowing up their precious fuel bowser.

Of the forty-seven Spitfires that had taken off from the *Wasp* at dawn, forty-six arrived in Malta, with one crash-landing in Tunisia.

A windowless bus decorated with postcards of the Virgin Mary drove the tired pilots up the hill to the Officers' Mess. As they prepared to sit down for lunch the air-raid siren sounded. The bombers would arrive in fifteen minutes.

Cloudbursts of anti-aircraft gunfire directed the intercepting force of a dozen Hurricanes and Spitfires onto a score of Ju88s.

From the mess balcony the new arrivals watched huge fountains of dust rise up from the aerodrome where the German bombs burst. In two places there was a thick column of black smoke billowing up from where two of the newly arrived Spitfires had been parked.[11]

'The Spits are getting into them!' someone with a pair of binoculars shouted. The pilots followed four Spitfires chasing the Ju88s. Puffs leapt from a fighter's cannons. Seconds later dark smoke streaked from a bomber's engines as it plunged towards the sea. Then the protecting Me109s streaked down and a dogfight ensued.

'Look out, Spit, 109 coming down on you. Turn man, for God's sake, turn!' The veranda erupted in shouts and curses, like a crowd at a football match. 'Good show! Now you've got him!' Then: 'Thank God for that!' as a fighter turned just in time to avoid a stream of 109 shells.

The Malta veterans, both Spitfire and Hurricane, then demonstrated just how determined they had become. One attacked a 109 head-on. Neither broke off and they collided. The German lost an entire wing, the Spitfire its wingtip. As the fighter made a belly-landing, with Hurricanes struggling to provide overhead cover, the pilot jumped out and dashed for cover. As he did so, bullets kicked up the ground around his feet.

The Germans were intent on destroying the new Spitfires before they could get into the air. Three hundred Axis bombers struck Takali airfield on 20 April 1942, the day they arrived.

Many of the new arrivals had not heard the whistle of a bomb before and some had not even seen an enemy aircraft. They were soon to have their fill. At teatime the Germans came to Takali again. Then at dusk too.

It was quite a change from the relatively peaceful skies over England. Air Vice-Marshal Hugh Lloyd, the Air Officer Commanding in Malta, noticed the shocked looks. 'There had never been such an exhibition of concentrated bombing. The newly arrived pilots were speechless. They had never seen anything like it.'[12]

Because there were more pilots than planes in Malta, Michael Le Bas had to wait four days before his first sortie. He was grateful to be in a flight led by Laddie Lucas, twenty-six, the excellent left-handed golfer who had been flying both Hurricanes then Spitfires in Malta for the last two months.[13]

Le Bas hung onto Lucas' wing as they lifted off from Malta in a steep climb to get to 20,000ft as quickly as possible. He felt the excitement of the chase. They had just been scrambled to meet a formation of Ju87 dive-bombers. And they were coming in with fighters. Just ahead of him, Lucas began waggling his wings. He gave a signal that his engine had failed and dived back down. Le Bas suddenly felt less confident. Lucas was a man of poise and experience and a true leader. Now he was gone.

The flight carried on up to 20,000ft. Then someone spotted the Stukas below. Le Bas' worries were left behind as he dived down on the Germans. He glanced at his airspeed. It was approaching 400mph. Surely too fast?

For a split second a Stuka came into his sights and then it was gone. The dive had been too quick for him to get a steady shot.

He looked over his shoulder. Now a horde of Messerschmitts was sweeping down on them. *Jesus*. Le Bas dived to the sea and began weaving furiously, as Lucas had told him. Fortunately, the 109s did not hang about for too long. Getting back to Sicily with enough fuel was always a worry for them.

Le Bas was drenched in sweat as he climbed out of the Spitfire and walked unsteadily towards the mess transport. Someone handed him a mugful of the dark-red local wine, officially called Ambete. He took a sip. A coarse film of liquid slid over his teeth and tongue, leaving behind a bitter taste. The back of his throat felt drier than before the liquid had entered. He took another gulp, hoping for a better reaction. It was the same. No wonder people referred to it as 'Stuka Juice'.[14]

The next morning he scrambled out of his tent to the sound of an Me109's cannons. He got outside in time to see the German fighter close on a Hurricane's tail and give it a final coup de grâce of gunfire. Smoke began pouring from the engine, followed by fire. Then the canopy came open.

He watched spellbound as the pilot climbed out of the Hurricane's smoking cockpit and jumped from 800ft. The well-meaning cheers for his survival were abruptly cut short. The parachute streamed forlornly behind the pilot, refusing to open. The only sound in the following silence was the crump of a body striking the ground.

He walked back to his tent, his pace quickening as he fearfully passed a 1,000lb bomb that had failed to detonate. Craters caused by those that did explode had been filled in overnight by soldiers working under arc lamps. Then, under cover of darkness, the only surviving steamroller emerged from its cave and flattened the strip, making it ready for aircraft by daybreak.

But Malta was in a losing battle. There were simply not enough aircraft. Within two days of the *Wasp* mission, nine of its Spitfires had been destroyed on the ground, eight in the air and twenty-six damaged by bomb shrapnel. There was just a handful left that could fly.

* * *

The *Wasp* Spitfires had heralded a false dawn.

It also soon became apparent that many of the new pilots lacked experience, with several Spitfires lost through accidents. Some wondered if the seventy-two squadrons currently defending England's tamed skies had taken the opportunity to offload green or unwanted pilots.

Hugh Lloyd sharply rebuked the chiefs back home: 'Malta is no place for beginners.'

While not noted for his air tactics, Lloyd at least provided some backbone and resilience for the airmen under his command. At his underground headquarters he hung a sign outside his office that read: 'Less depends on the size of the dog in the fight than on the size of the fight in the dog.'

If RAF resolve was stiffened, some Maltese seemed to be losing heart and stooping to low crimes. One pilot on his first operational sortie had crashed-landed and later died in hospital. He had not bailed out because a local had allegedly stolen his parachute to sell the silk on the black market. On hearing the news, Wing Commander Gracie ordered a gibbet erected on the aerodrome to warn of what would happen to anyone who stole parachutes.

Aircraft spares were also undermining efforts to get planes airborne. Mechanics pored over wrecked Spitfires, stripping them of anything that might prove useful. Engineers also had to work in stifling heat without proper workshops or heavy equipment, lacking even basic tools such as hammers and wrenches.

By the end of April only half-a-dozen serviceable Spitfires were left on the island.

A telegram marked 'Most Secret' was sent to the Chief of the Air Staff. It warned that there could be no guarantee of safe air coverage of convoys coming to Malta. If the island was to be properly defended a surge of 100 Spitfires was required.

Churchill used the information to ask Roosevelt for another *Wasp* trip, warning that otherwise 'Malta will be pounded to bits'.

News of the island's frailty also reached German High Command. The *Fallschirmjäger* – paratroopers – repacked their parachutes and studied the island topography with ever keener interest. Despite their losses they had prevailed in Crete the previous year. This time, with air defences destroyed, they would do so again. Furthermore, Sicily now boasted three new runways ready for glider towing. The airborne invasion was ready.

* * *

Morale was affected in an unforeseen manner. With the air battle fought directly over the island, the death of friends and comrades was witnessed first-hand.

'One cannot deny having rapidly built up a shell to insulate one's feelings, as lively and cheerful friends disappeared with the utter finality of death,' wrote one pilot a few weeks after arriving off the *Wasp*. 'A somewhat numbed perseverance took over. Laughter came a little less readily as time went on. There was no question of bolstering up our spirits in wild mess parties. There were no bar stocks.'[15]

Malta was at its darkest hour. 'The island was being pressed to the last gasp,' Churchill recorded as he made a second personal request to Roosevelt for 'another good sting' from the *Wasp*. It was granted, plus the British carrier *Eagle* had been fixed. Spitfires were coming.

Sixty-four of them.

Squadron leaders and flight commanders in Malta looked at each other in disbelief when briefed with the news. *Sixty-four! That's ten times our operational Spitfires.*

When the excitement subsided another realisation dawned: *Jerry will try his damnedest to destroy the lot.*

German radar could pick up the fleet of Spitfires at least 100 miles out and would put up every available fighter and bomber.

There was more news. Churchill realised that Malta required the sort of backbone that could tolerate the madness of annihilation and still fight on. Field Marshal Lord Gort knew how to tolerate pain and carry on. His Victoria Cross citation in 1918 noted that on being wounded he carried on leading an infantry attack. He was then carried away from the fray but recovered enough to get off his stretcher and lead another attack.

Churchill judged he was a man to get things done.

Gort flew into Malta on 7 May, two days before the fighters' expected arrival. He gave two orders: use the army to ready the new Spitfires for action within twenty minutes; throw a smokescreen over the harbour.[16]

Then he let it be known that the island's George Cross, awarded for acts of 'conspicuous courage in extreme danger', which had been awarded to the Maltese people on King George VI's personal direction, would shortly arrive.

Wing Commander Gracie added his own planning detail. As soon as a Spitfire landed it would be directed to a blast pen where fitters and riggers waited with fuel and bullets. Bren gun carriers were to be on hand to drag damaged Spitfires aside, stretcher bearers would take away the wounded and platoons of soldiers stood ready to fill in bomb craters.

'The turn-around had to be treated like a pit stop in the middle of a Grand Prix race where every second counts,' Laddie Lucas wrote.[17]

On 8 May a horde of Stukas struck. With just twelve Hurricanes and six serviceable Spitfires, few pilots could take to the skies. Lucas grabbed a Lee-Enfield rifle and began firing single rounds as the screaming Stukas dived down at them. Around him people scurried for cover, but other pilots joined in, hoping their knowledge of the 'deflection shot' – aiming well in front of a fast-moving object – might bring down a Stuka. They had little effect other than making the spare pilots think they were not a complete waste of rations.

When dusk closed in, thoughts turned to how much damage a *Staffel* of twelve Stukas could do to packed airfields.

As daylight broke on 9 May the anti-aircraft gunners broke open case after case of ammunition. On this day there would be no restriction to the standard fifteen-round daily ration.[18]

On the high ground radar operators stared at their screens, willing the first Spitfire blips to appear from the west.

There had been a rumour that the first aircraft would arrive around lunchtime. At 10am pilots spotted black dots on the western horizon. Worried glances were quickly replaced by grins as the familiar throb of Merlin engines approached. *Thank God, the Spitfires are coming!* someone shouted. There were cries of thanks and joy, clapping and a few back-slaps. The island was on its knees, in desperate need of reinforcements, and now they had come.

The sleek shadows of Spitfires lifted off the sea and circled the airfields. When they landed, a resident Malta pilot jumped on the wing and guided the pilot towards his pen. The propeller had barely stopped rotating before the plane was engulfed in personnel bearing fuel, bullets and oxygen. Michael Le Bas guided one to its blast pen, telling the pilot to unclip and give up his aircraft.

'That's jolly good, now where's the war?' the pilot shouted.

'The war hasn't started for you yet, mate,' replied Le Bas, who had only flown one operational sortie since arriving three weeks earlier. 'Now get out and be quick about it.'[19]

'You won't be seeing her for a while,' other pilots were told as their planes taxied out, just six minutes after landing.

The Luftwaffe was coming.

Le Bas was among those ordered to go up against a formation of Italian Cant bombers accompanied by Macchi 202 fighters. Five enemy aircraft were shot down. People from around the island watched the action overhead. They knew the difference between a Spitfire and the enemy. Every time an Italian or German plane went down there were cheers, whoops and clapping. By the end of the day there was a tangible change in the island's mood. The Maltese went streaming back to their homes wearing large grins and shouting up to neighbours' windows about the victories they had seen. At the RAF aerodromes there was some back-slapping too, along with excited hand-gesticulating as the Spitfire men related their own aerial accounts.

The German commander, Kesselring, could almost detect the optimism sweeping off the Mediterranean. Radar had shown the relief force slip unhindered into the besieged citadel. The *Generalfeldmarschall* was not a man accustomed to being outwitted. He ordered every available bomber to pound Malta.

At dawn the following day, the plucky Royal Navy minelayer HMS *Welshman* crept into Grand Harbour with her priceless cargo of ammunition and Spitfire spares. Pounding at her top speed of forty knots she managed to avoid warships and U-boats in the dash from Gibraltar.

At 11am a force of thirty German bombers with fighter escorts made for Grand Harbour. A solid cone of flak came up to meet them, tearing into men and machines, sending several plummeting into the sea. For a moment the Luftwaffe thought they had got through the worst of it as the AA guns went silent. The more experienced pilots knew this meant only one thing. They began urgently scouring the skies. It did not take long to see what was heading for them. A force of thirty-seven Spitfires and thirteen Hurricanes tore into the German force.

Kesselring was incensed and now threw everything he had at Malta.

RAF pilots flew sortie after sortie during the fiercest aerial combat seen over the island. Maltese civilians again refused the sanctuary of shelter to watch the overhead battle, cheering whenever a German headed down to destruction.

That night the Axis-run Rome Radio broadcast that thirty-seven Axis aircraft had been lost to forty-seven Spitfires. In fact, just three Spitfires were downed, with the loss of a single pilot.

The next morning's headline in *The Times* of Malta read: 'Battle of Malta: Axis Losses Heavy', followed by: 'Spitfires Slaughter Stukas'.[20]

One good day was not an assurance of campaign victory. They were trapped on a tiny, besieged island, which, at seventeen miles by nine, was smaller than Greater London. But, unlike the Battle of Britain, there was no steady replacement of aircraft, and troops had to fight on near-empty stomachs.

Malta's population, which now exceeded 300,000 with military included, was approaching starvation. No convoys had got through in April or for the rest of May. Aside from the *Welshman*'s fast runs, the only other supplies came from the submarine *Clyde*, which had been converted into an underwater supply ship. Steel and cordite were no substitute for calories.

While the Axis aerial attacks lost their ferocity, the blockade was throttling the island into submission. Malnutrition began to have a debilitating effect on the troops. Scores of pilots went down with 'Malta Dog', a violent form of dysentery caused by contaminated water. 'To put it crudely, the definition of the "Dog" was being able to shit through the eye of the needle 50ft away at least fifteen times a day,' wrote one pilot.[21]

There was little sustenance for those who could eat. 'The rations are terrible, just two slices of bread a day and some biscuit duff, which is the mainstay of the diet,' wrote an RAF fitter in his journal.[22] 'It can be flavoured, like mash. The tea is discoloured because the water is filled with chlorine. Some men think bromide is added to their tea to reduce their sexual longings and safeguard the local maidens. On our rations it is very debatable whether anyone could sustain an onslaught on the local ladies.'

Churchill recognised the peril, urging in a personal note to his foreign secretary that it was 'vitally urgent' to keep the island supplied. In June the Admiralty sent two convoys simultaneously from the east and west. Only two freighters out of a total of seventeen got through, delivering 25,000 tons of supplies. The planes were running desperately low on fuel. Malta was again on the brink of disaster.

* * *

Allan Scott, 1941

After his excursions on Rhubarbs, Allan Scott, who had lost his twin sister in the 1920s influenza epidemic, had come a long way from flying in a Fox Moth as an eleven-year-old and was eager to get on with the job of fighting in a Spitfire after ditching his career as an architect. Thus he was delighted to find himself on HMS *Eagle*, in July 1942, steaming eastwards towards the besieged island of Malta with dozens of badly needed Spitfires.[23]

At dawn on 21 July, Scott nervously took his place on deck alongside twenty-nine other pilots. He marvelled at the sight; he had never seen so many Spitfires crammed together in such a small area. It was a potent force. Now all they had to do was get off the damn carrier and find their way to Malta. He looked out over the ocean and again was assailed with doubt over whether he would be able to build up enough speed in the short distance to get off the deck. They had all heard stories of nose-heavy Spitfires that had failed to get into the air and had simply plunged into the depths, just a few bubbles marking their passing. It had kept Scott awake long into the night.

It was a fear harboured by many pilots and some lost their nerve. The morning did not start well.

A few minutes earlier Scott and the others had watched in horror as a pilot failed to pile on enough power on take-off. The Spitfire had reached the end of the carrier runway then simply tumbled over the ship's bow straight down into the sea. A wake showed momentarily then aircraft and pilot were gone. The sight left the next pilot, an Australian, thoroughly shaken. Halfway down the deck without enough power he slammed on the brakes. The Spitfire skidded and wrapped itself around a Bofors gun.

Burying thoughts of disaster, Scott fixed his eyes on the sailor wielding the take-off 'bats'. A circling sign was made. Scott opened the throttle. *More circling.* He poured on the power, watching the needle climb towards 3,000rpm.

He had to trust the deckhand implicitly. The sailor had the knowledge and experience to know the precise moment when there were enough revs for the take-off run.

The needle pushed over the 3,000rpm mark. The Spitfire's tail shuddered. It was desperate to fly.

Scott's stare remained fixed on the batons and the arms attached to them.

The batons shot forward.

Scott released the brakes and threw the throttle fully open. The Spitfire bolted.

To stay on a straight line he kept the white centre markings under the cannon on his left wing, building up speed as he rapidly approached the bow, partially obscured by the Spitfire's long nose.

The needle nudged 85mph as he staggered over the bows, dropped a few feet then powered upwards. He was off.

Scott joined the formation of twenty-eight Spitfires and set course for Malta. It was the tenth Spitfire mission off a carrier that year. The Luftwaffe *Staffel* based in Pantelleria by now knew that with only a few rounds of ammunition and limited fuel the Spitfires were a vulnerable target. On 3 June an inbound flight from the *Eagle* had been detected and the fully armed and fuelled Messerschmitts were waiting. Four Spitfires were lost.

Tense and sweating, Scott scanned the blue for dark specks. It was clear. An hour later he arrived over Malta to a sky full of 109s attacking Takali, the very airfield on which he was meant to land. Then a 109 loomed in his rear-view mirror.

Scott screwed up his eyes and thought through the options. 'Short of fuel, desperate to land and with a 109 on my tail there was no time to put the undercarriage up. I heaved the Spit into the tightest turn I have ever made in my life, the adrenaline gripping my body and helping me to evade his attack. He missed. I was able to out-turn him and shake him off. Only then could I attempt another landing.'

Scott dumped the Spitfire on the ground and tore towards the protected pen, parked, leapt out and headed for the nearest slit trench.

He looked over the lip to see his Spit already being refuelled by a string of men – army, navy and air force – passing tins of petrol from hand to hand and then up to the 'erk' who was straddling the fuselage as though on horseback. Desperate to get the aircraft ready for the next scramble, he was pouring the petrol into a large funnel to fill the tank. *Welcome to Malta.*

* * *

With almost sixty new Spitfires arriving from the *Eagle* during July, Kesselring knew he had to strike quickly to have one last chance at gaining air supremacy prior to invasion. Fleets of German and Italian bombers were assembled over Sicily then sent the fifty miles south to pummel the three RAF airfields.

The Spitfires were now really under pressure to see off the threat. Orders went out to the pilots to take down the enemy.

Allan Scott had been on the island for just two days when he was ordered onto a scramble against a formation of bombers escorted by Italian Reggiane fighters on 23 July. His mouth was dry with tension as he sped up through the sky to engage the enemy.[24] The

Spitfires' orderly formation evaporated as aircraft broke off to seek their own individual targets. Scott began looking frantically around to find his own enemy aircraft.

'In a split second the sky was filled with weaving and turning aircraft. I managed to get on the tail of a Reggiane fighter but at first could not fix my gunsights on him as he violently manoeuvred to avoid me. But as he broke to dive and turn for home I did manage to let fly a quick burst of cannon shells.'

Scott felt frustrated as he came back to land. He also felt some guilt at expending precious fuel and ammunition without landing a blow on the enemy.

In England, after the Battle of Britain, dogfights – something most pilots thirsted for – had been a rarity. In Malta, between snatched moments of sleeping under his wings and 'Malta Dog' lavatory trips, they soon became part of the daily routine for Scott.

'The sky would be filled with aircraft, all of them twisting, turning and diving, my head jerking with them, eyes flitting from one flick of a movement to another. All actions became instinctive and so rapid, from brain to body to manoeuvring the aircraft, that it is hard to imagine them separately. Ultimately, the machine became an extension of the mind, one pilot-machine against an enemy pilot-machine, each trying to outwit the other, each determined not to be defeated. Manoeuvrability was vital, and it was here that the Spitfire had the advantage. It was up to the pilot to use it skilfully.

'Called to scramble, the squadron would climb at full throttle to gain as much height as possible as quickly as possible, in order to be above the approaching bombers. We knew, and accepted, that the escorting 109s would always be above us. Nevertheless, on sighting the bombers we would individually pick our targets and dive to attack. At this point the Me109s would target the Spitfires. My tactic was to go for the bomber in a turn, as I knew this would give the turret gunners difficulty in getting the correct deflection on me. It would also give me sight of any 109 preparing to attack, as he would have to turn inside me in order to get deflection.

'The firepower I had was four machine guns and two cannons each firing twenty rounds a second which, in a three-second burst, would deliver 600 rounds, usually sufficient to destroy a bomber. In those brief three seconds it all became one movement – fire and break left. It was in the break that I could pick out an Me109 attacking, at which point the dogfight would start.'

Head-on attacks with 109s were the most fearful. Not only did they have a closing speed of 800mph, but the Germans had the advantage of being able to shoot through the Messerschmitt's nose cone, allowing them to fire sooner.

'These encounters happened in a flash and were far too close for comfort. Not only did the hair stand up on end, there was always the risk that a new pair of trousers would be needed on landing – as well as a cigarette or two.'

Scott soon found himself at the wrong end of the altimeter when he was engaged by two 109s at sea level. He had shot down one bomber but in doing so had expended all his ammunition. Then something extraordinary happened.

'I was sitting on the tail of one of them and unable to shoot. The German pilots realised this. All I could do was use the Spitfire in its defensive role and keep out-turning them as they came down. After several tight turns of getting nowhere, they decided it was a stalemate. To my utter amazement they came in and, at a reasonable distance, took formation on either side of me and waggled their wings. For that brief moment we were no longer enemies but fellow aviators.

'I often found that the Luftwaffe pilots had the same outlook as our own; of course we were at war and our take was to destroy enemy aircraft, but as far as I was concerned I was shooting at the aircraft, the pilot could bail out.'

Not all the combat above Malta was so chivalrous. Indeed, at times there were acts of murder by the Germans and retribution by the British.

Laddie Lucas believed that machine-gunning a parachuting pilot was the exception to the rule in the 'hard, clean, ruthless fighting in the air'. But he was eyewitness to one instance of dirty fighting earlier in the year.

Dougie Leggo, a Rhodesian pilot of 249 Squadron, had successfully bailed out over the sea after being hit by a German ace who was in turn downed. 'Leggo rolled his Spitfire onto its back and parted company. His parachute opened immediately. As he descended earthwards, a lone Messerschmitt, appearing seemingly from nowhere, sprayed the canopy with tracer bullets in a callous gesture of murder. It was over in seconds. There was no chance of retaliation.[25]

'No discipline will hold the blind fury of a squadron which has witnessed such cruelty to a comrade. I knew it could only be a question of days before one of the pilots surreptitiously would find a chance of levelling the score. It came within a week. A Junkers 88 had been shot down. The aircraft had ditched in the sea and now the crew of three were in a dinghy. Their chances of being picked up must have been good. As we headed home for Takali my eye caught sight of a single Spitfire away to my left, at the bottom of a shallow, fast dive, heading straight for the dinghy. A sustained burst of fire sent geysers of sea water creeping up on the tiny, inflated boat. Not content with one run, the pilot pulled up into a tight climbing turn to the left and dived again. In war one bad act will always beget another . . .'

* * *

The continuous dogfights were exhausting both pilots and machines, and draining the island's fuel, and by early August Malta was down to a fortnight's aviation fuel.

It wasn't just fuel for the aircraft. Food was again in increasingly short supply. Allan Scott had only been on the island for a month but had rapidly seen the mild excess of flesh around his belly pinched to nothing. As the pilots washed and shaved in the mornings, he looked at men whose ribs clearly showed. He saw extra notches added to trouser belts that now spilt out excess material over thinned-out waists. At other times he watched as pilots with 'Malta Dog' ran at full tilt into the toilet block, and then heard the groans of pain as they emptied their bowels for the umpteenth time that day. 'Bloody well lost four stone since March,' one angular-looking pilot croaked between loo trips enforced by the painful and debilitating diarrhoea.

There were further groans of dissatisfaction when it was announced that rations were to be reduced from four to two thousand calories a day. Scott soon discovered that a maggot-infested fruit and nut chocolate bar was considered a delicacy. 'If it's good enough for the maggots, it's good enough for us,' one pilot said. 'Boil the weevil-infested chocolate in water, skim off the bugs, then drink the rest.'[26]

Bombing had destroyed water pumps. All livestock had been slaughtered. The threat of starvation was very real. All the island's efforts to date would be for nought if supplies ran out.

Malta's biggest resupply convoy was assembled off British waters for what was codenamed Operation Pedestal. Fourteen merchantmen were loaded with fuel, aircraft spares, ammunition, food and medical supplies.

In their midst was the modern American oil tanker, the *Ohio*. Crewed by British sailors, the tanker, capable of sixteen knots, was carrying 170,000 barrels of fuel, enough to supply Malta's Spitfires for three months.

The Royal Navy escort was phenomenal in size and power. A fleet of four aircraft carriers, two battleships, along with thirty-nine cruisers and destroyers, would guard Operation Pedestal.

Both sides knew the stakes were immense.

Every available Axis warship sailed to meet them – heavy cruisers, motor torpedo boats, a dozen submarines and a force of nearly 300 bombers.

Operation Pedestal set out from the Strait of Gibraltar on 11 August. Within hours the attacks began. The ever-reliant *Eagle* was the first victim, sunk by submarine. The attacks became relentless. Ship after ship went down and with them their life-saving supplies.

Within three days there were only five of the original fourteen merchantmen left, including the *Ohio*. The Germans knew they had to sink the tanker.

At 10.45am on 13 August, the *Ohio*, which had suffered a torpedo strike amidships the previous day, came to a standstill sixty miles west of Malta. A Stuka lay on her deck, its bomb still unexploded. Elsewhere the damage was severe. The ship had been lifted out of the water and slammed back down when straddled by bombs. Another hit was scored on the same hole made by the torpedo, virtually breaking her back. The crew had to fight boiler fires to get the stranded ship's engines going again.

The big prize was in reach. Sink the *Ohio* and Malta was sunk. The order went out to Kesselring's bombers.

The first wave of Stukas came in shortly before 11am, a bomb sending burning liquid over her decks. Another three echelons of bombers approached. The Royal Navy destroyers lashed to the tanker to keep her afloat went to full speed, deliberately snapping the ten-inch hemp towlines.

The *Ohio*'s captain listened to the approaching drone of bombers, knowing all their sacrifice was about to become an irrelevance. Across his decks came the reek of burnt oil and rubber.

Suddenly he heard the approach of another engine roar over the stifling Mediterranean waters.

The crew shouted in delight and defiance as fighters tore into the bombers. Sixteen Spitfires from Malta were hurtling towards the enemy. Unnerved by the oncoming fighters, the first echelon of aircraft broke formation, followed shortly by the second. But a section of four bombers held firm and headed for the *Ohio*, determined to sink the tanker no matter the consequences to themselves. The Spitfires pushed their throttles fully open in a dash to rescue the tanker. Among the pilots was Allan Scott, who latched onto a bomber. 'As we came within range I spotted a bomber doing a run-in, carrying a full bombload. I fired a beam shot at it. My fire, from nose to tail, shot it out of the sky, and I flew through its debris.'

Other Spitfires joined in, along with the *Ohio*'s own AA gunners firing off with everything they had. Flak clouds clogged the sky around the RAF fighters but they carried on firing on the enemy planes, taking down two more.

But one German had made it through the wall of flak and the Spitfires snapping at his heels. As he flew over the ship a 1,000lb bomb slipped out of its cradle down towards the deck. Crippled and travelling at just five knots the *Ohio* was slow. But not too slow. The bomb landed in the wake just behind its stern. The force of the blast threw the tanker forward, buckling its plates and creating another great hole. But still she remained afloat.

Further attacks were beaten off by the Spitfires and Malta's shore batteries, now within range.

The *Ohio*, lashed once again between two destroyers, limped towards Grand Harbour. Crowds gathered to watch the scene, some cried, nearly all cheered. They all knew the significance of the oil tanker's arrival.

Scott had jumped with other pilots onto the bus that was heading down to Grand Harbour to witness the *Ohio*'s arrival. He wanted to see at close quarters the near-broken ship he had seen at sea. 'The efforts to protect its precious cargo and to get it into port had been heroic. Frantic in their relief, the jubilant crowds came out to wave the *Ohio* into port, knowing only too well that had this convoy not got through Malta would have fallen and the course of the war been dramatically changed.'

Smarting from Malta's defiance, Kesselring launched a final bludgeoning attack on the island. For seventeen days over October, Luftwaffe bombers once again came in waves and the Spitfires rose to meet them.

But with the fuel from the *Ohio*, the Spitfire and Hurricane pilots were able to push their throttles wide open to gain height. On 12 October, Allan Scott's squadron rapidly climbed to 10,000ft above a formation of 100 Ju88 bombers.[27]

'Seeing the bombers below we immediately dived down to engage. I got my sights on a Ju88 and opened fire with a good three-second burst. Bits flew off it and an engine was hit, smoke pouring out. I had to break hard then to avoid an Me109 on my tail. A dogfight was in progress, with Spitfires and 109s weaving all over the sky. I managed to destroy a 109 and damage another. With the need for the attacking fighters to reserve enough fuel to get back to base, these dogfights did not last long. It was not often three could be bagged in one sortie. It had been a very successful outcome.'

Within a week the game was up. 'Our losses were too high,' Kesselring admitted.

The German commander scaled back the attacks as more Spitfires, equipped with 170-gallon drop tanks, arrived in Malta after a five-hour, 1,100-mile direct flight from Gibraltar.

Victory had significant implications for both sides. Rommel's desert forces would contract and the British 8th Army would thrive. It had been an exceptionally close-run thing. Before the Spitfire arrived, Malta was near to surrender. While the fighter's presence by no means guaranteed success, it bludgeoned the Luftwaffe and lifted morale, an intangible benefit in war.

During the siege, the Axis lost 309 planes compared to 259 British fighters, destroyed in the air and on the ground, the majority of them Spitfires. A total of 120 RAF pilots were killed.[28]

Laddie Lucas succinctly grasped the implications had Malta been lost: 'In short, a chain reaction of hideous proportions would have attended the garrison's fall.'[29]

Once again the Spitfire was on the side of the victors. The fighter's iconic reputation grew ever more.

CHAPTER SEVEN

DIEPPE, AUGUST 1942

Alan Peart

Alan Peart glanced at the veterans' faces, eyes alert to the prospect of a serious dust-up. He felt for the tattered cigarette card in his pocket, to convince himself that he really was here, in England flying Spitfires with 610 Squadron and the renowned ace Johnnie Johnson as his squadron leader.

It was 18 August 1942. Almost exactly a year earlier, Peart's boyish features had appeared before the appeal board of three officers. He wanted to be a fighter pilot rather than fly bombers.[1]

Looking at their reactions Peart did not quite have the stomach to tell them that, actually, *I want to become a Spitfire pilot*.

Ever since the day he had seen the picture of a Spitfire on a card from his father's cigarette packet he had been spellbound. Although he lived among the mountains, lakes and glaciers of New Zealand, Peart had never seen anything quite so beautiful.

During the appeal he had thumbed the dog-eared card in his pocket, resisting the temptation to pull it out and slam it on the table.

At the end of elementary flying training his dream had been shattered. Assessed as an 'average' pilot and 'above average' navigator, to his horror he had been categorised as 'suitable for flying bombers'.

His request for an appeal hearing had been granted.

Bollocks. He placed the cigarette card on the table, the beautiful curved lines of the fighter instantly recognisable. 'That's why I want to fly single engines. I want to fly the Spitfire. It's that or . . .' He shrugged his shoulders and took a step back.

The three officers looked at each other and nodded.

Seeing the shaking hands of 610 Squadron's fliers as they lit their cigarettes brought back to him his mother's pain as he said goodbye a year ago. After a long drag the shakes stopped. Peart stared a moment longer at the group of men he'd recently joined, wondering what fears or horrors they had confronted in past battles. His thoughts again went back to his final farewell in New Zealand, at Hamilton railway station. 'My poor mother was convinced, not without good reason, that she would never see her son again. She said goodbye with stoicism but I never forgot the look of agony on her face as I parted from her. While I simply dismissed the dangers ahead, my mother certainly knew.'

And the shakes were there for good reason. Before dawn the next morning, 610 Squadron were to fly over the French port of Dieppe and draw as many enemy aircraft up to the fight as they could. It was going to be the fiercest air battle since 1940 and 25 per cent casualties were expected. *That's one in four*, Peart thought as he glanced around the dozen or so heads in the room.

Worse, as the squadron 'sprog' he was to be at the rear of the formation, the most vulnerable position, reserved for the most inexperienced pilot.

'I looked along the line of chaps next to me and wondered who was due for the chop. The awful truth dawned on me that from now on things were for real. Will I be an easy target for some German ace, before I could get enough experience to look after myself? All my past reading confirmed the likelihood of that scenario. It was a traumatic and sobering thought.'

His mind cast back to a few weeks earlier on his first flight in the Spitfire. It was not what he'd expected. As Peart sat in the small but comfortable cockpit, he felt the excitement built over years of dreaming for this moment overpower him. It felt like he was looking at the switches and dials for the first time. A momentary panic gripped him, as he tried to remember what to do to get the plane airborne. He took a deep breath and reached for the throttle lever, pushing it forward. The engine noise increased significantly, then the Spitfire was moving. But not in the direction he wanted it to go. It spun round in a complete circle. Peart felt his cheeks burn with embarrassment as he used the rudder pedals to control the tail and keep the Spitfire straight. It was his first lesson in the power of the Merlin engine.

He opened the throttle again and hurtled down the runway and into the air, experiencing the Spitfire's agility and its joy of being freed from the ground.

The Spitfire proved much more powerful and faster than anything he'd flown before. It would need to be. The Mark V might have been a match for the 109 'F's over Malta but it was really struggling against the Focke-Wulf 190.

The RAF desperately needed to find out what made the Fw190 so good. Supermarine's test pilot Jeffrey Quill was drawn into a plot by Philip Pinckney, an enigmatic SAS commando, to drop into France and steal a 190. The plans, marked 'Most Secret', were well advanced when a Luftwaffe pilot mistook the Bristol Channel for the English Channel and subsequently became totally lost, finally landing his Fw190 intact in South Wales in June 1942.[2]

Quill and others flew the captured 190 to discover its attributes. An official RAF report found that the German fighter was 'superior in speed at all heights' and could outclimb as well as out-dive a Spitfire V.[3]

The designers at Supermarine had been working hard to come up with a riposte. The answer was simple: improve on what we have. They developed the Spitfire Mark IX, arguably the greatest variant to come out of the Supermarine workshop.

When Jeffrey Quill viewed the Mark IX for the first time he was not that impressed. Yes, she had the same sleek outlines as previous Spits and yes, she had the dual cannons and he knew the new Merlin 61 engine lay under the cowling, but what else did she bring to the party?

Well, quite a lot as it proved. 'The performance and handling of this aircraft in its present form is quite exceptionally good at high altitude,' Quill wrote after fifty-seven hours flying the new model. 'It is considered that this machine will be a very formidable fighter.'[4]

The Mark IX also added 70mph to the Spitfire's top speed and 10,000ft to its fighting altitude. 'The performance of the Spitfire IX is outstandingly better than the Spitfire V,' the official test report read. 'Spitfire is considerably faster and its climb is exceptionally good.'[5]

The only structural alteration from the Mark V had been to elongate the body by nine inches to accommodate the Merlin 61. But what a difference those nine inches made. With its two-stage supercharger, in which air was doubly compressed before entering the carburettor, the Mark IX was given an astonishing 20 per cent increase in power.

Brian Kingcome, who at twenty-four was one of the RAF's youngest Wing Commanders and had been fighting in Spitfires since Dunkirk, was among the first to discover its powers. 'The effect was magical. I had expected an increase in power but nothing to match the reality. To enhance the dramatic effect, the second stage cut in automatically without warning. One minute there I was, relaxed and peaceful, as I climbed at a leisurely pace towards 15,000ft, anticipating a small surge of power as I hit the magic number. The next minute it was as though a giant hand had grabbed hold of me, cradled me in its palm like a shot-putter and given me the most terrific shove forwards and upwards. The shove was so great that I almost bailed out. It literally took my breath away. It was exhilarating, a feeling that I could never forget. I yearned at once for a chance to demonstrate the astonishing new tool to the Germans.'[6]

However, the new aircraft very nearly fell into the Germans' laps before it even fired a shot. Keen to share its qualities, Quill flew the brand-new Spitfire down to Hornchurch in Essex to let his friend Group Captain Harry Broadhurst have a go. Charismatic, independent and unconventional, Broadhurst took the Supermarine test pilot at his word. As Quill went into the Hornchurch ops room to watch a fighter sweep's progress over France, Broadhurst took the latest Spitfire for a flight above. While the wing headed towards Boulogne at 25,000ft, Quill noticed a single aircraft on the plotting table some distance behind.[7]

'What's that plot there?' he asked the controller.

'Oh, that's the Station Commander.'

'God damn it, he's in my aeroplane! Do you realise that's the most important prototype fighter in the country right now? What's more, the guns aren't loaded!'

'Well, there's nothing I can do about it,' the controller tartly replied. 'But right now he seems to be at well over 35,000ft.'

'Thank God for that,' Quill said, then resigned himself to an anxious wait as dozens of Luftwaffe fighters flew up to meet the Hornchurch Wing.

Quill wondered how to explain to his boss that he had taken off from the Supermarine test base at Worthy Down, Hampshire, that morning in a vital trial aircraft and before the day was out it had been shot down in France.

'Magnificent aeroplane,' Broadhurst told him on landing. 'Get as many as you can, as quickly as possible.' Then his dark gaze settled on Quill. 'By the way, you might have told me that the guns weren't loaded.' Quill stifled a reply.

* * *

Harry Strawn with his dog, 'Red', August 1942

On the same day Peart received his briefing, there was some nervous laughter among the American pilots of 309th Squadron as they listened to the Dieppe plans amid the lush, rolling hills of West Sussex at Westhampnett airfield.

The medium-sized port of Dieppe had been chosen as the place that an Allied amphibious force would land and hold a piece of occupied France for a day, proving that sea-borne invasions were possible. When they withdrew, the 6,000-strong ground force would destroy the port's defences and hopefully leave with useful intelligence. What was more, the British public would see the impunity with which the Nazi continent could be breached and that Britain was committed to liberating Europe. The summer of 1942 would be good for morale.

In the skies above would be squadron after squadron of Spitfires protecting all below. This time an umbrella of fighters would cover the sky. It would not be another Dunkirk.

The mission for the newly arrived American pilots of the 309th

Squadron, about to be tested in battle for the first time, was clear if somewhat contradictory. 'We are going to destroy the entire town and hold it for one day,' wrote Harry Strawn, the pilot who'd had careers in farming and advertising before finding his vocation flying Spitfires. 'Of course we will be fighting Fw190s all day. It should be a big show and my first fight. I'll need strength tomorrow.'

The RAF was about to unleash more than 600 Spitfires, although nearly all Mark Vs, as only four squadrons of Mark IXs were currently operational.

The Fighter Command chief Trafford Leigh-Mallory was convinced that a good opportunity lay in the Dieppe plans. The Rhubarb, Ramrod and Circus attacks into France were at a stalemate and Jerry wasn't playing ball. In fact, he was drawing them ever deeper into France only to strike when the planes had a few minutes' fuel left. It might have seemed a deadlock but in fact the RAF was losing. In the first six months of 1942 it had lost nearly five times as many aircraft as the Luftwaffe, 245 to 59.[8] And despite heroics among some French, nearly all British bail-outs ended up in capture.

Intelligence had suggested that if a French port was seized the German protocol was to assume it was the prelude to a full-scale invasion. The Luftwaffe would be ordered to mount a major operation to control the skies. RAF commanders saw an opportunity to give the 'Hun' a bloody nose.

There was pressure as well from the army, particularly the Canadians, fed up with exercises in the damp British countryside while there was a gargantuan clash of arms in Russia. They wanted to prove themselves in action.

There were demands too from Joseph Stalin, the Soviet leader, to open up a second front in Europe. With German forces penetrating deep into the Caucasus in summer 1942, he argued that the Germans would move forty of their 180 divisions off the Eastern Front to fight in France.

The Dieppe 'invasion' by a division of 6,000 men had the modest ambition of seizing a French port merely for 'the duration of at least two tides'.[9]

To provide overhead cover Leigh-Mallory had a total of seventy squadrons, almost double the number at Dowding's disposal at the start of the Battle of Britain. His squadron leaders and flight commanders were also all seasoned fighters from the previous two years of conflict.

Opposing them was a force of skilled German fighter squadrons, with almost 200 of the deadly Fw190s, a handful of 109s and a fleet of more than 100 bombers.

With the odds in his favour, Leigh-Mallory was content for the battle of attrition to begin.

* * *

The final briefings on the evening of 18 August gave pilots no room for doubt. They were told to fight it out to maintain air superiority over the beaches 'even if you are to remain alone there to the end'.[10]

A few hours later the task force of 237 ships sheltering in harbours along the south coast weighed anchor and headed into the Channel for the seventy-five-mile crossing to occupied France.

It was the middle of the night when Alan Peart felt a gentle tug on his shoulder. 'Cuppa cha for yer, sergeant. It's two-thirty.'[11]

He sat up and pulled on his still-new battledress. Around him others donned faded uniforms and old 'best blues'. Peart tied a silk scarf around his neck, followed by his New Zealand wool jumper.

His hand went to his face. *Should I shave?* He tramped to the washrooms, and splashed water on his face before applying shaving cream. A few minutes later he stepped back from the mirror and nodded to himself. *Ready for action.*

A light, warm wind brushed across West Malling aerodrome, nestling among the woods of mid-Kent, as he strode to the breakfast tent. Those who had not shaved were already emptying their plates of a rare feast – real eggs, chips, fried bread and margarine.

Stars still shone brightly as Peart walked to the dispersal hut. He glanced at his watch. *3am.*

Over among the green hills of the South Downs that looked down on Westhampnett, the American pilots shared the same thoughts. 'I guess this is the big day in my life,' Harry Strawn had time to note in his diary after his 3am wake-up call. 'The planes are warming up in the dark. Others are already in the air heading towards Dieppe for the big day. Most of us are joking and laughing, but I rather imagine it's to cover up nerves. I feel a bit on edge and a little shaky.'[12]

At sea, 3am was the cut-off time to cancel the invasion. British commandos and Canadian infantry waited in ships to embark on the new landing craft specially designed for putting ramps down on beaches to allow fast disembarkation. Their fears of being cut down were somewhat assuaged by the knowledge that alongside them lay fifty-eight of the new, powerful Churchill tanks, also using new landing craft. Before dawn they would all be storming up Dieppe's shingle beach, over its sea wall and into town, rounding up those Germans wise enough to surrender. Within twenty-four hours they would be back home with the opportunity to brag in bars and pubs of how they had set foot in occupied France, given Jerry a bloody nose and come back to tell the tale. The ladies, no doubt, would be swooning for a Dieppe hero.

The majority bobbing in the Channel did not want to hear any cancellation order. And no such order came. The signal was given and rope ladders went over the sides, and the infantry began clambering into the gently rolling landing craft. At 3.06am the first boats chugged towards the sloping shingle beaches of Dieppe.

Overhead, four-inch shells from the destroyers crashed into German concrete emplacements.

Undaunted, the landing craft ploughed on. As the minutes passed, troops could hear aircraft overhead. A few minutes later bomb blasts accompanied flashes on the cliffs and shoreline around Dieppe. The soldiers grinned and nudged each other. Jerry's gun batteries were clearly taking a hammering.

But so was the RAF. Among the first to suffer casualties were the eight squadrons of 'Hurribombers', Hurricanes converted to dive-bombers to drop 250lb or 500lb bombs minutes before the amphibious assault came in. Eight Hurricanes were lost with a further twenty damaged.

At 3.47am twelve Spitfire squadrons were sent up.

Pilots could see streams of tracer bullets pass to and fro from soldiers on the beach and German positions looking down on them.

It was difficult to concentrate when so much was going on down below. The Spitfires pushed around the sky, largely unnoticed by the Canadians now pinned down in a merciless crossfire on the beaches. The idea that Dieppe was going to be a walkover was quickly dispelled. German machine guns concealed in solidly constructed pillboxes sprayed belt after belt of bullets into the hapless infantry. Artillery from the surrounding area joined in, sending splinters of beach stones and metal among the troops. Some infantry got to the cover of the sea wall but few ventured over it. Waves began to wash in, flecked with red.

* * *

As demonstrated by his daring flight in the Spitfire IX to observe the fighter sweep into France, Harry Broadhurst was no shrinking violet. He also had a good nose for finding facts while absorbing detail, and a reputation as an acrobatic daredevil. Those attributes had served him well during the France debacle, the Battle of Britain and the Rhubarbs, where even a man of his skill had been badly shot up. He was already an 'ace' and had the decoration ribbons across his chest to prove he was not shy of a fight. Aged thirty-six, he was not going to be pushed around.

But he had just taken a beating. During the Dieppe planning, he argued against using 'stepped-up' wings of fighters set at designated heights – low level, mid level and high level – patrolling over the beachhead. Broadhurst contended that it would be 'too unmanoeuvrable' against the small, agile formations of German bombers or fighters.

His view went against that of the majority and led to Broadhurst venting strong disagreement. The matter had, in his words, 'left me in the doghouse'.

Doghouse or not, he was not going to be stopped from flying. Early in the morning, Broadhurst borrowed a Spitfire IX from RAF Hornchurch and went to have a look over Dieppe for himself. Just after 6.30am, flying at 20,000ft, he spotted groups of Fw190s in pairs or fours climbing up into the sun then diving through the stepped-up wings onto the aircraft and ships below before beetling back inland at low level.[13]

Broadhurst studied the attacks from afar for some time before his experienced eye picked out two Fw190s approaching. Manoeuvring rapidly he latched onto the 'number two'. He used the Mark IXs boosted power to close in on the German and then opened fire in a single, destructive salvo. The kill did little to soothe his discontent over ill-guided tactics as he landed at Biggin Hill.

Broadhurst strode out of his Spitfire to the operations room and its direct line to Fighter Command. He did not keep his mouth shut.

The bloody useless 'stepped-up' tactic was not working.

Why? A senior commander wanted to know.

Why? Why! Broadhurst was not going to hold back now. Because I've seen it with my own eyes! That's why.

At 7.05am, shortly after Broadhurst landed, radar plotters on the south coast began picking up large Luftwaffe fighter formations heading in a constant stream towards Dieppe. The wished-for battle of attrition was on.

A series of terrific dogfights began. The two Norwegian Spitfire squadrons, 331 and 332, were up high and ready to take on the Nazis who still occupied their country. The Spitfires dived down on the mixture of 109s and Fw190s. But they were still in Mark Vs and it was proving increasingly inadequate against the Fw190. Despite their bravery, Norwegian-piloted Spitfires splashed into the sea, but they also took a few Germans with them.

The stoicism of the Norwegian CO, Wilhelm Mohr, was evident as he walked with a fellow commander around the dispersal area to see what aircraft were available for the next sortie. When Mohr mentioned he wouldn't be going on the next flight the British officer looked surprised. Mohr set him straight: 'I am sorry but I am afraid I *haf* a bullet in my body.' He pointed to a hole in his boot. During a melee his aircraft had been hit and the round had burrowed into his right leg.[14]

Since 3am Alan Peart had been fighting back fears and doubts about what might happen in his first fight.[15] Was he up to the job? Would a German ace spot his inexperience and go for an easy kill? If his plane was hit, would he be unhurt? If he had to bail out, would he be able to get the canopy open? As the hours passed he began to wonder if 610 Squadron had been overlooked. Reports came in of others getting kills but also suffering losses. There were mutters about '190s' and 'why the hell haven't they given us Mark IXs?' The dispersal-room chatter stopped when Squadron Leader Johnnie Johnson's calm voice addressed them: 'Time to get up there, chaps.'

Peart tried to look nonchalant as he walked to his aircraft. But he could see the tension in his ground mechanics as they busied themselves around him, ensuring he was securely strapped in with parachute and Mae West life jacket. At the signal to 'go', Peart gave a thumbs-up and watched his flight sergeant mouth a 'good luck' then grin and make a motion of firing a machine gun with both hands.

Peart felt a surge of elation and pride as the entire squadron took to the sky as one. He felt safe too, among so many experienced and respected pilots. For a brief moment he embraced the idea of the coming battle and was curious about how he would react under fire for the first time. Would he be hit? Would he fly home in terror? Or just sit there and take it?

Then his mind settled on the concentration needed for rear-end Charlie.

The squadron climbed to 7,000ft and Peart was struggling to keep up with the other eleven Spitfires as they made their way over the Channel.

'Come on Red 12, stay with us.' Peart applied more throttle to catch up as he swept left and right, tracking the sky. As tail-end Charlie, he was in danger of drifting away from the formation and being picked off singly.

For a brief second Peart looked ahead and spotted a heavy pall of smoke towering over the coast. *Dieppe*. He could see flashes and explosions, vehicles at crazy angles, some in the water, some out. Tanks with dark smoke pouring out of their turrets. Anonymous shapes littered the beach. Bodies? *Dead men. Our men.* He had never before seen death and destruction on such a scale. He looked away.

Below were two other stepped-up squadrons, one at 3,000ft and the other at wave-top level. 610 were there to provide top cover. Peart concentrated on doing the best job he could.

Johnnie Johnson ordered them higher, to 10,000ft.

'Shit!'

'Fuck!'

Peart heard expletives then started desperately searching the sky overhead.

'Bandits. Fifty-plus. Coming down. 190s and 109s! Stand by.'

Aircraft began weaving about madly.

'Fight your way out.' He recognised the anxious voice of the wing leader. 'Get out. Watch those 190s above at six o'clock. All Elfin aircraft – get out!'

'Red 12 break port.' Peart immediately obeyed the command and turned the stick, diving hard left as Messerschmitts and Focke-Wulfs came down from astern and the flanks. He banked left and right, trying hard to stay out of enemy sights.

'Jamie, strong enemy reinforcements coming in. About fifty-plus. Over.' Johnson's calm voice warned a squadron leader down below.

'Red 12 you're under fire. Under fire!' Peart instinctively flung his Spitfire hard right and down. Still he couldn't see the enemy, let alone fasten onto one to fire his guns.

Around him Spitfires carried on fighting in pairs and fours. Down below he could still see the desperate fight for survival raging on the beach and in the waves. Men were dying down there but he had to focus his mind on the job in the skies.

He spotted a Spitfire hurtling at speed just above the wave tops towards a destroyer. Peart was puzzled. They had been carefully briefed not to fly under 4,000ft around shipping. The navy gunners would shoot at anyone who came close. Flak flew towards the fighter. Another aircraft was not far behind. At the last moment the Spitfire shot up and over the destroyer. The enemy aircraft veered away in a tight turn, unwilling to challenge the navy gunners.

To shake the superior Fw190 from his tail, Johnnie Johnson had resorted to the near-suicidal tactic of flying into his own flak by heading towards a Royal Navy destroyer. After fighting the Fw190 at close quarters he knew that the Mark V was really struggling. 'Our Spitfire Vs were completely outclassed by the Fw190s and on this occasion I was certainly lucky to get back,' Johnson recorded.[16] The 'V's simply did not have the power to take on the 190s. Only the Mark IXs could and it seemed the only person flying one was Harry Broadhurst, still monitoring the course of the battle from above.

Group Captain Harry Broadhurst was determined to do something about that soon after landing back at RAF Biggin Hill after his second Dieppe sortie. He telephoned Leigh-Mallory at 11 Group HQ and requested that Mark IXs be sent up in pairs or fours to counter the 190 threat. The reply he received was not encouraging. There were only four Mark IX squadrons available and they were detailed to escort the raid on Abbeville airbase by the American 8th Air Force.[17]

Broadhurst just about restrained himself from using an expletive against a senior officer before the phone was back in its cradle.

* * *

When 610 Squadron landed back at West Malling, Peart gratefully accepted the mug of tea handed up to the cockpit along with a spam and cheese sandwich. Suddenly he felt ravenous. 'Got your first taste of it today, Alan,' his section leader leaned on his wing.

'Yes,' Peart quietly responded.

'Lucky that 190 missed you. Seemed he was giving you everything he had.'

Peart nodded then took a large bite of sandwich. *I didn't even bloody well see him.*

He had to spot enemy fighters at a distance otherwise he'd be dead.

'Fuel your belly up,' the officer patted his shoulder. 'We'll be back up shortly.'

Ground crews worked hard to turn around the aircraft. It was like the Battle of Britain again. Rearm, refuel, polish the cockpit windscreen then patch up bullet holes and return the aircraft to duty. All within half an hour. Peart looked on in admiration.

'Come on, I heard they're serving something called "nearly-spam" and chips in the mess.'

Peart felt a slight wobble in his legs as he got down. He was grateful. Grateful for his luck and grateful to have experienced combat for the first time and survived. *Even if I didn't see the bastard!*

* * *

Harry Strawn waited for six hours before the scramble order came. As he lifted his Spitfire into the sky he felt certain, along with his fellow Americans of the 309th Squadron, that he was about to be tested in combat for the first time.

Despite the aircraft around him it felt lonely in the cockpit. He tightened the flap of his flying helmet, trying to cut out the sound of wind rushing past. His mouth and nose were enclosed in the mask containing his microphone transmitter. His broad shoulders brushed the cockpit sides as he glanced around looking for his fellow fliers. He felt shut off from the rest of the world, cocooned yet vulnerable.

Soon they would be in a fight. *Someone trying to kill me.* Certainly there would be flak. He tried to recall the lecture given by a veteran. White puffs on the ground meant AA was shooting at you; if puffs appeared in the air with red in them they were very close. All you can do is ignore the fact that a shell, three and a half inches across and travelling at speed, could make a severe mess of the cockpit.

Best to remember you're in a small space occupying a tiny piece of sky.

That piece of sky was not small enough for some in the 309th. Strawn watched as three of his fellow American fliers, men he'd been having breakfast with only that morning, were sent streaking downwards in flames in their Mark Vs. The only silver lining was hearing someone shout in glee over the radio, 'Got him! I've got him!' and seeing an Fw190 head down, emitting smoke.

Strawn swooped low over the Dieppe beach. It was not a sight he wanted to dwell on. Bodies floated in the surf or straddled obstacles. Men were clearly fighting for their lives as gunfire pummelled them from all sides. Seeing the bloodbath on the beaches made the dangers of flying easier to accept. 'Thank God I'm in the air, for there it comes quickly and easily. At least you don't have to witness wholesale slaughter.'

Because the tanks arrived late, the infantry were forced to press ahead. Some of the Churchills had flamethrowers, which could easily have wiped out the machine-gun nests and gun emplacements in the cliffs. Instead, it had become a scene of carnage and mayhem, with officers and men cut down. When the tanks finally arrived only twenty-nine got ashore, but a dozen were then bogged down on the soft shingle under their tracks.

Then the British commander unwittingly made the decision to reinforce failure.

At 7am he launched his reserves of two battalions into the hell of the beaches. As the landing craft approached, the Germans opened up with everything – machine guns, mortars and grenades.

The slaughter ashore grew by the hour. The idea of holding Dieppe for 'two tides' was simply not feasible. At 10.50am the decision was made to withdraw.

At 11am the RAF unleashed a heavy attack on German defences

around Dieppe prior to laying a smokescreen. Landing craft, supported by destroyers, began the hazardous operation of retrieving those who had survived the slaughter. As the ships came in close to shore and within range of German machine guns, the order was given to abandon all equipment, including the brand-new Churchill tanks. The Royal Marine landing-craft crews, hearing the clatter of bullets strike against their hulls as they pulled up the shingle, felt some relief. Their job had just been made marginally easier.

The German gunfire grew in intensity, as they fired blindly into the smokescreen knowing the British were on the back foot. Soldiers clambered onto a landing craft only to find themselves back in the water after it capsized or sank. The wave crests were streaked red. Then the smokescreen began to thin. Gaps appeared and the enemy machine-gunners poured everything they had into them.

A handful of Blenheim and Boston bombers came thundering across the Channel to lay down more of the precious smoke.

Sensing their chance, the Luftwaffe threw bombers and fighters at the ships and ground troops. The Spitfires engaged in a bitter battle to hold them off. For those at 3,000ft above the shipping, there was little room in which to manoeuvre from attacks above.

Myles Duke-Woolley, at just twenty-six, was a pugnacious Battle of Britain ace and leading his squadron on its third sortie of the morning. He felt like they were waiting to be picked off. Being able to spot an enemy fighter from far away was, as Peart was beginning to learn, a skill that required a lot of practice. 'The Duke' was good at it. He wouldn't have survived this long if he hadn't been. Yet in the turmoil of Dieppe and from his low position even he failed to see a lone German fighter that dived on them from a great height and out of the sun. Skilfully, the pilot steadied his dive until he was coming at the Spitfires head-on with a closing speed of 800mph. Confident in his marksmanship, the enemy pilot opened up from 600 yards away. It was then that Duke-Woolley spotted him. And he was too late.

With the German fighter closing at 400 yards a second, he simply did not have the time to react in the second and a half at his disposal.

'He shot down two aircraft in the squadron I was leading and both pilots were killed. We could do nothing but carry on and the squadron most commendably did not waver. The German's attack was skilful and came right from the eye of a blazing sun in a cloudless sky, and in those conditions quick positive identification is very difficult.

'I lost two pilots for nothing in return. It was bad and a sad business but part of the sort of price you incurred by being pegged on a leash with a small fixed area in which to "work". We were sitting ducks, really, and unfortunately were singled out by a first-class poacher.'[18]

At 12.30pm the Allied beachmaster controlling the Dieppe shore was given the order to leave. He'd got a few more off the beaches than expected, given the enemy fire. Some men who had been pinned down for seven hours behind large rocks or the beach wall had made a run for it. The beachmaster watched as men dashed down through the smokescreen to the promise of a landing craft and the thought of getting out of their nightmare and back home to safety. Some ran without weapons, some without helmets or any equipment. Some ran straight, others weaved. He watched as the German machine-gun fire cut through the smoke, snapping at the stones then thudding into flesh. Soldiers were sent sprawling onto their faces with bullets in their backs. They whimpered and cried for help. A few got through, their pinched faces telling a story of a harrowing morning of carnage and chaos. Gratefully, they splashed through the blood-tinged surf and up into the landing craft. Even then they knew they were not safe, as they waited anxiously for others to board before the engine roared in reverse and the boat backed away, all the time under fire.

Others simply stayed put under cover, forsaking the chance of dying while escaping for survival as prisoners of war.

As the last landing craft puttered away from the bloodied shingle, the RAF Hurribombers dived in to suppress the German guns.

Now it was a question of getting the flotilla back across the seventy-five miles of sea to home and safety. The Luftwaffe was not going to make it easy.

More than six hours after his first flight over Dieppe, Harry Broadhurst found himself on his third sortie shortly after 12.30pm. He immediately spotted the destroyer HMS *Berkeley* under attack from German dive-bombers. She had lost steerage and was drifting, at the mercy of the swooping aircraft. He radioed for the covering Spitfire squadrons to take position at the rear of the convoy. They were not in time to stop two 190s dive towards the destroyer, one scoring a direct hit on its stern. Broadhurst emptied almost all his ammunition into one 190 but it got away. The *Berkeley* began to sink but others got alongside, rescuing survivors.[19]

For an hour there was no sign of the enemy. But all involved knew the Luftwaffe would return, once they had rearmed and refuelled.

The indefatigable Broadhurst set out on his fourth sortie of the day at 3.15pm and flew directly to Dieppe as the clouds closed in. He was tired, having been up since 3am, and was aware he was pushing his luck. But he knew he flew a Spitfire superior to anything the Germans had. Which was just as well, he realised, when he spotted two Fw190s diving out of the sun. Despite his exhaustion, Broadhurst was able to pour on the power and the Merlin 61's supercharger did not let him down. Which was a good job. For very quickly the Fw190s doubled in number, eager to find one last prey before their day of plenty ended. With four Fw190s on his tail Broadhurst knew that in a Mark V he would have been dead or dangling from the end of a parachute. Instead, using the Mark IX Spitfire's high speed at altitude, he managed to keep out of range long enough to evade all of them by roaring up into cloud. The 190s did not follow. A few minutes later he came out of the murk and found himself close behind a Blenheim trailing smoke, its three-man crew doing their best to limp home. The twin-engine bomber would not have stood a chance against a German fighter. Broadhurst came alongside and waggled his wings, giving the crew a thumbs-up. The looks of gratitude softened some of the anger that was burning inside him after a day of poor tactics and misjudged leadership. He took up station above and behind the Blenheim, staying close until it landed at the coastal hub of Tangmere.

Broadhurst had flown eight hours during four sorties, destroyed one Fw190 and damaged three others. He was given a 'bar' to his Distinguished Flying Cross, awarded for bravery in the face of the enemy. 'I was no longer in the doghouse,' he noted drily.

In contrast to Dunkirk, the navy was effusive in its praise of the air force. 'The RAF gave us a wonderful defence, but for them there would have been more casualties and greater loss of shipping,' said one naval officer. 'They put up a grand show.'[20]

For the Germans it was more than a grand show. 'It was one of the happiest days since the Battle of Britain,' recorded one Luftwaffe pilot.[21]

He had a right to be pleased. In just twelve hours the RAF had flown 2,500 sorties and lost 108 aircraft, including sixty-two Spitfires. The Luftwaffe lost just forty-eight aircraft and only twenty of those were Fw190s.[22]

At the time the RAF claimed ninety-six enemy aircraft and a significant victory. It was not the case and the Luftwaffe was back at full strength a few days after the raid. After the Rhubarbs of the last two years there was still no knockout blow against the Luftwaffe.

On the ground the losses were appalling, with 900 dead, 500 wounded and nearly 2,000 captured among the 5,000-strong Canadian force. A quarter of the 1,000 British commandos were also lost.

By dusk the last ships limped towards the coast, watched by crowds who lined the clifftops from Eastbourne to Newhaven. Some cheered, while others looked on sombrely as the exhausted troops came ashore alongside the wounded. To some it seemed like a grim reminder of Dunkirk, from two years earlier. However, in the press it was reported as a great, albeit short-lived, victory.

One of the boats contained a scene that spoke of those strange moments of peace sometimes found amid the brutality of war.

Peter Scott, a renowned naturalist and artist who had joined the navy, commanded a gunboat that had picked up both a German Luftwaffe and Norwegian RAF pilot. As he approached England, Scott went below decks to check on the fliers. The German was sitting with the ship's cat on his lap next to the Norwegian pilot 'who only hours before would have quite happily killed him in the air'. The German's armed guard was sitting on the other side of his prisoner, fast asleep with his head on the pilot's shoulder. 'It is sights like this that makes one wonder why people go to war with each other in the first place,' Scott noted.[23]

Most of those involved thought Dieppe had been a victory at least for the RAF. But a number felt the frustration that without the most modern Spitfires, they weren't fully in the fight.

CHAPTER EIGHT

NORTH AFRICA

As he sped in his Spitfire over the Mediterranean towards the Algerian port of Oran in the late afternoon sun of 8 November 1942, Harry Strawn smiled broadly.

Even if it was the Spitfire Mark V rather than the latest Mark IX model, he was still in a glorious aircraft and about to enter a campaign in the exotic deserts and mountains of North Africa. It would be something he'd tell his offspring round log fires back in the States. Indeed, the idea of children made him grin again. In his pocket was a letter from the lovely Marjorie Asquith, the stunning brunette with sparkling eyes and coy smile he had met during flight training in Oklahoma. She promised she would wait for him.[1]

His smile did not change when he saw something glint over the harbour at Oran. He squinted and spotted four aircraft a short distance away. *Must be our Corsair fighters from the carriers.*

Strawn gave them a second glance then concentrated on following his section leader onto the airfield. As he pushed back his canopy and lined up for landing, the unmistakable 'rat-ta-tat-tat' of machine-gun fire filled the air. Clearly one of the more nervous guys had *goofed up* and let go with his guns.

Then he heard the sound of gunfire again. Much closer this time. He turned round and saw his wingman, Joseph Byrd from Texas, plummeting towards the ground, trailing smoke.

Jesus, where did that come from?

He looked again. The 'Corsairs' were in fact a flight of French Dewoitine 520 fighters and they were looking for easy Spitfire kills. The Vichy French clearly did not look upon the Americans and British as allies.

The Spitfire-flying American pilots of the 309th had as yet to experience a sustained campaign, the few short hours over occupied France during the Dieppe raid being the sum of their experience. Along with US ground troops, they were about to be tested in the unfamiliar terrain of North Africa. They were entering a crucible where they were pitted against unpredictable weather, the hardened men of the Afrika Korps and the Luftwaffe's latest planes.

But they did not expect to be fighting the French.

Strawn frantically considered his options. He was committed to landing. He just prayed the other flight coming in had seen the French ambush. He pushed the Spitfire hard down onto the tarmac and braked even harder. He spotted a ball of fire at the other end of the airfield where Byrd had gone in. Then he looked up to see the flight of four American Spitfires streak down on the French. Three Dewoitines were sent down in flames. Strawn smiled grimly.

As part of the French surrender in 1940, the Nazis allowed the government to administer the southern half of France and the colonies in North Africa under the 'Vichy regime'. Before the invasion, covert contacts had been established with the Vichy French and the Allies were under the impression Algeria would be taken without a fight. Clearly, some of the French thought otherwise and were unwilling to break with the Nazi regime.

As Strawn walked over to meet with the pilots who had landed he heard the crack of gunfire and a bullet zipping overhead. *Jesus!* He dived under a Spitfire, trying to shelter as best he could next to its wheels. Other rounds thumped into the runway around him. They were coming from the scrub, a few hundred yards away. The French snipers, it seemed, did not want the Americans there either. He heard a chatter of machine-gun fire and an infantryman shout, 'Got him!'

* * *

While Malta might have diverted a few hundred German aircraft and the 8th Army's campaign in Libya was tying down the Afrika Korps, the Soviet leader Stalin demanded much more. With 180 German divisions pressing down on Russia, he wanted diversions elsewhere to relieve the pressure.

Fending off bullish US commanders demanding an invasion of Europe, Churchill and his generals had argued instead to seize the French-held territories of Morocco, Algeria and Tunisia. If the entire North African coast were in Allied hands, this would tighten the navy's grip on the Mediterranean and allow for an invasion of southern Europe in 1943.

It would also be a good testing ground for US troops going into action in a western theatre for the first time, among the shrubland, forests and deserts of North Africa, set to the dramatic backdrop of the Atlas Mountains.

The plan was for the Anglo-American force to push from the west while the 8th Army drove from the east. Between them the Afrika Korps and Italians would be squeezed.

* * *

Shortly before dawn on the day after the invasion, Strawn was ordered back into his Spitfire at Algeria's Oran airfield, close to the city's Mediterranean port. It was 9 November 1942 and a signal had been received that a column consisting of a score or more French Foreign Legion tanks was heading up from the desert in the south to retake the airfield.

At 5.30am Strawn was revving his Merlin behind three other Spitfires ready to take off. He was eager to get at the French. The shooting-down of Byrd had been a dastardly act. The scores had to be evened.

He released his brakes and shot down the runway into the lightening sky.

The French column was not difficult to find. A large plume of dust thrown up by the tank tracks signalled their position at a pass a few miles short of the airfield.

The Spitfires carefully lined up on the column then one after another dived down, pouring fire into them as they went. 'They were little, bitty one-man tanks in the front. They looked like World War One vehicles. They just flew apart in pieces. We got those and their supply trucks and oil tankers and motorcycles. We caught them in a little narrow pass and it was like shooting duck pins, it was that easy.

'I saw this motorcycle guy coming towards me. He jumped off the motorcycle and hid behind it.' His flimsy machine would provide little defence. 'When you've got eight .303s with converging fire, that thing just went sky high.'

The Spitfires swept down again and again, coming in extremely low, so low that when Strawn got back to the airfield he found telephone wires wrapped around the fuselage.

It took another day for the Vichy French forces in Algeria and Morocco to realise that continued fighting against the US and British force of 100,000 troops was pointless. To Hitler's great fury the French surrendered. His anger was such that he ordered his troops into Vichy France, taking over the whole country. German and Italian reinforcements were rapidly sent to Tunisia.

But for Strawn and his pals it was a time to celebrate. Despite not changing clothes or shaving for four days, they went into Oran and bought some wine off the Arabs for twenty-five cents a quart, plus oranges and tangerines. A pig was killed and pork tenderloins joined the feast.

The German presence was not threatening enough to stop the men of the 309th from having a good time. A week into the operation was long enough to go without a party. Christmas was looming and who knew how long they would be around?

Strawn had heard that a few of his ground crew had served alongside some of the American big bands. He was delighted to discover that several of them had played with the likes of Glenn Miller and

Henry Busse. There were saxophonists, drummers, trumpet players – enough to form a fifteen-man band of their own. Inside the former French Officers' Mess, a row of tables and chairs was formed at one end of the room and a small stage built for the band at the other. Strawn and a few other officers grabbed a couple of French trucks and drove into the city of Oran. They found it well stocked with both drink and women. They packed the trucks with crates of champagne and fine wine then came back for the women. At least forty Allied nurses and thirty French women giggled coyly as they found themselves trucked into the airbase. The French women were in pretty polka-dot dresses; the Allied nurses had time to throw on a bit of lipstick but were still in their smart white uniforms. Everyone was in good spirits. The Americans certainly knew how to throw a party. The band played the latest numbers from across the Atlantic, while the aviators quaffed champagne from the French flutes and chatted to the women. As the night wore on, people found their partners and danced. With most of the French now throwing in their lot with the Allies, a handful of French officers sheepishly joined in the fun. 'Everyone had a good time,' Harry Strawn reported.

The next morning Strawn's fug quickly cleared when the mail came through and he spotted a letter from his sweetheart, Marjorie Asquith of Muskogee, Oklahoma. 'It was a swell letter and I believe she still likes me some,' he wrote, thinking back again to her lovely smile and the short dance they'd had after they'd first met. It had been a blind date but they'd hit it off straight away, even if some of his flying tales had been a *little* embellished. He certainly had some stories to tell Marjorie now. 'I shall have to keep writing for I think a lot of her, she would make a swell wife for me. I know I could love her more than enough.' He knew the thought of seeing Marjorie again would sustain him and push away memories of the loss and destruction he'd witnessed. And would inevitably witness again.

But as the Americans partied, the Allies were slow to push forces eastwards to take Tunisia. Hitler was determined not to let Tunisia go and began pouring troops in by air and sea over the short hop from Sicily.

* * *

Alan Peart (back left) with 81 Squadron in North Africa

Alan Peart was still itching for action. His only combat experience had been over Dieppe and even then he hadn't seen the Fw190 firing at him. North Africa was not going to disappoint.

81 Squadron was ordered to provide support from the coastal town of Bône (now Annaba) which had just been taken by the Allies. Bône was a delightful Mediterranean port city lined with boulevards overlooked by French colonial architecture, and the Roman ruins of ancient Hippo Regius lay on its outskirts. It was fifty miles to the Tunisian border and hence much closer to the front line. Peart carefully packed his personal possessions and clothing into the Spitfire's ammunition bays and the storage behind the cockpit.

He flew down the Algerian coast, delighting in the changed landscape of desert, mountains and sea.

Aware that he was still the squadron novice, he carefully aligned the Spitfire's nose on the long, rain-darkened strip at Bône, with the odd shell hole either side of the runway, and made a perfect landing. No one took any notice as he jumped down into the mud and headed towards the dispersal tent.

He had taken only a few steps when a Bofors anti-aircraft gun fired two rounds. He needed no second warning that a raid was inbound and sprinted to a slit trench fifty yards away.[2]

Peart looked over the lip in time to see three enemy bombers appear out of the clouds with their bomb-bay doors already open. They levelled out and then the bombs fell. A crump of explosions was followed by a blast of heat as Peart cowered in the bottom of the trench, hands over his head, willing the stick of bombs to stop short of his position.

The attack was over in less than a minute. As the drone of German engines faded, Peart stuck his head over the parapet and saw that the Spitfire he'd just flown into Bône was now a burning wreck with all his kit inside.

He was shocked at the proximity of death. 'The bomb hit the cockpit. I'd brought that Spit all that way and now it was gone. A few seconds before I'd been in the cockpit – this was the narrow gap between life and death I was learning about and one of my closest brushes with death. We had been pitchforked into real activity and this phase was to be the most vicious form of fighting I would encounter.'

It was indeed an abrupt introduction to frontline squadron life. The promise of African sunshine, palm tree oases and dashing Arab warriors had also not yet materialised. Instead, rain pounded down on the bleak and featureless aerodrome, where the only shelter was an old dull concrete passenger terminal. The pilots huddled inside, trying to stay out of the rain and wind that blasted through the windows. Chatting was the only pastime until a raid came in, then it was a race for the nearest waterlogged slit trench. The only relative comfort was sitting strapped into their cockpits.

Peart and 81 Squadron were also still flying the outclassed Spitfire Mark Vs, painted a desert sand colour and fitted with a large, ugly protuberance under its belly. The fine dust of desert conditions meant that aircraft had to be fitted with a filter to stop engines clogging up and so preserve them. The engineers came up with the

Vokes filter, an intake mounted under the nose that prevented much of the sand getting in but badly affected aerodynamics and led to at least an 8mph drop in speed.

Sitting in a replacement Spitfire, Peart looked up ruefully at the low clouds overhead. *Just like home*. For a moment his thoughts went back to his mother carefully arranging a neat row of dough to bake in the oven at their house in New Zealand. He had just turned twenty and was 12,000 miles from home. Operations were tough, his family and friends were at a great distance and there was no certainty he'd ever see them again. There had been very little news, just a handful of letters in the two years since he'd left New Zealand full of excitement, drive and hope. He pushed the thoughts of family and home away as he caught the familiar hum of the Spitfire warming up. He examined the clouds again and felt rising excitement as he waited for the signal to take off in pursuit of enemy bombers. It was 1 December 1942.

How the hell they were meant to find the enemy bombers somewhere up above was anyone's guess. He felt cold and hungry. They were surviving off the fourteen-man ration packs, whose delicacies included tinned meat or fruit and a powdered milk and tea mixture, with the edge taken off by chocolate and cigarettes. But he didn't mind. He was in his beautiful Spitfire, fully fuelled and loaded with bullets ready to take on the enemy.

At the signal to go, he opened the throttle, thundered down Bône's bumpy airstrip and quickly entered the clouds. Less than a minute later he came out into glorious sunshine.

And virtually smack into the middle of a formation of five Italian SM.84 bombers. Peart opened the throttle and dived towards the clouds into which the Italians had just disappeared. As he came out of the grey mass he saw the bomber immediately ahead. It was time to track down his prey.

Peart carefully placed his fighter in the mist at the base of the cloud then steadily began to overhaul the triple-engine bomber. The gap closed to 400 yards. He concentrated furiously as the turbulent air bounced him around, threatening to expose the hunting Spitfire.

Then he began to pull in the SM.84, getting the distance below 300 yards. He knew within a few seconds he would be able to open up. He got to 250 yards. Still he held off. This would be his first kill and Peart wanted to make certain.

Closer and closer he crept until he was just fifty yards behind, clearly able to see the rivets on the fuselage and helmeted heads of the rear crew, bobbing in the compartment, completely unaware of the guns trained on them.

Peart's thumb went down on the firing button and pressed hard. 'I opened fire with cannons and machine guns at point-blank range from dead astern. Great pieces flew off and the bomber appeared to stop in midair so that I nearly collided with it. The nose went down and I followed in a near-vertical dive, giving it another burst to make sure. I later felt rather bad about the second burst when the bomber was doomed anyway.'

As he watched the bomber crash into the sea, Peart pulled back on the stick and hurtled skywards to try to bring down a second bomber he'd spotted. The crew were now alert to their comrades' demise and readied themselves for the incoming attack. The SM.84 poured on the fuel too, but with a top speed of 268mph there was no chance of outrunning the British fighter.

But this time the gunners were ready. As Peart came up close the Italians opened fire from the tail and side machine guns. The Spitfire flipped out of the way then swooped back to attack. By now Peart had expended all his heavy 20mm cannon rounds. Instead, he had to pepper the Italian bomber with a long raking burst from his four Browning .303 machine guns until they too ran dry.

'Smoke was pouring from one engine. Reluctantly, I had to leave.'

As he turned to fly back to base, Peart reflected on the fact he had for the first time taken another human's life. 'This was the reality of aerial warfare – shooting down enemy bombers which also sometimes meant killing the half-dozen men inside. Fighting another fighter it was just a machine and you didn't think about the man inside – it was machine versus machine. But shooting down a bomber was when I realised I was killing people. There was no sense of guilt at all – I felt sorry for them but this was what warfare was about and it was our job.'

By now Peart was beginning to realise that the men fighting in the do-or-die combat of the skies came in three categories. 'The first was the type who simply wanted to stay alive and tried to avoid situations where that was put at risk. They didn't achieve very much. Secondly there were people who had a job to do, did it to the best of their ability but they fought within the rules and had humanity, understanding for the enemy. Then there were the killers. They were ruthless and killed without much thought – but they were the best, the aces. I think I was probably in the second type – I had a job to do and had to do it.'

Yet despite the killing, Peart was still eager to get into the action and follow to the letter the policy of 'attack at all times'. A few days later he was patrolling in clear skies close to Bône, with the Mediterranean shimmering below, as number two to his Flight Commander when he spotted a dozen Me109s.

Taking out the Italian bomber had been straightforward and it had also given him confidence that he could do the job.

'Green One, this is Green Two. Tally-ho.' He felt a rush of excitement as he opened the throttle and dived down on the Messerschmitts. He did not even wait to see if his wingman had followed.

He had not. Indeed, he had ignored Peart's battle-cry, shaken his head then turned back to base, firm in the opinion that the young pilot had committed an act of suicide.

The lone Spitfire now headed into the middle of the German pack. Before he could get a shot in, the wily Luftwaffe pilots had already broken formation, possibly sharing the same incredulity as Peart's wingman, in being attacked by a lone Spitfire. Their disbelief rapidly turned to delight as they realised that at least one of their number was a few short minutes away from adding a Spitfire to their tally of kills.

Peart was in very deep trouble. Me109s were coming at him from all sides and there was nowhere to hide.

The only good card he held was that he knew he was in a highly agile aircraft that, if they worked together, could possibly get him out of the almighty scrape he had just got them both into. The only other comfort was that he was behind his own lines. Even if he didn't have much chance of survival, *at least they'd find my body*.

At first he stayed at the same level as the 109s, using the Spitfire's incredible turning ability to keep inside his opponents. There might even be a chance that he could get a few shots off at them. As the first pair approached head-on, he squeezed off a few rounds then broke away. 'But this bunch had some really experienced and capable pilots. I soon found myself in dire trouble.'

Peart felt sweat pour down his face. He had no time to wipe it off. He was using every skill and piece of aerial combat knowledge to keep the enemy fighters off his tail. He pulled turns tighter than he'd ever made, feeling the G-forces press in on him. The sheer physical strain and mental application began to drain him. He knew the end was not far away. The Luftwaffe boys were far too good to let him get away with it.

Then a calm descended as he recalled the words of a First World War friend of his father's who had become a mentor to the young Peart. 'When cornered, son, give them everything you've got. Sell your life dear. They'll remember you after that.'

Peart was now set on one course. 'I decided that none of these bastards was going to get me without well and truly earning their victory.'

He used the Spitfire's agility to the full, pulling and wrenching it into extreme rolls and dives. The twelve fighters came at him in pairs but could never quite get him squarely in their sights.

A pair of 109s would execute an attack while the next pair got in position to follow on. Peart dived under their noses, watching the cannon fire streak from them and praying it would not hit.

The twisting and turning went down and down until the twenty-year-old pilot found himself close to the ground knowing now there was very little room left to use the Spitfire's superior manoeuvrability.

On one level he was pleased that he had managed to hold off the dozen Germans for so long. He had indeed 'sold his life dear'. As he broke to starboard to slip away from another pair of Messerschmitts on his tail with guns blazing, he felt sweat drip down through the sleeves of his shirt onto his wrist and hand. He did not want to die. He was good at this. He enjoyed it.

He flicked the Spitfire in a dummy roll to port then hauled violently over to starboard, glancing around as he turned. His mouth went dry. The sky was empty behind. *Where the hell are they?*

He braced himself for the inevitable onslaught of rounds pouring up through the cockpit after a 109 had finally got underneath him. Instinctively, he rolled the Spitfire again, searching the sky and ground as he did so.

Something caught his eye higher up. At first he could not take it in. A formation of twelve fighters heading east. German fighters. The 109s were going home, probably short of fuel and astonished at the Spitfire's ability to elude them.

Peart panted with elation, blinking the perspiration out of his eyes. He threw back the cockpit canopy, feeling the rush of air brush against his face. He had been given a second life, a second chance. Of that he was certain. And he would not waste it.

'It then occurred to me that the German CO would have some scathing things to say about his pilots' marksmanship, because apart from my initial opening fire I had had no chance to use my guns without leaving myself wide open to a burst myself.'

Peart looked around to get his bearings then set course for Bône. For the first time he wondered where his senior wingman was. He got his answer when he landed and walked into the dispersal area. The pilot officer at first looked shocked to see him then launched into a tirade at Peart for acting irresponsibly and endangering his own life and his aircraft.

The invective continued until one of the more experienced pilots held up his hand and signalled for the officer to stop.

'Tone it down, sunshine,' the Canadian flier said. 'It's a damned pity we don't have a few more like him.' Peart's humility was momentarily salved but then he was summoned to appear before the squadron leader.

'We have not been sent out here to become a shabby load of individual cowboys, do you understand, Peart?' the CO growled from behind his desk as Peart stood to attention.

'Yes, sir.'

'In future you're to follow your section leader's orders before going off charging into attack. Got it?'

'Yes, sir.'

The CO then waved him away but not before giving Peart a big wink.

Grinning to himself, Peart headed back to his tent. He arrived to find his personal kit being lined up for auction. It was tradition that, with such severe equipment shortages, if a pilot was killed in action, his military clothing and other flying kit was shared out among surviving pilots. His section leader had told everyone he had certainly been killed and here were his possessions about to be sold for pennies. Alan managed to persuade his friends he was indeed alive, took to his cot and shut his eyes, trying to block out the images of diving and swooping Messerschmitts firing at his tail. Within seconds he was asleep.

* * *

Since helping rescue the bomber crew who had ditched in the Channel in early spring 1942, Robbie Robertson and 72 Squadron had generally had a quiet time. When he received an arm-numbing batch of inoculations in November he was somewhat grateful. They were clearly off somewhere exotic.[3]

Freezing in a flimsy tent, wrapped in a thin blanket, was not how he'd imagined North Africa. 72 Squadron had arrived at the airstrip of Souk-el-Arba on 20 November 1942, a week before Peart shot down the Italian bomber. British paratroopers had captured the airstrip, eighty miles west of Tunis, the capital of Tunisia, just a few days earlier. It didn't take the Germans, based around Tunis, long to find 72 Squadron's base.

Robertson was deflecting the usual digs as he sat down to write a letter to his girlfriend Connie, whose name was lovingly painted on his Spitfire. He had taken some ribbing for his constant references to her but he couldn't care less. *Connie keeps me safe.*

His eyes drifted skywards at the dozen fighters in line astern circling overhead. Clearly it was the new squadron that was meant to join them. The planes descended as if coming in to land.

'109s!' someone shouted.

The pilots glanced at their parked aircraft. There was no way they'd be able to reach them in time to take off. There was only one option: run for it.

Robertson scattered with the rest, diving onto his belly as no slit trenches had been dug.

American .50-calibre machine guns stationed around the aerodrome blasted away but the Germans still came on.

The 109s screamed down, pumping cannon shells as they came. Bullets thudded into the dirt, running in a line up to the petrol and ammunition dump. In an instant the area ignited with a terrific whoosh. Lying on his stomach just 150 yards away, Robertson could feel the blast of heat burst over his face. Then he heard the fighters circle back round for another run. He cowered fearfully out in the open. 'After the first run I was scared stiff. It's no fun lying in the middle of a field where you can hear the bullets hitting the ground and ricochets going right, left and centre and you can't tell whether they are coming across you or through you.' He shut his eyes as he heard the scream of engines and violent throb of gunfire puckering the earth around him. Then the sound of enemy engines faded.

He got up and saw men at the petrol dump using mud and dust to put out the fire. Someone had a bucket they were using to scrape up the earth and chuck it on the flames; others used shovels or their bare hands. The smell of burning petrol and cordite was joined by another. It was the distinct, bitter odour of burnt bacon. As Robertson tossed another handful of dust into the flames he saw the grim outline of two withered arms, bent at the elbows, hands pointing upwards. The flames licked at the skin, sending slivers of fire along it. Two of their Arab labourers had unwisely hidden among the four-gallon petrol tins when the strafing began. Robertson turned away from their grisly remains. While aerial combat had its dangers, the war on the ground was dark, unforgiving and had a nauseating stench.

* * *

This is certainly not the African desert of bright sunshine, rolling sand dunes and palm-thronged oases, Flight Lieutenant Greggs Farish thought as they trundled over a landscape deadened by dark clouds overhead and pools of mud where insects hovered. At least the rain – which everyone thought had been left long behind in England – had relented after days of downpours.

Farish was the officer in charge of 72 Squadron's ground crew responsible for ensuring the Spitfires were serviceable. They had been travelling east for two days, keeping the Algerian coastline on their left and the interior on their right. The Allies had pushed rapidly into Tunisia and the RAF squadrons had to move up to keep the pressure on the Luftwaffe and protect Allied ground troops from air attacks. They were moving 72 Squadron 100 miles east from Bône to the front line. In the last few hours he had felt his spirits rise as the cloud base lifted to reveal the tall, dramatic sentinels of the Atlas Mountains lying to the south and distant pine forests. Ahead he could just make out Spitfires landing at their new base of Souk-el-Arba, in a land of rugged mountains separated by the fertile plains of northern Tunisia.

Farish was tall, studious and a man who cared for both machines and pilots. For the pilots like Robbie Robertson who had flown into Souk-el-Arba a few days earlier, he was a welcome sight. They knew that under his supervision they could fly with complete confidence in their aircraft.[4]

Sporting thick, round glasses, Farish, twenty-two, was to be found at most times of the day studiously examining a Spitfire, usually with his unlit pipe close to hand. Farish, nicknamed 'Spanner', had applied to become a pilot but his eyesight meant he was declared 'unfit for flying duties'. Undeterred, he still joined the air force. With an engineering degree from Imperial College London, he was commissioned into the RAF's engineering branch in 1941.

As they set out on convoy from Liverpool for North Africa, he had an inkling that he was in for interesting times and kept a diary.

Arriving at Souk-el-Arba, Farish encountered the RAF 'commandos', a group of rugged mechanics who had kept the muddy, puddle-littered airstrip and planes running before the squadron's mechanics arrived.

'These men, in tattered bits of uniform, dirty, long-haired, unshaven, tools sticking out of their pockets, were either cooking food over fires among the planes or dashing out to service aircraft as they landed.

'These were the RAF "Commando" servicing echelon. Two flights of them, about 200 men, keeping flying four squadrons of Spitfires, one of Beaufighters and some Hurricanes. They came in with the original assault and today are preparing to move out now that the squadron's personnel are coming up. They had done a damn fine job. These men are different from the average RAF airmen. Much more independent and *don't care a damn who you are* sort of attitude. They are tough too. I like working with them.'

Exhausted after the long drive, Farish had fallen onto his cot only to be awoken again by the sound of rain thrashing against his tent. He managed to drift off to the sound he found comforting under canvas. When he woke, there were six inches of water in his tent. It was not turning out to be the adventure he'd expected. But fighting through the rain, mud and bombing, Farish ensured 72's fighters were kept aloft to help push the Germans further back into Tunisia.

And among those whose aircraft he serviced was one of the most rakish men to hold rank in the RAF.

* * *

Harry 'Chas' Charnock was a character who would not have been out of place in a Flashman novel. Having missed out on the Great War, he joined the RAF after Harrow School in 1924, aged nineteen. Six years later he was booted out, ostensibly for a low-level flying incident over Tangmere. The fact he had pushed a senior officer into a pond had not helped. For nine years little was heard of him, until two days into the outbreak of war the shortage of pilots persuaded the RAF to forget the past and allow Charnock to return as a non-commissioned sergeant pilot.[5]

He claimed three Germans during the Battle of Britain and was shot down once. This Charnock used to his full advantage. Despite landing on friendly ground, he managed to persuade the RAF to pay out compensation for the loss of his entire kit bag, as well as pocketing the gold sovereigns kept by pilots to facilitate their return from hostile territory. Charnock was awarded the Distinguished Flying Medal. He'd also had a taste for action and wanted more. His request for transfer from Britain was granted and he joined 72 Squadron.

'If ever you saw a dissolute looking fellow, here was one,' wrote Farish. 'Even in his worn flying clothing one felt Charnock would be better placed propping up a night club bar. He usually contrived to have a bottle of whisky in his hand when on the ground. He was over thirty, by far the oldest pilot in the squadron. He had flown everything and had broken Spitfires up in the air with aerobatics. He was the maddest pilot I ever met, completely round the bend. And yet one felt he had seen the whole world. Perhaps he had and in his wisdom found only flying left. And he flew only to kill and be killed.'

No one knew what demons drove Charnock, whether it was violent hangovers or something from his past. As Alan Peart had noted, fighter pilots fell into three categories: the avoider; the 'get the job done' type and the killer. Charnock most certainly fell into the last category.

When he arrived over the steep mountains and occasional green trees of Algeria he went on a killing spree.

Over a three-week period from 25 November, he claimed five enemy shot down, an Fw190 and four Me109s, and one Me109 probable. For a time the rampage was put in abeyance, after Charnock was himself shot down on 18 December 1942.

Furious at the Luftwaffe's effrontery, Charnock was in no mood for niceties when he bailed out of his Spitfire and descended by parachute into no-man's land. He found himself among thin bushes and dusty tracks, up in the hills and some distance from the nearest town. Anxious to get back to his own lines and the bottle of whisky under his bed – which under the circumstances he was entirely justified in seeing off that night – he set out on foot.

But Shanks's pony was simply not quick enough. After walking a few miles, he came across an Arab leading a donkey and saw an opportunity for a swift ride back to his whisky.

'Can I borrow your donkey?' Charnock asked bluntly, pointing at the animal.

The Arab showed no understanding so Charnock repeated himself. This time the Arab wagged his index finger vigorously and shook his head.

Charnock moved in close, his hand resting on the pistol in its holster, and repeated his demand.

The Arab remained unmoved and pulled the donkey's rein tighter into him. At that moment a stray dog came past them, eyeing the scene. Charnock pulled out his revolver and shot the dog between the eyes. He then turned back to the Arab, smoke drifting from the gun barrel.

With shaking hands, the man handed over his donkey. Charnock mounted the animal and trotted towards British lines.

Within a few hours he spotted the sandbags and trenches of the British positions and with a kick sent the donkey trotting back home. Charnock scrambled over the sandbags and tumbled into the friendly trench. He dusted himself down, then looked for the nearest officer and the chance of a liquid reward for his efforts.

'I see you're a member of the rival establishment.' A clean-shaven captain in an ironed uniform emerged from a dugout. The words were spoken in a cut-glass accent by someone who could only have been to *bloody Eton*.

Charnock always wore his Old Harrovian scarf when flying in his Spitfire, in the knowledge that in his permanently unkempt state it would be a snub to the establishment in general and rival Old Etonians in particular.

The officer handed over a canteen. Charnock took a swig, half in expectation that his throat would be delightfully lit with the sting of something strong. It was water. He turned on his heel and left, still swigging the canteen.

At the rear lines, Charnock found a truck heading in the direction of Souk-el-Arba and got a lift. His irritation at the lack of a proper drink abated when an idea struck him as they drove past a monastery.

'Stop!' he shouted at the driver. He jumped out of the cab and, wearing his best grin, knocked on the monastery door. A monk opened it and, in the ensuing conversation – in a mix of French, Arabic, English and a smattering of Latin – Charnock discovered what he had suspected. *Monks make booze ... so they must have some spare!*

With the nose of a practitioner well-versed in foraging for alcohol, he struck up a rapport with the wine-making Christian monks and promised to return.

Charnock reappeared the next day in a 15cwt Bedford truck with a dozen washed four-gallon petrol cans in the back. The whole lot was filled with the monk's red wine and back at 72 Squadron he invited everyone to a party. By this time Robbie Robertson had become his wingman and felt a degree of trepidation with Charnock both on the ground and in the air. His fears were to prove correct and Charnock poured out mugfuls of the dark-red liquid. 'The only thing we had to drink from were large, white enamelled mugs and if you pour red wine in those you have to pour a lot before it looks as though you've got any in at all. We half-filled these mugs and sat around enjoying ourselves.'

Charnock had bought a prodigious amount of wine and insisted everyone should celebrate his safe return. Toasts were made to the Spitfire, monastic orders, donkeys, Arabs and finally the Luftwaffe for making it all happen. The toasts were inevitably followed by singing around a fire made from wood, debris and aviation fuel. Then Charnock stripped off and began a gyrating dance with Indian-like ululations. As darkness headed towards dawn, Robertson managed to find his tent and slumped down on his cot. For once the sun was out and its blaze turned his hangover into something he had not experienced before.

'I woke up in the morning not really with a headache, but my head just wouldn't leave the ground. I felt like death. Red wine wasn't for us if we were to go on flying.'[6]

A few days later Robertson was on patrol with Chas Charnock for company, escorting Boston bombers on a raid on German positions in Tunisia when 'twenty-plus' fighters appeared out of the sun. The rest of the squadron failed to spot the diving 109s and Fw190s. Robertson looked at the Spitfires then back up at the diving enemy.

'Go for the bastards,' he heard Charnock shout.

'Roger,' Robertson replied.

Rather than present their backs to the enemy, the Spitfires turned and sped upwards to meet the 'wad of enemy aircraft'. Robertson pulled hard on his stick and opened up the throttle to stay as close as possible to his Flight Commander. Charnock steamed ahead, letting go a full burst at an Fw190 as it closed within range. Robertson watched as the aircraft went from a clean dive into a flat spin.

Robertson overtook Charnock, then suddenly, without any apparent reason, his speed suddenly dropped off and he went into a spin. Trying to correct the spin so high up would have left him a 'dead duck' with so many enemy around. Despite the growing dangers of spinning all the way down into the ground, Robertson saw it as the best of bad options.

'I continued spinning down until I got closer to the ground.' Fighting hard and seeing the ground looming, he managed to pull out of the spin and regain control. But he was still being closely followed by two 109s.

'My engine was coughing and spluttering and not going as fast as I'd have liked it to go. So I got right down on the deck and was belting for home as fast as possible, weaving like mad, in and out of valleys, frightening the life out of camels and odd bodies I passed over, still pursued by the 109s who were taking potshots at me every now and again. All I could do was keep turning the minute they came within range.

'Eventually, after one of these turns, I managed to get a fairly good shot in at the leading 109 and he shot straight past me onto the deck. I thought by this time the other one would have cleared off, but he was a bit of a keen type and he went on chasing me all the way back to within a few miles of the aerodrome. He finally gave up but did manage to put seven bullet holes in my aircraft. When I finally landed at Souk-el-Arba I had no ammunition, very little petrol and was absolutely drenched in perspiration! Most of it, I must admit, due to heaving the aircraft about at low level and doing all sorts of things that the Spit wasn't meant to do, but probably quite a percentage was due to the fact that I was scared stiff.'

* * *

Sergeant Robbie Robertson lay back in a slightly damaged wicker armchair, enjoying some rare sunshine at Souk-el-Arba. His thoughts were sometimes gripped by memories of his spinning Spitfire heading downwards with two Messerschmitts on his tail, but he had learned to put them out of his mind by dreaming of England and his girlfriend Connie. On the gramophone next to him Vera Lynn's beguiling voice sang 'Do I Love You'. Warmed by the winter sun, he felt at peace with the world, looking forward to some Christmas cheer in five days' time. He sipped his tea as his gaze took in the empty skies then he looked across to his parked Spitfire. Its sleek line had an addictive quality, demanding to be flown. It was time to go so, grabbing his parachute, he joined another sergeant pilot for an overhead patrol.

They had been airborne for just five minutes when a 'twenty-plus' raid was reported heading towards a nearby aerodrome. Gaining height, the two Spitfire pilots knew they had a chance of getting a good 'bounce' on the Germans.

Just before they got within range of the bombers, Robertson spotted an Me109 creeping up towards the vulnerable underbelly of his wingman's plane 200 yards away.

'Break, break! Enemy below!' There was no response.

'As the Jerry started shooting I could see the flashes all over the place from his guns. I pulled in to try and head him off and with luck have a crack at him. I'm not sure whether I hit him or not, but the next thing I knew there was a hell of a bang and I got hit in the head and started bleeding like a stuck pig.

'I couldn't see out of my right eye and was feeling a bit groggy so the only thing I could do was crash-land. It was 4.40pm, a Sunday, and I was at 1,500ft. So I pushed the aircraft down; it was doing about 180mph by that time. I landed with the wheels up and the engine still going.

'I came to a grinding halt and, by the time I'd finished, the engine and fuselage were pointing off to the left and I was staring from the cockpit out over nothing.'

Robertson could smell the distinct odour of high-octane fuel. For a moment he flailed around the cockpit trying to focus on what was important with his one functioning eye. He knew at any moment a spark could ignite the entire aircraft into an inferno which no amount of fire tenders could put out in time. His hand reached up to the hood and he managed to pull it open. Then, as blood flowed down his face, he felt for the pilot's door handle at his side and opened it.

'I crawled out and crawled as far as I could from the aircraft, because the Huns were great ones for coming back and shooting you up on the ground.'

Ground crew then came running to pick him up and get him into an ambulance to the field hospital.

Like many pilots who had performed a belly-landing, Robbie had discovered that the Spitfire was resilient in protecting its pilots as it broke up. Only his shoulder was bruised from the crash. 'The Spitfire could take an enormous amount of punishment without any damage to the pilot.'

But Robertson's right eye had been lacerated with shrapnel from the German bullet. The surgeon told him it would have to be removed.

'I pleaded with them not to and asked if they could take the bits of shrapnel out that were in and around my eye but keep the eye in. If I could just keep the eye in and look normal I might wangle myself back on flying.'

The doctor reluctantly agreed. For the next two days the wound was treated and Robertson was given morphine to keep the pain at bay. But the throbbing in his head became unbearable. A screaming, constant headache made sleep near-impossible and the only relief came for just an hour after his morphine. He finally realised that his eye, vital for a fighter pilot, would have to be removed. Resigned that his Spitfire days were over, he asked the surgeon to carry out the operation. And he was lucky. The excruciating pain in his right eye had been caused by it becoming infected by the shrapnel. Septicaemia was spreading to his remaining eye. If he had waited much longer the surgeon would have been forced to remove both eyes.

He sank into a morose state. He would be taken away from his good friends on the squadron and he would never fly the Spitfire again. And, of course, his face was now disfigured. The full onset of the 'miseries' was complete when he realised what Connie would see. *A scarred, one-eyed ex-fighter pilot with few prospects.*

For a brief moment the miseries lifted when an official letter with RAF typed letterhead arrived, informing him he'd been awarded the Distinguished Flying Cross for his bravery.

He smiled grimly. There was one letter that he now had to write. It was only proper to release Connie from their commitment. 'It was hardly fair to keep her to our engagement. It is one thing to be engaged to someone who is all in one piece and certainly something else to be engaged to someone who is hardly 100 per cent. She could call our proposed marriage off and there'd be no hard feelings.'

Connie would not hear of such a thing. Within a few months of Robertson's return to England they were married.

* * *

As the early days of New Year 1943 passed, the British and American forces that had thrust into Tunisia, coming to within forty miles of the capital Tunis, suddenly found themselves confronted by fresh German divisions. Reinforcements had been rushed over from Europe from mid-November 1942, across the ninety-mile stretch of water between Sicily and Cap Bon, elbowing out from the Tunisian coast. The plan to sweep into Tunis had been largely thwarted after the French commander there had failed to prevent the Germans using the ports and airfields to rapidly reinforce. Now the Germans were able to launch a counter-attack against the poorly prepared Allied positions. The Luftwaffe had been reinforced too. On the back foot, the RAF, still equipped with the battle-weary Spitfire Mark Vs, were taking a battering and struggled to provide the army with adequate air support.

When Greggs Farish arrived just inside Tunisia at Souk-el-Arba a month earlier, 72 Squadron had formed part of a wing totalling forty-eight aircraft. Against the Axis onslaught, the wing had now been reduced to just twelve serviceable Spitfire Vs. They were also up against superior Me109 'G's and Fw190s, which had the advantage of flying off the tarmac road between Tunis and Carthage rather than muddy strips.

The relentless bombing, dogfights and sorties were beginning to have strange consequences.

Following the dressing-down after his solo charge at twelve Messerschmitts, Alan Peart had seen 81 Squadron numbers decline at their airfield outside the coastal city of Bône from thirty pilots to ten and only a few serviceable planes. Half-a-dozen had been killed, more had been wounded and a number had reported sick. But the intensity of operations against superior aircraft and living in austere conditions was proving too much for others. Some pilots were cracking up, either through exhaustion or the stress of waking up each day knowing it might be their last.

It was not only seeing friends killed or absent that made Peart more cautious. After his experience of taking on a dozen German fighters, Peart was understandably wary. Thus, when in the circuit preparing to land at Bône, he was aware of the Luftwaffe penchant for attacking aircraft at their most vulnerable. He was not ready for a fellow Spitfire pilot's aggressive moves. As Peart settled to come in to land, with flaps down, speed indicator showing 85mph and altimeter 300ft, he took one last look to check for enemy. There was no Luftwaffe plane in sight but less than 100 yards behind him was a Spitfire and its pilot's intentions were clear. *He's bloody well lining up to take a shot!*

Peart pulled up the flaps, poured on the power and wrenched the stick back and to starboard, immediately aborting his landing. As he climbed back up into the sky, he heard over the radio a pilot in a 242 Squadron Spitfire shout, 'Johnnie, what the hell are you up to?'[7]

On landing, Peart wanted to ask the very same question and strode over to 242's dispersal area. But the pilot, an experienced Flight Commander, had already been whisked away for medical evaluation after hallucinating that Peart was an enemy aircraft.

A few days later, Peart witnessed a more horrifying incident. He was chatting to an army lieutenant supervising three men filling in a bomb crater when a Spitfire came in to land. Peart, the officer and three men all stood on the side of the airstrip as the fighter lined up for landing. Its wheel bounced on the soft ground then Peart watched as the tail lowered and the plane settled onto the runway. As it approached their position, he instinctively took a step back. Suddenly, from the corner of his vision, he saw the Spitfire lurch round as a wheel hit a poorly covered crater. The scream of the propeller along with a rush of wind brushed past his face. Then he heard the sickening whack of a wing slicing through flesh. Blood splattered down his front. Peart stared at the bloodied wings and nose of the Spitfire. Bits of human body, including what appeared to be an ear, hung from a gunport. He felt his gaze drawn to where the three soldiers had been standing. On the ground were three men in uniform, all missing their heads.

Jesus!

'You bloody idiot!' The army lieutenant was screaming at the pilot. 'You bloody, damned fool.' He began walking menacingly towards the aircraft.

Peart put a hand firmly on his shoulder. 'Calm down, mate. It was an accident. Calm it down.'

Men came running along with an ambulance. Peart jumped onto the Spitfire wing among the blood and gore. The canopy slid back and he looked upon the pilot's ashen face. The realities and intensity of warfare were draining morale. It was clear he would not be flying for some time.

It was not the first time Peart had seen pilots be taken off frontline operations after the stresses of constant warfare got on top of them.

'This was a nerve-wracking period and quite a few pilots suffered nervous breakdowns which manifested themselves in a reluctance to get into combat, irrational behaviour, mental disturbances and hallucinating,' Peart wrote. 'These pilots were rapidly moved away.' Some of them were given the label LMF – lacking moral fibre – essentially accusing them of cowardice at a time when they were suffering a mental breakdown through combat stress.

'All of us were under considerable nervous tension and, like front-line soldiers, looked upon the dawn and wondered if we would see another tomorrow.

'Small things like the sunlight, trees, birds and other living things assumed an unusual importance, clarity and value in our limited world and helped us to keep a sense of what was normal. I suppose it could be called sanity. One felt seriously vulnerable and mortal.

'We all understood what LMF could mean though it was rarely mentioned. We were losing people hand over fist and a few people had nervous breakdowns; it was the worst time for losses and we all felt it. It was a real period of stress and strain and it took a toll on all of us.'

The question of mortality took a tighter grip as the Luftwaffe counter-attack developed from their bases in Tunisia and advanced into Algeria. The RAF had little in the way of riposte. Greggs Farish used bulldozers to ram wrecks off the airfield as every flyable aircraft was put in the air. Pilots flew five sweeps a day. Some mornings, the wing would start with fourteen aircraft and by dinner time they were down to two.

Replacement planes arrived and were adopted by whichever squadron area they taxied into. Their 'acceptance check' for combat was straightforward: they were declared airworthy simply by being refuelled and having a letter chalked on the fuselage.[8]

To cut down the number of Spitfires nose-diving into the mud, Farish ordered airmen to climb onto the tail during taxiing. In the course of one scramble, a pilot forgot about his tail-man as he opened the throttle at the bottom of the airstrip. 'The poor bloke must have been too frightened to fall off as the Spitfire gathered speed and the next thing they were airborne,' Farish wrote on 20 January 1943. 'Imagine the pilot's consternation when he, unable to trim the aircraft, looked in the mirror and saw an airman waving in the breeze around his rudder! He managed to stagger round the circuit on full power while the terrified man hung on like grim death.

'On touching down, the airman was thrown clear and broke his leg. That was all . . .'

* * *

Rommel, having been pushed from the east into Tunisia by the British 8th Army, decided to make a decisive thrust against the untested Americans on his western flank. At the end of January, in the first major battle between Germans and Americans, the inexperienced and poorly led US troops were pushed back. The speed

Engineers from the RAF Battle Of Britain Memorial Flight working on the Rolls-Royce Merlin engine of the Spitfire Mk IIa at RAF Coningsby, Lincolnshire.

Squadron Leader Duncan Mason displays the RAF BBMF Mk IIa Spitfire. This is the only Spitfire that fought in the Battle of Britain in 1940 that is still flying.

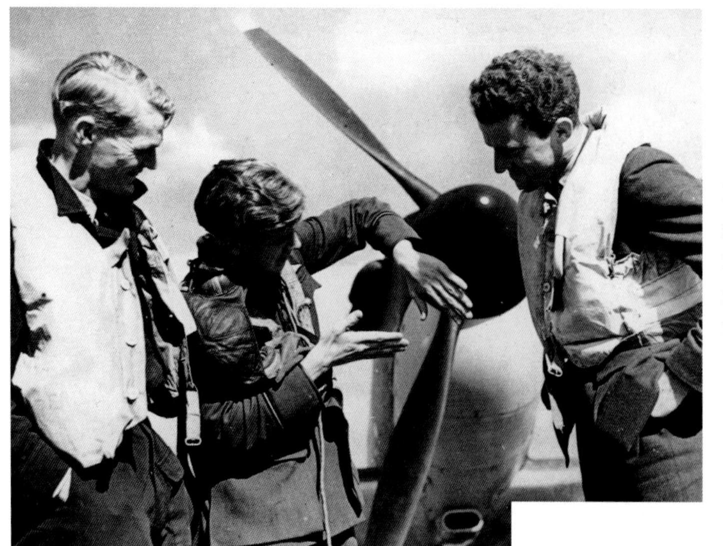

Pilots of 19 Squadron at RAF Fowlmere relive a dogfight after returning from a sortie in summer 1940.

Spitfire engineer Joe Roddis and the author at Goodwood airfield in 2016.

Spitfires of 222 Sqn at RAF Hornchurch scramble to meet an incoming raid during the Battle of Britain, Summer 1940.

Engineers prepare a batch of Spitfires prior to delivery to squadrons in 1944.

A Spitfire and Hurricane from the RAF BBMF at Gloucester airport. Spitfire veteran Ken Farlow looks on and fulfils a final wish to see his beloved Spitfire one last time.

When the RAF BBMF groundcrew were told about Ken's service history, they were delighted to give him a personal tour around the Spitfire.

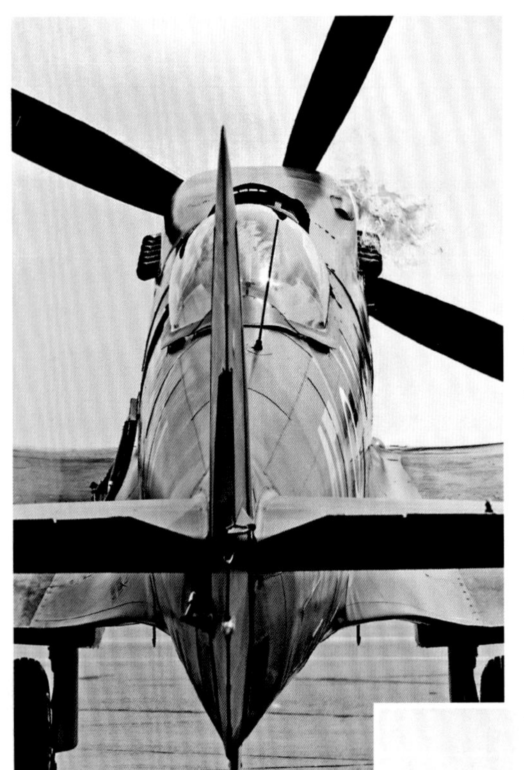

The RAF BBMF Spitfire Mk XVI starts its engine at RAF Coningsby.

A cockpit view of Spitfire TD314, built at Castle Bromwich in late 1944 and still flying with Aero Legends.

Engineer Joe Roddis *(right)* and pilot Terry Kearins, who had returned to duty after being shot down, relax on the wing of a Spitfire at Merville, France, in 1944.

US pilot John Blyth's Photo Reconnaissance Spitfire Mk XI PA944 *(top)* and *(below)* after he escaped a crash-landing in it on 12 September 1944. John *(centre photo, far left)* enjoys a well-earned cigarette.

ATA pilot Mary Ellis celebrates her 100th birthday in 2017 by taking the controls of a twin-seat Spitfire over Sussex. Shadowing her is one of the Spitfires she delivered during WWII whilst in the Air Transport Auxiliary.

Photo Reconnaissance Pilot Jimmy Taylor, who was shot down over Holland on 19 November 1944, with one of the RAF BBMF's PR Mk XIX Spitfires at RAF Coningsby in 2016.

Squadron Leader Duncan Mason in the RAF BBMF Spitfire Mk IX over Derwent reservoir.

Spitfire engineer Joe Roddis and former WAAF Betty Wood at Goodwood airfield in 2009, five years after the wartime friends had been reunited.

Alan Peart with his niece Heather Peart, then a RNZAF pilot, on Anzac Day 2006 in Hamilton, New Zealand.

Veteran Allan Scott, 96, prepares for another Spitfire flight at RAF Biggin Hill in March 2017.

ATA pilots Mary Ellis *(left)* & Joy Lofthouse with the author at a reunion in 2017.

Brian Bird in 1946 *(left)* and *(below)* with Air Vice Marshal Cliff Spink before his Spitfire flight in 2014.

Ken French at home in 2016 discussing his Spitfire experiences with the author.

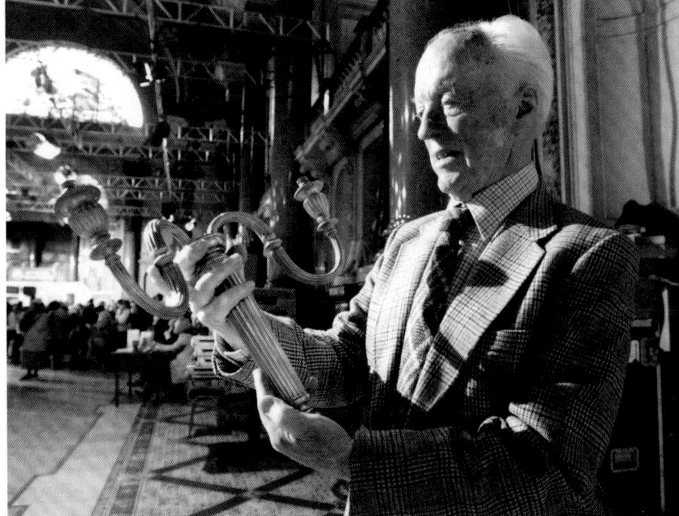

Ray Holmes appears on an episode of the BBC's *Antiques Roadshow* in 2002 with the chandelier he removed from the Reich Chancellery, scene of Hitler's last stand, in 1945.

of Rommel's advance meant his troops were bearing down on airfields that had been behind the front line. By 10 February 1943, the German force had advanced to within sixty miles of the main Allied airbase of Thelepte, just inside the Tunisian border.

When Harry Strawn had arrived at Thelepte a few weeks earlier with the 309th, rumours began to grow that the Germans would soon advance on them. At night Strawn cowered in a dugout, listening to the distant thud and blast of artillery rounds while clutching Marjorie's letter close to his chest. He had little faith in the Americans being able to hold off the advancing battle-hardened Afrika Korps. On the night of 10 February, he used candlelight to write his diary as he sat shivering in the dugout. 'They say the Germans are headed this way so we may have to move out of here for our army could never stop Rommel.'

As he wrote he cleared his throat for the umpteenth time. What had started that morning as an irritant at the back of his throat had developed into a constant pain that felt like a razor blade against his tonsils. Worse, his only handkerchief was sodden from constantly blowing his nose, which was beginning to turn red raw from the cold and constant attention. The medic had given him a couple of painkillers but could spare nothing more. He shivered again and ran his hand across his wet nose. Campaign life was turning out to be very different to the nights of champagne, big bands and the pretty girls of Oran.

Four days later the tanks of the 21st Panzer Division began their main assault on American lines, twenty miles from Strawn's position. For the first time, the Tiger tank, with its formidable 88mm main gun, appeared on the desert battlefield. Allied Sherman tanks were no match. The Germans poured through the front line, threatening the airfields.

On 15 February Strawn wrote: 'Things are really cooking now. The Germans are moving up closer to us. They are just 15 miles south of here.' A major tank battle was raging between the German panzers and Allied tanks. The Spitfires of 309th were sent up to help stem the attacks, but there was little they could do against the thick Tiger armour. The best they could do was prevent air attacks on Allied lines. When they returned to base there was little chance of relaxing, with the gunfire growing ominously closer. Strawn began to think more of Marjorie and home, as well as the prospect of being overrun in the middle of the night, taken prisoner or killed.

That morning he had been eating breakfast outside when an AA gun fired off two warning shells and everyone scrambled for cover. Strawn threw down his plate of powdered eggs and had just made it into his dugout when a dozen Me109s came screaming over the airfield, strafing everything in sight.

But the Messerschmitts had failed to notice the twelve Spitfires that were patrolling high above the airfield for just such an attack. They screamed down on the Germans, knocking out two and damaging two more. Harry decided he was far safer in the skies with his Spitfire than in the trenches waiting for his German foe to bomb him.

The next day, 16 February, the sound of enemy gunfire appeared much closer as Rommel's tanks advanced from both the north and south in an attempt to capture Thelepte in a pincer movement.

'They say we are laying a trap for the Germans but so far they seem to have avoided the trap and instead have almost encircled us. They are so close now that we can hear the report of their guns as they battle just over the mountain from here.' Rumours abounded about how fast the Germans could move. Strawn began to double-check his Spitfire's fuel tanks to ensure they were full. He also got together extra food and water to put in the compartment behind the pilot's seat. Among these provisions he included one of Marjorie's letters. He fought back the melancholy as he gave the pale-blue notepaper a final kiss then tucked it into the canvas bag. 'I got my things together this evening just in case we have to pull out in a hurry,' he wrote. 'They tell us we will have forty-eight hours' notice so I guess they know what the situation is.'

That forty-eight hours' notice was a little optimistic. Within hours the situation had dramatically changed.

'I was woken at 2.30am when we were told we would have to

evacuate Thelepte by noon that day.' Strawn had been struggling to sleep anyway. His sore throat throbbed and the artillery from both sides crumped through the night. And he was in a state of constant terror at the prospect of being stuck in his bed when a German grenade rolled through the doorway.

As he stumbled into the night air he could make out the distinct outline of the row of Spitfires parked on the runway's edge. He went to the one with 'Marjorie' lovingly painted on the side and ran his hand over the writing. For a moment he relaxed and forgot about the approaching guns and dull throb in his head.

As dawn approached, he heard a distant crash followed by the dull thud of an explosion and a flash of light. *Shellfire.* It was just over a mile away. Surely it was time to get out? The order to leave at noon must have been overridden by events on the ground?

He heard a Spitfire engine start. It was just the mechanic checking it over. Around the airfield there were fuel bowsers, trucks and signalling equipment. They would never be able to get that equipment away in time.

More shells landed in the coarse scrubland in the distance. He glanced over his shoulder. The looming bastion of the Atlas Mountains stood behind, barring the way back to Algeria from where they had arrived a month earlier. At least the mountains might hold up the Germans. *If we get away in time.*

But still no order came. Strawn went to the mess tent for a breakfast of dry bread and thin black coffee. A blast shook the canvas, sending the tent flaps inward.

'Jeez, time to go boys!' someone shouted. All the pilots jumped to their feet and jostled their way out of the tent.

Strawn sprinted outside to see a cone of earth spiral upwards from the impact of a shell a few hundred yards short of the airstrip. The German artillery observers knew precisely where Thelepte airfield was and were zeroing in their guns. He ran towards 'Marjorie', praying that he would get to her in time, before she became a smoking wreck. One of the ground crew was already in the pilot's seat firing up the engine. *Thank God!*

Strawn leapt onto the wing, then stood aside to let the airman get past. He gratefully jumped into the seat and the airman strapped him in. Strawn gave him a thumbs-up and taxied his Spitfire to the end of the runway, away from the incoming shells. He felt his heart pound and his grip tighten on the stick as a salvo erupted just inside the perimeter wire.

'Buster,' the squadron leader called over the radio. It was code for emergency boost, borrowed from their Spitfire instructors who were veterans of the Battle of Britain days.[9] A dozen Merlin engines rose to a crescendo as pilots threw their throttle levers 'through the gate' then hurtled down the airstrip towards the gunfire.

Strawn felt his Spitfire kick forward as he released the brakes and in just a few seconds the speed needle was registering close to 90mph. He pulled back and lifted off, tucking in the wheels as he did so. Then he gave a silent prayer to the plane's inventor as he flew straight and fast into the sky, the Spitfire spiriting him away from the dangers below.

Down beneath them was the road to their new base at Tébessa, eighty miles to the west. It was packed solid with trucks, tanks, men and equipment.

The Spitfires slipped over the mountains and the 309th headed to Tébessa. It was a town surrounded by snow-capped peaks and steep valleys with freshwater rivers. There was no accommodation, no mess, just the ground under the Spitfires' wings. After landing, Strawn gratefully lay down under a blanket and tried to forget about his cold and sore throat. He was just happy to be away from the dangers of Thelepte.

It was almost too cold to sleep, but he managed to drift off dreaming of his sweetheart Marjorie, waiting for him back in Oklahoma.

* * *

Two days later, the threat of a major German breakthrough increased dramatically. Rommel's panzers had smashed through the Americans at Kasserine Pass, just seventeen miles away in the hills north of Thelepte. The entire front line was now under threat.

'We listened to the news, none of which sounded very good; it seems the Germans are not content with just running us out of Thelepte for they are still coming,' Strawn wrote on 20 February. 'We didn't sleep much for all night their bombers were over the airfield.'

The rain was beginning to turn the landing strip into a dangerous quagmire that could flip a plane on take-off or landing. It could also ground the entire squadron, denying the pilots the most effective escape route.

On 22 February, the 309th's Spitfires escorted an armada of bombers heading to pulverise German frontline positions close to Thelepte in Tunisia to halt Rommel's offensive.

'All day long our air force bombed and strafed the German lines,' Strawn recalled. 'I have never seen so many planes operating in one day. If our army can't stop the Germans at least our air force will give him something to remember. Of course the Spits are always used for top cover, protecting the bombers.'

Under the force of the aerial onslaught, the Allies were able to retake lost ground and the Axis advance was finally halted before they could progress far into Algeria.

Better still, the 309th now had a fresh batch of Spitfires; although still Mark Vs they were at least brand new and had wings with cannon fitted. The Americans quickly spotted that the fighters were fitted with a different type of propeller. They had the Jablo blades from the Castle Bromwich factory, which were wider and made from compressed wood, and gave the fighter much better performance in thin air or at high altitude. They were also fitted with a gun heater intensifier system that piped additional heat into the gun bays, reducing jams.[10]

Strawn immediately noticed the difference. 'My new Spit and she really is a honey. The new type of prop gives her much more speed,' he wrote on 13 March. 'I had two guns taken out to give it more manoeuvrability and I am going to call this one Marjorie again. Perhaps it will change my luck and get me at least one Jerry.'

His excitement spilled over into a letter to his girlfriend. 'Yesterday, my ground crew named my Spit after a very lovely girl. Therefore, I have now flown about four hours in "Marjorie the 3rd". Of course, the 3rd meaning number three Spitfires!' Even in his letter writing, Strawn was careful to avoid any misunderstandings. 'My armament man did the painting and it is very good. Of course I had to let him paint his girl's name on the ship also, for he takes as much interest in my plane as I do.'

With their new aircraft the pilots were warned that they could soon be flying five sorties a day as a major offensive was launched in the west to take the pressure off the 8th Army in the east. The Afrika Korps was pushed back and the Americans advanced all the eighty miles back to their old airfield of Thelepte, which had now changed hands four times in two months. Strawn was heading back there.

As his Spitfire came in to land he felt a shiver. A month earlier the runway had been erupting in plumes of artillery smoke.

In a pause between the near-continuous two-hour sorties he found time to sit down on an empty ammunition crate and pen another letter to Marjorie.

'We are now at the same field we started out on. It's rather strange, for I imagine that not too long ago some German boy was probably writing to his girl back home. Of course we have to take many precautions, for they planted mines all over the field . . . One boy went to get a piece of firewood and when he picked up the log, he set off a mine and was killed instantly.'

The Americans were quickly into the action, escorting A-20 bombers targeting dug-in infantry. The Luftwaffe was there to meet them and Strawn knew he was in with a chance of his first kill. 'At 8,000ft we saw four Me109s on the deck and then four more at the same level that we were. Well, they hit us from above and how they hit. I was shot at three different times, but each time broke soon enough to miss his fire. Once an Me109 passed over my head so close I could see all his markings, white wingtips, white nose, white crosses and grey body. They really have a ship in this new Me109G for they can run away from us in no time at all.

'They shot down two boys in our squadron, Early and Juhnke. Juhnke crashed in our territory and came back this evening. Early we haven't heard from and no one saw him go in or get hit. We got three damaged but not by me for I was too busy making sure I wasn't going to get hit.'

Strawn had been away from the States for almost a year and on continuous operations for seven months yet, despite his best efforts, he had still to close in on his first kill and feel he had contributed something to the war. He was also not being helped by flying the Spitfire Mark Vs.

* * *

Greggs Farish with a Spitfire Mk V, 1944

Despite being brand-new machines, the Mark Vs were proving to be no match for the powerful 109 'G' variant. The Spitfire in North Africa was being outclassed.

RAF commanders recognised that the threat of superior German fighters had to be countered.

Greggs Farish was summoned to his CO at 8pm on 25 March at their new airfield of Souk-el-Khemis, a dusty strip inside northern

Tunisia.[11] 'I've got a job for you, Spanner. Bags of work now.' He pointed on the map to where Strawn's 309th were based at Thelepte, 200 miles by road to the south. 'You have got to be there by tomorrow morning with a servicing party.'

The new Spitfire IXs of 72 Squadron were flying to the front-line airstrip to replace the now outdated Mark Vs to counter the Me109Gs. With the massive power that the IXs brought to the battlefield, the RAF would have a plane far superior to the 109s and very much on equal terms with the Focke-Wulf 190s. But the battle-winning Spitfires would need immediate refuelling and rearming as soon as they landed at Thelepte.

Farish was 'pleased as punch' at the chance of getting some front-line action but he knew he had to move fast – 200 miles overnight was a hell of a way, even along the desert's straight roads. After a rapid conference with his NCOs, he decided to take forty men and seven three-ton Bedford trucks loaded with ammunition, signalling equipment, petrol and oil. Farish borrowed a rifle and a Jeep then grabbed a quick bite in the cookhouse.

By midnight they were ready to move. Under the headlights of his trucks parked at the end of the runway, feeling the chill of the desert night, Farish gathered the drivers round for a final briefing, spreading his map over the bonnet of his borrowed Jeep. 'Get these names down – Souk-el-Arba, Le Kef, Kasserine and Thelepte, which is just here.' The screwdriver he used for pointing at the map thumped down on the location. 'The kites take off here.' The screwdriver moved right over the map to their current location far to the north. 'They leave at 8am tomorrow so we've got to move fast. First lorry can use headlights, the rest only tail lights. After dawn keep well spread out so you can only just see the man ahead, at least 400 yards, and have a spotter on top. OK? Right. Let's get going.'

By 3.30am they had reached Le Kef, the halfway point, and stopped for tea and sandwiches.

As they moved south, with the ramparts of the Atlas Mountains on their right, the sky got lighter.

'We carried on through the Kasserine Pass and here and there we passed a smashed-up lorry, riddle-holed and burnt-out,' Farish recorded. 'In one place there was a Churchill tank surrounded by three German tanks, all wrecked, and nearby a little bed of wooden crosses growing in the desert scrub.'

The convoy was about eight miles from Thelepte airfield when the lead truck stopped for a five-minute breather. As the drivers checked fuel and oil, the rest stretched their legs. A dead donkey on the side of the road attracted the attention of several airmen, some prodding it with their feet. Suddenly there was a blast and half-a-dozen men collapsed to the ground.

After months of air attacks everyone instinctively threw themselves to the ground. But there was no aircraft. It was a landmine hidden by the Germans during their retreat. Everyone turned to the sound of grunts, groans then screams. One of the mechanics, Aircraftsman Hitt, was writhing in the dirt and dust. His trousers were a ragged mess of material and torn flesh. Bright red blood pumped from his thigh. A severed artery. He needed medical attention and he needed it fast. An armourer who had been an air-raid warden in London wrapped a tourniquet tight around his thigh, managing to stem the flow of blood.

Farish, who'd been driving the last truck in the convoy, immediately took control. He sped down in the Jeep to a nearby American hospital then escorted two ambulances back. As he did so he spotted 72 Squadron's new, modern Mark IX Spitfires overhead. After giving the ambulance drivers directions, he dashed to the airfield, arriving just as the first fighter taxied in.

For a moment Farish stood back to admire the clean, fresh lines of the brand-new Spitfires. There were no bullet holes patched up, no dents or scratches from AA fire, scrapes from rough landings. *Brand spanking new.* There was something about them, perhaps the slightly longer nose, that suggested menace.

Farish ensured the Spitfires were refuelled then drove off to check on his wounded. He discovered that an American surgeon had already repaired Aircraftsman Hitt's severed artery.

'We found him in a ward of gravely wounded men. On either side was a close row of beds and in them men in all conditions, with limbs, hands, even faces missing. There was a queer smell of chemicals and around the beds there moved American nurses – women! – in smart uniforms who gave hope and cheerfulness to the place. Up and down the middle walked a doctor who, when he saw us around Hitt's bed, exclaimed: "You can't kill an Englishman."'

Farish drove back to the aerodrome to be told that the newly arrived Spitfire IXs had already downed two Germans.

Harry Strawn, who was at Thelepte when 72 Squadron flew in, was fulsome in his praise of the new fighters. 'They are much faster than ours, have a better rate of climb and a higher ceiling. In fact they can outclimb the latest Me109 and Fw190s. They did OK too, for on their first mission they shot down two 109s and damaged two more. The Hun can't tell them from our Mark Vs so he tries the same tactics on them that he uses on us which proves fatal, for the Nines just climb up behind them and let them have it.

'They soon learn, though. In the afternoon we took some bombers over and the Hun wouldn't attack us because he was afraid we were Nines instead of Fives!'

In reciprocation for the air cover, the British enjoyed the Americans' generous hospitality, gratefully taking armfuls of peanut butter, honey, sweetcorn and fruit juices.

* * *

While the fight was raging, Hugh Dundas had arrived on operations at Souk-el-Khemis, an airstrip bulldozed from the mud in northern Tunisia, as the acting Wing Commander of 324 Wing after its boss had been injured. Aged just twenty-two, he was the equivalent of an army lieutenant colonel in rank. Dundas had demonstrated excellent leadership qualities, having recovered from Bader's loss and the dark days of the Rhubarbs a few months previously. He had even finally proposed to his long-standing girlfriend Diana. 'She had no qualms – she was for taking our happiness while we could. My longing to do the same was overwhelming. I would fight my private battles against fear when the moment came.'[12]

The wedding was planned for February 1943, but days before the event a wing leader was incapacitated in North Africa and Dundas was summoned to go back on operations.

He found the conditions of the waterlogged North African airfields a shock. He had been expecting endless stretches of sand, rolling desert dunes and a generally parched land. Furthermore, those under his command had been fighting since November and were not overly impressed with someone fresh from England. A DFC and Battle of Britain experience counted for little among those who had been bombed and strafed for four months while living in mud.

When the wing leader returned from sick leave Dundas was not left kicking his heels for long. In the midst of the Allied counter-attack of early April 1943, he was sent on a curious mission to win over a force of French airmen. The pilots were from the former Vichy regime, ostensibly on the Germans' side, but after the Vichy surrender they had been uncertain over whose side to take or how to approach the Allies. So they took what they considered the best option – to stay put and do nothing, lying low at Bou Saâda oasis, 250 miles south of Algiers. It was understandable. This was the Africa that all the British had imagined back home. Shimmering waters of an oasis, the sun-dappled shade of palm trees, white-washed Arab homes and veiled, exotic women. Dundas' task was to lure the French away from this paradise and persuade them to join the fight, using Spitfires to complete the seduction.

He flew to Bou Saâda with another pilot, crossing mountains and deserts until he spotted a landing strip two miles north of the rich, green oasis. 'A white house and massive *Beau Geste* fort lay like a bright splash of paint on the empty brown canvas of the desert. A couple of small, old-fashioned planes stood by a tent in one corner. As we circled I saw a man walk out of the tent and stand with his hands to his eyes, staring up at us.'

With some trepidation Dundas came in to land as his colleague circled above. The man on the airstrip, dressed in a French lieutenant's uniform, waved in a friendly fashion.

When they were taken to the grizzled commanding officer, he did not press too hard on why Dundas was there, instead offering dinner and a bed for the night.

As the wine went round some of the younger French officers confessed their admiration for the Spitfire and their desire to get into action.

When the Spitfires had arrived, a couple of pilots had gone outside to look at the fighters from a distance. They had moved closer in, finally running their hands over the smooth lines of the elliptic wings, bending under the slender undercarriage and then stepping back to admire her from the front. There had been nods, in a Gallic fashion, which seemed to suggest approval.

The wine influenced Dundas too. He decided to tell the officers the nature of his mission, that he was authorised to ask them to join the fight to liberate Tunisia from the *sale Boche* – the filthy Hun.

The offer was greeted with enthusiasm and clearly called for celebration. Dundas was driven into town to a single-storey house where young women in flowing robes danced seductively.

Next, a beautiful Arab woman came in and danced, accompanied by a man playing the flute. The middle-aged female proprietor then spoke in the French commandant's ear. The woman reappeared, only this time completely naked.

'She danced in a voluptuous way, increasingly so as the tempo of the music quickened. The atmosphere in that little room became charged, as that desirable naked body gyrated before us in practised erotic rhythm.'

The music stopped and the girl left behind a febrile atmosphere. The commandant approached Dundas. 'Madame's compliments, *mon colonel*. The girl is yours for the night. You will be happy. She has great beauty, no?'

Dundas politely refused. 'The vision of that voluptuous body swam before my eyes. She had great beauty, yes. And I would be happy, no doubt; but I remembered that I had come to collect a new squadron into our ranks, not to spend the night in the arms of an Arab girl. To the undisguised amazement of my hosts I declined the offer.'

However, the French went on to join the fight.

* * *

In April 1943 the Americans of the 309th finally received their own batch of Spitfire IXs, having previously watched with envy as the British got first dibs on the new mark. Four men from the 309th had flown their old Spitfires to Algiers to bring back the new planes, which had been shipped into the North African port. They were from the 5,600 Spitfire Mark IXs assembled at Castle Bromwich.

'With a Merlin 61 engine and a four-bladed prop, we will be able to outclimb the Me109s and Fw190s,' Strawn reported.

Within a week the entire squadron was equipped with Mark IXs flown down from Algiers. Strawn was overjoyed after his first flight. 'What a ship it is! It has a 1,600hp engine with a supercharger which will take you up to 40,000ft or more if you need it. It is faster and has more climb than our old Fives. The Germans are scared to death of them for they know we can outclimb them.'

On 17 April Strawn sprang out of bed happy in the knowledge that he'd soon be leaping into the domineering Mark IX. Hopefully he would be able to test the new Spitfire in action. He gulped down his breakfast of a lumpy oatmeal and powdered milk mix washed down with a mug of sweetened tea. Their mission was to fly top cover at 25,000ft over southern Tunisia for a force of B17 Flying Fortresses – heavy bombers that had recently entered the campaign.

The Germans were quick to notice the new threat in their midst and were determined to inflict a big psychological blow by shooting the bombers down. They would throw everything they could at them, from 109Gs to their prized Fw190s. Strawn and his comrades knew they would have to work hard to keep the bombers safe.

It did not take long for the first interceptors to arrive. A thought crossed Strawn's mind that finally this could be the day he got his first kill. He was desperate to prove his fighter pilot credentials. Days earlier he'd had a 109 cold but his cannons jammed. Now his flight dived down at some 109s but they got away in the melee.

In the skies above the enemy lines in southern Tunisia the American Spitfires had climbed back to their station above the bombers when a flight of Fw190s was seen streaking up to the Fortresses' bellies. The men of the 309th rolled over and dived.

Strawn spotted a lone Fw190 below and swooped down towards him. The German saw the danger heading his way and went into a near-vertical dive. Strawn followed and the new 'Marjorie' held her own, matching the 190 for speed.

Strawn suddenly found himself in the unusual position of having an Fw190 in his sights. He had him cold. *Surely his first kill would follow?*

The gap was just close enough to open fire. Strawn gave him a burst then another burst. Cannon fire streaked towards the German, clipping his wings. A few seconds later Strawn saw white smoke come out of the fuselage.

He glanced down at his altimeter: 10,000ft. He was low, well within range of the accurate 88mm German AA fire. He had to do the sensible thing and regain height. He pulled back on the stick and searched for his squadron and the bombers. *Nothing.* The sky that had been full of bombers and whirling fighters minutes earlier was now empty.

Feeling a growing sense of isolation Strawn turned his aircraft in the direction of the bombing mission. As he began climbing back up to 25,000ft he looked below at the rugged mountains that gave way to flat plains. It all seemed empty and endless.

He had just climbed through 22,000ft when he felt the Spitfire lifted by a giant force and tipped over. He heard the jarring sound of metal striking metal. The aircraft juddered and shook. Above him the canopy partially disintegrated.

By pushing hard on rudder pedals and elevators he managed to drag the Spitfire the right way up. He looked to his right. Two feet of the starboard wingtip had been blown clean off. The aircraft was wobbling erratically. He started sweating as he fought to keep her stable. He looked down at his instrument panel. It was completely demolished. He felt sharps pains in his right arm. It was lacerated with shrapnel and blood seeped through his uniform. Worse, his oxygen tube was cut and he was at 22,000ft. Then the plane caught fire.

Have to get out quick before I pass out.

The terror of being burnt alive pushed him beyond the limits of pain as he used his damaged arm to get out.

'I reached up to release my seat harness, pulling the release pin out of the right-hand side.' He was moving faster now, the pounding adrenaline pushing aside his fears. 'I reached up to pull the canopy release pin, which was a little ball that hung right up at the top of my head. When the canopy flew off it sucked off my oxygen mask. I took two deep breaths.'

The Spitfire inverted and Strawn fell out. Somehow, while semi-conscious, he managed to pull the ripcord on his parachute. Then he lost consciousness and drifted down, a limp body hanging at the end of a piece of silk.

Strawn's rag-doll-like body bundled into the ground. Afrika Korps troops who had seen his plight rushed over to the billowing canopy attached to the slumped American pilot. They turned Strawn over and saw he was still alive.

'The next thing I remember is two German soldiers standing there with rifles pointing at me. I passed out again. When I came to I thought, "Oh gee! I've died and gone to heaven." All I could see was all these beautiful white clouds. The soldiers couldn't figure out how to get my parachute off so they simply picked me up, parachute and all, and put me in the sidecar of a motorcycle.'[13]

For the next eight hours, a German surgeon operated, skilfully sewing back together Strawn's ulnar nerve in his elbow.

The pilot awoke on a straw mattress and under coarse sheets in a ward filled with injured Germans. The surgeon came in to see him. 'He could speak English. He thought I was English and said he hated the English but had had to operate on me just the same. When I told him I was American his whole attitude changed and he began to talk very freely with me. He said I would soon be well and then taken to Germany where I could fish and live a very quiet life.

'I thanked him for being so good to me and from then on we were really good friends. He came to see me twice a day after that.'

Whenever the surgeon came in the orderlies would snap to attention with a Nazi salute. It was Strawn's first taste of the rigid control the Germans had over their men.

After more than a week in the Bizerte hospital, and as the Allies advanced into Tunisia, he was moved to another hospital in Tunis, where fifty men were packed into a room.

'In the daytime it was swarming with flies and at night stinks of blood and sweat. Very few of us sleep. The windows had to be closed so as to have a good blackout, for at night the English bombed anything that showed light. The air raids were very frequent and more than once we could hear the bombs as they whistled overhead, dropping just across the street from us and breaking the windows. It was hell to think that one of your own bombs might blow you sky high.'

He survived by smoking strong French cigarettes. As the Allies got closer the Germans began evacuating their wounded by air, including some American pilots. Strawn was afraid. He knew his fellow airmen would pounce on the German transporters. He wasn't wrong.

* * *

After the loss of Stalingrad two months earlier in February 1943, Hitler refused to be humiliated again. The airlift to resupply the iconic Soviet city had failed, but Tunis was different. It was not surrounded by fanatical Russians, just a gentle stretch of the Mediterranean a short 150-mile hop to the western end of the island of Sicily, where the Germans had numerous airstrips. Junkers 52 cargo planes were joined by the mammoth Me323 transporters. Tunis could easily be resupplied.

The Messerschmitt 323 'Gigant' – Giant – was a further testament of German ingenuity and audacious engineering. With six engines, a 180ft wingspan, a top speed of 130mph and the ability to carry 130 troops or ten tons of supplies, they heralded a step change in airborne logistics. By comparison, the Junkers 52s could carry just 2.5 tons of supplies.

The Luftwaffe was now making 150 transport flights a day and this did not go unnoticed. Harry Broadhurst, who had demonstrated his tactical acumen in Dieppe, was now commanding the Desert Air Force with considerable success. He understood the importance of transport aircraft. Neutralising them would bring a rapid end to German resistance. Broadhurst knew too that Hitler was determined to keep the corridor to Tunisia open. The Me323s were giants and giant targets, and taking them out of the sky would not only stop supplies getting in but provide another dent to Nazi morale. A man sculpted by years of warfare had become ruthless in thought.

On 18 April, from forward bases in Tunisia, he assembled his most experienced pilots, men who for the last year or longer had fought in scorching heat, cold nights, sandstorms and whatever else the desert could throw at them. They were hardened men and grimly determined to get the job done then go home.

To some, the idea of bagging a massive transporter carrying a host of crack German soldiers was a satisfying prospect. For others, it was nasty but necessary.

From their bases in Tunisia the Spitfire squadrons assembled high in the sky, with radar vectoring them precisely onto targets over Cap Bon, the Tunisian peninsula that jutted out into the Mediterranean, pointing towards Sicily. The German transporters were flown the 150 miles from airstrips in Sicily to supply the capital Tunis. But from a long way out the giant transporters were not hard to miss, filling the sky like a flight of prehistoric birds.

Then the Spitfires and Mustangs fell upon them in their scores.

It was an uneven fight, a bloodbath that even the likes of Hugh Dundas found shocking.

'The carnage was so ghastly that our pilots had difficulty in giving coherent reports or estimates of planes destroyed,'[14] reported Hugh Dundas. 'The unfortunate Germans were helpless, like sheep caught in a pack, swiftly broken up and massacred by hunting wolves. The only return fire came from the troops inside the transports, shooting with their sub-machine guns and rifles from the doors and portholes. The convoys were flying at very low altitude and the planes could not weave or manoeuvre violently without crashing into each other or into the sea. Some men dived from the doors, without parachutes, without hope, to escape from the inferno of flame and fire. Some German pilots just pushed the nose down and crashed into the water rather than wait for the final certainty of destruction by our fighters.'

The only respite came when the fighters ran out of ammunition. Just half the transports got through.

The Luftwaffe tried to answer the threat by sending up hordes of fighters over Cap Bon when the next convoy came in. Broadhurst countered by sending his wing of veteran fighters against them, allowing the slower US Kittyhawks and some fighter-bombers to tear into the transporters. This time the 323s were carrying petrol for the panzers. Plane after plane went down into the sea, streaming an inferno of burning fuel, aircraft and bodies before crashing into the water and subsiding with a hiss. 'Thirty-one of them fell, trailing fire across the sky and burned on the calm surface of the sea,' Dundas reported.

In a final act of desperation, the transports went in at night. And again they were slaughtered. Heavily armed Beaufighters, equipped with advanced radars in their noses, were able to track then home in on the planes. The surviving German transporters arrived singly into Tunis, the looks on their crews' faces showing men who never wanted to take to the skies again.

Cut off in the capital Tunis, other ports and in the mountains with no supplies to continue the fight, the Germans capitulated en masse. By 13 May, 240,000 Afrika Korps and Italians had become prisoners.

The Luftwaffe lost a third of its total strength in the campaign from November 1942 to May 1943, with some 2,400 aircraft destroyed. By comparison, the RAF and USAAF lost just 849.

* * *

Fortunately for Harry Strawn he was not put on a flight to Germany. During the last few days of German resistance the fighting intensified, but then on 9 May 1943 the hospital commander surrendered to a British captain captured a few days earlier.

The surgeon Strawn had befriended handed over his Luger pistol then said: 'I once told you the war was over as far as you were concerned but now it is over for me. However, I am glad for I am tired of it all and at least I know I will get home to my wife after it is over.'

Strawn felt the relief of surviving the campaign wash over him. At last he could seriously contemplate returning to the States for a joyful reunion with Marjorie. Ever since their first date two years earlier, he had been smitten, every minute spent in her company relived in detail during the quiet moments on operations. After a few months in hospital in England, Strawn was well enough to cross the Atlantic and return home. Their reunion was indeed joyful, the romance instantly rekindled as Marjorie threw herself into his arms after he walked down the gangplank. They returned together to Muskogee, Oklahoma, where they were married in October 1943.

But Strawn also reserved a deep and enduring affection for his Spitfire. In a magazine interview after his return he said: 'The Spitfire was very simple and easy to fly, it was almost like a trainer. If you got into trouble all you did was take your hands off the controls and let it go. It could literally fly itself. All in all, the Spitfire was a great aeroplane.'

* * *

Hugh Dundas had been in the fight for three and a half years since the days covering the British withdrawal from Dunkirk. He had seen the enemy only fleetingly, the flash of a man behind helmet and goggles before they engaged in a do-or-die struggle. Or seeing them come down by parachute in the distance. He had not particularly wanted to get too close. The enemy to an extent had to remain dehumanised. But now there were hordes of Rommel's fabled Afrika Korps taken prisoner. Dundas got in a Jeep and drove to the encampments outside Tunis where the thousands of German prisoners stood behind barbed wire. He relished the trip.

'It was a curious and almost solemn experience to drive out and see this hitherto impersonal enemy herded together in hordes of living, beaten human beings. I sat in my Jeep and stared at them in their ugly uniforms and forage caps as I might have stared at animals in the zoo or men from another planet. There they were, in their tens of thousands, Hitler's invincibles, disarmed, dejected and looking pretty ordinary and harmless in defeat. There they were, the long and the short and the tall, as per the barrack-room song.

'Well *fuck 'em all*, I thought, taking the lyric one line further. They were the defeated ones but they were safe. That was more than could be said for me and my friends. We had won so we had to go on and start all over again.'[15]

Hugh 'Cocky' Dundas was right. There was still plenty of fighting, and dying, to be done before Hitler's Nazi forces were defeated. And he, and the Spitfire, would be at the heart of it all.

CHAPTER NINE

THE RELENTLESS FIGHT IN EUROPE

With the majority of their bomber force now in Russia, the Luftwaffe was keen to make some kind of response to the RAF and Bomber Command's pulverising of German cities and factories. They came up with the *Hohenkampfkommando* – the High Altitude Bomber Detachment. While long in name, this consisted of just two Junkers 86Rs. They were effective, however. By injecting nitrous oxide into the engines and extending the wingspan by 20ft, the Ju86 'R' could reach 48,000ft carrying a single 550lb bomb.[1] The aircraft could thus enter RAF airspace with impunity. Goering could now boast that revenge attacks would start on Britain. It was not an idle threat.

Back in late August 1942, Ju86 crews bombed Britain at their leisure, looking on with disinterest as Spitfire Vs surged towards them then dropped away because their engines simply lacked the power to go much higher than 37,000ft, unable to get within attacking range.

Because the Junkers were only single aircraft rather than a fleet that could cause severe damage, and deemed to be on reconnaissance missions, no air-raid warning was given on their approach. The disruption was too costly to the war economy. Thus, during morning rush hour on 28 August 1942, the streets of Bristol were bustling with commuters. Three packed buses were caught in the middle of the Ju86's 550lb detonation which landed in the city centre. The single bomb ripped open the buses' thin metal skins, cruelly striking those packed inside. Hot shrapnel and flying glass tore indiscriminately through the early-morning commuters. Limbs were strewn across the bus decks, a scene of carnage that even hardened rescuers struggled to deal with. The bomb killed forty-five and injured fifty-six. It would not go unpunished.

A response was demanded. The RAF hastily formed a high-altitude interception flight using the new Spitfire Mark IXs, which could climb high, and with the Merlin 61 they were able still to generate 600hp at 40,000ft – substantially more than earlier Merlins.

Among their number was Prince Emanuel Galitzine, twenty-four, the great-grandson of Russian Emperor Paul I. The prince was a baby when his parents, with the assistance of the Royal Navy, fled the Russian Revolution in 1919. Galitzine joined the new Special Service Flight, the name given to the hoped-for high-altitude interceptors based at RAF Northolt, west London. The prince enjoyed a diet of chocolate, eggs, bacon and fresh orange juice, food unobtainable during rationing but considered necessary for high-altitude flying. He underwent tests in a decompression chamber in Farnborough, where pilots were starved of oxygen to demonstrate what it was like to work at high altitude. He was given lectures on how to conserve energy at height by making movements slowly and deliberately. 'Everything', the pilots were told, 'should be done in an *icy calm* manner.' He would be relying on pure oxygen to breathe and his heated suit to combat the extreme chill of high altitude.

A week later he was in the cockpit of a Mark IX that had been made significantly lighter to gain the extra altitude. To lose weight, a wooden propeller was refitted, there was no armour and the four machine guns had gone, leaving just two 20mm Hispano cannons that could fire sixty rounds a second. All further equipment not essential for high-altitude flying was removed and the plane was camouflaged in 'Cambridge blue' paint.

Unfortunately, the Spitfire with the pressurised cabin – the Mark VII – was still undergoing development and was not yet ready for operations, so the high-altitude pilots had to make do with the Mark IX, which had been rushed into service. With so many technical changes, and the ongoing development of the various models of the Spitfire, differing 'Marks' of the aircraft would be introduced in different theatres of war, to meet ongoing threats, and not necessarily in numerical order.

The 450lb reduction in weight was instantly recognisable, Galitzine reported, as he took her up for a test flight. 'She had plenty of power and was very lively. I stayed above 40,000ft for some time and found it quite exhilarating. It was a beautiful day and I could see along the coast of England from Dover to Plymouth and almost the whole of the northern coast of France as far as Belgium and Holland.' The temperature around 40,000ft could be as low as minus 60°C so he also 'wore an electrically heated flying suit which kept me warm and comfortable'.

On his second flight Galitzine took the Spitfire up to 43,400ft and, to ensure they worked in the extreme cold, tested his cannons. All was well.

Two days later he was wrapped in his high-altitude suit, waiting at high readiness, when a suspicious high-flying raider was reported climbing to height over France. The prince took to the skies.

'Climbing away at full throttle, the Spitfire went up like a lift, but there was a long way to go – 40,000ft is 7½ miles high. I climbed in a wide spiral over Northolt to 15,000ft then the ground controller informed me that the incoming aircraft was over mid-Channel and heading towards the Portsmouth area. I was ordered onto a south-westerly heading to cut him off. After several course corrections I finally caught sight of the enemy aircraft as it was flying up the Solent. I was at about 40,000ft and he was slightly higher. I continued my climb and headed after him, closing in until I could make out the outline of a Junkers 86. By then I was about half-a-mile away from him and we were both at 42,000ft.'[2]

Inside the Junkers, the crew gazed with their usual disinterest as the fighter climbed towards them. After a few minutes *Leutnant* Erich Sommer, the observer, watched with growing concern as it got closer and closer.

'Aircraft approaching, starboard side,' he reported to the captain.[3]

'OK, observer.' *Oberfeldwebel* Horst Goetz did not pay much attention as fighters had constantly tried to harry them without success.

'Enemy fighter climbing fast,' Sommer warned again. 'Approaching our altitude. Still climbing . . .' Goetz noted the concern in Sommer's voice and leaned over to his side of the cabin to see for himself. To his horror he saw the Spitfire, a little above them and still climbing.

He had to act quickly and immediately gained some height by jettisoning the 550lb bomb. He then pushed the nitrous oxide injection lever to full, increasing power on the two engines. He also partially depressurised the cabin, avoiding the possibility of an explosion if it was pierced. Then he opened the throttles and tried to outclimb the Spitfire.

Prince Galitzine knew he had been spotted when the Junkers' bomb was released. 'The German crew had obviously seen me because I saw them jettison their bomb, put up its nose to gain height and turn round for home.'

Prince Emanuel Galitzine

He was not going to let it get away. It was time to test the Mark IXs capabilities to the full. The war's highest aerial combat was about to begin.

'I jettisoned my 30 gallon external slipper tank, which was now empty, and had little difficulty in following him in the climb and getting about 200ft above the bomber. At this stage I remember telling myself: *Take it easy, conserve your strength, keep icy calm.*

'The grey-blue Junkers seemed enormous and it trailed a long, curling condensation trail. It reminded me of a film I had once seen of an aerial view of an ocean liner ploughing through a calm sea and leaving a wake.

'I positioned myself for an attack and dived to about 200 yards astern of him, where I opened up with a three-second burst. At the end of the burst my port cannon jammed and the Spitfire slewed round to starboard; then as I passed through the bomber's slipstream my canopy misted over. The canopy took about a minute to clear completely, during which time I climbed back into position for the next attack.

'When I next saw the Junkers he was heading southward, trying to escape out to sea. I knew I had to get right in close behind him if I was to stand any chance of scoring hits, because it would be difficult to hold the Spitfire straight when the single cannon fired and she went into a yaw.

'Again I dived to attack but when I was about a hundred yards away the bomber made a surprisingly tight turn to starboard. I opened fire but the Spitfire went into a yaw and fell out of the sky.' A yaw occurs when an aircraft twists and oscillates around a vertical axis, making it very difficult to control, particularly at high altitude. But Galitzine, despite the fear of blacking out and plunging seven miles earthwards, managed to recover the tumbling Spitfire.

'I broke off the attack and turned outside him, climbing back to 44,000ft. I carried out two further attacks. On each my Spitfire fell out of the sky whenever I opened fire with my remaining cannon and my canopy misted over whenever I passed through the bomber's slipstream.'

Sweating, exhausted and slightly nauseous from the gut-wrenching yaws, the prince glanced down at his fuel gauge. After four attacks in an action that lasted forty-five minutes flying at full throttle, Galitzine saw that his tank was almost empty. He lined up for a final attack.

Despite the outside temperature of minus 60°C at high altitude, inside the Ju86 Goetz was sweating profusely as he fought to keep out of the Spitfire's reach. Already the bomber had juddered alarmingly when an armour-piercing round penetrated the wing. As the Spitfire pulled out of a yaw he spotted a patch of cloud and dived into it.

Galitzine glanced again at his fuel gauge as the Junkers' tail was swallowed in the murk. He was well over the Channel, about twenty-five miles from Cherbourg. He broke away, cursing his jammed cannon which denied him an almost certain kill.

Goetz gratefully managed to land the bomber in Caen and checked it for damage. The crew got out and slapped each other on the back, lit cigarettes and looked skywards, thankful for surviving the Spitfire attack. As they walked around the aircraft the damage was instantly recognisable. In the middle of the port wing was a hole the size of a beer bottle, where an armour-piercing round had gone straight through. It was the only damage but that single bullet was enough. Goetz knew that it was now clear that the Junkers' period of immunity over England was at an end. There could be no more stratospheric attacks by their bombers without running the risk of being shot down. The Spitfire had again prevailed, winning a small but important strategic victory.

The War Office was also quick to let the British public, and vicariously the Luftwaffe, know that their number was up in the high-altitude fight. The aviation cartoonist Chris Wren captured the victory in a picture showing a worried Junkers 86 pilot leaning out of the cockpit and looking over his shoulder to see Spitfires above him. Underneath he penned a verse:

> 'Than Doktor Junkers eighty-six nothing can fly higher,'
> The pilot thought and preened himself until a glance behind
> Reminded him that out of sight does not mean out of mind.
> And if the sky should fill with lead, the likely clue is 'Spitfire'.

* * *

Fearing the Spitfire threat, the Luftwaffe largely confined itself to the skies over occupied Europe, though the German pilots occasionally deigned to cross the Channel in search of prey. Bad weather was usually the best weapon to sneak through the home defences undetected for a hit-and-run strike.

Having learned her lesson about flying in poor weather, Diana Barnato Walker had wisely put down the aircraft she was ferrying at Whitchurch, Hampshire, as a heavy band of rain, moving across England from west to east, approached on 2 January 1943. Rain was pelting down as she went into the dispersal hut to find a dozen other ATA pilots who had come down and were waiting for a lift back to base.[4]

She was pleased to see the Anson was piloted by her friend Jim Mollison, who had flown a record-breaking solo flight from Australia to England in 1931 and gone on to marry Amy Johnson, the renowned female solo pilot killed on ATA duties in 1941.

Twelve of the ATA fliers climbed into the twin-engine Anson, slightly overloading it. Diana took the co-pilot's seat next to Mollison, thirty-seven, who had flown for the RAF since the 1920s. Mollison told her that by the time they got back to headquarters at White Waltham the weather front would have cleared there, allowing the ferry pilots to spend a night in their own beds.

They flew towards Reading just under the cloud base with the sun behind them and the dark weather front looming ahead. As they passed over Reading's rail tracks, Diana noticed smoke billowing from the railway yard below.

Probably smoke coming off a locomotive below, she thought.

She looked up at the looming dark covering ahead and caught her breath. 'Suddenly, from the mass of cloud in front of us, out popped an aircraft, just like a cork from a bottle, going like stink. Not only that, it was coming straight for us.' It wasn't smoke, it was anti-aircraft fire.

'At first I thought it was a Mosquito with some thick ATA pilot flying in the muck who had still got his head down on instruments without realising he had cleared the weather.'

The plane's shape grew rapidly and became more defined as it quickly closed the distance between them. Then she noticed something sparkle from the aircraft's nose. Something distinctive. *Bullets!*

'Against the dark cloud, I saw tracer coming out at us from what appeared to be the guns of the silvered aircraft. I then noticed the huge black cross on the fuselage and swastika on the tailplane. An Me110!'

Jim Mollison saw it too. 'Jeez!' he yelled. 'It's a Jerry!'

He yanked the Anson up into the overcast to hide as the German flashed past. 'It was very close, on our port side, its guns still blazing.'

They were then gratefully swallowed up by cloud and came in to land at White Waltham to find everyone running around in tin hats shouting, 'Air raid!'

Diana Barnato Walker also had the odd mishap of her own making. In good spirits, she had left RAF Benson in a lightweight PR Spitfire Mark IX fitted with the new bubble-type canopy for better vision. Flying in clear blue skies she decided to finally attempt a roll. After a few unsuccessful tries, she managed it.

'I promptly got stuck upside down! In this attitude, while wondering what to do next, from out of my top overall pocket fell my beautifully engraved, round, silver powder compact. It wheeled round and round the bubble canopy like a drunken sailor on a wall of death, opened, then sent all the face powder over absolutely everything.

'When I found myself the right-way-up again, the inside of the canopy was like a frosted lavatory window. I wiped away to clear a view but just smeared it into an awful mess. I was very hot and sticky and brushing my overalls made the stuff fly up again, sticking to my face and neck. It was amazing how much powder there seemed to be. It rapidly spread over the whole inside of the cockpit, instruments, windscreen, knobs and switches – just everywhere! To add to my discomfort, as I righted the aeroplane that dear little powder compact dropped down into the fuselage beneath the control wires under my feet. It was just sitting there, shining up at me. There was no immediate danger of it jamming anything but I couldn't reach it to make certain.'

When Diana landed she taxied close to the watch office. As she was shutting down the plane a tall, handsome RAF flight lieutenant approached. With a jaunty step, he was up on her wing, wearing a charming smile. When Diana pulled back the canopy his expression changed to one of disbelief.

'I was told,' he gasped, 'that a very, very pretty girl was bringing us a new aircraft. All I can see is some ghastly clown!'

Diana was a touch disappointed. 'He jumped down from the wing like a maggot from a bait tin, turned on his heels, then fled away to a parked car, clanked the gears and was gone. It might have been the start of a beautiful friendship, even a romance . . .'

* * *

John Wilkinson, 1944

Meanwhile, John Wilkinson, who, as a sixteen-year-old, had witnessed the Battle of Britain unfold in the skies above his school in Sussex, had just been awarded 'Best Flying Cadet' after completing a year's training in the safe blue skies of Florida before returning to England in 1943. For advanced fighter tuition he was sent to Northumbria and onto battle-weary Spitfire Mark Is. But the weathered fighters still retained a seductive quality for Wilkinson. 'I found a great joy in flying which was greatly enhanced by the graceful and powerful Spitfire. Just like a bird, it was perhaps the one machine in that period that was most incredibly attuned to flight.'

Despite the odd mechanical failure, the trainees threw their Spitfires into mock dogfights, underlining that action was imminent for God-fearing Wilkinson. 'These exercises were the pinnacle of my preparation for one-on-one mortal combat. They magnified the seriousness of close-in aerial fighting where we were to engage the enemy at point-blank range, as close as 100 to 250 yards, knowing that one of us was about to die.' Wilkinson knew that his own God-given attributes would also stand him in good stead in the fight. 'The Lord blessed me with an uncanny ability to see things faster and at greater distances than my contemporaries.'

When Wilkinson moved south to join 41 Squadron he found himself on the grass airstrip of Lympne and accommodated in the sumptuous surroundings of Port Lympne mansion where, a decade earlier, the glamorous Auxiliary Air Force pilots had rested and played during the carefree days in the Kent countryside. During his flight training in America, where much pilot training was now being carried out in the clear, enemy-free skies, Wilkinson had developed a strong friendship with a Jamaican pilot called George 'Bunny' Henriquez. He regularly visited Bunny's family, who had moved to Clewiston, Florida, and spent long Sundays entertaining his young daughter.

Of course, the war intruded on their friendship: Bunny was posted to fly Lancaster bombers with 630 Squadron, based in East Kirkby in Lincolnshire, and Wilkinson onto Spitfires with 41 Squadron in southern England. One day in the summer of 1944

Wilkinson had an urge to visit Bunny and got permission to fly from Lympe in a repaired Spitfire that needed testing. The trip was an enjoyable diversion from the war and Bunny took great pleasure in showing his friend around the Lancaster. Neither discussed the losses that Bomber Command was experiencing in daily missions over Germany. When Wilkinson took off to return south he circled over the base where Bunny was standing by his Lancaster. Then he felt an overwhelming sense of doom. 'I had a strong premonition that Bunny would soon be killed.'

Aside from the strange surroundings and premonitions, Wilkinson's journey from the ruins surrounding St Paul's Cathedral to becoming a Spitfire pilot had been fulfilled. Soon he would be needed for the fight. But it would not be in the way he had imagined.

* * *

In a few short months a strong romance had blossomed between the taciturn fighter pilot Terry Kearins and bubbly Lancashire lass, Edith Bardsley. Both had volunteered for the services. Kearins was the apprentice farmer-turned-Spitfire pilot from New Zealand with the thatch of jet-black hair who had volunteered for the air force. Edith had joined the Royal Navy as a nurse.

In the spring of 1943 they met at a club after Edith had been asked to join a friend who was courting another New Zealander. Edith was immediately attracted to Kearins' quiet charm and the big hands that pushed through his thick hair. His chequered silk scarf and pilot's wings on his chest also helped. Kearins was similarly infatuated. He could not resist being drawn to Edith's warm, enthusiastic conversation and ability to find mirth in most situations. They were very happy. Then one night, Kearins' usually serious features creased into a broad smile when Edith gave a firm 'yes' to his offer of marriage.

A few days later, on 15 July 1943, he found himself patting his breast pocket for the umpteenth time, checking Edith's picture was still there as he settled into the Spitfire's cockpit.[5]

Kearins had listened attentively as 485 Squadron's boss, Johnny Checketts, ran them through the plan for a Ramrod bombing mission near Amiens, seventy-five miles south of Calais, escorting USAAF Boston medium bombers on a daylight raid. On only his second operational mission, Kearins was to fly as Checketts' number two.

Shortly after 4.30pm, the Bostons dropped their load on the railway network at Poix and were on their way back when they were jumped by twenty Fw190s. Kearins and Checketts managed to destroy one between them but then Kearins was hit. Checketts watched in dismay as the Spitfire plummeted towards the ground without seeing a parachute deploy.

When Checketts got back to base he glumly wrote up an official report: 'Flight Sergeant Kearins was seen to go down in flames and crashed on land. He did not bail out.'

* * *

The cockpit began to feel very small and tomb-like to Terry Kearins as his Spitfire rolled over and began a headlong plunge to earth. Flames shot out of the engine cowling and over the cockpit hood. Fire licked at his boots. Kearins knew that very soon the flames would reach the fuel tank, with catastrophic effect. Momentarily, he shut his eyes to focus. There had been challenging and dangerous times before. Especially on farm machinery that went wrong and could brutally wrench off an arm or chop a man in half. *If you remain calm*, his father had told, *you'll do OK*.

The sharp pain of burning in his legs made him catch his breath. Kearins pushed aside the fear of incineration, unhooked his helmet leads then loosened his seat harness. As the plane buffeted down on its final flight, he released the cockpit canopy, feeling the flames lick against his legs. Then he was out of the aircraft. The cool breeze and silence were a welcome change from the inferno he had just left.

Descending under his parachute canopy, Kearins landed in a

field close to three children. Biting back the pain from his burns, he used his schoolboy French to ask them to hide his dinghy, parachute harness and flying jacket. One of the children led Kearins to a wood 500 yards away, where the pilot hid his Mae West, tunic and English money under some blackberry bushes,[6] close to the village of Le Quesnoy-en-Artois, thirty miles north of Amiens and twenty miles from the Channel coast.

German search parties were not far behind and with them came vicious Alsatian dogs.

I stink of burns, they'll sniff me out, Kearins thought as he lay between a tree stump and a hedge, trying to control his racing heart and the thought of capture or worse. The barking came closer then receded. Despite the excruciating pain in his burnt legs, Kearins kept silent.

Fortunately, dusk was only a few hours away. As the adrenaline ebbed away he felt his body throb with pain. He looked at his legs. Some of his clothing had been burnt onto his skin. The burns bubbled and blistered. He bit down on a thick piece of wood when the pain became unbearable. Thankfully, the summer weather was warm. There was no way he would have survived a winter's night.

For the next two days Kearins managed to avoid German patrols, but with his strength beginning to drain away he had to find help.

In a desperate situation, he risked everything by exposing his position and calling out to a passing woman from behind a tree, where he'd found some unripe apples. She ignored him. As Kearins turned to hobble off, he stumbled then collapsed. The woman turned around. Emilie Forgez had made a decision which could have fateful consequences. She took the airman into the farmhouse. An hour later her husband returned and agreed they should give him shelter.

When they stripped off his uniform they found his legs had become a festering mess. Their local doctor was a German sympathiser so their only option was to nurse him themselves.

Over the next six weeks M. Forgez discreetly visited several chemist's, picking up bandages and burns ointment. At one point a fever gripped Kearins so severely that they believed he would die. They decided to secretly bury him in their grounds so no word of his presence could leak out. The penalty for harbouring Allied airmen was execution or a concentration camp.

Luckily, Kearins' burns slowly began to heal; the festering was defeated by M. Forgez's constant cleaning and changing of bandages. Soon he was on his feet and eager to get outside. M. Forgez quickly realised his skill as a farmer and soon Kearins was helping harvest his tobacco. At times he would lie down amid the thick, tall greenery and look up at Allied aircraft crossing the sky and dream of one day being back in a Spitfire.

He also put the foliage to another advantage. M. Forgez had mentioned that a new secret rocket site was being built nearby. Kearins made sure he got close enough to observe the 100ft-long steel elevated ski ramp built for a long, rocket-like missile. Alongside it were fuel and other storage facilities, all carefully camouflaged from above.

With the Gestapo wary of prying eyes a cover story was invented for Kearins and put to good use. In answer to why he hadn't been drafted as a construction labourer, Kearins was to be a deaf and dumb farmhand who was the boyfriend of M. Forgez's daughter. Kearins' long and dishevelled beard and hair added further plausibility to the role.

During one Gestapo visit, Kearins was shunted quickly into the tobacco barns amid all the harvested plants. For half an hour his heart thudded furiously as he listened to the secret police speak to M. Forgez on the other side of the wall.

Kearins knew he would be endangering both his French hosts and himself if he continued to stay any longer. He also wanted to get back home. His thoughts were occupied with Edith. Had she been told he had made it out of the burning aircraft? Did she think of him? Had she found someone else? Kearins knew he had to get home. He asked M. Forgez to contact the Resistance.

On a mild day early in October 1943, three months after Kearins had parachuted from his Spitfire over France, M. Forgez's twelve-year-old nephew appeared at the farm saying the Resistance was ready to activate his escape.

A few days later, Kearins, M. Forgez and his nephew set off on bicycles. Once they were stopped by a German staff car asking for directions. As the Frenchmen spoke amiably to the Germans, Kearins felt helpless and terrified. These brave French people were risking their lives for him in the full knowledge that betrayal or discovery would lead to dreadful torture and death. At least 20,000 French were executed resisting the occupation and helping the Allies.

The German officers seemed content, gave the cyclists a cursory wave and drove on. Then they came to a village filled with German armoured vehicles. Kearins' stare remained straight ahead as he passed lounging soldiers, hoping his beard and long hair would ward off questions. After cycling six miles, they arrived in the hamlet of Le Ponchel, close to the medieval battlefield of Crécy, at the home of a teacher who led the local Resistance. Issued with forged papers, Kearins was placed in the hands of the Bordeaux-Loupiac Resistance.

A few days later the door to the house where he'd been given refuge opened and in walked Squadron Leader Checketts, the pilot who had been Kearins' wingman and who had reported him shot down in flames.

'Johnny!' Kearins exclaimed.

'Terry? Terry Kearins?' Checketts stared at the long-haired, dishevelled man before him; he could not believe the pilot he had reported going down as a 'flamer' had somehow survived. The pair shook hands, then Checketts brought him into a tight hug.

Checketts described how seven weeks after Kearins' apparent demise he had been leading his squadron of Spitfires over Abbeville, close to the Channel coast and a dozen miles from their location, when he found himself surrounded by six Fw190s. 'I managed to bag one, possibly a second and certainly damaged a third. But the buggers kept coming at me. I had to bail out.'

Checketts had also suffered burns and injured his spine but had been spirited away into the capable hands of the Resistance. And now, here he was!

The next day a Frenchman arrived at the house in a pre-war car not expropriated by the Germans. The plan was to drive the airmen the twenty-five miles to Amiens where they would catch a train to Paris.

Kearins and Checketts looked at each other. *Surely it was a hell of a risk?* But there was nothing like Gallic bravado and hiding in open view.

They had only got a few miles down the road when they were stopped at a German army checkpoint. The two Spitfire pilots glanced at each other, exchanging nervous looks as the driver wound down his window. It was the first time their fake papers would be tested.

The young, freckled German soldier studied their papers for a moment, leaned in the window, glanced at Kearins and Checketts, then handed the documents back. Kearins could not help thinking that the driver would have been shot on the spot had they been rumbled.

An hour later the driver pulled up close to the train station then went inside to purchase tickets. By now Kearins had picked up a passable amount of French for basic inquiries but felt a growing fear of discovery as they waited. The car door opened and the French driver got in and drove a short distance, then stopped and handed over their tickets.

They were told the train left in one hour, so rather than hang around the station with its French and German security forces, they should move into town. The pair nodded in understanding. He shook their hands. *Bonne chance.*

Carefully avoiding cafes full of Germans and police patrols, the pair ambled around Amiens then, a few minutes before departure, strode purposefully to their platform and got on the train without being challenged.

White smoke drifted out of the engine boiler as it remained at rest. Kearins and Checketts sat in their wooden third-class seats wondering why the train remained stationary. A glance out of the window showed soldiers marching down the platform then boarding. A minute later a whistle blew, the driver sounded a bell and smoke floated past their window as they rolled towards Paris. The pilots exchanged worried looks; their situation was becoming more perilous by the minute.

They spent the journey largely in silence as Kearins went over in his mind the description they had been given of the woman they were to follow at Gare du Nord station. She was in a black beret and red coat with lavender in the lapel. *But what the hell happened if they missed her? If she didn't arrive?* They had been told no more information. No names, no addresses, nothing. They'd just have to take their chances in Paris.

Gare du Nord bustled with civilians in dark clothing, the field grey of German troops and dark blue of gendarmerie. Kearins exchanged a look with a dark-eyed young woman with distinct cheekbones. He stared at her red coat, beret and the purple foliage in her lapel. Without a nod she turned and began walking towards an exit. Kearins put his hand on Checketts' back and followed. They had been told to make no physical contact but just to keep her in sight. The station was alive with security as they followed her to the metro station by a route that avoided the checkpoints.

The woman then led them across Paris to the Porte de Versailles in the 15th arrondissement to a building where another twenty escapees were being sheltered. There were back-slaps and animated conversations as the men shared their experiences, but all were careful to avoid mentioning any names.

For two days the airmen rested, making food together with the rations they were given, including a big batch of French onion soup that one serviceman had learned to cook during his time on the run.

Then one morning Kearins and Checketts were taken aside by a grey-haired Resistance man who told them the Spitfire pilots were considered a priority. They would be sent to Brittany and then picked up by Royal Navy submarine to get home. The man held out his hand and wished them luck.

The journey to Brittany would take two or three days, with several changes of train and the constant chance of someone spotting a mistake in the forged documents or their poor French, or simply that one would crack. To lessen the chances of discovery they travelled overnight.

Kearins found himself fast asleep on Checketts' shoulder when the carriage door slid open and the dreaded word 'papers' was barked. Two French policemen stood at the doorway holding out their hands. Kearins scratched at his beard, muttering some unintelligible French, then reached inside his jacket for the document that had been forged in Paris.

The policeman asked where they were going and appeared satisfied by the response. The papers were thrust back into their hands and the door slammed shut. Despite his languid demeanour, Kearins took a few deep breaths then thrust his shaking hand into his coat pocket.

Running in a circuitous route, and after several days spent in safe houses, the Spitfire men had nearly completed their 400-mile journey to the Brittany coast. Kearins looked out of the window at the rolling countryside and allowed himself to relax and dream of England's green pastures and Edith.

'Monsieur.' The word was hurried and just above a whisper. Kearins looked into the big brown eyes of a young French boy. A crumpled piece of paper was thrust into his hand and the boy was gone.

Checketts carefully unfolded the scrap of paper. They were to get off the train immediately. At the next station.

They were two stops from Quimper and both tired from the long hours of travel and living under the constant danger of discovery.

Kearins stared at the floor. *Damn it.* They were so close to their destination. After Quimper there would be no more long, dangerous train journeys, no more heart-stopping demands for papers or imagining what the Gestapo would do to extract every morsel of information they knew about the Resistance and Spitfires.

The train slowed and came to a halt. There was no security on the platform. As they walked out of the station they heard footsteps behind. Kearins glanced over his shoulder at a middle-aged French woman in black shawl. She held his eye momentarily then quickened her pace. As she passed, they heard the word *'Allez'* from under the shawl. The pilots kept their distance as she escorted them to a church deep in the countryside.

At the weathered church door they were told that, as a result of Resistance sabotage, the Germans were everywhere and in particular searching people coming off the mainline trains. The pair would be put on a local train.

By the late afternoon, the men found themselves on a small train that chugged along the line, stopping frequently before it reached Quimper. No attention was paid by the police to the local people who got off.

By now Kearins and Checketts had got used to being contacted by someone after leaving a train station. But for a good half-hour they walked nervously around Quimper until a look was given by a stranger and they were taken to a cafe. The owners gave them a room upstairs and, for the first time in a week, the men lay down on a bed and fell into a deep sleep.

Kearins could see it was dark outside as he opened his eyes. There was rapping again at the door. Nerves jangling, he bolted upright as the frightened face of the cafe proprietor's wife appeared. Security police were at the door! Kearins heard some loud thudding come from down the stairs. She ordered them to go out the back door.

The men tiptoed down the stairs and out the back door into a vegetable garden, which had a large chicken coop. The woman whispered for them to hide. Kearins joined the chickens, crawling into the excrement-stinking henhouse. At first there were a few disgruntled clucks from the birds but as Kearins crouched silently they gradually subsided. Checketts, meanwhile, lay flat among the abundant cabbage patch.

After what seemed like an age the owners came outside and whispered their names. The Gestapo had barely searched the cafe after they realised they were at the wrong address.

The men were then taken to a bakery in the coastal fishing village of Camaret-sur-Mer, at the end of a peninsula across the water from the big naval port of Brest. They were led to a long room at the back of the bakery where they found themselves inhaling the body odour of a group of twenty-six scruffy and unshaven men. All evaders like themselves.

A fresh-smelling baguette was thrust into their hands and Kearins chewed carefully, savouring each mouthful.

The pilots were told to *forget about the sub* as the best they could hope for was a fishing smack to get them back home. They were also warned that the Germans were highly vigilant, checking every boat that left and returned to harbour, as well as any dinghies going out to moored vessels. The entire fishing fleet had been told they would face reprisals if just one single boat failed to come back within the twenty-four hours they were permitted to fish.

Kearins nodded as he absorbed the information. Getting out of there would require someone to take an incredible risk.

A few hours later the baker came in and went straight to the Spitfire pilots. It was dusk outside and a dinghy was waiting to take them out to the boat.

Cloaked by the gloom, the fisherman carefully dipped the oars in the sea, propelling them silently over the water to the boat looming against the darkening sky. Kearins could make out the name *Suzette* along the side of the 30ft lobster boat. Thick netting covered its decks and the smell of dried shellfish drifted out of its deck planks.

The men were shown down into a small cabin, which had a bunk bed, small table, bench and a bucket for a loo.

Kearins went to lie down on the bed.

'Non.' The Frenchman pointed back up through the hatch. *'Ici.'* The fisherman indicated the thick pile of netting, motioning for the pilots to crawl underneath. The smell of seaweed, the ocean and lobsters was strong but not overpowering as Kearins tunnelled his way into the middle of the netting. *If it takes me back to Edith, it can stink to high hell for all I care.*

Terry Kearins disguised as a French farmworker

Kearins knew the journey would be 150 miles out over the Atlantic and across the Channel on a single engine at the risk of autumn gales. Still, if it got him back home into the arms of Edith and a decent bed, he would take his chances.

Checketts was in agreement. He also wanted to return to Spitfires and get back at the *Huns* who had shot him down. The pair did not remain alone for long. Over the next few days another eleven men came aboard before the crew called a halt, saying they were overloaded. Then the weather closed in.

They waited day after day under the nets as the wind blew and a swell lifted the boat at anchor. 'I bet you £5 that we escape,' Kearins whispered, scratching his thick moustache.

'I bet we bloody don't and I look forward to spending your five quid in a POW camp,' Checketts fired back.

On the fifth day a crew member on board demanded total silence. A German security patrol was approaching to inspect the boat prior to departure. Kearins could hardly breathe as he heard the distinct sound of jackboots on wooden decking. The odd kick was given to the ship's insides and someone lifted the nets but despite there being thirteen escapees on board none was discovered.

Kearins listened as the last jackboots left the deck and boarded the launch back to Cameret-sur-Mer. He was lying in the foetal position, cramping in the agony of needing to empty his bowels. Their diet of dry bread and cold fish soup had not agreed with him and the necessary trips to the stinking bucket in the hold, filled with the twelve other evaders' faeces and urine, were becoming a wretched experience.

He hurriedly crawled out of the netting through the roughly shaped tunnel they had made. Still on his belly he slipped down into the hold and saw to his delight that no one else had made it to the bucket. *Thank God*.

He sat down and emptied his bowls in relief. Thankfully, the bucket was unsoiled. Checketts had ordered for it to be cleaned after use, where possible, in case its contents made the police think people were living aboard. Kearins had been on the loo for less than a minute when others arrived, asking him to hurry. He used a large piece of newspaper to wipe himself then left the bucket for the next man to dispose of the contents. The man in line was only too grateful to have its use.

The next day, their sixth on board, the *Suzette* moved to the outer harbour where she was boarded again prior to being allowed to go out and lay the lobster pots. The Germans carried out a cursory check and the boat was allowed to putter out of Camaret-sur-Mer into the Atlantic.

As dusk approached, the crew allowed her to drift out to sea under cover of darkness. When some distance from land, Kearins heard a rumble from the engine room. After a few tentative coughs, the spluttering turned into something more substantial. It was not the roar of a Spitfire's Merlin engine but just as welcome. If the engine failed they would drift onto Brittany's cruel rocks and share the fate of many thousands of sailors.

As the boat crept away from France, shrouded in the blackness of night, Kearins climbed out from his cave inside the netting to stand on deck. For the first time in over three months he breathed in air that tasted of freedom. If the autumnal Atlantic storms held off and the engine remained constant, they'd be home within two days. Sitting under the moonlight he allowed the dream of being in Edith's arms to settle over him. He could not help the playful grin that came to his cheeks.

The pent-up fear of the last week was released as others joined him on deck, slapping backs and swapping stories of near-discovery, a week of frozen nights and unpleasant trips to the 'heads'. They knew they would soon all be back home, in the company of sweethearts and family, some of whom may well have given them up for dead. Then another realisation came: *we'll be back in the war.*

They all agreed on one thing. They would return to help fight for the cause to liberate Europe because more than most they had seen the hideous nature of the regime that now gripped it. And they could repay the debt they owed to the many courageous French men and women who had risked their lives to help them.

On 25 October 1943, the distinctive rocks of Land's End came into view. Within a few hours the *Suzette* was chugging into Penzance. Kearins found himself waving at other fishing boats and a small navy patrol vessel as they motored in. The weather had been kind and the engine had throbbed without interruption. They were home. He imagined what it would be like if Edith was waiting for him at the docks. Not that there was a chance of it, but it was a nice fantasy all the same.

As they tied up in port, there were handshakes all round, then hugs for the three French fishermen who had risked their lives and livelihoods in Brittany to save the British and Allied servicemen.

Kearins knew he had important information that he had to pass on quickly. At a debrief by MI9 military intelligence officers, he gave them the details and precise location of the rocket launching site he had spotted near M. Forgez's farm. It was added to the flow of information the security services were receiving that the Nazis had a deadly secret weapon with which they hoped to win the war. The location was added to the growing list of rocket sites on the Allied targeting list.

When Kearins had finished his debrief he jumped on a train to Biggin Hill to rejoin 485 Squadron. A few hours later he was standing at the bar, still in his old French clothes, complete with rope-soled shoes, and sporting a thick moustache.

'Kearins? Terry bloody Kearins?' One of the pilots came over to him, staring as if inspecting a curious animal at the zoo. He immediately offered to buy him a drink. The beers kept coming until Kearins realised he had to stay half-sober. He had an important date the next day.

He spotted Edith waiting on the platform the moment the train glided slowly into the station. He watched as her eyes searched frantically, peering into the glass panes of the carriage. *She hasn't seen me.* He slipped out of the carriage and walked towards her. She was a few steps away, side-on to him. Then she turned and almost fell into his arms. Tears fell down her face and her chest heaved with sobs. Soldiers walking past grinned.

She gripped his arms and his face like she couldn't quite believe he was there.

A few days later a coded message went out over the radio to those listening in occupied Europe: 'Jacques Lenoir has returned.' The Resistance was able to tell Madame and Monsieur Forgez that their charge was safely back.

It would be some time before they learned that the Spitfire pilot they had risked their lives to return back to health and sent on his way home had married the woman whose name he had muttered in fevered sleep. Three months after his return, the couple were wed at Edith's local church in Shaw, Lancashire.

* * *

The wolf-whistles grew in volume as the increasingly self-conscious section of young WAAF women marched towards the Spitfires at 485 Squadron's dispersal. In their smart light-blue RAF skirts and tight-fitting tunics, the half-dozen women cut quite a sight.

Marching at their front was one completely unfazed by the attention. Joe Roddis rested his spanner on the Spitfire's wing as his gaze fixed on the striking brunette. For a moment their eyes met and she held his gaze. Joe grinned and was rewarded with a fleeting smile before she returned to her professional demeanour, leading the girls into the flight office.

Joe picked up the spanner and continued to work on the aileron. But he couldn't concentrate. He jumped off the wing and strode into the office.

He introduced himself to the woman who had marched at their front. She was Betty Wood, the corporal in charge of the Motor Transport drivers.

She gave him a brief smile then Joe turned on his heel.

Outside, he took in a big lungful of air. Suddenly the burden of work at Biggin Hill seemed to lessen. He took in the surrounding green countryside with its low hills and spreading oaks and breathed in again. Life felt good. He rather liked Betty Wood.

Over the coming days the WAAF women worked alongside the men, delivering their 500-gallon fuel bowsers to wherever they were needed, night or day. The catcalls had swiftly been silenced and Joe made sure his men curtailed their swearing.

He came into frequent contact with Betty and their friendship grew during the autumn of 1943. They were both at ease in each other's company, talking about Spitfires, the war and anything else that came to mind.

Betty had just finished refuelling a Spitfire Joe was working on when he looked up from under the engine cowling and asked if she'd like to join him for a drink later. Still holding the fuel nozzle, Betty gave him a quick nod and a grin. Betty had already told him that she was engaged to her childhood sweetheart, an RAF sergeant serving in the Middle East, and wore the engagement ring with pride. But it seemed her commitment to someone else allowed them to step out together without pressure. Joe honoured her rule of no 'hanky panky' and it made for a magical time.

Most days they would be working on Spitfires from dawn, allowing them to finish in the early afternoon. The pair would then board the Biggin Hill train to London where evenings would be spent dancing to the jazz bands at the Hammersmith Palais or at the Covent Garden Opera House. They had fun, laughed a lot and for a moment forgot the war. 'Betty loved life and lived it to the full,' Joe recalled. 'I don't know why we became such good friends, we just hit it off. Our time together was an escape from the war and the military. It was pure friendship. Nothing else.'

Betty's intolerance of immature behaviour became more apparent after she met a group of American pilots sent to Biggin Hill to gain tactical experience. One took her on a flight in a Miles Magister trainer then proceeded to throw the plane about in a series of acrobatics with the obvious intention of making her vomit. Betty managed to retain her dignity but back on the ground she gave the American a hammering kick to the shins. The officer and his friends took it in good humour and nicknamed her 'Butch' in grudging respect.

It was a blissful time for Joe and Betty until the war stepped in. Like everyone else in Flight Command, 485 Squadron was suffering losses during the cross-Channel sorties, although thanks to the French Resistance at least some had been recovered, including Johnny Checketts and Terry Kearins. By late 1943, the squadron needed a rest and was moved to Drem, Scotland.

When a few months later they moved back south to Selsey on the West Sussex coast, Joe discovered that Betty had just been posted up to Inverness. Fate was conspiring to keep them apart.

One day Joe was sent to work away from his base. That very same day Betty arrived down from Scotland on leave and decided to go to her home in Worthing, West Sussex, and hopefully pay Joe a surprise visit at Selsey. Yet again they missed each other, so she left a note asking him to meet her the next day. Joe eagerly jumped on the train to Worthing the next morning. When it pulled into the station he was leaning out of the window, keen to see Betty after months apart. Their eyes met but there was something different in her face, something mournful.

Joe asked her what the matter was after they briefly embraced.

Her fiancé was coming back home from the Middle East. She looked down the line. He'd be back in a few days.

She took Joe's hand, saying there was a tea dance on at Worthing town hall.

As they sat down with a cup of tea, Betty was quiet as Joe chatted. Then a slow foxtrot came on. Their favourite number. They looked at each other and without speaking slipped onto the dancefloor.

When the foxtrot finished, tears streamed down Betty's face as she rested on Joe's shoulder. He took her hand and led her off the dancefloor and outside into the fresh air. They walked the short distance to the train station, both turning together when they heard the distant purr of a Merlin engine as a lone Spitfire streaked over Worthing Pier.

Joe fumbled in his pocket for his train ticket. Betty squeezed his arm. For a moment he was lost in her gaze. Should he ask her to go with him, to be with him? He instantly quashed the thought. He had given his word that he would respect her commitment.

The whistle of the arriving train broke the moment. Joe sighed then gently released her fingers clinging to his arm.

Her cheeks were damp as they embraced next to the carriage.

Carriage doors slammed behind them. The guard's whistle sounded.

Joe pushed himself out of her arms and boarded. 'Goodbye, Betty!' he shouted through the window, waving.

He saw her lips quiver. She turned away.

Joe shook his head. 'Goodbye, Betty Wood.'

* * *

The tall stands of Lord's Cricket Ground struck Brian Bird as symbolic of power and authority. He stared in awe, imagining what they had witnessed. Under their shadow Len Hutton had made 196 against the West Indies two months before the war began; Bradman had scored heavily here too ...

'Snap out of your bloody civilian coma,' a flight sergeant shouted as Bird gawped. It was March 1943 and he had been summoned to the RAF's Aircrew Training Centre based at the HQ of cricket.

Bird had come a long way since hiding among the corn from Luftwaffe bombers while working as a sixteen-year-old farmhand in Kent during the Battle of Britain. It seemed a long time too since he'd ridden his bicycle to church on 3 September 1939 to tell his stepfather that war had been declared. But his plan to get back at those who attacked his country was still on track. He was passed fit for flying and after basic training he sailed to South Africa where he qualified as a pilot.

A few months later he was sitting in a Hurricane outside Cairo in Egypt waiting to go solo in his first ever fighter. 'In my hands were the controls of a mighty fighter which had played such an important role in the Battle of Britain and almost unexpectedly I felt entirely at ease.

'As if providing icing to a rather special cake, the view from my cockpit was utterly staggering, with the full length of the Suez Canal stretched out beneath my port wing and vast areas of the Sinai Desert to starboard.'

Bird spent the next fortnight notching up ten hours solo in the Hurricane then it was time for the main event: the Spitfire. He immediately noticed subtle differences. 'The Spitfire was a lighter aircraft than the Hurricane, both in weight terms and aerodynamic handling. Whereas in the Hurricane small pilot errors escaped unpunished this was not the case with the Spitfire. But it was an aircraft which gave even the most nervous of pilots a quick shot of confidence.'

Bird, determined to get in the action before the fighting ended, took to the advanced operational training with enthusiasm. As a young farmhand in 1940 he had seen Spitfires and Hurricanes fight for Britain's survival in the skies of Kent. He now had the chance to fly them into combat himself.

His skill and determination were noted by instructors as he practised battle formations, steep climbs, dive-bombing, air-to-air firing and, of course, aerial combat. He was sent to advanced fighter training. Brian Bird was going to war.

* * *

Victory in the Battle of Britain bought the RAF time in which to properly train its pilots. No longer were men thrown straight into the front line with just a dozen or so hours in a Spitfire under their belts. Instead, thousands were sent to America or Canada to train in clear blue skies free from marauding Messerschmitts. Then they were swiftly transported home past the hunting U-boats in the relative luxury of the *Queen Elizabeth* liner.

Thus Ken French had already had experiences beyond the gushing trout streams of County Cork when he arrived back in England after a year in America. The Protestant Irishman, whose family had been targeted by the IRA, had seen a bit of the world since leaving Ireland just before the outbreak of war to get a job as a clerk in Southend, Essex, prior to being accepted into the RAF.

On the six-day Atlantic crossing, the pilots constantly speculated about what it would be like to fly a Spitfire. By March 1943, Ken French had arrived at Eshott in Northumberland, where he was confronted by a long line of Spitfires waiting for their pilots.

His impatience and anticipation to get airborne in a Spit were held up as they relentlessly practised on the ground, learning how to use the instruments blindfolded then tantalisingly being allowed to taxi down the runway.

Then, on 31 March, French found himself strapped into a Spitfire with its Merlin engine purring. *Here I am, a young lad from Cork, in the world's finest fighter!*

'Green One to tower, permission to take off?' French tried to sound calm as his heart thudded, waiting for the response.

'Permission granted, Green One. Good luck.'

French pushed the throttle lever forward and the Spitfire responded instantly. 'I was aware of a greater power than I had on any other aircraft. Once I got moving I raised the tail by easing the stick forward to allow me to see where I was going and in a very short time I was in the air and climbing away. I stayed up for just over an hour and found it a real pleasure to fly. But what goes up must come down and I knew this would be the difficult part. The Spitfire landing speed was faster than anything I had experienced before. It also had a very narrow undercarriage, which called for extra care once you touched down. If you did not keep it straight it could spin around on the ground and do what was called a "ground loop".'

French need not have worried. He made a perfect landing, emerging from the cockpit with his usual grin spread broadly across his face.

'My first trip in a Spitfire was a glorious experience. I was part of this beautiful machine and it almost flew itself. I spent an hour in the air and felt so wonderful looking all around me and down at the earth far below me.'

But in wartime, learning to fly a Spitfire also came with the necessity of having to fight it. French would have to go to war in Spitfire Mark Vs that were outclassed by the Focke-Wulf 190, which was earning the nickname of the 'Butcher Bird'.[7]

He was posted to 66 Squadron based in Kenley, Surrey, and on 11 September he was strapped in his plane and battling with nerves minutes before his first operational sortie escorting Mitchell bombers over northern France. The new pilots had been told in no uncertain terms that they would be up against the more capable 190s and that casualties were inevitable.

French tried to wear his customary grin as his flight sergeant strapped him in. 'Knowing it was my first trip he helped me, which was a nice gesture. His parting words were that he would say a prayer for me. I was not religious but I'm sure most of us said a quiet prayer from time to time.'

No Fw190s came up to meet them but over Le Havre the German AA opened up, sending accurate shells towards the planes.

'This was my first operational sortie and here were people trying to kill us, which was a strange thought. Most of the flak was centred on the bombers but I was very aware that if one of those puffs of smoke hit me there was a good chance I could die. It was a sobering thought.'

The sorties continued, along with the inevitable casualties. In early October, French's room-mate Alan Edwards failed to return from a mission over France. Despite an effort to find any sign of a crash he had simply disappeared and was reported 'missing in action'.

It was yet another sobering moment for French but not much time was allowed for reflection. 'Alan was a friend of mine and it hit home. It was funny really, one minute we'd be flying, perhaps someone dying, then we would land and if there were no other ops, we'd pile into cars and head out to the pubs or to a party. We would have a few drinks together. I don't think we got that close to anyone as people would arrive and sometimes be missing a few days later. Everything was always changing. Just because someone was shot down didn't stop anything – we were back in action a bit later that day.

'Alan's mother kept writing to me, desperate for information, but there was nothing I could tell her. It was a very sad situation. Of course we felt sorry for them, but we also made light of it – the attitude was, "I'll have his flying jacket; he won't need that any more!" Someone came to take Alan's things away and that was that. You didn't have time to dwell on it – there was a war to be fought.'

It was only months later that they were told Edwards had survived the crash, been captured and now languished in a POW camp.

There was one relief from the stress of continuously flying in the knowledge that the next day you might be the unlucky one. A good party.

'We lived life to the full. You had to – you didn't know if you'd be around to have a drink next day! After a few drinks, it took the edge off the reality, the war and what it meant. One minute we were battling Fw190s or seeing bombers shot down, next we'd be partying in the mess. It's daft to think like this now, but the partying took your mind off what might happen the next day. You could die the next day.'

Some of the antics were perhaps inevitable for young men living under immense pressure. During one such party, French found himself hanging upside down from the rafters of a pub.

'Don't ask how I got there but all the money fell out of my pockets. This was quickly gathered up and used to buy the next round of drinks. It might sound frivolous but it was fun and I am sure we all felt much better for it. If we were flying the next morning and still had a hangover we would plug into our Spitfire's oxygen supply and this usually did the trick.'

Oxygen was fitted to the planes so that pilots could fight above 10,000ft with all senses fully functioning. During training, they were given a demonstration of the effects of oxygen depletion. They were put in a chamber which gradually had the oxygen reduced, as would happen in a climbing aircraft. 'All but one of us were fed with oxygen to compensate for this and we watched the behaviour of the one who was not getting any. He was given a pencil and paper and asked to keep writing his name and address. He did this quite normally at first but his writing gradually deteriorated as he was starved of oxygen until it eventually became no more than a scribble. When they turned on his supply and showed him what he had written he could not believe it as he thought he was writing quite normally right up to the end.'

French was to experience himself the potentially fatal effects of oxygen depletion. Poor weather had forced the squadron to 30,000ft to escort back home a large force of Flying Fortresses and Liberators, which was returning from a Berlin raid.

The intense cold of high-altitude flying was the first thing to hit home. 'Our only heating was what we got from our engines and the planes were by no means draughtproof. I wore four pairs of gloves but my hands still went dead and I lost all feeling in my feet. I had frost on my eyelids and I could see ice forming on my wings. My windscreen and hood were frosting up, making it difficult to see out. Then I blacked out. I fell some distance before coming round. I fought to get the plane under control again. I increased my oxygen supply and rejoined my friends.

'The danger with lack of oxygen is that you get no warning. In fact, you think you're functioning normally right up to the point you black out.'

French knew that he had to learn fast. Soon the assault on Europe would begin. They started training hard to use the Spitfire in its evolving ground-attack role.

* * *

Nigel Tangye and Ann Todd on their wedding day in Chelsea, October 1939

The actress Ann Todd had suffered many sleepless nights wondering if her Spitfire pilot husband Nigel Tangye would return home safe. She had had a curious war, giving birth during a bombing raid, and performing on stage, including one show in front of Queen Mary.[8]

Tangye had also done well from the proceeds of *Teach Yourself to Fly*, a book he had written in 1938 and that the Air Ministry recommended to all trainee pilots. Together they purchased a London home.

Tangye was a man of adventure, who had covered the Spanish Civil War as a journalist and as an MI5 agent spying on German forces. During the war, he had been appointed as the chief liaison officer between the RAF and the US 8th Air Force operating out of Britain. To do so, he had been given his own personal Spitfire to get about.

Tangye was the type of single-minded man who, when he wanted something, generally got it. Being in his thirties, he found it difficult to get onto an operational fighting squadron and instead found himself during the Battle of Britain and afterwards either as an instructor or doing liaison jobs. He was itching to see some sort of action. He had a friend in charge of the PR Spitfires at RAF Benson in Oxfordshire, who agreed to give Tangye a trial. It seemed a perfect fit for the Cornish adventurer. 'By doing this I would expose no one to danger but myself. I could be working at my Air Ministry desk in the morning, flying over Europe in the afternoon and, rather grotesquely, home for dinner in the evening. Further, flying under the conditions of extreme isolation suited my loner temperament perfectly.'

His first mission in the reconnaissance Spitfire high over occupied Europe gave Tangye an unforgettable experience. 'A quarter of an hour of briefing and I was off in this superb machine. I was not prepared for the awesome majesty of flying really high and alone. The paradox of being poised as on a cliff edge, between a dark night-blue sky and the sun flooding the earth's surface far beneath.

'The air is so rare that the controls are flabby, making flying and stalling recognisable only by a hair's breadth.

'After half an hour of feeling my way, the majesty of the scene won over its awesomeness and I felt a great wonder at the privilege of being equipped to enter such a realm of the gods.'

After several missions Tangye's celestial experiences came to an abrupt end when he collapsed from high-altitude sickness. The high flying did not, however, sufficiently scratch the itch for adventure.

One night as he lay in bed at their Chelsea flat in London holding Ann tight, her son David from her first marriage sleeping peacefully next door, he began asking her about what it had been like during the bombings.[9] Ann described the horror of trying to protect her child then the intense feeling of relief when the attack was over.

Tangye promised to finish the Anderson air-raid shelter in the garden as soon as he could. Then he brought up the subject of flying on a bombing mission himself. An opportunity had come up with the Americans to go in one of their mighty Flying Fortresses. Nigel thought it would be different to being alone in a Spitfire as he'd have six other crew for company. He also suggested it might help him be more in tune with the RAF's daylight bombing problems. Plus it was only a propaganda leaflet-dropping mission, not a bombing run.

Ann knew better than to argue with the man who, even before their marriage, had earned the reputation of a swashbuckling adventurer. She turned over and went to sleep. Tangye lay awake, imagining himself in the bomber's cockpit.

A few days later his American contact phoned to say his flight as an observer on a B17 Flying Fortress had been confirmed. They were to drop three tons of propaganda leaflets over St Nazaire, the heavily defended dry dock on the north-western coast of France.

Tangye felt both excitement and nerves as he landed his Spitfire at the USAAF airfield outside Nottingham. The sense of imminent adventure was once again upon him. He spent the afternoon getting kitted up, trying on the big bomber-crew overalls, boots, helmets and thick gloves. For at least an hour he went through the emergency drills of exiting a crippled aircraft. The prospect of being entombed inside the burning hulk of a B17 as it plummeted earthwards was brought home. It contrasted with the relative ease with which you could escape from the Spitfire cockpit. The very bulk of his flying kit coupled with parachute made it seem an impossible task to squeeze through the escape hatch. Hopefully the adrenaline would see him through. And at least he had others for company.

His thoughts turned back to the Spitfire, where everything was down to just the pilot's responsibility. There was no one else to consult or to rely on.

'Chow time, sir.' A grinning head popped up through the hatch. Tangye checked his watch: 5pm. In three and a half hours he'd be airborne and committed to whatever the crew faced.

As he sat down in the 'chow hall', a mighty dish of stew, creamed carrots, sauté potatoes and beetroot was put in front of him. Despite the impending mission, he found his appetite and ate the lot, then the pineapple that followed, finishing with the excellent coffee the Americans always served.

An hour later they were called in for a mission briefing. Tangye squirmed in his seat nervously at the intelligence officer's conclusion. 'You'll have vapour trails all the way so keep a sharp lookout for cat's-eye fighters.'[10]

Tangye went to the crew room where conversation turned to the near-misses of the previous night's operation. While the Fortress could take a pounding, losses were high. Tangye wondered if he'd made the right decision to swap his comfortable and manoeuvrable Spitfire for a lumbering bomber. And, with thirty minutes to go before take-off, he began to reflect on whether his desire for adventure was entirely misplaced. Surely he should be at home, there for his young family?

Negative thoughts were pushed aside as the crew were bundled aboard a truck and driven to a tent close to the bomber. 'Here we enrobed in the complicated paraphernalia of high flight. We were given escape kits for use if we had to bail out, along with chocolate and chewing gum. Then we walked out in the inky blackness to the great shape that stood before us. I was amazed that so large a thing should have such small holes to squeeze through. I clambered up to my position behind the two pilots. I was to have no space as I was squashed between the pilot seats and the upper turret. I couldn't stand up straight and directly beneath me was a hole so that I was forced to lean slightly forward over it. At all costs I couldn't lean back as the turret would be revolving all the time.'

He began to wonder if he could possibly remain in the cramped and painful position for the next five hours. It might have been feasible perhaps in a pleasantly heated room at sea level, but flying in the turbulent, cold air at 26,000ft was a different prospect. And, at thirty-three, he was no longer young when compared to the age of the pilot, twenty-two, and his twenty-year-old co-pilot.

Despite his misgivings, Tangye felt a thrill of excitement as the four turbo-supercharged engines thundered into life. At precisely 8.30pm the eighteen-ton Fortress rolled down the runway and pulled up into the night sky, circling the airfield to gain height. After fifteen minutes they reached 10,000ft and set course for St Nazaire, a hundred miles inside enemy territory.

With a flier's curiosity Tangye looked out of the port window to see if he could spot London and observe how good the blackout was from the air. He knew they would pass in close proximity to Ann and their Chelsea home as their course lay five miles to the west of the city.

London, to his surprise, was not at all difficult to find. For all the wrong reasons.

Searchlights scoured the sky and endless flashes came from AA gunfire in Hyde Park and every other piece of open ground, shooting up into the night. The cold realisation hit him. A major air raid was in progress and his wife was in the middle of it.

Most people in London had grown complacent over the Luftwaffe's ability to mount another Blitz. By winter 1943 there had been no heavy raids over London for a year and a half. Now it looked like the biggest barrage of the war had begun.

'The old home town looked as though hell had broken loose,' Tangye recorded. 'Flares falling, staccato flashes of guns, leisurely flashes of bombs, a huge red rose of an explosion as a gasometer was hit and the crew over the intercom shouting: "Jesus, did you see that?", "Christ, poor old London!", "Aircraft at 3 o'clock" and so on.

'I felt truly sick at heart and cursed myself for choosing that night of all nights to leave Ann and David to fend for themselves. It was a tremendous experience of helplessness to watch that battle from the skies. I thanked God for the Anderson shelter that had only just been completed at my home a few days before.'

It was into that Anderson shelter at their Chelsea home that Ann Todd now fled with her young son. The curved corrugated iron shelter was designed to accommodate six people. Ann took advantage of the extra space to put in a few cushions, a table and toys for her son. Despite her attempts at airing it, the shelter still smelled damp, being dug 4ft down into the garden. On the outside she had planted flowers but they seemed of little importance as she sat fitfully while the bombs rained down.

'It was a terrifying air raid on London. I was alone as Nigel was on duty, so putting a tin hat on my small son and one on myself I carried him across the back yard as bits of shell fell like rain around us. We jumped down into the underground shelter. I had tried to make the place as comfortable as possible by painting the walls and covering everything with pictures but it was very damp and dismal.'[11]

Ann had cuddled up on one of the bunks with David in her arms and was trying to shut her eyes to ward off the sound of detonation when something strange happened.

'I suddenly heard Nigel's voice calling me and his well-known whistle. I thought he must be outside the back gate which was locked and that I must let him in immediately. I practically crawled the short distance and above the noise of gunfire shouted: "One minute, darling" and unlocked the gate. There was no one there.' Whether it was the terror of the bombing or an overactive imagination, she was certain she had heard her husband's voice. She stood for a minute in the garden listening to the crash of AA fire and the groaning impact of bombs. The ground shuddered under her feet as a bomb landed a few streets away. She suddenly remembered David and rushed back to the shelter, taking him into her arms in a smothering embrace.

Meanwhile, Tangye, now certain he preferred Spitfires, was sweating through his own ordeal as he watched the great flashes of fire as bombs burst on the city. He asked the pilot what part of London they were over.[12]

'West London. I think, over Kensington or Chelsea,' the pilot answered.

'Bloody hell. My wife is down there!' Tangye could not believe he was on his first trip in a bomber looking down on his family being bombed. He felt a wave of nausea.

The pilot's masked face turned towards him: 'Christ, I am so sorry for you!'

Somehow Ann felt his distress from her bunker down below. 'Mentally, Nigel called out to me and I picked it up at the same moment that they flew over our house.'

The Fortress trundled southwards, heading out over the Channel and climbing to 20,000ft. 'Enemy and friendly shapes loomed up, our own guns were firing from immediately beneath us. Then we were coned by a mass of searchlights and felt very exposed and naked, for who would expect to see an American Fortress over the night skies of London?

'I was left alone with visions of my house with its ceilings down but I was sure that my tough little wife would be equal to any occasion.'

Tangye's fears rose again as the rear gunner reported vapour trails forming as they headed into enemy territory. 'That meant we left a stream of mist reflected in the starlight for any fighter to see and follow up to its starting point which of course was us. You feel quite conspicuous enough alone in the night in the knowledge of radio-location devices without such a companion.'

The plane crossed over the occupied Channel Islands, reaching 26,000ft. He looked at the faces of the two pilots and the shadowy outline of the snouts of their oxygen masks. In front of them was the vast instrument panel with its myriad of luminous dials. Through the bullet-proof glass of the cockpit he could clearly see the night sky. 'The stars bright and clear and below nothing but unfathomable depths. I went through in my mind all the emergency operations I had learned that afternoon – ditching drill, bailing out, oxygen failure. Then the navigator would burst in on the intercom: "Navigator to speak to pilot, please."

'"Go ahead."

'"Give me five degrees to port please."

'Or the pilot would speak: "Rear gunner, how are the contrails?" [referring to the telltale line of vapour that the engines emitted usually over 20,000ft].

'"Still there, all right."

'"Keep a sharp lookout, fellers."'

Suddenly Tangye was struck by nausea and anxiety but the enemy coast was ahead and the Fortress lumbered on.

'At 22:20 we passed over the French coast. The blackout was none too good. I could plainly see clusters of lights and individual lights and the headlights of a car. We had a hundred miles to go. A few searchlights probed the sky and a couple of guns flashed.

'At 22:50, I had the thrill of hearing the bombardier say: "Bombardier to pilot."

'"Go ahead."

'"Bomb doors open please."

'And then what seemed a second or two later the Fortress gave a great lurch as the three-ton load was dropped. The pilot swung the plane north and we were on our way home. It was odd to realise the psychological effect this change of course had. We were heading for home. The job was done. The fact that we still had forty-five minutes over enemy territory meant nothing. Then the pilot said: "Keep a sharp lookout, fellers."'

Later that day Tangye arrived home to find the ceiling still up and his wife shaken but unharmed. He grabbed her in a smothering embrace, feeling her soft skin against his grizzled cheek. Looking into her melting eyes he said he would not to do a bombing run again.

It was a wise decision. The Bomber Command losses were horrific. Nearly 56,000 were killed out of a force of 125,000. With more than 8,000 wounded and almost 10,000 taken prisoner, it meant a Bomber Command airman stood a one-in-two chance of getting through unscathed.

As Ann leant against his chest, Tangye made a silent vow never to leave the comfort of his Spitfire again.

CHAPTER TEN

ITALY

Greggs Farish

The island of Sicily sat at the toe of Italy, poking far into the Mediterranean Sea. Since 1940 it had been used as an enemy base to harass shipping, bomb Malta and more recently for the desperate resupply of Tunisia.

In May 1943, with the North Africa campaign concluded, British commanders argued that taking Sicily would secure Mediterranean shipping lanes at a time when Atlantic convoys were being hammered by U-boats. It would also be a natural springboard for the conquest of Italy and mainland Europe. An invasion date was set for July.

After a sustained assault on Sicily's air defences, on the night of 9 July 1943 an armada of airborne troops and landing craft headed towards Sicily's shores.

Spitfires from Malta fifty miles away were to provide continuous patrols overhead to protect the beachheads. Fuel allowed only thirty-five minutes on station per squadron, so twenty-five minutes after the first squadron left, the young Wing Commander Hugh Dundas, now confirmed in post as 324 Wing's boss after his adventures in the North African oasis, took off.

'We crossed great convoys of landing craft and supply ships churning through the wind-flecked sea. Even from 12,000ft it was possible to see that the waves were breaking hard against and often over them. I felt sorry for the men who had spent hours of darkness squatting miserably in those pitching, rolling little boats, wet and cold from the spray and the wind, with nothing to do but contemplate their arrival on a hostile beach. I thought that our way of fighting a war was not so bad. Probably there was danger just ahead but we had risen from comfortable beds, with sheets and pillows, and we could hope and expect to go back to a hot breakfast far from the sight and sound of battle.'

Despite being only twenty, Alan Peart was now an experienced hand, especially after surviving his foolhardy, almost suicidal, one-man attack on a dozen Me109s in North Africa. *I'll never do that again*, he told himself constantly. He was now patrolling overhead in his Spitfire, looking down on the mightiest amphibious operation yet undertaken in the history of warfare with 160,000 men ready to land. 'I had never seen so many ships together at one time. It was said that there were 2,000 of them, of all sizes, from landing craft to liners with warships spread around them. They were contending with heavy sea and I wondered how the troops must have been feeling, cooped up below decks as they were.'

It was the Allies' first full-scale assault on western Europe since limping off Dunkirk's beaches three years earlier.

The troops landed successfully and, as they pushed through Sicily's rugged interior, airfields were seized and the Spitfire squadrons flew in. With little opposition in the air they had time to pick over abandoned German aircraft. The engineer officer Greggs Farish had arrived with 72 Squadron in Sicily via landing craft. His friend, the Spitfire pilot Tom Hughes, persuaded him to look over an Me109 that looked in fine condition left amid the small trees at Comiso airfield, twelve miles inland from the southern Sicilian coast. With some help from a German dictionary, Farish got it ready to fly.

As the Wing Commander of 324 Wing, Hugh Dundas was given the honour of being the first to test the German fighter. He was in high spirits, elated after entering occupied Europe. 'A moment to remember and a memory to treasure.'

Dundas was strapped into the enemy Me109. It had been painted bright yellow and decorated with RAF roundels in an attempt to keep their own anti-aircraft gunners' fingers off their triggers. At 6ft 4in he found the cockpit unpleasantly cramped. 'The seat was positioned in such a way that the pilot was, so to speak, sitting on the floor in a semi-recumbent attitude, legs sticking straight out in front. Such a position had its advantages because a pilot whose legs and head were at the same level would not black out as quickly as one who was seated in an upright position. But the unfamiliarity increased my anxiety as I sat listening to the engineering officer explaining the functions of the various knobs and dials. Furthermore, it was very evident that the 109 had not been tailored for pilots of my height. When I closed the cockpit canopy I found that it pressed down on the top of my head and when I turned my head to right or left my long nose was liable to come in contact with the Perspex hood.'

Uncomfortable and with the airstrip lined by interested RAF spectators, Dundas was not entirely disappointed when he discovered the engine revolution counter was faulty and taxied back in.

Farish took the Me109 back and soon made it serviceable for the next attempt. Another Spitfire pilot, 'Sexton' Gear, an experienced flying instructor, was very keen to fly the 109 and, on a hot Sicilian afternoon, took off after the required messages were sent out to the army AA gunners surrounding the airfield that the German plane, painted yellow and with RAF roundels, was a 'friendly'. In his excitement Gear had, unlike Dundas, forgotten to ask for a Spitfire escort, to ensure no one in the air, on land or sea fired at him.

As he flew out to sea a navy destroyer ignored the bright yellow paint and RAF markings and gave him several AA broadsides. Gear put his nose down and headed for home with flak bursting in the sky around him.

The army gunners now took their cue from the sailors. Farish looked on in horror: 'All the guns for miles around opened up at this Me109. We were in mental agony lying on our bellies with shrapnel pattering down. A Spit took off in the middle of it all and flew into the gunfire.'

The Spitfire was flown by his friend Tom Hughes, twenty-one, the Rugby-educated man who, with his elegant attire and neatly trimmed moustache, exemplified a gentleman pilot.[1]

Hughes had quickly realised that Sexton was in real trouble and made a hundred-yard sprint to his Spitfire, taking off at full boost. 'I quickly found Flying Officer Gear in the Me109 being skilfully flown among the treetops amid a barrage of anti-aircraft fire from our troops.

'I was terrified by the tracer but managed to get fairly close behind the "friendly" enemy, waggling my wings violently and hoping the Army would be kind enough not to hit me in the Spitfire or my friend in the Messerschmitt. By then, all Flying Officer Gear wanted to do was to get his mount back to our landing strip as quickly as could be.'

On landing, the Messerschmitt was found to be completely untouched by AA fire. 'Much to the officer commanding the Royal Artillery's consternation there was not one bullet hole in it,' Farish said.[2]

Despite the experience Tom Hughes was still keen to fly an enemy plane himself, to compare the speeds at level flight between a Spitfire and a Messerschmitt, particularly the 'G' version which was said to be the Luftwaffe's favourite.

He found another Me109G and, after alerting the AA gunners and with a Spitfire for escort, he took off.[3] 'We climbed together to 6,000ft and I flew westwards at cruising speed. As I opened the throttle to maximum and increased the revs the engine sounded horrible. I thought it would be sensible to return and land at once so turned back eastwards. Suddenly there was a fearful escape of steam from under the instrument panel, some sort of leak in the coolant system had developed and I found it not only hot, but choking to breathe. I immediately jettisoned the hood and was pleasantly surprised with the excellent arrangement of it, which allowed quite easy escape.'

But the steam was building around his legs and was unbearably hot. He would have to abandon ship.

'I undid my straps and started to climb out. I had a sudden change of mind – were my parachute straps tight? I tried to climb back in and somehow knocked the control column. In a trice I was catapulted straight up and clear of the cockpit and somersaulted over and over. I pulled the D-ring without bothering to count to three, which was part of the training advice. As the parachute opened I was startled by the shock from dropping freely. I was now supported underneath the canopy and saw galaxies of stars before my eyes, but what a joy it is to be safely lowered to the ground on a silken thread.

'I drifted down in the summer sunshine with a relief approaching ecstasy. I saw the German fighter crashing and exploding in a vineyard down below. I landed perfectly in soft volcanic soil up to my ankles in the vineyard. I pulled on the lines and collapsed the canopy quite easily.

'Two Sicilians appeared by magic. They took me to a little shack nearby and I was introduced to a tiny, ancient, shrivelled woman who must have been their grandmother. They gave me a glass of wonderful red wine and soon I was as cheerful as they were. With my parachute rolled up I got on their donkey cart and headed for the main road back to Pachino. A Jeep driven by Greggs Farish rounded the corner and I was trans-shipped and returned to base, but only after we had all been back and had another drink of their famous wine.'

* * *

Gallons of Sicilian wine had been assembled by members of 81 Squadron to celebrate the joint twenty-first birthday of Alan Peart and his new boss, Squadron Leader William Whitamore, who was a mere one day older.[4] The squadron had been sent to the airstrip at Lentini, near the town of Catania on the eastern coast, surrounded by low hills where they pitched their tents away from the malaria-carrying mosquitoes. Whitamore had been nicknamed 'Babe' on his promotion to Squadron Leader aged just twenty. Despite his tender age and youthful looks, Whitamore had proved his worth, destroying more than five aircraft since joining the RAF soon after his eighteenth birthday in 1940.

By 24 July 1943 he was already an 'ace', with a Distinguished Flying Cross to boot. The party on a hill overlooking the airstrip had just started when a parachute flare descended over their airfield. After weeks of quiet it was apparent that the Luftwaffe had regrouped for a counter-attack. The pilots went haring for the nearest cover just in time to hear the rushing whistle of bombs descending. Peart was among those left stranded in the open. He dived to the ground as a crackle of giant fireworks broke out all around. The earth shook with explosions, lifting him off the ground. Peart lay flat, waiting with dread for the next bomb to land. It came seconds later, obliterating a fellow airman lying next to him.

'The guy was shredded by one of the anti-personnel bomblets; his body was lifted in the air and he landed beside me with a thump. I was shocked as he had shielded me from the blast.'

In the bursting light of an explosion Peart looked in horror at the wrecked body. He did not want to die. He needed to find shelter. *Fast*. He remembered a partially dug slit trench at the edge of the airstrip.

He felt the heat from the bomb blasts as he sprinted to the hole, terrified of being obliterated in an instant.

'I found it empty and dived in. Meanwhile, more heavy explosive and anti-personnel bombs were falling and everything seemed to be in flames. The protection to my body provided by the slit trench was most comforting. Then someone dived in on top of me.

'The feeling of cover over my back was welcome. Then a third chap joined and immediately complained that his backside was showing above ground. Could we get lower? We couldn't. I felt perfectly safe with two bodies on top of me and I certainly could not get any lower. Next, the topmost fellow slid down the side of the trench and squirmed his way under me in spite of my strenuous efforts to stop him. Then I was second. The chap above me started to complain and did exactly the same thing. I was on top now and could vouch that protection was indeed extremely limited. I was also not amused as I had got there first. I did the same thing and fought my way under the bottom chap.

'With much swearing and cursing at each other we changed places I don't know how many times while the bombing was going on.'

When they heard the last of the bombers' engines disappear back into the distance they gingerly emerged from the trench and dusted themselves down.

'Jesus Christ!' Whitamore exclaimed. All around them were the burning wrecks of Spitfires, some flattened on their bellies and wingless, others with fire streaking from their engines. One had been skittled over by a blast, lying on its back with wheels in the air. 81 Squadron had not one single flyable Spitfire.

'The place looked like Dante's inferno, with rising columns of smoke and dust illuminated by the flares, burning aircraft, exploding ammunition and AA guns firing,' Peart said.

'There was not much we could do until daylight so we returned to our hilltop campsite and continued our party. So ended our birthday celebrations. I became twenty-one years old the next day.'

Peart subsequently discovered that an unexploded anti-personnel bomb lay at the bottom of the slit trench in which the three of them, including Whitamore, had been squirming. Their luck seemed to be holding out. For the moment.

* * *

This new German aerial offensive was the result of a Goering diatribe against the Luftwaffe as Sicily slipped from Nazi control. A message sent to his pilots accused them of cowardice and threatened Eastern Front postings.

> I can only regard you with contempt. If an immediate improvement is not forthcoming, flying personnel, from the Kommodore downwards, must expect to be reduced to the ranks and transferred to the Eastern Front to serve on the ground.

But the Luftwaffe had been kept quiet for good reason. As one pilot put it: 'We lacked everything necessary to a fighter unit's operations – skilled personnel, spares, ammunition, even petrol.'[5] Added to this was the 'quality' of Allied aircraft.

Helped by the renewed bombing offensive, the Germans conducted an orderly withdrawal from Sicily. As in North Africa, 72 Squadron moved up with the advance in their trucks. Greggs Farish was delighted to find a decent spot to camp near the ancient port of Augusta on the east coast, next to a battery of Bofors gunners he had befriended.[6]

'We thought we had done rather well. We had our evening meal cooked for us and sat round after dark pleasantly talking in a camp circle with the gunners. Then we retired to bed, as ever around our truck, which was parked a little way from any one gun, in the middle of the field.

'I woke up and heard the awful drone of aeroplanes, enemy bombers, invisible, close. Cursing, we all scrambled under the truck and the din got louder. All that night we heard the bombing of big guns, the rat-tat-tat of machine guns, the banging of pom-poms and cannon and then the scream of a plane diving through the flak and the earth-shaking *crump, crump* of bombs landing. Sometimes there would come a whistle, growing louder as it neared the ground so that you would swear it was going to hit you. Also there was, every now and again, the rattle and whispering of shrapnel falling, bits of shells from the guns. One time a big piece came whistling down and landed about five yards away. It put an awful fear in us; we thought it was a bomb.'

The bombing raid provided Greggs Farish with the opportunity he had been seeking for almost a year. In Algeria one of his corporals had once suggested that a piano would allow them to have a good sing-along after a tough day in the field. He had scoured most of North Africa and then Sicily without success.[7]

Farish was working on a Spitfire at the small airfield outside Augusta when one of his flight sergeants approached with a grin. He thought he'd found what Farish had spent six months looking for.

Everyone in the squadron knew about Farish's quest. The flight sergeant told him that Augusta was deserted and there was a lovely upright piano upstairs in a house.

Farish stood on the Spitfire's wing holding his spanner. Looting was punishable by death, but *to hell with it*, they'd been fighting the damn war long enough. And he could count on his daring Spitfire pilots to get away with the caper.

He gathered a group of pilots together and they took a flatbed truck to the outskirts of Augusta. Then the flight sergeant guided them to the deserted townhouse.

While inspecting the piano they heard a noise and were horrified to see two military policemen looking down on them from an upstairs window in a house opposite. The policemen grinned and waved. They were doing their own spot of pilfering.

However, Farish's RAF lorry had been foolishly parked outside the Provost Major's HQ. The officer in charge of military discipline demanded to know what was going on. The pilots made some excuse about engine blocks. The officer was unimpressed. 'If I catch any of you looting, you'll be shot.'

But Farish was too close to finally achieving his quest. He carried on regardless.

'The pilots got the piano downstairs with great shushes, bumps and curses. I drove up fast with the tail-board down and a tent ready. Quickly we had the piano out of the front door, on its back, all together with superhuman strength lifted onto the wagon, tent over, tail-board up and away before anyone else saw us – except the two MPs opposite laughing. We drove gaily and with what were, we hoped, innocent expressions, through the guard at the main gate.'

But their adventures were not entirely over. On their way back the driver, Sergeant North, stopped the lorry and allowed two Italian women on board.

One got up front with him and the other got in the back where she set about trying to seduce an airman called Fergus. Farish looked on with amusement. 'Now Fergus is rather serious where girls are concerned and reciprocated by practising Italian which he was learning. She winked, laughed and sang at the rest of us, settling herself comfortably on Fergus' lap, to his surprise. He didn't know his Italian was so good.

'Evidently the girl in the front, having only two airmen to contend with, had aroused greater passion for suddenly North pulled up and shouted, "Anyone else want to drive?"

'I took over again and realised as I let in the clutch that this seduction was meeting with more success than that of Fergus, for I was shaken by the sight of a pair of knickers on the floorboards. I hurriedly suggested that we stop at the next copse for a few minutes. This was heartily approved. North and his girl disappeared among the trees, while the rest of us had a bite to eat and a smoke.'

With North's liaison completed, they returned to camp and unloaded the piano.

It proved to be a great boon. 'Never before had the squadron gone in for any sort of communal entertainment. There hadn't been time but now a series of concerts were started. Talent sprang up from all directions, from Spitfire pilots to fitters and drivers.

'Almost every letter I censored at that time mentioned these weekly concerts with great approval; many told mothers and wives about the piano, which some said the Engineer Officer had given them, like I was a fairy godmother.

'As I left the Officers' Mess tent after dinner one evening I heard in the distance the sound of voices singing.' As he walked up the slope, there, in the moonlight reflecting off a Spitfire wing, was a great circle of dim shapes; men lying, sitting and standing. 'Here and there a cigarette glowed red and a match lit up faces. The piano suggested a tune which was quickly taken up by the assembled crowd':

> The other night dear,
> As I lay dreaming . . .
> I dreamt that you were by my side
> But when I awoke dear
> I was mistaken and held my head and cried.

* * *

For Alan Peart the Sicily campaign was also going to provide him with another 'first'. With the fighting quietening down, he was sent off for a rare few days' leave to the sandy beaches overlooked by the ancient hilltop town of Taormina, in southern Sicily.

The relaxation was a most welcome change. 'It was curious to be dragged out of intense combat and sent on leave. It was strange to enjoy life to the full and then return to the skies and to the killing. We could sleep, relax, stay in bed all day if we wanted – it was wonderful and such a contrast to my life of war.'

But then something else happened one day as they lay on the beach. A striking young Italian woman stripped off her clothes and entered the water. It was the first time the young Spitfire pilot, bloodied in battle, had seen a naked woman. Peart was dumbfounded. He had been in the heart of fighting and dying for more than a year yet still remained naive in other matters. 'I was just twenty years old and a very inexperienced young man. I was thousands of miles from home, fighting in a world war but knew little of worldly matters! I had killed, watched friends die. I was battle-hardened but I had never before seen a naked lady.'[8]

It was a curious existence; contact with home had been minimal and letters were few and far between. 'Because of the censors, there was very little to write anyway – the sun rose in the morning and went down at night. Perhaps I'd heard a bird singing or something like that – you were not allowed to mention the war at all in case it affected morale back home. I didn't have time to be homesick, though – I was always thinking ahead about what I might have to face and how best prepared I might be to counter every possibility. I wasn't thinking of home; just staying alive until I could get home.'

* * *

The Sicily campaign was rapidly drawing to a close and in many respects it was a success. Sea lanes were opened to Allied merchant ships, Mussolini was toppled as Italy's dictator and Hitler had been forced to divert forces from Russia just a week after the massive Kursk tank offensive had begun on 5 July.

But with good leadership and their usual discipline, the Germans managed to withdraw more than 50,000 troops, mainly at night by ship over the two-mile-wide Strait of Messina into mainland Italy, along with forty-seven tanks, ninety-four guns and 14,000 vehicles. While some of the fighting had been hard, with the Allies losing 5,500 dead, the troops knew that taking Italy was going to be a real test. By not entrapping the German troops, the Allies had made it that much harder.

* * *

The arguments to mount a rapid Allied invasion of the mainland proved irresistible: a quick military victory would trap the German army and hasten Italy's surrender.

As late summer 1943 approached, the Americans accepted the postponement of Operation Overlord – the invasion across the Channel into France – and relented to British pressure to invade Italy.

Many wanted to follow Napoleon's maxim that Italy should, like a boot, be entered from the top. However, the short range of the Spitfires and other fighters restricted their choices. They chose the narrow beaches with good surf conditions around Salerno, south of Naples and not far from Italy's 'toe'.

The Allies' hand was significantly strengthened by the Italian surrender, announced publicly on 8 September. But the Germans were never ones to sit on their hands and reinforcements were mobilised before the Salerno landings began the next day.

The planning for Salerno was rushed. Among other theories it was argued that in order to achieve surprise there would be no naval bombardment.

A force of nearly 200,000 Allied troops and more than 600 ships set off from ports in North Africa and Sicily to seize the heel of the Italian boot and planned to press onto Rome and beyond before Christmas. At 3.30am, as the landing-craft ramps splashed onto the surf, a German officer speaking through a loudspeaker in excellent English told the wading troops: 'Come on in and give up. We have you covered.' Then the surf rippled to the impact of machine-gun bullets and broke apart to the impact of shells. The Germans had guessed correctly where the landing might come. Salerno was about to get bloody.[9]

* * *

Nine days after the invasion of Italy, Hugh Dundas' Spitfires were still lugging the 175 miles from Sicily as the Germans remained entrenched within a few hundred yards of the Salerno beachhead in southern Italy. The promised temporary airstrip, cleared by bulldozers and laid with steel matting, had only just materialised. However, it was still right under the shells and bullets of the enemy. Landing there was a terrifying prospect. Not only was it under enemy fire, but there was no organised air traffic control. It was every man for himself.

Despite the dangers, 324 Wing was ordered to base itself on the airstrip, which ran parallel to the beach with an olive grove between it and the sea. With some trepidation Dundas lined up to land.

'I was nearly frightened out of my wits by a series of explosions which sounded loud above the noise of my engine and were accompanied by many flashes from the olive grove.[10] As soon as I stepped onto the ground my eardrums were split by another tremendous blast from behind me. When I had picked myself up, dusted myself off and regained some dignity, I asked what the hell was going on.'

The extremely close artillery fire was coming from the British battery of twenty-five-pounder medium artillery field guns lined up in the olive trees between the runway and sea. To keep the Germans at bay, their firing was almost constant.

Dundas was not best pleased. 'Before landing I had thought that German artillery would constitute a major threat to our safety. Now it seemed to me that we were in even greater danger from our own guns. I was not given to pessimism but I was quite unable to suppress the fear that if they persisted in blasting away directly across the landing strip while our planes were in the circuit, it could only be a matter of time before a Spitfire and a shell came into the same bit of sky at the same moment, with unpleasant consequences for the pilot.'

Dundas listened to the crash of rounds coming out of the olive grove and sailing straight over the runway towards the German lines. A few seconds later a Dakota came in to land in roughly the same airspace as the twenty-five-pounder's shells. There was no collision but Dundas was not going to let his men's lives be endangered by their own side. *They face enough bloody risks as it is.* He grabbed a Jeep, drove down the runway then into the olive trees to find the Royal Artillery commanding officer. A lieutenant colonel, dressed in white corduroys and cream-coloured shirt, emerged from a tent among the olive trees.

As he walked up to the RAF officer a gun roared nearby. Dundas could see a muzzle flash among the greenery, just over 100 yards from the airstrip perimeter. 'Wing Commander Hugh Dundas,' he introduced himself. 'Would you mind . . .' Dundas paused as another twenty-five-pounder fired. 'Would you mind if your guns stopped firing when my Spitfires come in to land and take off?'

'Stop firing, my dear fellow? What on earth do you want me to stop firing for? My orders are to fire flat out, round the clock. Terribly sorry, old man, but I can't possibly stop firing.'

Dundas explained that he feared one of the gunners' shells and one of his Spitfires would eventually come into contact. The officer looked at him as though he was absolutely mad.

'Shoot down a Spitfire? Good God, who's ever heard of a twenty-five-pounder shooting down a Spitfire! *Hey!*' He called over an officer standing nearby. 'The Wing Commander here thinks we may shoot down one of his Spitfires. Take him in and give him a drink, will you?'

Dundas was not amused. 'Still muttering in amazement at the extraordinary prospect I had envisaged, he withdrew. The interview was at an end. The guns went on firing – flat out and round the clock.'

* * *

During the first week of the Salerno landings, at least half-a-dozen warships had been hit by a mysterious bomb that penetrated their armoured decks, all the way down to their hull. An Italian battleship had been sunk and a device had torn a large hole in an American light cruiser's bottom, killing 200 sailors.

With troops still pinned down on the beaches, the British battleship HMS *Warspite* was ordered to use her massive fifteen-inch guns to bombard German positions.

She was about to become the next victim of the Nazis' latest secret weapon, the *Fritz X*, the world's first guided anti-ship missile. Developed in great secrecy, the Germans had created a 3,000lb device that could penetrate five inches of armoured decking then burrow down to explode under the keel. It was mounted on Dornier 217 bombers and guided onto the target by a bombardier who used a transmitter to adjust its large fins in flight via the bomb's receiver. A skilled aimer could guide the missile to within at least 50ft of his target 50 per cent of the time. Being launched from three miles out it also gave the Dornier crew a good chance to get away before a ship realised it was being attacked.

The *Warspite*'s sailors had felt reasonably secure operating under the umbrella of Allied aircraft above. In the mid-afternoon of 15 September, just as they were about to launch another salvo, the unmistakable scream of a bomb was heard coming from the sky above. For a millisecond the crewmen looked at each other. How could this be? There were no bombers about; no thump of anti-aircraft guns.

Then they heard the cruel rent of metal being struck and torn.

A *Fritz X* struck a funnel, pierced through six decks then detonated in the hull, creating a 20ft hole. The *Warspite* shuddered to a halt. The smell of burning and screams of the wounded rose from the decks below.[11] The orders went out – the Dornier 217s were to be intercepted and destroyed.

* * *

Alan Peart could not help glancing again at the fuel gauge and feeling a sense of irritation. It was almost 200 miles from their base in Sicily to Salerno and already he'd used more than a quarter-tank of fuel. Even with their drop tanks, they still had only thirty minutes' patrol time with little to spare if they got into a dogfight. Of course, there was the emergency strip at Salerno, but they'd been warned that it was under constant shellfire, as 'Cocky' Dundas had already discovered, and only to be used *if you're really desperate*. He'd even heard rumours that it was close to being overrun.

His eyes scanned the horizon ahead. Navigation at least was not a problem. The long columns of smoke, the wake of ships and the shadows of aircraft above all signposted Salerno.

As he got closer Peart's gaze swept the sky and the sea. Something was wrong. Instinctively he knew his superb eyesight had picked up something amiss.

He squinted, searching the ocean. Dark smoke belched from a battleship below. He looked in the sky. *Nothing.* He focused on the water around the ship, searching for the telltale sign of a torpedo foam trail. Again, nothing. He turned back to examine the blue overhead. He thought he'd glimpsed them before and dismissed them for being too far away, but two dots in the sky, just a few miles away, were streaking northwards. And they were bombers. German bombers, he was sure of it.

He knew this was why his boss 'Babe' Whitamore had put him in charge of 81 Squadron's flight of six Spitfires. Peart had the best eyesight and the most experience to lead half the squadron.

'Dog One, enemy bombers bearing 280 degrees.'

Peart squinted ahead at the distinctive pencil-shape outline of a fast Dornier 217. The sky was thick with Allied fighters and bombers and yet the Luftwaffe had managed to sneak in and attack a warship unnoticed.

He pushed the throttle wide open and felt the Merlin power him forward, quickly gaining on the Germans. Peart knew the new Dornier 217s could nudge over 300mph, but the Spitfire IXs were whippets; travelling at nearly 400mph they closed fast. The German crews were clearly no mugs. Within a minute they had spotted the six Spitfires closing on them and split up.

Peart ordered three aircraft onto each bomber then tore after his target with his two wingmen. As the gap closed he felt his heart pound once again with the excitement and trepidation of impending combat. He scanned the sky and then his instruments, took a few deep breaths and felt the familiar icy calm settle over him.

He silently urged the Spitfire forward, closing the distance on the German plane.

The range reduced from 400 yards to 300 yards. He flicked the gun switch from 'safe' to 'fire', then brought his aim to well ahead of the Dornier, calculating the deflection shot needed to strike a target moving ahead at speed in a flank attack on the port side, away from the rear gunner's bullets.

The distance shortened to 250 yards. Another two seconds and he'd open up with everything he had, sending a thick stream of lead that would shred everything in its path.

His focus fixed on the gunsight.

Then it was empty.

Peart blinked. He glanced left and right. *Bloody hell, these boys are good.*

At the last minute the German rear gunner must have called 'break' and done it with perfect timing. The Dornier had banked hard to starboard just as Peart was about to fire.

As the Spitfire again chased it down, the pilot weaved from side to side. They would know he'd flown from Sicily and had limited fuel. If they could stay out of harm's way for long enough they'd survive.

But the Spitfire could easily outmanoeuvre a twin-engine bomber, albeit a fast one. Peart closed again to within 300 yards. A yellow flicker came from the back of the Dornier. A split second later Peart saw tracer rounds zip over his canopy. *Damn close.* He'd not come up against such a skilled crew before.

He flipped his Spitfire left then right, throwing off the gunner's aim. Then he straightened up and set himself up for a quarter flank attack on the Dornier's port side. He grimly focused on the target, aiming a deflection shot fired from 300 yards. He'd have liked to have got closer but the distance was well within his capability.

He pressed down on the firing button, letting go with his two 20mm cannons and four machine guns. The Spitfire juddered and slowed marginally as the guns forced their projectiles out of the wings. For a second the Dornier flew on untouched. Then Peart spotted flashes of bursting cannon shells pucker the port wing. The Dornier dived hard to starboard. Peart saw his two colleagues' Spitfires flash overhead, their guns spurting bullets towards the bomber.

They missed.

Peart cursed at their inexperience then hauled himself round for a second approach. This time the rear gunner was firing almost constantly but now with little accuracy.

'I then made my second attack adopting the same approach tactics while the bomber pilot did his best to dodge. I opened fire again with both cannons and machine guns and this time my fire hit the bomber solidly. A large piece flew off and there was a big bang as my aeroplane flew into it.'

Slowly the Dornier began to lose height, the pilot fighting at the controls to find stability. He managed to nurse it down towards the ground and make a good crash-landing on the side of the hill. Peart waited for flames followed by black smoke. Nothing came. There was a good chance the crew had survived. They had fought well. He was pleased.

A transmission from a wingman requesting a strafing run on the downed Germans broke into thoughts.

Peart denied the request.

The wingman argued that they were behind enemy lines.

Peart again declined. 'The bravery of the crew in carrying out an operation unescorted by fighters in the face of overwhelming odds was most impressive. They had defended themselves with great determination and skill. They deserved the chance to live.'

Before they could argue further an urgent voice came over the radio.

'Mayday! Mayday!'

It was Bill Fell, the twenty-year-old who had recently joined the squadron. Peart knew panic would be seizing hold of the pilot trying to exit the small cockpit with the growing terror that he could be trapped inside and burnt alive.

Abandoning an aircraft was a procedure that had to be precisely sequenced. They practised it almost every day, especially with the new pilots, and usually blindfolded. But doing it for real was entirely different.

'When the temperature in the cockpit is searing and things are burning, it can be expected that the sequence can become a little hurried, even essential bits can be overlooked. The imminent probability of an almighty explosion could ensure a too-rapid execution of the exit procedures. Bill had all of these problems to face.'

Flying close by, Peart began to relay the instructions Fell needed to hear.

'Trim your nose down, Dog Four. Undo helmet electrical connections.' Peart rapidly went through the drill. 'Unclip oxygen tube.' He could hear Fell panting frantically over the radio. 'Stay calm, Dog Four. Jettison canopy. Release harness. Good. Now roll your aircraft. Good luck.'

Fell rolled the Spitfire onto its back and dropped out of the cockpit just as it started to dive. Immediately his parachute caught on the tail rudder, the Spitfire dragging him down with it. Peart looked on helplessly as the plane with its pilot attached to the tail plummeted towards the earth.

'The machine with Fell trailing behind was diving vertically to the ground. We watched in horror at the certain loss of a well-liked colleague.'

The Spitfire was just a few hundred feet from impacting with the ground when to everyone's amazement Fell separated from the doomed fighter and his parachute spilled open.

'Just before reaching the ground Fell broke free and to our surprise his parachute opened. His plane went in with an explosion and a great gout of flame and smoke, while Bill did one swing in his harness before his body disappeared through trees to hit the ground close by.'

Peart breathed in shock and joy at seeing his comrade spared from death at the very last moment. It was turning into a good sortie after all.

Then he looked down at his fuel gauge. Chasing down the Dornier and following Fell had left him with a fuel tank nudging empty. He glanced down at the smoke and explosions coming from the Salerno beachhead. Small, dark shapes of fighters and

Dakota cargo planes buzzed around the great mushroom of dust and debris. Clearly the airstrip Hugh Dundas had landed at a few days earlier was in heavy use despite being in the midst of the maelstrom.

They were out of choices. There was at least a chance of finding a bowser of aviation fuel down there, then getting the hell out and back to the peace of Sicily.

Peart pushed the stick down and ordered his colleagues to follow. There was no air traffic control; planes were just piling into the airstrip when they could.

Peart lined up for his landing when from nowhere a Dakota suddenly filled the airspace in front, cutting him off. Peart banked hard, coming round up behind another Dakota. It was terrible flying but he was out of fuel and had no choice. He leapt over the Dakota in front and dived for the airfield.

'I gave him my slipstream. He wobbled badly and gave way and I entered the dust pall on my landing approach.'

A seemingly clear and straight landing strip appeared ahead. Peart felt his wheels touch down on the dirt and breathed out in relief. As he began to brake, the dust cleared ahead. He gasped, feeling adrenaline pump around his body. A Spitfire that had stalled on take-off was straddling the runway 100 yards ahead. Peart jammed on the brakes. His aircraft skidded then slewed round, veered off the strip and went onto its nose. Peart braced himself for a potentially lethal overturning. The tail waved in the air then slammed back down, right way up.

Peart knew he had to move fast. He threw back the canopy, jumped onto the ground and ran to the stricken Spitfire. The sound of aircraft engines overhead was joined by something else. *Shellfire.*

He had no time to worry about the dangers: they had to get the fighter out of the way before someone collided with it and made the entire strip unusable. He spotted the pilot frantically tugging at the cockpit controls.

'No time,' Peart shouted. 'We have to push her off. Release the brakes.'

The pilot jumped down and they took a wing each. Peart felt his flying boots skid in the dirt as they inched the three-ton Spitfire forward. He heard a plane fly low overhead. Remembering his rugby days in New Zealand, he bent low at the knees, as if in a scrum, and pushed hard. The inches turned into feet as the fighter built up momentum. He quickened his pace to keep up the speed. The aircraft trundled over some matting then slipped off the runway.

As they were tinkering with the engine, Peart could make out the distinct chatter of machine guns nearby. Bullets streaked overhead. The scream of an artillery shell pushed through the air. Two seconds later it was followed by the thump of detonation.

He could see flashes not far off in the foliage less than a mile from the airstrip. He glanced left and right. There was no fuel bowser in view and no one about. It was becoming obvious that the airstrip was close to being overrun. He had to sacrifice his machine and get out. They had been warned that it was vital that their latest 'Identification Friend or Foe' device should not fall into enemy hands. Peart ignored the incoming rounds and sprinted to his Spitfire. He climbed onto the wing, leaned into the cockpit and activated the IFF self-destruct button. As he ran back into the cover of the trees he heard a small crump of detonation from the plane.

Then he heard the rumble of a Dakota's Pratt and Whitney engines. He had an idea. He ran down the side of the runway, hugging the treeline as the leaves twitched from bullet strikes.

The chatter of machine guns spurred him on. He began sprinting, regardless of the mayhem around him. He waved frantically at the pilot, who slid back the cockpit window as Peart got alongside.

'Where are you going, mate?'

The pilot glanced down at Peart's flying uniform. 'Sicily. Need a lift?'

'Absolutely,' Peart gasped. 'Thanks.'

'Jump aboard and come up front.'

Peart gratefully leapt through the cargo side door. As he made his way to the cockpit, he felt the cargo plane lurch forward. He staggered into the cockpit where the pilot's total focus was on getting the plane aloft.

Peart suddenly realised that their direction of travel over the end of the runway would take them directly over the German lines. 'I could just about see the whites of their eyes. At any moment I expected to see holes sprouting in the bottom of the aircraft as their gunners homed in on us. Perhaps they were otherwise engaged for no holes appeared.'

He relaxed marginally as the Dakota began its slow, steady climb away from the inferno of Salerno but could not stop himself from scanning the sky for Fw190s in the hunt for easy prey. He felt for his parachute.

When he arrived at 81 Squadron's aerodrome on Sicily he discovered that only one of his pilots had got back. 'Darkness came and there was no word from the others and we began to have grave doubts as to their safety. Because of the appalling operational conditions at the Salerno landing strip, what with its lack of any flying control, the dust, low visibility and the signs when I left of the enemy possibly overrunning the strip, I really did wonder.'

With a grim face, 'Babe' Whitamore told him that one of their pilots from the flight had been killed during a collision at Salerno shortly after Peart left. The accident had a feeling of inevitability about it.

It had not been a successful sortie. Just one Spitfire had returned intact, one had been shot down and four destroyed or abandoned.

The Allies just managed to hold off the Germans from the beaches at Salerno during three weeks of hard fighting. But only just. If Hitler had released reinforcements from northern Italy they might well have been overrun. As it was they suffered 5,000 dead, and eighty-five ships, including several hit by *Fritz X* guided bombs, were lost or badly damaged. In the end it was Montgomery's 8th Army, pushing up from the heel and toe of Italy, that forced Kesselring to withdraw in the face of overwhelming numbers, as well as Allied air and naval superiority.

But the campaign for Italy was still in its early stages. Soon the Allies would find themselves confronted by a series of well-prepared defences running across the country.

* * *

The winter weather and defensive terrain slowed the Allied advance to a crawl that stalled at Monte Cassino, 100 miles south of Rome. The Allies decided to outflank the Germans by launching a seaborne landing behind German lines, just south of the capital. The beaches around Anzio were chosen and on 22 January 1944 a force of 115,000 mostly American troops landed. But they were slow to break out and German reinforcements arrived in the surrounding hills in time to bombard the bridgehead, pinning down the Americans.

A temporary airfield was laid at Nettuno, next to the Anzio beachhead, using pierced steel plating, but under the bombardment it soon became untenable, only to be used for emergency landings.

On 14 February 1944 a Spitfire IX from 111 Squadron, flown by Bamby Taylor, suffered engine failure and was forced to land at Nettuno. A new batch of 'IXs' had been consistently breaking down.

The Nines' failures caused no end of worry for Greggs Farish, who had been injured in an accident in Sicily and had returned to active service as 111 Squadron's engineering officer, based at Lago airfield, near Salerno. Farish gave another pilot some spark plugs for Taylor's aircraft and he flew off to Anzio in the squadron's reliable Spitfire V. The pilot returned to Lago alone and clearly shaken. Nettuno was under constant shellfire, the American engineers had evacuated the runway, so Bamby had no one to fix his plane. Furthermore, the shell holes and crashed aircraft were making the airstrip increasingly tricky. [12]

Knowing that one of his pilots was stranded under shellfire on a hostile landing ground set Farish contemplating a wild scheme, something he had gone through in his mind as he sat at the controls of a Spitfire during engine checks.

As an engineer officer, Farish lived cheek by jowl with the fighter pilots, forming strong bonds that made him double-check that every Spitfire they took airborne was in the best possible condition.

'Living with the pilots in the mess was a great privilege, even when one lost a good personal friend. Indeed it was perhaps wise, being a ground officer, not to become too friendly with the pilots. But how could one avoid that with people like Tom Hughes, Sexton Gear and Chas Charnock? It would not be untrue to say that without showing it, I loved and worshipped all pilots.'

Tom Hughes, June 1943

Farish had dearly wanted to become a flier but his poor eyesight made him ineligible. However, he had done a couple of hours' tuition on a dual-control Italian biplane under the instruction of his friend Tom Hughes. Hughes realised Farish had talent but found landings difficult because of his thick glasses. 'He could not see the "blades of grass" so his judgment was never very good near the ground.'[13]

Farish stood next to a Spitfire and rubbed his thumb along his chin. He was gripped by an urge to get Bamby Taylor off the airstrip before he was killed because an engine had failed.

'Damn it.' Farish took off his glasses, cleaned them with a dry rag then set off with a purposeful stride towards the operations lorry. There, he casually took out a Mae West life jacket and a parachute. Nothing particularly out of the ordinary for an engineer officer. He next visited the hut used by his ground crew to store their tools, taking a spanner, screwdriver and other bits.

As he walked over to his Jeep he passed a pilot lounging in a comfortable wicker chair in the shade of some leafy trees. 'Spits' landing speed is around 90mph, isn't it?' he asked innocently.

'Yes,' the pilot responded, 'and with the flaps down you could do it at 85mph.'[14]

Farish mumbled a 'thanks' then got in his Jeep and drove to the squadron's Spitfire V, which he knew had never broken down.

With his heart racing, and striving to appear normal, Farish slung the parachute into the cockpit, donned the Mae West then told his flight mechanic to strap him in. His men were used to carrying out orders. No one asked any questions. It wasn't that unusual for the engineer officer to taxi a Spitfire to test its engines.

However, one or two shared the odd glance. Why was he wearing a Mae West and a parachute?

Firmly strapped in, Farish looked around the runway, taking in the light green of the olive orchard, the birds arcing in the sky out to sea. He felt a gentle breeze against his cheek and double-checked the wind direction.

The aerodrome was quiet and peaceful. There were no aircraft in the sky or coming in. All the pilots were in the mess having their afternoon tea.

If he was going to do it, now was the time.

'I was outwardly calm but inwardly cold, shivering all over, yet clear and absolutely determined now.

'I looked around the dispersal, nobody seemed to be taking much notice, so I started up and taxied out fast to the runway.'

One or two heads had turned at the sound of the Merlin breaking the afternoon siesta. Farish hurried the Spitfire to the end of the runway. As he turned into the wind he knew now he was committed. The Merlin's roar increased and people began running out of tents and the Officers' Mess, waving their arms furiously. A flight sergeant got to within a few yards, making the sign for Farish to switch off.

'I just looked him straight in the face and pushed the throttle open.'

The Spitfire lurched forward. Farish was thrust back into his seat by the immense, almost overpowering acceleration. He had seen many Spitfires take off, but to experience the power of the Merlin pulling him like a bolting horse down the runway was something different.

As he fought to hold the plane on a straight and steady course, he felt a lightness in the wings. He glanced at the olive grove flashing past. *Must be fast enough for take-off.* He pulled back on the stick. The Spitfire lifted momentarily then slammed back down, drifting alarmingly off to port. Images of the tyres bursting and the legs collapsing underneath him terrified Farish as he fought to correct the drift.

Then he was going straight and true again. Within seconds the speed built. The wings vibrated, seemingly demanding to get airborne. Farish carefully pulled back on the stick again. Instantly the Spitfire was in the air. Freed from the ground it flew skywards. And sky was all that Farish could see. He had lost the horizon. Greggs Farish, an engineer with no formal flying training, was airborne in a Spitfire Mark V.

It felt like the fighter was in a near-vertical climb, just hanging in the air by the sheer power of the propeller. The tail began buffeting violently. Farish knew he had to do something. He took a breath and pushed the stick forward.

The Spitfire responded instantly. Quicker than Farish was prepared for, far quicker than the biplane he had flown with Tom Hughes. The nose flicked down and the horizon all too quickly came into view. The engineer officer found himself hurtling towards the deck.

He did not have time to wipe a smear of sweat from his glasses. Gently, he pulled the stick back.

The Spitfire's nose came up and she soared up again, but not as steeply as the first time. Farish glanced down at the altimeter. *1,500ft*. That was good. He had some room below at least. But the aircraft still felt like it was fighting against something. He looked down to his right and saw the undercarriage lever. He admonished himself. It was still in the down position.

He then reached up and closed the canopy. The noise of howling immediately abated.

He was in the air and he was flying. His first ever solo flight and it was in a Spitfire. The elation of being in such a beautiful, responsive machine that he knew by every rivet, screw and bolt stayed with him for a long moment. But the most difficult and dangerous part lay ahead. Getting to Nettuno and down on the ground.

'I was terribly shaken by the take-off. I couldn't get my map folded in the right place. I couldn't find the flying instruments at a glance. I was in the cloud base at 3,000ft and it looked thicker ahead. I could just see the coast on my right, but knew it was enemy and didn't know where I was. I was all alone, never been so lonely before. I seemed already dead in a way. And I didn't see how I could possibly go through with it. Yet I was committed – no going back. I was very near hysteria in the cockpit and it would have been so easy to put the nose down into the sea.'

Farish began to take a detached professional interest in how the Spitfire actually flew. And it saved him.

After years of working on the machine, talking to pilots and imagining how it would be to fly, if these were to be his last moments he might as well enjoy them.

He made gentle turns left and right. The response was astonishing. Then he dived briefly, feeling the thrill of the plunge wash over him. He climbed back up and played with the throttle lever, increasing and decreasing his speed.

'Slowly I started to live as I had never lived before, an absolute singleness of mind came over me: I was *flying*!'

Then below the starboard wing he recognised the big rock that marked the end of the Pontine Marshes, over halfway to the Anzio beaches. He broke off from the weaving and began to practise gliding with his throttle closed and flaps down. Soon he would have to land. And the thought made him shiver in the sweat that had soaked his back.

But he was not there just yet. As every minute passed he grew in confidence. Why not try the guns? It would be his only opportunity to fire a Spitfire's weapons. He grinned mischievously and dived to the sea. At around 600ft he loosed off a short burst. He was delighted. 'The cannons shuddered, emitting a little blue smoke.'

On Farish flew, throwing in the odd manoeuvre as he followed the Italian coastline northwards. After forty flying minutes he looked ahead and saw that the sea was filled with a cluster of boats. *Anzio*. Knowing the navy's appetite for shooting at aircraft that came close, he gave the beachhead a wide berth.

Strewn with wrecked or abandoned aircraft, the landing strip was not difficult to find. Farish was by now handling the Spitfire in the air with confidence. But the biggest test now awaited. First he decided to fly up and down the metal landing strip a few times, to see if it was even possible to land on. Although one end looked torn up, it appeared clear enough.

Farish climbed up to 1,000ft, searching the sky above for enemy aircraft, briefly wondering what he would do if it came to a dogfight.

He turned, took a deep breath then began the descent heading into the wind, repeating in his mind what was required for landing. Immediately, he dropped the undercarriage and throttled back. As the speed dropped off, the aircraft began to buffet. Hurriedly he lowered the flaps, steadying her again as the nose tried to drop. He glanced at the altimeter. *500ft.*

He came in on a glide. The airspeed indicator hovered just above 90mph. His eyes locked onto the runway ahead. His height dipped below 300ft then 200ft. He could clearly make out debris on the airfield. Then he was at 100ft, fully committed to hitting the ground one way or another.

'The ground came rushing up to meet me. I waited to the last moment, then pulled the stick back. The huge nose of the aircraft came up and obscured my vision entirely. I bounced once then settled down, then felt a violent swing to starboard and jammed on full brake and rudder. I was very surprised the legs didn't fold up.'

He jumped out of the cockpit onto the ground and looked at the aeroplane with sheer surprise. *My God, I've done it.*

Unsteadily, he walked towards a group of American soldiers and asked if they'd heard anything about Bamby Taylor.

Yes, they had, the 'Limey guy', they said, had 'gotten' a ride in a DC3 transporter. For a moment Farish felt his spirits sink. All that for nothing. Then he smiled. But what a nothing!

He looked across to the Spitfire IX that Bamby had been forced to abandon then felt in his pocket for the spanner and screwdriver. There was nothing else for him to do. He walked over to the Spitfire, rolled up his sleeves and threw open the engine cover. *From fighter pilot to 'erk'*, Farish grinned to himself.

He was peering into the carburettor when a familiar sound came from outside. A V12 Daimler Benz engine. *Me109s.* And they were heading straight for the airstrip. Farish leapt off the Spitfire and dived into the dirt, looking up in time to see the first Messerschmitt release its bombs. A blast thundered across the runway, spraying dirt and dust over him. *They're getting debris all over my bloody engine*, the thought flashed through his head as machine-gun fire tore into abandoned aircraft at the other end of the strip.

Farish stayed on his stomach for a long minute as he waited for the Germans to go.

He dusted himself down and went back to work when a few minutes later he heard another familiar sound. This time a friendly one he knew very well.

A Spitfire crabbed towards the landing strip and came in to land. To Farish's eye, something looked amiss. The pilot stepped out. It was his friend, 'Screw' Rivett of 93 Squadron.

'What the bleeding hell are you doing here, Spanner?' he asked.

'Never mind that, blast you, it's bloody hot round this joint so the sooner you get out the better.' Farish looked from the Mark IX he was repairing to the Mark V that he had flown in and then at Rivett's aircraft. 'Listen, Screw, you need to get out of here. There's a Five over there. Take it back and tell them I'm OK.' There were now three Spitfires on the ground, two IXs and Farish's Mark V.

'What's wrong with it?' Rivett said. 'Will you give me your word it's serviceable?'

'Of course the bastard thing's serviceable. I've just flown it up here! And tell them I'm not going to fly anything back myself.'

'What?'

'Don't ask.'

They walked to the Mark V, Farish running his hand across the wing as he helped the pilot strap in. Then he stepped away as Rivett fired her up, watching with a degree of remorse and pride as the first and probably only Spitfire he'd ever fly faithfully took to the skies.

As darkness closed in, Farish was taken in by some American aircrew sheltering in a dugout nearby. With a couple of blankets and a jumper for a pillow he got his head down, in a sleep of elated exhaustion.

His eyes came wide open. The bright flash of yellow and the short ripple of thunder came again. He sat up. He heard another screaming whistle of a shell hurtling through the air. There was little he could do about it. He put his head back down and went to sleep with the rumble of gunfire in the background.

In the morning, after a few dry biscuits and some American black coffee, he decided to stroll back to the airstrip and work on the Nine.

Again his head was turned by the welcome sound of a Merlin. This time the arriving Spitfire looked in a fragile state. No undercarriage was showing as it came in to land. Farish stepped down from the Nine. At the last moment the pilot threw the nose up then the belly sank down, bringing the aircraft to an abrupt halt.

Farish ran over. From out of the cockpit came his old acquaintance, 'Richy' Richardson, a Flight Commander from 93 Squadron.

He looked around the airfield, at the Spitfires and other aircraft left there. 'Christ, like Piccadilly Circus here!'

'Morning, Richy.'

'Morning, Spanner. What the bloody hell you doing here?'

'Fixing Spits.'

'Course,' Richardson retorted.

'I have a spare one over there. But it still needs a bit of fixing.'

Richardson took a look around at the various wrecks, shell craters and dark smoke drifting from the Anzio beachhead. 'Marvellous idea.'

Both men went to work on the fighter, with Richardson passing up tools and holding pieces of Merlin for Farish. As they were doing a spark plug change, Farish heard the now familiar sound of a shell whirring through the air. This time he knew it was close.

'Run!' he shouted.

The pair sprinted towards the dugout next to the beach, about fifty yards away, diving in as the ground shook and earth rained down.

They waited a short time then gingerly made their way back to the Spitfire. Only a few minutes had passed before another salvo came in, making them duck and again run back to shelter.

'You might as well stay put,' Farish ordered Richardson after their fourth trip to the dugout. He trudged back to the Nine and carried on working. 'It was strange being the only person in sight, on top of a Spit standing on that open airfield littered with wrecks, in a frightfully exposed position. I thought of what Mother would say if she saw me and of the sunlit peace of our aerodrome among the trees of Lago. But I was absolutely determined to get that plane away, never been so fixed of purpose before in my life, a sort of cold anger.

'I noticed that the shells were falling into the sea between us and some ships. They were probably trying to hit the ships and couldn't quite reach them. By a conscious disregard of everything going on around me I worked on, until the last plug was in and the last lead connected.'

Finally, the Nine was ready. With Richardson and a couple of Americans sitting on the tail, Farish jumped into the cockpit and fired up the engine, taking it to a high boost to ensure it could get off the torn-up and congested runway.

'She's ready,' he said, standing at the lip of the dugout.

'Marvellous. Well done, Spanner. Bloody good work.' Richardson got in the cockpit and Farish helped strap him in. He knew the plane had received a bit of shrapnel but he was certain she could fly. With a beating heart he stood back and watched the last serviceable Spitfire leave Nettuno.

As he stood watching the fighter disappear into the sky he heard the sound of a Jeep speeding onto the airstrip. It was carrying white-helmeted American military policemen. They were friendly and understanding but insisted orders had been radioed over to put Farish under immediate close arrest. 'For stealing a goddam Spitfire', one of them said, shrugging his shoulders, like it was the craziest thing he had heard.

At that moment everyone turned at the sound of an incoming aircraft. Farish smiled broadly. It was another Spitfire. And it was a Spitfire from 324 Wing in need of repair. A minute later it was joined by a second.

'I think these chaps might need some help before you clap me in irons,' Farish said. Then he nodded towards a Fairchild four-seater that had also flown in. 'Maybe he can escort me back?'

The military policeman had a quick word with the pilot and came back wearing relieved grins. 'You've got it, buster, he'll take you back.' They shook hands. 'Helluva war,' one shouted as they took off in their Jeep, eager to avoid an awkward arrest and the incoming shellfire Nettuno was attracting.

As the engineer went back to work he thought of putting up a sign: *Farish School of Flying, Aircraft Repairs – done while you wait.*

Another flight of Me109s hurtled in, dropped their ordnance and then sped away. By now Farish was feeling exhausted after the marathon repair effort.

The pilot of the Fairchild looked grateful when Farish finally said goodbye to the two Spitfires and their pilots. Farish was grateful too; he was only too pleased to get back to the 'trees, sun and peace of Lago'. The Fairchild took off and had climbed just a few hundred feet when Farish closed his eyes and then slept for the entire hour-long flight.

On landing, Farish was immediately taken to hospital. Doctors there asked a series of questions as they attempted to analyse why a seemingly sane officer had committed an act of outright madness. But Farish's answers were level-headed and rational. Not content, the medics took an X-ray of his skull. Still they could find nothing wrong. The next day he was released into the custody of the military police, who, after questioning, told him he faced court-martial.

No one acknowledged that Farish, at immense danger to himself, had flown a Spitfire with no formal pilot training to rescue a valuable pilot trapped on the battlefield. What was more, he had repaired not one but three Spitfires, all the while exposing himself to enemy fire. Instead of court-martial documents, Greggs Farish should have been reading a medal commendation for the highest of honours for his incredible skill, dedication and courage.

Perhaps RAF chiefs did not want to admit that a mere engineering officer could possibly fly something as complicated as a fighter.

A few weeks later Farish stood to attention before a senior officer as the charge was read out to him.

'When on active service in the field in not being a qualified pilot you improperly and without authority took off and flew an aircraft.'

A second charge read: 'Your conduct was to the prejudice of good order and discipline.'

Farish pleaded not guilty to the latter. In mitigation the court heard he had got four pilots airborne and saved three Spitfires from destruction by working single-handed on them while under fire. 'This scarcely seems to be prejudicial to good order and discipline,' his defending officer argued.

The court-martial board was made up of five officers with, between them, one Distinguished Service Order, for outstanding leadership on operations, and three Distinguished Flying Crosses for bravery. To Farish's surprise, the pilots on the board took great interest in the details of the case. 'When we got to the nitty gritty of the facts I found to my pleasure and surprise that, judging by the voluminous questions, the pilots who really constituted the board were far more interested in how I had managed to fly a first solo in a Spitfire landing it safely than they were in hanging me.

'I had offended every rule in the Pilots' Union it seemed to me and yet these pilots were all empathetic.'

But despite a strong case Farish was convicted on both counts, receiving a Severe Reprimand and six months' loss of seniority, meaning delay to any potential promotion. 'I went away somewhat disappointed, to put it mildly.'

However, there was some solace when the court's findings were published a few months later. They read: 'After careful consideration the Air Council have formed the opinion that the sentence was too severe and have decided to exercise their power to remit that part of the sentence relating to loss of seniority.'

Saving three Spitfires and four pilots was quite a feat. It needed other such acts of individual heroism for the Allies to eventually break out of Anzio three months later in June 1944 and liberate Rome. But the country was still proving difficult to conquer.

Italy, Churchill had earlier pronounced, was the 'soft underbelly of the Axis'. An American general was later to acerbically comment that it was 'one tough gut'.

CHAPTER ELEVEN

Spitfires Out East

Alan Peart in the Imphal Valley, 1944
(fifth from left on back row with hand on belt)

The landing at Broadway in Burma was going to be tricky. The temporary airstrip was just 700 yards long, the minimum landing distance for a Spitfire. At one end there were tall teak trees, the other a swamp.

To land safely required what was called a 'precautionary let-down' at minimum flying speed, aiming to touch down right at the start of the available landing run after a steep approach to avoid the trees. Maximum safe braking was applied in the hope that they didn't end up in the swamp at the far end. With the Spitfire's long, heavy nose, braking had to be very carefully applied.

Alan Peart could already feel sweat drip down his new denim shirt which he'd just managed to grab from stores before taking off. Denim was by far the best material for the jungle. Everything else just rotted away in the wet and humidity.

Below him a sea of green stretched away, punctuated by the odd bare hilltop. Somewhere in it was Broadway, the thin stretch of cleared jungle that they might just squeeze into. There was going to be no room for mistakes.

* * *

The plan was for the Spitfires to join the Chindits, the highly trained jungle soldiers who operated far behind enemy lines sabotaging enemy supplies and bases. It was early 1944 and the Japanese were planning an offensive on British imperial India. Fighters operating from jungle strips had proved a success in hitting supply lines while protecting vital Dakota transport planes.

Replacing the outclassed Hurricanes in 1943, Spitfire Vs had proved a match for the Japanese Mitsubishi Zeros and the swift Nakajima 'Oscar' fighters. Although the Oscars only had a top speed of 333mph, they were light and highly manoeuvrable. But they did not have armour or self-sealing fuel tanks and carried just two 12.7mm heavy machine guns.

Worse, the Japanese aircraft, being mostly constructed of wood, made them easy 'flamers'. But their planes were agile and their tactics were brave as well as clever. A British intelligence report warned against dogfights as the Japanese liked to be 'jumped' because they could 'rely on their very superior manoeuvrability at low speeds to keep them out of trouble'.[1]

When the Spitfire VIII arrived in early 1944 it was more than a match. It could outclimb the Japanese aircraft and, being twice their weight, could out-dive them as well.

There was very little difference in performance between the Spitfire VIII and IX marks, except that the VIII's extended wingtips made it perform better at high altitude.[2] However, the new 'tear-drop' canopy gave the Spitfire a vastly improved rearward view when the pilot looked over his shoulder, so much so the rear-facing mirror was removed. Its all-round performance was superior to the standard Japanese Nakajima Ki-44 'Tojo' fighter. The Mark VIII was to fight predominantly in the Far East and 1,658 were built by Supermarine in Southampton. As the Mark IX was rushed into service in mid-1942, it came out even before the pressurised Mark VII and when the Mark VIII was still being constructed and tested by the Supermarine engineers. The Mark VIII, from a pure flying point of view, was Supermarine test pilot Jeffrey Quill's favourite model of Spitfire.

In 1942, Singapore and then Burma had been lost in the swift and ruthless Japanese conquest. Counter-attacks by the Allies the following year had held the line against a potentially disastrous invasion of India. By 1944, the British had finally managed to work out how to fight jungle warfare, with its challenges of supplies and good preparation.

Alan Peart's 81 Squadron had been posted from Italy to India to join the campaign. Memories of lost friends and the near-misses in Italy and North Africa were left behind as he enjoyed the privileges of British imperial India.[3]

'I had my first encounter with the life of wealth and opulence enjoyed by some members of the community, when I visited the swimming complex in Calcutta. I had just started undressing myself in a changing room and had my shirt over my head, when I felt fingers fumbling with my belt. Expecting to find a rogue about to rob me, I ripped my shirt off to find a uniformed bearer protesting that the *Sahib* was undressing himself and it wasn't done in this club. I explained to the bearer that I preferred to undress myself.'

However, Peart was at least able to celebrate the Christmas of 1943 with some indulgence, even if Calcutta was within striking range of Japanese aircraft. 'At Christmas we had a wonderful party, at which everyone got blotto, or at least nearly everyone. Four of us were on early morning readiness so we had to go to bed early. The rest of our group came in during the early hours of the morning carrying one of our four, in an alcoholic comatose state. When we tried to get him up at dawn we couldn't rouse him. Walking him around the room just elicited his comment that his "shank" wouldn't work. Finally we put him back to bed and got some other poor blighter. Later, when we returned we found out that he had a broken leg. Thereafter he was known as "Shanks" McLean.'

After a few weeks' acclimatisation, 81 Squadron, equipped with the formidable Spitfire VIIIs, moved forward to support the Chindits.

Like many independent units, such as the SAS, the Chindits had been born under a charismatic leader intent on inflicting maximum damage behind enemy lines. With the Japanese counter-offensive looming in early 1944, Orde Wingate was given the task of harassing the enemy's rear in north Burma, to hamstring their assault on India. Wingate decided to create fortified bases from which he could send out raiding columns to wreak havoc. Unlike the first Chindit incursion, when they infiltrated the front line on foot, this time they would fly in gliders then be supported by Dakotas.

To protect the vulnerable transport aircraft, it was decided that a half-squadron of six Spitfires should fly from the 14th Army headquarters at Imphal 200 miles behind enemy lines into the main jungle base, codenamed 'Broadway'. Here they would refuel and if necessary rearm then defend the base from air attack during the day before flying back to Imphal after dusk.

81 Squadron was selected for the task. The pilots, led by the strong-willed twenty-two-year-old 'Babe' Whitamore, were already chipper. In their first combat in February 1944 they had intercepted a mass of Japanese fighters and, by using their superior climb rate, damaged a number. While the Japanese proved very aggressive, several were subsequently lost on the way home either from damage or running out of fuel.[4]

* * *

Peart checked his compass heading, map and watch. By his calculation they should be four minutes out. *How the hell are we going to find the strip? And what are we going to find down there?*

The idea of joining the vaunted Chindits seemed at first rather glamorous but the Spitfires would be far from any help. They were just six aircraft 200 miles from the nearest friendly base and now a damn sight closer to the enemy.

In the end, Whitamore gave it to them straight: *You're going to be out there on your own, with no reinforcements. Get on with the job as best you can. You're all experienced and in Spitfire Mark VIIIs, the best aircraft about.*

Whitamore also told them a Dakota had just brought into Broadway a new mobile radar set which would be capable of picking up an enemy raid from up to forty miles out. That would at least give them eight or nine minutes to scramble. Enough time to get off the ground and gain some height.

Peart's eyes readjusted momentarily as his gaze switched from green to the deep blue as he scanned the sky. He saw Whitamore waggle his wings and head down to the treetops. They'd found the landing strip.

The six Spitfire Mark VIIIs did one circuit then took the steep approach to land. Peart held his breath as he came in sharply over the teak trees, half-expecting his tail to catch a branch in its wake. He bounced then braked hard. Thick green foliage dashed past him on either side. Ahead he could see glinting patches of the swamp's brackish water. He came to a halt a good 100 yards short of the runway's end and allowed himself a brief grin. Whitamore had halted fifty yards ahead.

Peart taxied over to what looked like dispersal, shut down and jumped out. The heat on the ground immediately closed in on him.

'Breakfast over there, sir.' One of the ground crew pointed towards a green tent, a trestle table outside with chopped logs for seating. Broadway had been used as an advanced base in a previous operation, making the engineers' work less onerous.

Peart looked down at the plate put in front of him. It was insipid fare. A couple of anaemic soy link sausages sat next to something white and lumpy. He sniffed a sausage. It smelt of sawdust. He took a bite. *Tastes like sawdust.* He reached for the mug of dark tea. Thank God. At least that tasted half-normal. For once he looked forward to the dinner they'd have after flying back the 200 miles north to headquarters at Imphal that night, after their day spent protecting Broadway.

'Sir, you have to move your aircraft.' The corporal had a thin bead of sweat on his brow. 'Immediately, please.'

Peart looked down at his plate then stood up, his back already wet with perspiration. What was the problem?

His Spitfire was parked on top of an unexploded bomb. Probably one from a previous attack.

Peart looked over at his friend, Whitamore, then down at his spartan breakfast. He was sure it would still be there when he got back.

The fin protruded from the ground by a good few inches and was right under the Spitfire's belly. A couple of bomb disposal men were already leaning over it. Peart asked if he needed to move the plane. He was told not, so went back to 'breakfast'. The tea was lukewarm but someone had added sugar to it, which helped as Peart felt sapped by the humidity.

Peart and Whitamore had just found the shallow trench that had been dug for urinals when they heard a shout behind them. A Royal Artillery soldier stood panting.

Radar had picked up four enemy aircraft thirty miles out.

They both began running towards their Spitfires, doing up their button flies as they went. Peart made a quick calculation in his head. If the Japanese were doing 360mph that would be six miles a minute which gave them five minutes to get some height. Still, at least it was only four Japanese. *We've got six Spits.*

He looked across at Whitamore as they strapped in. The squadron leader pointed at him, then upwards. The two of them were to go up to check the radar was right while the other four waited on the ground, saving fuel.

They taxied fast towards the teak tree end then threw their throttles wide open. Peart watched Whitamore's wheel go up seconds after lift-off. He glanced down at his speed indicator. The needle hovered just below 90mph. He pulled back on the stick. As he did so a shadow swooped over the cockpit canopy. He looked up in time to see the distinctive red sun painted on the wings of a Japanese Oscar fighter just a few feet overhead.

Followed by three other fighters, it streaked towards the four stationary Spitfires, its guns already chattering.

Ahead, Whitamore did a very risky stall turn, virtually off the ground, to try to follow the Oscars. Peart pushed his throttle right through the gate for absolute maximum engine power and tried to follow. Neither managed to get sufficiently round to attack the Oscars so they clambered for height.

Pushing the Merlin engines to the extremes they managed to gain some altitude. At 2,000ft they rolled out from an inverted position then looked around.

They were surrounded. Peart scanned left and right, above and behind. The smooth outline of Oscar fighters was everywhere. He felt his mouth go dry. Despite the heat and the clammy sweat, he felt himself shiver and go cold.

There must have been at least another sixteen Oscars undetected by the radar. They were the top cover for the four initial attackers. Peart swore softly. They had been taken completely by surprise and they were deep in the mire.

'Green One to Green Three to Green Six, get off. Repeat, get off the deck!'

Whitamore's order was half-pleading, half-scream. Peart reached for the transmit button but the squadron leader was still speaking.

'He was obviously aware that we had more company than the originals and he was firing at an Oscar right in front of him, unaware that three more were right on his tail firing at him. In terms of time there were fractions of a second to assess the situation and act.'

Peart turned hard to come in behind the three assailants on

Whitamore's tail. Despite the panic gripping him, he did not neglect the basics.

He craned his neck round to quickly sweep his 'six o'clock'.

Shit!

Not only were three Japanese locked on Whitamore's tail, but Peart had his own three Oscars for company, lining up to take the shot.

'One was so close that I could see the yellow strips along the leading edges of his wings and smoke dribbling back from his guns as he fired at me. Before I could even get close to Babe the aeroplane he was firing at burst into flames.'

Peart tried transmitting again to Whitamore. There was no answer. He searched the sky. *Nothing.*

He tried the radio again. There was no reply. In that moment he knew his friend and leader had been killed. He had no time to dwell on it. There were twenty enemy fighters in the sky around him, all bent on his destruction.

Peart was about to embark on the most intense combat of his life, where both pilot and aircraft would be tested to the furthest limits. If he was to survive he would need every skill he had ever learned and for his Spitfire to serve him as faithfully as she ever had.

'The Japanese seemed to be everywhere, above, beside and more importantly behind. I felt acutely aware that I had nowhere to go and hoped that the superior performance of my machine would see me safely through.'

While the Spitfire could outdistance the opposition by going high, that became irrelevant as the Japanese were already above and in great numbers. It would have to be a classic low-altitude dogfight with the Oscars more manoeuvrable but not nearly as fast as the Spitfire.

Peart's advantage was power and speed. Plus, with his mixture of cannons and machine guns, he carried better armaments. *Only if I get the chance to use them.* It was going to be far tougher than the twelve Me109s he'd faced alone in North Africa.

The battle was to take place at little more than between zero to 2,000ft. The enemy had him hemmed in.

Within a few seconds an Oscar was lining up for a head-on attack. Peart peered over his gunsights and fixed his stare on the approaching enemy. They were closing at a combined speed of more than 700mph and a few hundred feet above the treetops. He had to time his shot to perfection. Too early and he'd as likely miss; too late and he'd either collide or the Japanese would be past him.

Whites of their eyes, boys, he remembered Whitamore's advice. Peart's thumb lingered over the firing switch. Ahead, the Oscar's cannon twinkled. Peart braced himself for the strike of rounds on the fuselage. There was nothing.

The Oscar was closing to 400 yards, 300 yards.

The silver fuselage loomed. Now 200 yards.

Peart's right thumb pressed down hard on the firing button. His eyes followed the stream of cannon shell and bullet strikes that thudded into the Oscar. A split second later it was over his head, streaming smoke. He pulled up and looked over his shoulder to see it hurtle down into the green canopy. *That one's for Babe.*

But there were another nineteen enemy planes in the sky.

'I was flying by instinct but you were also thinking at a tremendous rate in combat. I was always trying to work out how to make myself a bad target and how to change the situation to my advantage so I could bring my guns to bear. These thoughts happen in fractions of a second.

'I was in mortal danger and there was not a fraction of a second to think about anything other than flying for survival and to kill the enemy.'

Downing one enemy fighter had a negligible effect on the others intent on destroying the Spitfire. Peart knew the chances were stacked massively against him. He had bought a few seconds of respite but knew the reality of death could be close at hand. He was determined to survive.

'I really felt as though I was facing death. It would have been such a waste to die this way after everything I'd been through. I fought the rising panic. There was no hope and I had no chance of survival.

I just fought that panic and did everything in my repertoire to stay in the air.'

Peart's top priority was to prevent anyone getting on his tail. One telling burst and he'd be finished. His predicament called for desperate measures. He would have to fly the Spitfire beyond all known limits if he was to get out in one piece.

'I hauled my Spitfire into a steep, spiralling climb whilst skidding and slipping to make myself a hard target to follow. At the top I flipped over into a steep dive at full power. At the last moment I pulled the aeroplane out at maximum G-force and with satisfaction saw that I had lost the chap on my tail. But each time I attempted to out-speed them others came from altitude to latch onto my tail again. The same occurred when I tried to outclimb them.

'The whole combat became a melee of mad flying on my part with no chance of hitting back.'

He felt as though he was in a boxing ring fighting nineteen other opponents. He was using every bit of inner strength to stay on his feet, but the physical exertion was draining him of the will to continue. If the enemy bullets did not get him then a mistake through exhaustion almost certainly would. 'As in a boxing ring with no round breaks, fatigue began to set in. The business of such combat took considerable physical effort with the use of arms, legs, eyes and head. It wasn't long before I began to feel really tired. I worried lest through fatigue I finally became a victim to the enemy efforts.'

Then he began to contemplate the only other route left to him – a landing in the jungle that, one way or another, would almost certainly prove fatal.

'I preferred a possible escape from a crash-landing in a clearing rather than through sheer fatigue have some Japanese achieve the thrill of shooting me down, so I began to watch for a suitable gap in the jungle.

'But before seriously contemplating such an escape, I decided to attempt one last desperate shot at my opponents but couldn't see any. They had simply called the whole thing off and disappeared, probably because of fuel shortage.'

Peart pulled back the canopy and stripped off his oxygen mask, gratefully drawing in great lungfuls of air, like a drowning man who had just broken the surface.

A sudden panic gripped him as he looked down over the endless acres of green for the Broadway airstrip. It did not take long. Long streaks of smoke threaded up into the blue sky where the Japanese had hit the Spitfires on the ground. He searched the surrounding area for any other smoke plumes that might give away Whitamore's location. There was nothing.

He was running low on fuel and there was nothing more he could do. He took a few deep breaths and, with the canopy still open, he set up the plane for the precautionary let-down. Again he gave the brakes a hard dig, just as he had done so an hour earlier, but this time as he came to a halt all around him was the smoke and fire from burning Spitfire wrecks. Of his old friend and Squadron Commander, 'Babe' Whitmore, there was no sight.

'I returned to the airstrip to find fire seemingly everywhere. I landed without mishap and got out of the cockpit in a very tense condition which I relieved by running around until my nerves quietened down.'

He had spent an exhausting forty minutes fighting in the air. The four Spitfires on the ground had been destroyed, with one pilot mortally wounded.

A feeling of exhaustion gripped Peart as he returned to his aircraft to check for damage. He then saw the stress he had put the aircraft under. Both wings were bent, scores of rivets had sprung free from the sheer G-forces he had been forced to pull. The engine was damaged by the power demanded of it and, last of all, he saw that a cannon shell had entered the cockpit but by luck or otherwise had struck nothing vital.

In a few hours it would be dark. Peart looked around at the destruction and the encroaching jungle that he knew would probably keep the secret of his friend's final seconds for eternity. He had no desire to stay. And his Spitfire was still flyable. *Just.*

Peart was now going to fly home to Imphal in his Spitfire alone.

As he climbed into the late afternoon sun he contemplated the loss of his friend and leader. For the last two years, the twenty-two-year-olds had shared the same dangers, the same birthdays, the sadness and intense camaraderie of frontline warfare.

Peart looked wistfully towards the softening afternoon haze. He felt very alone in the Spitfire that had taken such a beating for serving him so doggedly. His eyes flicked down to the northerly bearing on his compass then fixed on the horizon. He knew it would be down to him to pack Whitamore's kit and write to his family. He blinked away a tear.

Whitamore had seemed godlike and indestructible and now he was gone.

Peart had just survived one of the most astonishing feats of aerial combat witnessed in the entire war. A lone Spitfire had managed to dodge the bullets of twenty highly agile enemy fighters. Reliving those events from his retirement home in New Zealand, Alan was sanguine as he related his incredible feat. 'I still don't understand how I survived that fight,' he told me. 'I suppose I was lucky and this was a case of divine intervention.'

Peart put his survival down to luck, but his modesty hid the fact that he was a pilot with great gifts and of supreme skills. Those qualities, married to a superlative machine, ensured his survival.

'I had a friend who was in the infantry in WWI – he told me his great fear was being bayoneted so he had trained until he was an expert in bayonet fighting. He survived. I did the same with the Spitfire – no ruddy Japanese was going to get the better of me!'

If there was one consolation, it was that his faith in the Spitfire, which was already high, had now been redoubled. 'I had to do things with that aeroplane which must have exceeded the aerodynamic and physical limits and it never let me down.'

As the fight for Burma continued, the Japanese, suffering from disease and lack of supplies, faltered in their attack. The attempted invasion of India had been their biggest defeat to date, costing them 55,000 casualties including 13,500 dead. It also meant that by the next year they were weakened to the point of defeat in Burma. Alan Peart's courage and skill, and 'Babe' Whitamore's sacrifice, had ensured the Spitfire had triumphed in the Far Eastern skies. And it was also in action in even further-flung corners of the globe.

* * *

Hauptmann Günther Rall was told by his group commander in no uncertain terms not to report what he had just seen over the Eastern Front.

'Perhaps you are mistaken, Rall?' he told the experienced Luftwaffe pilot. 'And all this will only do is alarm your comrades.'[5]

Rall was adamant. He had seen Spitfires. Six of them. And he had shot one down.

The commander had to respect his opinion. Rall, twenty-five, was an ace with more than 100 victories and had fought in France, the Battle of Britain and the Balkans. But most of his kills had been in Russia, flying his Me109 against the inferior Yaks and other Soviet aircraft.

It was 28 April 1943 and the Red Army had unleashed its offensive against the Nazis, who had penetrated the Caucasus as far as the Kuban district on the eastern shores of the Black Sea.

Months earlier the first batch of 600 refurbished Spitfire Vs had been ferried to Russia via Iran. The Spitfires had arrived after the Soviet leader Joseph Stalin personally requested them from Churchill in 1942. The Soviets received a further batch of 143 overhauled Mark Vs, many the veterans of dogfights during the Rhubarbs over France.

But they were supplied without any British instructors, manuals or mechanics. So the Russians managed to learn to fly and maintain the Spitfires by trial. And error.

The Spitfires' first appearance on the Eastern Front, attacking a dozen Stukas, had not ended well in terms of victories but it had landed a psychological punch on the Luftwaffe pilots who had been notching up easy kills.

Rall immediately typed up a report but was then asked by his commander not to discuss what had happened. The ace did not concur. 'Is it not more likely that tomorrow we will encounter a large number of Spitfires in our sector on the front?' he argued.

He was right. The same day another Luftwaffe ace, Alfred Grislawski, twenty-four, had been confronted by eight Spitfires outnumbered by two to one in his flight of Me109Gs.

'*Achtung,* Spitfire!' was heard over Russia for the first time as Grislawski warned of the danger to his young wingman, who had only ever seen the fighter in aircraft recognition books.

Seconds later the fighters engaged in a swirling dogfight and the Germans knew they were up against an entirely different foe. Even the experienced Grislawski could not manoeuvre into a decent firing position behind the agile fighters.

Initially, Grislawski's commander also did not believe his report that they'd encountered Spitfires.

The next day the first Me109 fell to a Spitfire piloted by *Kapitan* Viktor Chernetsov leading eight former RAF fighters against four Germans.

While the German army might have suffered a massive defeat and the loss of 730,000 men following the capitulation of Stalingrad in February 1943, the Luftwaffe at least until now had been the undisputed master of the skies.

What type of Spitfires did the Reds have? How many and how many more would they get? The questions swirled around Luftwaffe messes for a week, then on 7 May they got into a proper dust-up with the Red Spitfires.

Viktor Chernetsov, leading six fighters, spotted a squadron of Ju88 bombers heading towards Soviet lines and immediately dived on them. But in his excitement he had failed to spot the Me109s high above providing top cover. Alfred Grislawski led the Messerschmitts down in a screaming dive and hit Chernetsov with his first burst of fire. As the German closed in for the kill he had to break away and fend off another attack. Chernetsov's wingman had flipped his Spitfire round and got on his tail. A savage dogfight ensued, with one Spitfire lost when attacked by two 109s.

Grislawski was desperate to match Rall and get his first Spitfire kill, and doggedly remained on Chernetsov's tail. But the Spitfire persistently refused to settle in his gunsight. Grislawski had to break away, allowing the Russian to make it back to safety, albeit via a skilful belly-landing.

The Soviets decided to put their best pilots in the new aircraft, as Chernetsov proved. 'These pilots were not your average Russians. These fellows know their business,' one Luftwaffe pilot reported.[6]

After a month of intense combat over Kuban during spring 1943, just four of the initial twenty-seven Spitfires in Chernetsov's unit were serviceable, with thirteen lost in aerial combat. But for once the return for the Russians was favourable, with a claim of forty-eight victories that included twenty-five Me109s. Another Soviet Spitfire unit, the 821st Fighter Regiment, claimed thirty-two victories with a loss of sixteen fighters in combat.

But a lack of spares and an inability to properly maintain the complex Merlin engine meant that the Spitfire was withdrawn from frontline action. It was moved instead to a defensive role around major cities such as Moscow, where it proved successful at intercepting the high-altitude Ju86 bombers.

However, the Russian pilots had proved they could master a sophisticated aircraft and the Spitfires had a psychological impact out of proportion to their limited numbers.

While 1,331 Spitfires were eventually sent to Russia they did not prove as successful as the 10,000 American fighters shipped under the Lend-Lease agreement. Their mechanical complexity made them a struggle for technicians used to simpler aircraft and the freezing winters, along with poor logistics chain, made them difficult to keep in the air.

The roar of the Spitfire engine could be heard in almost every theatre of war by late 1943. But the biggest challenges it, and its crews faced, were still to be found in the skies, and over the beaches, of occupied Europe.

CHAPTER TWELVE

A Foothold in France

On the night of 5 June 1944 Derek Walker paced restlessly in his wife's Chelsea flat as a terrific gale blew outside. As his new wife Diana Barnato Walker lay in bed watching him with half an eye open, she had an inkling of what was making him *jumpy as hell* and keeping her awake. As an ATA ferry pilot she had flown over the south of England, where lanes were crammed with tanks and landing craft jammed the Solent.[1]

She watched Derek's pacing and worried. The invasion of occupied Europe was imminent. She observed her husband closely, trying to capture his features, feeling the ache of love and fear.

They had been married only a month. Diana had met Derek after dropping off a Typhoon fighter at Tangmere. When she went in to get her 'chit' signed, Derek was the duty officer.

It had been a whirlwind romance. 'Derek had a blue-eyed twinkling gaze and the habit of throwing his head back into a proud commanding stance then dropping his eyes.

'He was as brave as they made 'em. A leader of men. He had the ability to raise a laugh and could lift people up out of any desperate situation or mood.'

Derek proposed on her father's estate at Ridgemead House near Egham, Surrey. For just a few moments Diana played for time, then accepted.

'Many of my admirers had, by then, been killed in the war, so I thought I should hook him quick, in case one or the other of us got bumped off whilst flying.'

If Derek Walker, twenty-eight, knew anything about the invasion he said nothing to his wife. She acted likewise. But the ATA pilots knew more than most.

Joy Lofthouse, who had ferried more than one hundred aircraft over the last year, found her workload intensified in the lead-up to June.[2]

'We were delivering planes upwards of twenty fighters a day, Typhoons, Tempests and Spitfires flown straight to the squadrons on the south coast airfields. For a few months beforehand no one had been allowed to travel to the south coast of England for pleasure. From the air we could see all the mechanised vehicles stacked up in the lanes; you could have walked across to the Isle of Wight on the landing barges. The Germans had high reconnaissance aircraft. But they still thought we'd go the shortest Pas-de-Calais route. No one dreamed we'd take the longer route into Normandy.'

* * *

Ken French

On that stormy June night, Ken French, the affable Irish trout fisherman-turned-fighter pilot, had been ordered with the rest of 66 Squadron into a briefing.[3] On the wall was a large map of Normandy. They were told at that very moment an invasion fleet of 5,000 ships and 287,000 men was heading to five beaches in Normandy. The RAF's job would be to cover the dawn landings, particularly the American beach of Omaha. It was clear to French that they were going to be part of the largest and most complex amphibious operation in history.

'We had waited a long time for this so there was a feeling of excitement tinged with a certain amount of apprehension, for, although we knew that this was going to be the biggest day of our lives, we had no idea what to expect. Now the chips were down they would throw everything at us.

'It was clear we would not get much sleep as the first squadrons would be taking off before dawn and this was June when dawn comes early. Then from midnight onwards there was the constant noise of planes passing overhead – heavy bombers attacking the coastal defences and others pulling gliders packed with airborne troops and transport planes full of parachutists.'

Sleep proved difficult. French could not help thinking about the men crossing the rough seas, including his brother Phil, a soldier on one of the landing craft. At dawn he boarded his Spitfire, which, like all invasion aircraft, now had black and white stripes painted underneath to identify them as friendly.

'When we arrived over Normandy we had a panoramic view of everything below. We could see the landing craft running up onto the beaches. I seemed strangely detached from the reality of it all, so it was hard to imagine the terrible noise that must have been going on and the fact that thousands of men were dying on Omaha beach below us. I had nothing but sympathy for the men dying below and was glad that I was flying above it all. Their sacrifice was truly amazing. A terrible time.

'As it took us about half an hour to get to Normandy and the same to get back we were only able to stay on patrol for about one hour. I made three trips that day and we met with no opposition.'

* * *

Tony Cooper had wanted to be a pilot ever since, as a five-year-old, he had sat on his sister's lap for a ride in a biplane during the visit of one of those flying circuses that had inspired so many youngsters to learn to fly. He did not let two RAF medical failures put him off and persevered, becoming a flying instructor. But he wanted operational experience and, by June 1944, he had got his wish.

Flying in his battle-worn Spitfire V, with his newborn son's name 'Peter John 1' painted on it, he took off from Deanland, a forward landing strip in the South Downs, at 4am on 6 June. Like everyone in 64 Squadron, he felt the excitement of a significant step being taken to bring the war to a close.

The Spitfires soared over the Channel to cover the massive fleet below at the American Utah Beach.

'Opening up into battle formation we reached the beaches over in France at 05:20 and as dawn broke we were able to survey our patrol area,' Cooper said. 'Our feeling of pent-up excitement turned into one of total awe at the scene below us. The coast and beaches were covered in a pall of smoke from the softening up by our bombers and the naval bombardment. But below us as far as we could see was a multitude of ships, thousands upon thousands, formed up in a tremendous, gigantic armada.'

At first an inquisitive single Junkers 88 made for the fleet. With scores of aircraft above and heavy flak below it was a suicidal move. A barrage of hot metal tore up from the sea into the bomber, making it shudder in midair. Pieces of airframe broke off as the plane was eviscerated by the vicious groundfire then sent plummeting in flames down into the sea.

The biggest danger was to come from overanxious naval gunners below, as Cooper, twenty-eight, recorded in his logbook. 'Navy shelling beaches. First landing made by infantry troop at 06:20. Nearly shot down by a [Allied] Thunderbolt. Spitfire in front of me actually was. Another Spit hit by naval shellfire blew up.'[4]

* * *

The Luftwaffe failed to turn up on D-Day. With just over 300 serviceable aircraft it was outnumbered twenty to one.

Later in the day, Diana Barnato Walker ferried an Albacore on the short hop from Hamble to Eastleigh with a splendid view of the invasion force. 'I saw tanks moving on the roads, going to be loaded onto ships in the ports. Ships seemed to stretch as far as the eye could see across the Channel. I also made out the huge Pluto [Pipeline Under the Ocean] "cotton-reels" holding up the oil pipeline, bobbing about in the rough sea, as well as some of the Mulberry pre-fabricated harbour being floated out towards France. The Allied planning people had decided against taking an enemy-held port: Dieppe had taught them that lesson. This time they were taking their own harbour with them.

'This was it! The invasion – to push back the enemy into their own country. So many people I knew were in those tanks, those ships and those bombers and fighters. I wondered how many friends I would ever see again.'

Nigel Tangye was back in his Spitfire to do a spot of photo reconnaissance on the Argentan railway junction. Like French, he watched in awe as thousands of troops struggled 25,000ft below.[5]

'I was so aware of the contrast in our tasks. The men far below on the white-flaked blue-green of the Channel were seasick and, I imagined, numbed by the long-drawn-out and increasing intensity of anxiety as they approached their unknown fate on the beaches of France.

'And there was I, sitting in the cockpit of my Spit, clean and civilised, speeding through the heavens, my main anxiety being the low clouds over the battle area that might prevent my pinpointing my target.

'In only a couple of hours, compared to the months of campaigning ahead for those stalwarts in boats below, I would be back in the mess with a gin in my hand and later would be having supper with Ann, after her show, at the Berkeley.'

The deception plan leading the Germans to think that Normandy was a diversion and that Pas-de-Calais was the real target proved effective. While the casualties at Omaha Beach were particularly high, by the end of D-Day a beachhead had been established. At D-Day 'plus five' 326,000 troops had been landed along with 54,000 vehicles.[6]

The advantage of having airstrips close behind advancing troops had been long recognised and landing grounds sprung up across Normandy.

Aircraft mechanic Joe Roddis, now of 485 Squadron with the likes of Terry Kearins, was among those flown over to set up camp before the Spitfires came in. Only a few months earlier he had stood on the platform at Worthing station and waved goodbye to Betty Wood. Now he was on operations in France where day and night he could hear the crack of artillery and the occasional whine of enemy aircraft. The fear of being in the heart of the war zone was coupled with the sense of adventure, finally being in occupied Europe and taking on the Nazis. 'I was excited to be on French soil. This had been our aim for so many years and now it was happening. There was also a real sense of danger; it was a war zone with equipment and vehicles everywhere.'[7]

There was also an intimation that some of the French were not as friendly as expected, with rumours that some pro-Nazis were taking up arms against the Allies.

'The few locals we encountered were openly hostile as they had suffered during the invasion. Snipers were everywhere and some very unsavoury characters calling themselves "Werewolves" were intent on doing us harm. Sometimes when we went through crowds of French civilians some waved but some spat at us.'

However, the intensity of operations at least allowed him a little time to reflect on his separation from Betty Wood. But he could not prevent the images of their last dance and tearful farewell coming to him as he lay awake at night. He knew he had to let her go. *Find someone else and move on.* And Joe had other matters to concern himself with. After D-Day, keeping the troops equipped with vital supplies was a huge challenge, and there was little flexibility in the logistics chain for luxuries. Hardened troops were distinctly unimpressed by the French lagers on offer, so the Spitfire came to the rescue for men starved of their beloved beer. A Mark IX, fitted with pylons under the wings to carry bombs or fuel tanks, was duly modified to carry beer kegs. If the Spitfire flew high enough, the cold air ensured the beer was ready for consumption as soon as it landed. In a bid to attract much-needed positive media coverage, the modification was designated 'XXX' and pictures appeared in the newspapers to illustrate the efforts being made to keep the invasion force happy.

* * *

On 17 July, Spitfires from 602 Squadron pounced on a German staff car hurrying along a lane. Among the wounded was the veteran commander Field Marshal Rommel, on his way to direct operations. Alongside its role as a beer carrier, the fighter had now found another great use as a ground-attack aircraft.

Ken French was flying his Spitfire in a low-level patrol seeking targets of opportunity when he spotted a German car hurtling along. For an instant he hesitated. He had practised low-level strafing many times and knew, after much live-firing practice, the devastating effects the Mark IX's mixture of cannons and machine guns could have, but now he was about to fire upon another human being. He was in the dive and committed. As the gap closed with the speeding car he could see a soldier inside look over his shoulder. French was fixed on the target now, his thumb went onto the 'fire' button and pressed down. A stream of gunfire kicked up a few yards behind the wheels then strode forward, puncturing both vehicle and occupants.[8]

'Once in range it was all over in seconds,' French said. 'Fighting in the air, although you know there's a pilot inside, you are still just shooting at a plane not a person. This was killing people close up on the ground and it feels different. I pondered many times as to who was in that car but of course I will never know – that was war and you didn't have the luxury of overthinking what you were doing.'

The risks of low-flying missions were high, as it brought the fighters well within range of groundfire, as French discovered when a shell burst just in front of him. 'I banked the plane steeply so I could look down to the ground and there in a field on the edge of a wood I saw the gun which had fired at me. I asked myself what should I do? His gun was bigger than mine so he could hit me before I could get to him. It also crossed my mind that perhaps there were more troops in the wood lying low which could give me a hot reception, so I decided that discretion was the better part of valour. As the Irishman once said: "It's better to be a coward for one minute than be dead the rest of your life!"'

* * *

The Allies knew the secret weapons would soon be unleashed. Intelligence had picked up chatter of *Vergeltungswaffen* – vengeance weapons – from numerous sources. And reliable eyewitness accounts of V1 sites had come from shot-down pilots like Terry Kearins, who had spotted the distinctive rocket 'ski jump' launch rails while on the run in northern France.

But no one really quite knew what was about to hit them. Certainly the Nazis had committed huge amounts of money and manpower to the projects, but until they were launched speculation filled the vacuum in military circles.

As a liaison officer to the US 8th Air Force, Nigel Tangye had connections that went to the top and he knew the Germans had something up their sleeve. 'The authorities have wind of a large expendable aeroplane with a range of 5,400 miles carrying six tons of explosives,' Tangye wrote in his diary shortly after D-Day. 'This presumably can be used against London, New York and Moscow, but even so one cannot imagine the Hun High Command believing that it would change the course of the war. They would be considerably easier to intercept than flying bombs.'

The RAF and the wider British population were about to find out just how difficult the 'flying bomb' would prove to knock out.

One week after D-Day the first V1 bombs landed on England. Initially, the government tried to hide from the population that a new savagery had been unleashed. The sudden explosions around the capital were put down to gas leaks, but the sheer volume of flying bombs meant the British public quickly discovered the truth.

After years of surviving Luftwaffe bombing, a new terror had arrived. Hearing a 'doodlebug' drone overhead, civilians waited fearfully for its engine to cut out, followed seconds later by the detonation.

The two-ton rocket that could travel at 400mph quickly proved its devastating effect when, on 18 June 1944, 500 V1s were launched on London.

In the Guards Chapel at Wellington Barracks the sound of choir and congregation singing a hymn filled the packed interior. A few worshippers picked up a strange, intermittent buzzing noise. They halted mid-verse and prayed for the Lord's protection. Soon the whole congregation stopped singing as the sound of the approaching menace grew. Then it stopped. Stunned looks filled the church. 'Take cover!' someone shouted.

Seconds later a blast ripped through the roof, sending tons of bricks and mortar onto the worshippers below.

A few straggled out of the choking, thick dust and screams, but 121 were left dead in the rubble.

The V1 swarm had to be stopped. While the ranks of anti-aircraft guns took out a few, something else was needed.

The new Spitfire Mark XIV, powered by the Griffon engine that gave it a top speed of 446mph, became an early ballistic-missile interceptor. The Mark XIV was a beast of an aircraft, loved by many pilots for its brutal power provided by the Griffon 65 engine which produced 2,050hp – almost double that of the original Merlin.

In late 1943, the test pilot Jeffrey Quill flew the first production Mark XIV and was impressed. 'A very fine fighter it was. It fully justified the faith of those who, from the early days in 1939, had been convinced that the Griffon engine would eventually see the Spitfire into a new lease of life ... It was a splendid aeroplane in every respect. It was powerful and performed magnificently. The only respect in which the XIV fell short was in its range.'

The thirsty Griffon drank up fuel but it was able to climb to 20,000ft in just five minutes, compared to the original Spitfire Mark I's eight minutes.

Being able to climb almost vertically greatly unnerved the German pilots. 'It gave many Luftwaffe pilots the shock of their lives when, having thought they had bounced you from a superior height, they were astonished to find the Mark XIV climbing up to tackle them head-on, throttle wide open!' reported one pilot.[9]

The operational test report also concluded: 'The Mark XIV has the best all-round performance of any present-day fighter.'[10]

Along with the powerful Hawker Tempests, Mosquitos and Mustangs, it made for an excellent missile interceptor.

Flying a Spitfire XIV Diana Barnato Walker felt frustrated that there was little she could do even when she sighted a V1.

'When we first saw the buzz-bombs we ATA women were flying Spitfire XIVs or Tempests – the aircraft with the speed to stop them – but it wasn't our job to shoot at anything.

'I enjoyed watching a successful chase, our RAF fighters catching up the shiny tail of the V1. Even in the sunlight the explosion was bright and impressive as it blew up or hit the ground. If it was flying near enough and low enough, my aircraft wobbled with the blast.'

By high summer the sheer numbers of V1s were beginning to overwhelm the home defences. Fighter Command threw everything it had up at them, which included the Spitfire XII, carrying the first Griffon engines and the forerunner of the Mark XIV but with less speed. The American-trained John Wilkinson found himself in a Mark XII on 11 August 1944, scrambled for an intercept.

As he powered up into the sky, Wilkinson felt growing excitement that finally he was going into action for the first time, albeit against a machine.

A radar controller vectored him onto an approaching missile.

'The best way to stop a V1 was to get your wingtip under its wings and tip it up, thereby toppling the gyros that controlled it, causing it to dive out of control before reaching populated areas.'

But a diving Spitfire XII was not quite fast enough to accomplish this so Wilkinson had to think fast to stop the bomb.

'I was pressing my aircraft to the limits as I had seen what the V1s could do during some leave in London. They were killing hundreds of people. I was determined to stop it. I was thinking of the poor people on the ground who would die if I was not successful.

'But I could not quite reach the V1's wing so I had to wait as it pulled ahead of me. I remained at full throttle and slid in behind it as soon as I could then started shooting straight away.'

As the cannon kicked out its bullets Wilkinson felt its recoil kill off the excess speed he had over the rocket, making him fall behind. He built up his speed again, this time determined to get in close to do the job.

'I was dangerously close but determined to stop it. I fired again. I pressed the gun button so hard, as if it would increase my firepower, that my thumb was sore.

'This time I hit the V1's controlling mechanism. The missile rolled over and dived, exploding in a field below. I felt a wave of satisfaction that I had saved some potential victims from its intended death.'

There were other Spitfire pilots who went even further than Wilkinson to save the civilians below.

Aligning a gunsight on an object travelling at 400mph required skill, and judging the right distance to open fire even more so. Too close and there was a good chance your plane would blow up in the detonation. The courage of pilots was tested to the full.

The Free French pilot Jean Maridor had shown his determination to fly from an early age. His parents were poor so he had funded flying lessons in Le Havre by working part-time as a hairdresser. He had just qualified as a fighter pilot when France surrendered in 1940, so he escaped to England to carry on fighting the Nazis. Flying Hurricanes and Spitfires with 91 Squadron, he shot down four enemy aircraft. By the summer of 1944 he had a reputation as a V1 killer after shooting down six.[11]

On the afternoon of 3 August, Maridor spotted a V1 coming in over Rye, Kent, and dived down in pursuit in his Spitfire XIV, making repeated attempts to shoot it down from the safety of 200 yards away. But his bullets kept missing and it was now clear the missile was heading towards the military hospital at Benenden School in Kent. Spotting the large red cross on its roof, Maridor, twenty-four, made a final, desperate manoeuvre to take out the missile. He closed to under fifty yards from its jet engine and let go a salvo of 20mm cannon shells. The V1 immediately blew up, the explosion engulfing the Spitfire, tearing off its right wing. Maridor was sent to his death, spinning into the ground close to the hospital. But the Frenchman had undoubtedly saved scores of lives.

* * *

Nigel Tangye (on right), 1943

After his return from the Flying Fortress bomber mission, Spitfire pilot Nigel Tangye had a greater insight into what Londoners went through in the attacks, not knowing when they went to work if their home would be standing on their return.

Tangye had had a few close shaves, having to dive under his desk in the War Office when 180 V1s were launched at London over a twenty-four-hour period in late July. While the RAF shot down sixty and AA around the city got sixteen more, the rest got through.

One unintended consequence of the V1s falling short of London was the effect upon the Kent countryside. Nigel Tangye reported in his diary: 'The hopping season is approaching and the hop growers are wondering with considerable anxiety whether the hoppers will feel quite the normal zest for the usual excursion to regions where the bombs are being shot down in large numbers to explode on or near the ground.'[12] Without the hops harvested, Britain's thirsty troops were in danger of going without a key ingredient for their beer.

Tangye, like many others, developed a hatred for the bombs. 'They were a vile, indiscriminate weapon with a devilish sound preceding them which for a few seconds gave no evidence of crescendo so you did not know if it was coming your way or not. Soon you heard it develop into an approaching string of rapidly repeated obscene expletives until it stopped and the air was filled with a cavernous silence that you could hear as you wondered if the bomb was falling toward you. An aspect of evil about it was that during the silence of a few seconds that seemed like an age you could not help wishing it onto some other area, in effect for it to kill other people. And the relief when that wish came true. One hardly felt proud of oneself.'

The bee-like whine of the V1's engine and its distinctive cigar shape of stubby, square-cut wings with the jet engine mounted at the rudder began to haunt Londoners.

While Spitfires could be used to intercept the missiles, they also played a vital role in the most effective method of quelling the threat.

The light, agile and unarmed Spitfire XI photo reconnaissance planes were sent on the dangerous missions to take photographs of the V1 launch sites and factories. Their pictures were crucial in planning for immediate bombing raids to flatten them.

John Blyth

The American reconnaissance pilot John Blyth, who had come from an impoverished background on the US West Coast where his English father had sold tree bark to pay for school clothes, was among those who flew the PR missions in the days after the first V1 attacks. The pilots not only had to fly into the teeth of German defences, but in order to get the best pictures they were ordered to drop from 30,000ft to 15,000ft, making them even more vulnerable to fighters.

On one of his first missions, Blyth realised he had to develop astute tactics if he wanted to stay alive. He had just reached German airspace when he spotted an Me109 diving down on his tail. Coolly, he acted as if he hadn't spotted the threat. 'If you panicked and reacted too soon they might get a better line on you. The 109 disappeared behind me and I figured he was just getting ready to open fire when I pulled straight back on the stick – going straight up in the Spitfire which I could never have done in the American P38. I got up to 35,000ft and rolled over to see him still sitting below me trying to see where I'd gone – I could see him weaving around trying to figure out where the hell I was and what the hell had happened!

'I watched him disappear then continued on the mission. That was the power of the Spitfire for you.'

While Blyth enjoyed the solitude of the cockpit and loved flying, it got lonely on missions with no one else to speak to. 'But you were also very busy – navigating, keeping an eye on your maps, watching the engine instruments and fuel, getting ready for photo runs, always on the lookout for Germans. It was a wonderful experience to be up there, almost God-like looking down on the world. I loved flying the Spitfire and was confident if I was ever intercepted.'

The low-altitude flying to hunt for the V1 launch sites also put them in range of AA fire, which proved a challenge when they had to fly straight and level to photograph. All the pilots could do was hold their nerve. 'You could see the flak coming up; the puffs of smoke, the black clouds blooming outwards,' Blyth said. 'You knew you were being shot at, someone trying to kill you, but you just had to go through it as best you could. You couldn't let it stop you. It's hard to say what being scared means. You just got on with the job.

'For this job I really loved the Spitfire because it was so manoeuvrable and a pleasure to fly at high altitude. I never had any problem with it – it just kept ticking along. It carried me through hostile territory and I trusted it with my life.'

After a mission in July 1944 Blyth found himself in the rather extraordinary position of being targeted by the very bombs he'd photographed. After flying over the Pas-de-Calais, he beetled back to London for a date with his English girlfriend Betty Peck at the Savoy Hotel. They were in a taxi heading towards the hotel when they heard the dread approach of a missile. 'We looked at each other and then the driver sharply pulled over. We knew when the engine quit two tons of explosive would be heading our way. I dived onto the floor and tried to pull Betty down with me. But she was having none of it as she didn't want to get her dress dirty on the taxi floor. A few seconds later we heard a big explosion a short distance away. So I just got up, dusted myself down and we went our way.'

Recalling those heady days seventy-two years later from his home in North America, John was clearly delighted to be reliving his wartime experiences. His son had warned me that his increasing dementia and deafness meant that it may be too difficult to interview him, but once we got going the memories flooded back and his love of both the Spitfire and Britain shone through. Sadly, he died a few months after our interview, but his son wrote to tell me he had thoroughly enjoyed our discussions and he was in no doubt that reliving his wartime exploits had prolonged his life.

Diana Barnato Walker was another who had a dangerously close encounter with a V1. Lying in bed at her Chelsea home in Tite Street during a spot of leave in London, 'I was lolling around when a buzz-bomb went gliding past the window of the third-floor flat. Tite Street isn't very wide and the bomb went between my house and the house opposite. The engine had already cut out as it came over the Thames and it swished past, exploding at the top of the street. I was glad it was time to get back to Hamble and the safety of ATA flying.'

Of the 9,000 V1s fired, 1,999 were shot down by fighters. Many others crashed, or were brought down by AA guns and barrage balloons. The V1 Diana had seen exploding was one of 2,400 that got through to England, killing 6,000 and injuring 19,000 people.

* * *

The benefits of invading France, alongside access to one's own Spitfire, soon became evident to some of those who had been living under strict rationing. On an afternoon in late July, a Spitfire landed at the ATA base in Hamble and taxied up to the mess, where Diana

Barnato Walker had gathered with the rest of the curious pilots. She was astonished to see who the pilot was. 'Out climbed my Derek. I tried to look nonchalant.'

After a quick embrace he warned her: 'Don't go anywhere near my plane. I'm afraid there's a terrible smell in the cockpit!'

Diana looked at him in shock, wondering if something awful had happened. Was there something dead in there perhaps?

The war had been on for a long time and food rationing in Britain was drastic. People weren't starving but they were hungry. She watched as Derek went back to the Spitfire, fished out a large circular parcel and brought it over with a big smile on his face. 'He had been over to Caen and brought back a huge Camembert cheese,' Diana said. 'No such cheese had been seen in England since the fall of France in 1940. Derek said: "Diana, darling, this is something I liberated especially for you." We all fell upon it and munched away.'

* * *

Despite German counter-attacks using the near-invulnerable Tiger II tank, the Allied advance began to gain momentum. US General George Patton led the break-out, entrapping 50,000 Germans in the 'Falaise Pocket', south of Caen in Normandy, where they were killed at will. Vehicles, pack horses and men littered the battlefield, all of them dead or destroyed.

Ken French visited the area after strafing it from the air.[13] 'The aftermath of the fighting in the Falaise Gap was horrendous. We had witnessed it from the air but down here was the reality. Mile upon mile of destruction, quite literally the death of an army. As far as you could see, burnt-out lorries and tanks and the bodies of soldiers and horses lying about everywhere. The weather was hot so you can imagine the terrible smell and this was going to get worse before time was found to bury all the dead.'

As the advance continued, so the airfields moved deeper inland. French's 66 Squadron arrived five miles north of Caen in late August as the British attempted to push eastwards.

When not flying, Ken French took every opportunity to explore the countryside and meet the locals. On one occasion lorry loads of German prisoners trundled past. 'They looked very weary and frightened and I am sure most of them were glad to be out of it as they must have had a very hard time. Even though they were under guard it put a shiver down your spine seeing them at close quarters.'

After a week of Spitfire sorties, French was given a day off to do as he pleased. He wanted to experience more of the ground campaign he had observed so much from the air. He and a couple of pals hitch-hiked their way forward, driving past pleasant woods and hills until the peace was shattered by the crack of artillery. 'It was a sharp reminder that we were getting close to the action. We saw a number of soldiers in various poses of readiness. When one found out this was our day off he said: "Blimey, when we get a day off we go in the other direction!"'

The troops were from the Duke of Wellington's Regiment, who took in the RAF sightseers, giving them a briefing on the battle situation.

The Spitfire pilots found themselves on a ridge of high ground just west of Lisieux, a small town twenty miles east of Caen. 'The enemy down in the valley were at that moment counter-attacking to try to throw our troops back across the river, which was a bit alarming as they were less than half a mile away. It would have been very embarrassing if we had been captured! The CO said the enemy force was about 200 men, which was roughly the same as ours. They were putting down mortar fire in the area of the river crossing so our troops were having difficulty in getting supplies across but he assured us everything would be all right in the end. The major then took us out into the orchard where the noise was deafening with a constant whistle of shells going over which, he informed us, were ours, which was comforting. He then picked out another sound which he said was mortar shells falling just the other side of the hedge about 100 yards away. If we would like to crawl under the hedge we could watch the battle going on down at the river.'

The Spitfire pilots decided they preferred war in the air rather than on the ground. 'We were mindful of the mortar shells landing just the other side of that hedge so made our excuses that it was getting late and we had to get back before dark. We took our leave and thanked our host for going to so much trouble to make our visit interesting.

'Before we had gone very far along the road our progress was stopped by a staff car from which a general emerged. He expressed surprise at seeing the RAF up near the front and when we explained ourselves I think he thought we were daft, but we also felt that he was pleased we were showing an interest.'

On the same day, 25 August 1944, Paris was liberated. The German army was on the run, albeit in its usual orderly fashion, managing to extricate nine out of eleven panzer divisions from France.

But the Allied air-to-ground attacks had hampered supplies getting to the potentially devastating panzer divisions. The Allies' overwhelming numbers had also kept the Luftwaffe at bay and away from the huge supply stockpiles on the beaches.

As the Allies began to rapidly push forward through France and into Belgium, growing evidence of German atrocities emerged.

Ken French's Spitfire squadron had advanced with the rest of the Allied forces to an airstrip outside Lille. Still eager to explore his surroundings, French found himself at a fort where eighty men, women and children had been taken hostage then executed in retaliation for Resistance activity. 'I had noticed a very unpleasant smell and saw a number of people in the vicinity of the graves and an ambulance standing by. A Frenchman approached and told me the bodies were being exhumed to be given a proper burial. One grave was open, hence the smell, and he asked me to see for myself so that, when I went back to England, I could tell people what the Germans had done to them. I went with him to the graveside and it was a horrible sight, the bodies of four men with their hands tied behind their backs. It was a most unpleasant experience but they were right to involve me as these things should not be forgotten.'

* * *

By September, the Belgian capital Brussels had been liberated. Derek Walker flew again into Hamble with a proposition for his wife, Diana Barnato Walker. A photo reconnaissance Spitfire was needed in Brussels to take pictures of the German lines fifteen miles away but he had no spare pilot to fly it. As Diana had four days' leave, could she bring it over?[14]

It was music to Diana's ears. While ATA men were now allowed to ferry aircraft over the Channel, the women, who had proven they could fly anything from a Tiger Moth trainer to heavy bombers, were not.

'Oh no, *girls* can't go! There aren't any lavatories for them,' had been the excuse.

Anticipating her answer that she wasn't permitted to go, Derek told Diana that as she was on leave it was an RAF job not ATA. He then produced a letter from his boss giving her permission to 'travel to Brussels'.

For a moment Diana was speechless. This was truly a momentous opportunity. As far as she was aware, never before in the history of aviation had a husband and wife couple flown together into a country at war. It would be truly unprecedented, and the fact it was in the most sleek, beautiful and seductive aircraft made it doubly so.

'Of course,' she blurted out, her eyes shining with excitement.

On 2 October 1944, Diana turned up at Northolt where she was given the Wing Commander's personal Spitfire Mark VII, the model fitted with the early pressurised cockpit for high-altitude flying to intercept high-level reconnaissance planes over Britain and Egypt. She was about to embark on a truly astonishing adventure.

As Derek sat in his idling Spitfire, under the gaze of RAF mechanics Diana gingerly slid open the cockpit canopy and slipped in behind the controls. The mechanics looked on with doubting expressions as she crammed her weekend bag in the cockpit, complete with a make-up carrier. The apprehension left their faces as she expertly fired up the Spitfire then waved them away.

As the two Spitfires soared into the air, Diana remembered Derek's last words to her. 'Whatever happens,' he warned, 'don't land anywhere else. If anything crops up, get yourself back to England.'

Flying wingtip to wingtip over southern England on an easterly heading to Brussels, a grin of sheer elation swept across Diana's face. 'As we headed out over the Channel I marvelled at the scene. This had to be a unique event: a husband and wife flying two operational Spitfires across to the continent in wartime. Other husbands and wives may have flown together, but our set of circumstances left them all standing.'

After just an hour's flight in clear weather over liberated Europe, the two Spitfires came in to land at Brussels. There were a few baffled looks on the ground as the two Spitfire pilots landed in perfect formation then left their aircraft together holding hands.

The husband and wife then entered Belgium's capital city which was still revelling in the joy of liberation, exactly a month earlier. Diana was quickly gripped by the party spirit. 'Everyone hugged and kissed everyone else, while the streets were full and noisy. There was the near-distant rumble of guns but no one seemed to take any notice. I kept bumping into all sorts of friends from the army as well as the RAF.'

The next day Derek agreed that Diana should be allowed to fly the Spitfire around Brussels and the surrounding area for a 'test flight'. With the front line not too far away, she decided to see it from 20,000ft up on her side of the line. 'I had a look at where I was told the Germans would be. It all seemed quiet to me and I couldn't make out from high up where the so-called front line lay. Nobody took a pot shot at me.' She came back safely then returned to the capital to enjoy its legendary hospitality.

'We had glorious days of fun and food. The Belgians had sugar, sweets, wine – all sorts of things that we in Britain hadn't seen for years. They had leather shoes and handbags in the shops and no clothes rationing – their war was over.'

With her flight home delayed by persistent fog the couple extended their stay. 'Derek and I had now been together for longer than on our May honeymoon. In fact, this whole episode seemed more like a honeymoon for us, in a foreign country, foreign city with friendly foreign and British friends.'

Despite the fog, after six days' holiday the couple took off for RAF Northolt with Derek promising that if things were bad they would turn back. Derek flew at high speed on the RAF's high fuel consumption rate rather than the ATA's more restrictive, fuel-saving one. Unaccustomed to the speed, Diana found herself struggling to keep up in the tricky weather. 'I could scarcely see anything except now and then a flash of light underneath from the water when we crossed a dyke or canal. All the rest was just yellow muck. I was unable to map-read so I kept hoping Derek would stick to his word and turn back, now he had had a look at the weather. But he plunged on so I had to stay beside him.'

Diana concentrated furiously on keeping up with her husband's Spitfire. Suddenly, the glamour and romance of their week away was being swallowed by the dangers of the dense mist. After twenty minutes the visibility worsened and then the worst happened. 'Derek disappeared into dense muck beside me. When I looked again he wasn't there.

'Suddenly I was on my own but where in heaven was I? I went down low to circle, trying to pinpoint my position, but there were no features, only open farmland. I didn't dare stay in one place very long because I didn't know where the Germans were. I certainly didn't feel like being shot down.'

Diana had flown in harsh weather before and now recalled the advice given by her two Spitfire pilot friends a year earlier. *Think.*

She throttled back to conserve fuel then set off on a north by north-west course, estimating that within seven and a half minutes she'd hit Dungeness on the south Kent coast. Then she flew into thick sea fog. Not being good on instruments she went up to 4,000ft into glorious sunshine. She spotted a plane and turned towards it, thinking it was Derek. It was a Dakota.

Like Hugh Dundas after his first dogfight over Dunkirk, Diana thought she might now be totally lost and heading into oblivion.

Fighting back the panic, she readjusted her course to due north. After fifteen minutes of flying low she experienced a feeling of utter joy as she spotted a beach running east to west. 'There, right behind it, looming up beside me with a rusty grin, was the huge gasometer of Bognor Regis.

'I flew round the gasometer, crept up the river to Chichester then turned right into Tangmere circuit. My, it was foggy! All the runway lights were on, while green and white Very flares were being fired up through the murk. "Just my luck," I thought, "they're bringing in a squadron and I'll have to wait my turn." It was now so thick that I stayed quite close to the circuit while keeping a good lookout for other aircraft, which I thought would jump out at me from the muck at any moment.

'After a few minutes, not having seen any sign of other aircraft I decided it was now my turn before I ran out of petrol.

'Feeling the ground beneath my wheels was terrific. I taxied in, parking next to the watch office, where, to my amazement, I saw Derek's Spitfire. He came running out, his face as white as a sheet. With an air of wonderment and relief, he said: "How on earth did you get here? Do you know that this is the *only* airfield in the whole of the south of England that is open?"'

He had also sent up the cascade of Very flares in the desperate hope his wife would see them.

That night she slept soundly in a Chichester inn. Derek heard the church clock strike every fifteen minutes.

CHAPTER THIRTEEN

THE BEGINNING OF THE END

Jimmy Taylor

The cavern of deep blue blanketed the sky above Jimmy Taylor's head. He reached up to the cockpit canopy to touch it. He smiled. The blue was everywhere but untouchable.

Taylor was happy. He was flying a sky-blue Spitfire Mark XI that had been lovingly polished by his mechanics to give it an extra few miles per hour. To be in a Spitfire and on operations had been a boyhood dream. As a teenager, he had first seen a Spitfire's alluring shape as it swept over the bracken of Aldershot in 1938. Now he was flying one of its most graceful models. After two years of training, which included a stint in America, by September 1944 Jimmy Taylor had left behind Eton and his fleet of model aircraft to fly the real thing.

Better still, he was in a clean war. The photo reconnaissance Spitfire of 16 Squadron carried no weapons. Just four formidable cameras which some argued were more effective than any gun or bomb.

Taylor's gaze lingered over the sleek wing then checked the rear-view mirror for the umpteenth time. His eyes went beyond the plane's elegant tail, ensuring there was no giveaway condensation trail or that a 'bandit' was about to jump him from the rear. The sky was clear, pure and beautiful.

What an exotic bird of prey rather than a weapon of war. Taylor was happy in himself. *This is a really good job. The cleanest way to fight.*

He checked his altimeter again. It was steady at 30,000ft.

Time to commence another run.

Below him was the key road artery around Salzwedel that linked Berlin to the cities of Hamburg and Bremen. The order had come from Supreme Headquarters Allied Expeditionary Force (SHAEF) to photograph forty miles of the highway. They wanted to know its condition and who or what was using it.

Taylor lined up the Spitfire for a straight run and pressed the exposure button. Every two seconds the two sophisticated F52 cameras, mounted just behind him in the plane's belly and pointing vertically down, took pictures.

The 36in focal-length lenses were capable of taking 500 photographs. On a good day the cameras could snap 1:12,000 scale pictures, allowing the photo interpreters to spot a man on a bicycle from the 8 x 7in prints.[1]

Taylor's 500 frames would each be minutely examined by the expert photo interpreters at RAF Medmenham, in Buckinghamshire. It was whispered that his Photographic Reconnaissance Unit provided a better form of intelligence than that which came from secret intercepts, giving commanders almost real-time intelligence of precisely what the enemy was up to. The Germans knew the PR Spitfire's strategic importance and were determined to stop them. Taylor had to take his chances with radars, radar-guided flak and jet fighters.

He checked the sky as he finished the run then looked down at his map. The reconnaissance pilots were very much on their own, deep over enemy territory, so their navigation had to be superb to find and photograph the target.

Taylor nodded to himself then turned to the west, heading back to friendly airspace.

He looked overhead, behind, then glanced below. His eyes instantly caught double contrails disappearing under the Spitfire's nose 2,000ft lower. His mouth went dry and his heart raced.

Messerschmitt 262.

The jet fighter with the long sinister nose and twin jet engines had developed a grim reputation since appearing in the skies a few months earlier. Its reputation was earned from the sheer power of its jets which thrust it to 560mph, a good 100mph faster than the Spitfire XI. It also came with the awesome firepower of four nose-mounted 30mm cannons.

It was Taylor's first encounter with the enemy. He took deep breaths of oxygen to control the adrenaline rush. The jet was speeding off to his right. Perhaps it hadn't spotted him? *No.* Slowly the German began to turn in a big circle, homing in on the Spitfire.

'This is where young James starts for home,' Taylor said to himself.

The clouds were a good twenty miles away. He had no choice but to climb up as fast as possible and hope to hold the jet off before he reached safety. The enemy aircraft started climbing up in pursuit.

'I felt a horrible dread in my stomach when I imagined the cannon and machine guns he obviously packed in his nose. I opened the throttle wide and climbed at the fastest possible rate, heading for distant France and using up precious gallons every minute.

Meanwhile, "Joe" swept from side to side, but never really dropping far below. And so it went on for five minutes.'

Suddenly the confident roar of his faithful Merlin engine subsided into silence. Taylor's eyes swept over the stilled propeller then his instrument panel. He thought frantically. Thirty vital seconds passed as the Spitfire slowed.

Got it!

The wing fuel tanks had run out. 'Frantically, I turned onto mains and it seemed ages before the old Merlin picked up again. Then on I went, scared to find the German getting closer behind. At 37,000ft I levelled off and turned slightly to see how "Joe" was coping. The devil was still coming on, so I had no alternative but to go on climbing and found myself at 39,000ft. Here I levelled off again, thinking that "Joe" could not make it, for it was devilish high and I'd turned my oxygen on to full. I was too excited to feel or notice any ill-effects, but I got a shock when I turned to look for "Joe".

'Now he looked most menacing, being just underneath my tail about 1,000 yards behind but still fortunately 2,000ft beneath. His speed brought him level with me. Then he turned to the right and made off into the distance. I expected him to come back again but the last I saw of him he had put his nose down and was losing height, soon becoming a speck then invisible. I suspected a trap – it was too good to be true – but, though I searched the sky in all directions, I could see no sign of him or any compatriots.'

Taylor finally got home after four hours' flying, with fifteen gallons, or about twenty-five minutes' flight-time, remaining. Unlike the Luftwaffe's jets, which had a maximum flight-time of ninety minutes, the Spitfire XIs did not guzzle fuel.

But the threat from the German jet fighters on Allied control of the skies was considered high enough to merit bombing missions against Me262 factories and aerodromes.

As Taylor made his way home, his thoughts turned back to the classroom lectures during training. It was a German general, Werner von Fritsch, whose quote from 1938 was drummed into their heads: 'The military organisation with the best aerial reconnaissance will win the next war.'

The request for a PR mission to get the very latest information on the ground came variously from SHAEF, the Air Staff or Bomber Command.

The order rapidly filtered down to intelligence, meteorological and briefing officers along with photo interpreters. The command then went out to the engineers, flight mechanics and tradesmen who would start readying 16 Squadron's Spitfire XIs while the pilot went into a briefing. After preparing for his flight, the pilot would board and carry out the sortie.

It all seemed clear-cut and possibly those who examined the black-and-white stills had little idea of what pilots experienced to get them.

The Mark XI could carry 218 gallons of fuel, more than three times the original Spitfire Mark I, and the pilot relied on its high speed, manoeuvrability and camouflage to stay out of trouble. With the pressurised cockpit, it could also go high, 45,000ft, without causing the significant effects of high altitude. Though the thin air still had an effect on the brain, as Taylor noted in his diary:

1. I tried to talk over the radio but couldn't produce enough air to produce gutturals.
2. Difficulty in sucking: no palate to mouth, coughs are hollow, and sneezes produce agonised exhausted feeling in face and lungs.
3. Windscreen in front freezes completely over, blocking vision.
4. Bags of snowflakes appear in cockpit in quick descent.
5. The plane is extremely touchy and unbalanced. 1/8 inch movement of stick produces a steep bank or dive.

There was something about the photo reconnaissance Spitfire XIs of late 1944 that would surely have impressed R. J. Mitchell, the aircraft's designer, who had not lived to witness the Spitfire's remarkable evolution after dying of cancer in 1937. Without cannons or machine guns, its lines were clean and graceful. It was painted sky blue and had a touch of the glorious Twenties and the Schneider Trophy about it. It was fast and it could go high. More importantly, it had the sharpest pair of eyes on the battlefield.

The PR Spitfire pilots were entrusted with the most sensitive secrets and brought back golden information that could turn a battle.

The reconnaissance squadrons used experienced fliers, a close-knit group of men whose bonds were formed in dangerous, five-hour missions. There was little of the excitable chatter common in combat units.

They worked alone and were vulnerable. Many perished in poor weather, through oxygen failure or the enemy's sophisticated air interdiction system of good radar coupled with fast jets.

* * *

For Jimmy Taylor the brutal reality of war was becoming ever more apparent. By mid-September 1944 his unit had lost three pilots. Taylor had sat with the rest of the squadron looking on glumly as they were told of the losses. One had spun down from a great height, probably due to oxygen failure, and two flight commanders had disappeared in bad weather. The deaths had a chilling effect on the pilots. They had all experienced 'close calls' and knew that death ran in close proximity to the PR job.

Flying over northern France, Taylor, who had holidayed in Europe with his father in the pre-war years, was shocked by the devastation. 'What I saw overshadowed by far anything I've seen in England. Everywhere you look you can see craters, some older and grass-grown, others with the brown earth quite freshly disturbed . . . What hurt one most was not the damage to military objectives but the awful toll taken on the farms, villages and chateaux that were so unfortunate to be in the vicinity. A chateaux, once the pride of some wealthy owner, desolate with one wing shattered or like a sleeping giant, with all its shutters closed, except maybe for a servant's window at the top, waiting for the return of the master.'

Jimmy was just grateful he would never have to face the savage reality of war on the ground.

* * *

After a week of low cloud and poor weather, on 19 November 1944 every Spitfire in 16 Squadron was sent into the skies. Taylor was given the specific task of overflying a jet base at Rheine, close to Germany's border with Holland.

He took off at 11am from Melsbroek airbase in Belgium, gaining height as he headed over Germany. Flying at 26,000ft he noticed contrails developing so he lost altitude before photographing the jet airbase. 'Suddenly, while I was in the middle of a run, there was a loud bang from the engine. It stopped momentarily. I tried to continue but a cloud of smoke filled with oil came out of the exhausts, followed by a sheet of flame. I switched off my cameras and juggled with the controls to try to get the engine to run properly. But the smoke continued to pour out and my windscreen was soon covered in oil so that I had to open the hood to see out. I called up Melsbroek on the radio and reported that I had engine failure. They told me to try to get back by gliding at 140mph on a course of 230 degrees, although the wind of 60mph at my height was against me and reduced my speed over the ground by that amount.

'I was leaving a trail of dirty grey smoke behind me which would soon attract the Germans' attention. There was an eighty-seven-gallon petrol tank between me and the engine so when smoke began to come up from the cockpit floor I felt that the whole plane might explode at any moment and decided to bail out before I was blown out. I made careful preparations and told Melsbroek what I was doing, then when the radio cut out at about 14,000ft I turned the aircraft upside down, released my harness and dropped out.

'Unfortunately either I hit the tail or the wing. I felt as if I had been cut in half and lost consciousness. I was woken up by a small voice urging me, *pull the ripcord, pull the ripcord!* I did so and saw the parachute begin to open, then I lost interest in proceedings.

'The next moment the ground rushed up, the same voice called, *knees together, knees together!*' Jimmy Taylor, the Eton pupil and vicar's son from Portsmouth, was now alone, and on the run in enemy-occupied territory.

Jimmy had been evading the Germans for five days when he rounded a corner, cold and dirty, but just a few miles from the Allied front line. He was in good spirits and feeling confident about getting home.

His escape kit, tucked in a plastic box inside his tunic, had sustained him through the cold November days. Water purification pills, biscuits, chocolate, twenty-four Horlicks energy tablets and a rudimentary compass had all proved useful.

The only downside was that he had been shot down near the town of Borne, in Holland, on a Sunday and had planned to be home within two days as he had a date in Brussels on the Wednesday.

It was a fine Friday morning. The crump of frontline guns was getting closer and thoughts of being back in 16 Squadron's mess grew. The sound of artillery fire increased. Taylor, dressed in a scruffy civilian coat, rounded a corner and found himself looking at a battery of 88mm guns. He shuffled on, eyes down. He was almost past the last gun when an officer approached him.

'Don't you know there's a battle going on and there's a good chance of your being killed?' the man said sternly.

'Yes,' Taylor replied in German. 'I want to leave here as quickly as possible.'

'*Gut*. The sooner the better for your own sake.'

'*Danke*,' Taylor replied then walked on, sensing that the officer was suspicious. After walking fifty yards he could not resist stopping to look back.

The officer was standing still. Their eyes met and Taylor instinctively felt the game was up. But he carried on.

A minute later he felt a hand on his shoulder. A grim-looking German soldier with a sub-machine gun hanging round his neck stopped him.

'*Komm mit mir!*' the soldier demanded.

Taylor looked at him blankly.

'Come with me!' the soldier repeated.

'Why?' Taylor replied, trying to play dumb.

'Just come.'

A few minutes later the soldier asked whether he was Dutch or German.

'Dutch,' Taylor replied, knowing he could not bluff being a German.

'Then why don't you speak Dutch?' the soldier smirked.

By now he was surrounded by a group of twenty German artillerymen.

'Take off your coat.' Taylor did as he was told, revealing his blue RAF battledress from which he had removed his wings.

'What's this uniform?'

'My working clothes,' he replied.

'Where did you get it?' The questioner moved threateningly forward.

'From the Germans,' Taylor responded, sticking with his story that he was a labourer.

As the tunic was removed they found other pieces of equipment that Taylor claimed to have found in a ditch.

Then the German officer arrived. He took one look at the flight lieutenant stripes and Taylor knew further bluffing would be useless.

'Bad luck, old man,' the man drawled in perfect English. 'You nearly made it!'

As a photo reconnaissance pilot, Taylor knew he might have information about PR Spitfires that would be useful to the enemy, so when he was transferred to an interrogation centre he resolved to keep strictly to 'name, rank and number' despite threats of being handed over to the Gestapo.

At one point one of his interrogators became aggressive, shouting and thumping his desk. The door opened and an immaculately dressed colonel with grey hair entered.

'What's all this noise about?' he asked in faultless English.

'It's this man, he's shouting at me and making threats,' Taylor replied.

'Oh dear,' the officer said. 'We can't have this sort of thing.' Then he turned to the interrogator. 'You mustn't treat Taylor in this way, he's a gentleman.' Then he turned back to Taylor. 'I see you've been to Eton. I'm most interested in the English public schools. You must come and talk to me about them.'

Only later did Taylor learn that a technique the Germans used was for a prisoner to be 'rescued' by a senior officer after a harsh interrogation, which sometimes made them talk. However, all Taylor ever gave them was a made-up number for the squadron he was in. Then he was sent to a POW camp on the Baltic coast. For 16 Squadron Spitfire pilot Jimmy Taylor, the war was over.

* * *

John Wilkinson (standing second on left)

It was not just up high that the Spitfire was proving its worth. As a counter to the German 'Battle of the Bulge' offensive, it was needed in the ground-attack role.

John Wilkinson had waited almost three years to become an operational fighter pilot on joining the RAF, aged eighteen, in 1941. After a few months' operational flying he had an 'assist' in shooting down a V1 in 1944 to his credit.[2] The God-fearing Wilkinson, whose father had committed suicide during the 1930s financial crash, was posted along with 41 Squadron to Ophoven in Belgium. He was soon flying the powerful Spitfire XIV, whose five-bladed propellers driven by the Rolls-Royce Griffon engine could get them to 20,000ft in just five minutes.

He had already felt the 'hand of the Lord' upon him in recent weeks after several near-misses, including an attack on a 'flak train', which had hidden AA guns.

In late January 1945, Wilkinson, now twenty-two, spotted a German ammunition truck trundling along a road and dived to attack. 'While I damaged the truck I was not satisfied with the results and circled around for another attack. As I approached I saw men running for the ditch dragging another man with them. Ignoring the men, I opened fire once again on the truck and there was an enormous explosion, such as I had never seen. I quickly pulled up to avoid the blast and debris and returned to a cruising altitude. It would have been an immoral waste of life to attack the men in the ditch who survived and who I presumed were probably lowly conscripted privates.

'One does not feel any animosity towards these targets, just the need to destroy the enemy's ability to wage war. Such is the futile waste when one must engage in war to prevent the destruction of our way of life and preserve our freedom.'

On 2 February 1945, Wilkinson received a battered letter, posted several months earlier, from the family of his great friend, Bunny Henriquez. The news was devastating. Bunny had been killed shortly after John had visited him at his base, when his Lancaster was shot down by a German night fighter over Pomerania.

On the same night Bunny's daughter had woken up screaming, asking her family to 'pray for Daddy'. As Wilkinson walked across the frozen grass of the airstrip he felt bitter at the loss of his closest friend and resolved never again to form strong bonds with flying companions.

Anger seized him as he pressed the starter engine. The Spitfire

XIV's powerful Griffon, despite the cold, emitted a deep roar. Wilkinson thrust the throttle forward and took off from their snow-covered airfield in Belgium with his squadron leader. Their mission was to shoot up anything on the ground. Wilkinson made an oath that that day he would find the enemy and exact retribution. 'Bunny's death made me incredibly angry. Of course people were dying all the time but he was a real friend. We had trained together, laughed together and I had been welcomed into his family home.'

Flying at 12,000ft, Wilkinson had already made several strafing runs on trains and trucks when suddenly he spotted the black outline of a German staff car. 'They were a choice target since it meant high-ranking officers capable of the decision-making that could result in casualties on our side. They saw me coming, halted the car and ran into a field. I destroyed their car and then I went down after the officers. It was the only time I fired my guns in real anger and I fired on these officers because they were the ones running the war. I don't know how many I killed or injured but I made sure I strafed them with everything I had – 20mm explosive cannon shells and .50-calibre armour-piercing incendiary bullets.'

Bunny's death had not gone unavenged. But his passing did make Wilkinson think for once about his own mortality. 'I knew that I could possibly die but simply didn't think about it. I don't even remember talking about death with my comrades. If people had their own fears they handled them on their own and in private.'

Moments after mowing down the officers Wilkinson found himself on the receiving end of heavy groundfire as he passed over a hidden grass airfield. 'In such cases the best defence against anti-aircraft fire is to use the full climbing ability of the Spitfire XIV. Heading up at 8,000ft per minute, one can usually climb out of trouble. However, in this case I could see the tracers and explosive shells gradually catching up with me. I instinctively flipped the Spitfire on its back and pulled a high "G" manoeuvre to dive just as I felt the bullets hitting my machine. There is no mistaking the sound of it. The engine was screaming as I headed down with the ground racing up to me at over 500mph. I pulled out of the dive very sharply, almost at ground level, and levelled off – one of the many fine qualities of the Spitfire – thereby avoiding disastrously mushing into the ground. I could see the tracers going over the cockpit hood but I was so low that if they depressed their guns any further they would be shooting each other. In a split second I was over a hedge and away.'

The near-miss left Wilkinson shaken but grateful to be alive. 'Until one experiences combat, no matter how well trained, it is utterly unpredictable how one will react. Being shot at fine-tunes the senses beyond description. The sounds, smell and feel of combat are absolutely unparalleled by any other endeavour on earth. Only those who have experienced it first-hand can truly appreciate and understand the power of adrenaline as it courses through the body, raising every nerve to the peak of efficiency.'

As John spoke to me from his home in Spearfish, South Dakota, recalling his brushes with death, it was clear that his faith in both God and the Spitfire was a major factor in sustaining him through those dark days of war. 'In my opinion the Spitfire is the greatest flying machine ever built,' he told me. 'I loved that aircraft so much, and flying them was such a great joy for me.' It was also his trust in God that saw him through. 'The protecting hand of the Lord regularly guided me away from harm. It was He who shepherded me safely through the war.' Sadly, John died in early 2017, another of the veterans I had interviewed who passed away as I wrote this book.

* * *

The adrenaline of combat had been coursing through Hugh Dundas since his days over Dunkirk, in the Battle of Britain, on Rhubarbs over France, in North Africa, Sicily and now Italy. He had had an incredible wartime career and it was starting to take its toll. He was now a Group Captain in charge of the Spitfire Mark IXs of 244 Wing in Italy – at the age of twenty-three, the youngest ever in the

RAF to hold the rank equivalent to an army full colonel. Whether it was his youth or sense of responsibility, Dundas still insisted on leading from the front.

'It was my job to ensure that fear was held within restraint. If it took hold it would quickly spread through every squadron of the Wing. And yet there was no one who felt more afraid than I, so the job was a hard one.'[3]

Like most who had lost their boyhood glorification of war, Hugh Dundas had to contend with the possibility of death on operations, along with the memory of his brother John, killed in 1940. 'The old struggle was raging within me – the struggle between the knowledge that I should fight on and the desire to call it a day and stay alive.'

Since the Salerno invasion of Italy in late 1943 the Allies had fought long and hard on their way up Italy, struggling through the seemingly endless German defensive lines. Dundas insisted that his Spitfires play their part by using them as ground-attack aircraft to harass supply lines. Thus, when a bridge north of Rimini needed to be destroyed in the late summer of 1944, he was at the forefront, leading his formation of Spitfires. The fighters were in their fighter-bomber role, a task for which they were well equipped, so much so that one commander had said they 'out-Stuka the Stukas'. Dundas looked over his shoulder and took pride in the glorious formation of twenty Spitfires behind him, in the blue summer skies. The picture had been completed as they soared over the evocative Italian countryside of vineyards, sharp mountains and ancient hilltop towns. He savoured the moment. At some point the war would end and such experiences were unlikely to happen to him ever again.

The moment of idyll fell away as he lined up to dive on the target, knowing that yet again his life could be decided in mere millimetres by the accuracy of a single AA gun below.

He also hated the Rimini bridge, which they had attacked before, as the flak around it was particularly intense. 'We flew out through a clear sky, no cloud to hide our coming. North of Rimini I turned and led the way in. The black puffs burst all around us before we had even crossed the coast and the target was still four or five miles ahead. The temptation to swerve was almost overpowering. I felt naked and exposed and was sure that I was going to be hit. The target passed under my wing and I rolled over into a dive. Down through the black bursts, down heading into the carpet of white, where the 40mm shells came up in their myriads to meet me, down further into the streaking tracer of machine-gun fire. I dropped my bomb and kept on down – safer on the deck than climbing up again – and used the R/T to tell the others to do the same, everyone to make his own way back across the line. Just after I had transmitted there was a thudding explosion and my Spitfire juddered.'

Bloody hell!

Dundas felt a shudder of fear and the realisation that his foreboding had proved right. After years of luck in dodging bullets, his time had now come, as it had for the many friends he had lost.

A great hole had been ripped in his port wing, halfway between cockpit and wingtip. But somehow, despite the damage, his 'faithful' Spitfire kept on flying. 'I held my course and speed, gaining height as soon as I had crossed the line.'

Dundas nursed the crippled Spitfire home, fearing that at any moment the wing could fail or the damage would make him plunge uncontrollably earthwards. Finally, the aerodrome came into view. He was committed to landing now, far too low to bail out. Gingerly he let down the undercarriage then very slowly eased down the flaps, his eyes constantly glancing at the port wing.

He lined the Spitfire up then descended, feeling a huge release of pressure as the wheels kissed the ground. He carefully applied the brakes, bringing the speed below 80mph. Suddenly there was a loud bang and the aircraft slewed round. A tyre puncture. There was nothing he could do but wait until it came to a halt. The Spitfire remained intact and Dundas climbed out, shaken but unscathed.

He went to the caravan he shared with the veteran fighter leader Brian Kingcome, who had invited round the equally illustrious Group Captain Wilfrid Duncan Smith, DSO and bar, DFC and bar and Spitfire ace with seventeen kills.

'They both treated my adventure as a huge joke – quite rightly, too. But for once I was not feeling jokey. I told them to go to hell and lay down on my bunk and thought, *Oh Christ, Oh Christ, I can't go on like this.*'

* * *

Ray Holmes, 1936

Ray Holmes had been in the war from its very start and now, having converted to reconnaissance Spitfires, hoped to be there at the finish. He justifiably thought he'd done his bit, particularly after ramming the Dornier heading towards Buckingham Palace in 1940.

In January 1945 he joined 541 Photo Reconnaissance Squadron at RAF Benson in Oxfordshire. Experienced pilots were needed to fly the long solo flights 500 miles behind enemy lines.[4]

'Now's your chance for a few gongs,' his training officer had told him. Holmes was aware that at Benson a whole new manner of flying lay ahead. 'I was now to become a lone ranger. A scout. A spy in the sky. I was to be taken to a briefing room, shown Top Secret maps, given highly classified information about a target and set to photograph it.'

With the bad weather of February and early March 1945 clearing, the squadron was put to work, sneaking deep into German territory. Within four days, four experienced pilots were lost either to enemy action or by being forced to ditch in the North Sea with little chance of rescue. Holmes could not help reflecting on the tragedy of their loss as the war was coming to a successful conclusion.

Flying day after day, the surviving pilots became fractious and tired.

'The danger signs were showing in the Flight. Chaps were getting edgy. The trips were growing longer. Four or five hours was quite a spell up there alone, relying on a single engine and your own navigation while you play a game of cat and mouse with a ruthless enemy.'

Regardless of any fears, and the notion that the war might be entering the final stages, there was no respite for the Spitfire photo reconnaissance pilots. Holmes was given an overview of targets over Germany, prioritised by the colour of the pins on the map – submarine bases, airfields, railway yards and oil refineries. All targets for Bomber Command. All needed photographing.

Among them was the port of Hamburg, not photographed for three months. 'The weather this winter has been bloody lousy and not one pilot who went in good weather came back,' his squadron leader, Tim Fairhurst, said. 'The Hun is fighting like hell to keep our recce planes away.' Holmes felt irritated by the remark. Of course he bloody knew the enemy was fighting like hell. He lived it every day. And he did not need reminding that 541 Squadron had already lost three pilots on the Hamburg run alone. They were all friends and colleagues.

Fairhurst then told him the Met Office had an 'unusual' forecast. Cloud covered the skies over Germany all the way to Hamburg, but a freak temperature inversion from the Alps had created a circular clearance about twenty miles in diameter. 'This pocket of clearance is moving north-west at 15mph,' Fairhurst said. 'Around midday Hamburg will bask in sunshine for at least half an hour.'

Holmes glanced at his wristwatch. 'I'll need to get cracking.'

'It'll be a lousy trip to Hamburg,' sympathised Fairhurst. 'Even lousier arriving back at Benson with no visibility for landing.'

Holmes at least drew some comfort on looking at the polished outline of his new, lightning-blue Spitfire XIX. The latest photo reconnaissance version was one hell of a beast. The Mark XIX was driven by a 2,100hp Griffon engine that had twice the power of the first Merlins. It could carry 256 gallons of fuel, three and a half times that of a Spitfire I. A total of 225 were built and were to see service for another decade in the reconnaissance role.

Holmes closed the canopy quickly, hearing the rain thrash down on it as he went through his instrument checks. It felt to him that he would not only be operating against whatever the Nazis could throw at him, but that he was up against the weather gods as well.

The Griffon burst into life and lined up on the rain-splattered runway. He glanced at his watch: 10.28am. Time to go.

His Spitfire hurtled down the strip. He could barely see the control tower. Water streaked off his wheels then ceased as they left the ground. Within 150ft he was in thick cloud. He flew on and up knowing at least no one else would be flying in this muck. Up and up he went, watching the altimeter climb through 10,000ft then 20,000ft, and still he was in thick, clawing cloud. It persisted even when he levelled out at 28,500ft, a height just below that at which his Spitfire would likely produce giveaway contrails if he entered clear weather.

He settled down to a cruising speed of 410mph, taking a few deep breaths to relieve himself of the tension of being in thick cloud relying solely on instruments. Over the North Sea, he switched on his radar detection device, which could pick up whether the enemy radar signal was tracking him. He smiled grimly when he heard a noise he recognised only too well.

'Almost immediately there came a familiar faint wail as the enemy's invisible radio beam swept past. It was repeated a second or so later, as the beam came back, then again, fast, as with each sweep the radar operator came nearer to fixing my position.

'The wails merged and became louder as a second beam then a third locked onto my position, a plot on the German operations board. They could now follow my every move, noting any change of track, speed or height. From the course I was steering they would anticipate the target was Hamburg, reckon my time due over it and have fighters sitting, waiting.'

He knew from now on he had to rely on his years of flying experience, his wits and pure instinct. It had become a game of chess. The wailing grew louder.

Sod that noise. He switched off the detection device.

'There was still nothing to be seen outside but swirling, wet cotton wool. It was hard to imagine that five miles below people lived in houses and drove motor cars or tended their animals on farms. All wishing me dead.'

Holmes checked his map, noting he was halfway to the target with another sixty-nine minutes to go. *A lifetime. Maybe my lifetime.* He began visualising the Hamburg landmarks so he would not have to consult the map if there were fighters waiting over the target.

Then he started a game of cat and mouse, gradually altering his course to starboard, knowing the radar operators would in a few minutes pick up the change and possibly believe he was in fact heading to Bremen. 'This would mean bringing up more fighters from airfields around Bremen or diverting the Hamburg defenders. I hoped for the latter, because that would leave Hamburg unprotected.'

He jettisoned the drop tank positioned under the cockpit belly which carried the extra ninety gallons of fuel. As it tumbled earthwards, the Spitfire felt lighter and more mobile. He now had greater manoeuvrability for whatever trouble lay ahead. He went to the compass and set course again for Hamburg.

'Now the cloud was quite suddenly thinner, becoming even wispy. The rain stopped beating the windscreen. It looked as though those Met wallahs might be right after all.'

Ahead he could see that the dark, horrible cloud was giving way to a much lighter and thinner covering. He felt a growing feeling of utter joy as the grim, rain-filled gloom was suddenly lifted.

'All at once I was sitting on a shimmering white eiderdown, the sun blazing down, dazzling my eyes and warming up the cockpit. The quilt exploded and there through straggling cloud wisps was the ground.

'Not only the ground! By heaven my navigation, despite the changes of course, had worked like a dream. There was the River Elbe, a shimmering snake dragging its lazy way over green fields and through dense woodland. Not three minutes' flying to the north the fields ended at the docks of Hamburg.

'Suddenly my heart gave a bound. Above the Spitfire was a contrail, a twin stream of condensation. Probably an Me262 jet, fast and armed with four 30mm cannons. The reception committee was in attendance. They were circling, waiting patiently for me. My ruse hadn't been so clever after all.'

It appeared at least that the jet had not yet spotted the Spitfire 5,000ft below, so Holmes dived down towards the quaysides. Even from five miles up he quickly noticed something was amiss.

'It all appeared bare and white, as if under a blanket of snow. Then, as I was starting with my cameras, I realised what was lacking. The quays were a mass of dust and rubble. There were no buildings. The ground was pockmarked with bomb craters. This was Bomber Command's revenge for the Luftwaffe's blitzes on Coventry, Liverpool and London.'

But the Messerschmitt pilot had spotted him and was diving angrily from the rear at a tremendous overtaking speed. With no guns to fight back and no chance of outpacing the German jet, the Spitfire's only chance was evasion.

'I slammed the throttle closed. The engine backfired as though it had been shot.'

Holmes focused on the airspeed indicator, willing it to slow. The speed dropped to 300, 250 then 200mph.

He looked over his shoulder. He could make out the clear lines of the Nazi jet, its sharp, sleek, predatory nose and the cigar-shaped twin jet engines, sitting below the wings, firing it along. The gap was now 2,000 yards and the fighter was closing fast. In another few seconds he would close to 1,000 yards and the pilot would be able to engage with all four 30mm cannon.

Holmes' focus went back to his speed. He had to time his next move to perfection. If he didn't, the cockpit would shudder to the impact of the high-explosive 30mm shells, themselves the thickness of a cigar.

He felt the Spitfire slowing rapidly. The needle dipped to under 200mph. He counted. *One, two, three.*

'I yanked the Spitfire into a vertical right-hand bank then hauled the control column back into my belly until my eyeballs seemed to be rolling down my cheeks.

'I blacked out completely with the centrifugal pull. Then I kicked on hard right rudder. The aircraft went into a fit of convulsions at this ill-treatment. Streamers flew from its wingtips as it spun down vertically off a high-speed stall. The Messerschmitt, at three times the speed of the Spitfire, was firing futilely because he could never turn tightly enough at his speed to get the deflection on the Spitfire. The whirling tracer from the four 30mm cannons was passing behind me. Surprisingly, I even heard the throaty bark of the guns. Then the Me262 flashed behind as I eased out of the spin.'

The German fighter might be incredibly fast but it was a wallowing whale when it came to agility. Holmes knew it would take the jet at least ten miles to complete its turn and come back at him. He had bought himself time. Lots of time. Certainly just about enough for another run with plenty of exposures left in the cameras. He swept over the west side of Hamburg, clicking pictures of the damage below as he went.

As Holmes finished his run he looked up. Still there was no enemy in sight. He grinned broadly and pushed the Spitfire up into the thick cloud which only moments earlier he had been cursing.

He glanced again behind. A second Messerschmitt, probably answering the call of its leader, was positioning for attack. But he was too far away. Holmes felt a wave of relief as he sped into the thick blanket of cloud.

'I sang most of the way home. Crazy songs, made-up words, mostly rubbish. I was jubilant. The sound of my own voice, which came back loud and clear through the radio headset, eased the tension. I did not care that I had to land at my base in the sort of weather that made the birds walk.'

When the photographs were developed Bomber Command was delighted. Holmes' pictures showed there was nothing left to bomb. The war was nearing its final weeks and the lives of hundreds of bomber crews need not be risked for a return trip.

Holmes was given a set of the pictures as a memento and awarded with a fresh egg for lunch.

* * *

Brian Bird

Brian Bird's courage had not yet been tested in combat although he was not entirely green to warfare after sheltering in the Kent fields during Battle of Britain raids with teenage female farmhands for company. To his constant astonishment and delight, he was now flying the Spitfires he had seen tackle Messerschmitts, Dorniers and Heinkels in the skies of 1940.

In April 1945, the twenty-year-old pilot flew in a Dakota transport plane towards his frontline squadron, watching distant puffs of smoke on the ground as shells burst along the front line. He was heading to join 185 Squadron outside Pisa in Italy.

As the aircraft doors opened he was greeted with the sound of gunfire in the distance. He felt his heartbeat quicken. Finally he was in the war zone, where the action was. His grin broadened at the roar from a flight of Spitfire fighter-bombers taking off for a mission.[5]

'One was quickly getting the message that the weeks ahead were going to be like nothing ever before experienced. Quite clearly one's survival was questionable, but this, in a strange manner, soon became a secondary consideration.'

Walking into the weather-beaten farmhouse that had become the squadron headquarters, he became conscious of a war-footing atmosphere.

This is where the serious, life-and-death decisions are made, Bird thought to himself. The atmosphere was low-key but highly professional, with conversations taking place where lives would clearly be affected. He felt elated at finally arriving on a frontline operational squadron even if the war's end was in sight. He knew that within days he would be flying into action, where people wanted to take his life and where he might have to kill. It was daunting but absorbing. He wondered, too, how he would react in combat.

He entered the room and found the duty officer sitting behind some discarded ammunition boxes, which served as his desk. 'An unshaven Flying Officer greeted me and introduced himself as the Squadron Adjutant. With the battle raging a few miles away there was obviously little time for ceremony or courtesies. I was immediately passed on to the Squadron Intelligence officer who wasted no time in familiarising me with the current position of the front line.

'One supposes that in peacetime I would have been allowed a day or so to settle in but this was war and there were no such niceties. Within thirty minutes of my arrival at squadron headquarters I was transported in a Jeep down a shell-cratered road to the squadron's landing strip to be introduced to my ground crew.

'Only thirty-six hours earlier I had been completing my final instruction course in southern Italy and now here I was, climbing into the cockpit of my first squadron Spitfire in the forward war zone.'

Bird was about to be thrown straight into action. His first operational sortie with 185 Squadron would be at dawn the next day. 'But not before we give you a good send-off,' the officer said with a wink as he led him towards the bar.

At some point after midnight and before dawn, Bird found himself staggering through the dark trying to locate his bunk. He found a water pump, put his head under it and drank from the glacial waters that rushed over his head. Slowly he made his way to bed, hoping that the light showing in the distance was not the dawn. Tomorrow – or was it today? – he was going to war.

This unorthodox form of preparation for his first patrol at least gave him a bit of Dutch courage as he awoke a few hours later, on 17 April 1945, and was taken to the 'ops' trailer for a briefing. An American division had been held up by a battalion of SS troopers dug in around a warehouse north of Bologna. The squadron was to patrol at 10,000ft until contacted by radio controllers on the ground. Bird felt his heart quicken at the prospect of experiencing combat for the first time, but as he entered the cockpit his emotions changed. 'I was suddenly conscious that all the butterflies which had been so rampant in my stomach for the last twelve hours had melted away, to be replaced by an air of clinical discipline.'

'Clear to go, Dragon Two.' The call came over his helmet

earphones. Bird felt a surge of elation as he opened the throttle and hurtled down the airstrip in his Spitfire IX. He was about to see action, to be in the war and do his bit. To help pay back the Germans who had attacked his country. The war's end was close but at least he was now part of it. He pulled back on the stick and soared into the sky, excited, nervous, but more than ready for what was to come.

Within ten minutes he had reached the patrol height of 10,000ft above the Apennines, where the sun was reaching into a cloudless sky. Just in front of him was the comforting sight of his leader's aircraft but no words of comfort came over the wireless. Silence would be maintained until the frontline Ground Control Unit called up.

Far below there were long lines of dust clouds twisting and turning through the Apennines and onto the roads of the Po Valley. No imagination was necessary to realise that this was the Allied troops in hot pursuit of the Germans in retreat.

It was a sight that made Bird realise that the long years of the war were coming to a successful end.

'Suddenly the wireless broke into life and I could hear Ground Control giving my leader a map reference for a new target. It was a rule that all pilots on this type of operation should individually acknowledge to their leader that they too have identified the target. With a swift glance down I was able, to my great relief, to identify the warehouse and quickly acknowledge the fact to "Dragon Leader".

'I turned my aircraft on its back and followed him down in almost a vertical dive. Beyond the long nose of my Spit I could see our target, a warehouse, getting nearer and nearer.

'With one eye on my altimeter, I could see the needle passing the 7,000 the 6,000 and the 5,000ft marks with alarming speed. The next second or so I was at dive-bombing height of 2,500ft. I pulled the nose of the aircraft through the target and pressed the "bomb" button on the control stick.

'Moments later, having pulled up to a safe height away from the flak, I quickly glanced down and saw my bomb bursting alongside the warehouse. A "near-miss".

'Acting on instructions from the ground we went in to strafe the warehouse with our 20mm cannons from a height of 500ft. This time one could see shells bursting inside the warehouse and we were to hear later from the forward troops that this attack helped to dispose of the SS anti-tank guns and help our own troops capture the location.'

Although Bird was in action for the very final days of the war, death could still strike with little warning.

He found that the dangers of ground attacks were extreme, with the SS determined to fight for every yard of ground. As they went to strafe a column of tanks passing through a village near Parma a barrage of tracer came towards them. 'One such shell hit our leading aircraft which crashed in front of the leading tank which then proceeded to drive straight over it. All this unfolded before my eyes yet in that split second of battle one's mind is strangely galvanised into suppressing emotion and pressing home your own attack.'

As the pilots gathered back at base there was sadness and bitterness at the loss of an excellent and brilliant colleague when the war's end was close. For Bird, the memory and thought of the arbitrary nature of war stayed with him. 'The picture of that aircraft sliding beneath the tank remained an unhappy memory.'

But with the Germans in full retreat over the River Po in northern Italy it was vital to keep up the pressure.

Intelligence had come in that the retreating Germans were, against the Geneva Convention, using ambulances with red crosses to move operational troops. The order was given to fire on them. The squadron was hunting the vehicles over Spezia, on the north-west coast of Italy. Bird was concentrating hard to stay in position on his leader's wing when he saw neat little clusters of white cloud around his aircraft.

'After dredging my mind for knowledge of such a meteorological phenomenon my thoughts were quickly dismissed by the voice of my leader in my earphones bellowing: "Weave, you stupid bastard, it's flak!"

A few minutes later they spotted a convoy of vehicles with red crosses in the mountains and Bird swooped to attack one on a precipitous hairpin bend. Before he could fire a shot the driver had jumped out and the vehicle went plunging hundreds of feet down the mountainside.

Bird then followed his patrol leader, who had spotted an 'armoured car', following behind on the strafing run. As he saw his leader's cannon strikes burst around the vehicle Bird lined up his gunsight to follow suit. 'The instant I pressed the firing button I got a closer focus on the target and realised too late that it was a peasant's horse and cart hell-bent on reaching cover.'

Bird felt shocked by his part in taking the life of a non-combatant. 'It made me feel sick to realise that I had slaughtered an innocent animal and human but such is the cruelty of high-speed war.'

Bird was about to experience for himself what the true reality of war was like for those on the ground. With his Spitfire unserviceable after a long patrol, he had to go by truck to their next airstrip outside Bologna. What he saw stayed with him. 'The houses in each village were virtually piles of rubble. I was probably seeing a microscopic reflection of what was happening in thousands of European villages at the moment. Nobody who has experienced such a journey can ever forget the utter desolation.'

He then witnessed a sight that made his spirits rise. 'Moving southwards along the same road were hundreds upon hundreds of lorries carrying German POWs being taken rearward to prisoner cages. As we passed through each village square the whole area was a grey mass of squatting and demoralised German soldiers waiting to be taken into captivity.

'On that journey through the war-torn devastation of northern Italy, I realised quite forcibly that the end of the war was very close at hand.'

* * *

The Germans were now in full-scale retreat across Europe and, as more land was liberated, the true horrors of the Nazi regime were being witnessed by Allied troops.

Joe Roddis, who had followed his squadron through France and into Belgium, was driving back to his latest Spitfire base in Holland when he ran out of petrol close to the Dutch concentration camp at Amersfoort. The Canadian troops who provided him with fuel showed him around the site.

'We ended up at a long, unending row of brick ovens with mountains of ash by each one. It had been a concentration camp. That shook us all.

'There were human bones, remnants of bodies. It was a real shock. This was the horror of what the Germans were capable of and I hated them for it. It made what we were doing, fighting the war, even more important.'[6]

Nigel Tangye had parked up his Spitfire near Leipzig in the heart of Germany in order to visit a concentration camp. His American friends had told him about the horrors being discovered there and he wanted to verify them for himself. It was an experience that would live with him forever. It was mid-April 1945, a few weeks before Germany's surrender, and the Americans had liberated Buchenwald concentration camp a few days earlier. They took Tangye through the neat brickwork of its front gates into the horror beyond.

'The very air seemed to become murkily tainted as one got within a radius of a few miles.' Despite the food and medical supplies that were arriving in vast quantities, inmates were still dying, with 400 being buried a day.

'Around mounds of blankets, clothing, cases of food and fresh fruit, there milled busy American GIs and solitary relics of human beings dressed in the inexpressibly doleful striped pyjama-like garment of the camp prisoner. They hobbled around bemused, living skeletons with a thin layer of yellow parchment over their bones, lifeless eyes sunk into huge black sockets between forehead and cheekbone.'

However, there was one inmate who stuck out from the rest, standing at 6ft 8in and extraordinarily emaciated. Tangye wrote: 'On his one-time huge frame the effect was horrifying, the more so because he had a large but very narrow head, a head with length but no width, like a plate on its edge.

'I knew I would never forget this man, not because of his grotesque shape after privation and years of fear, nor because of the hint of a smile he contrived to summon. I knew I would remember him for his spirit. He was Dutch and could speak English, French and German and a little Polish so that he was of great value to the liberators. One saw him all day, head and shoulders above a group of officers, GIs, generals surrounding him and he pointing, talking, hobbling, the very mouthpiece of the silent death camp abandoned by its jailors.

'In those first days he must have been responsible for saving scores of lives, hovering on the very threshold of death, by the miracle of his presence and uncanny energy in briefing the Americans as to what was what, where to go, what the priorities were.'

Long after the nightmarish days at Buchenwald, Tangye would remember this Dutchman, 'a star against the black night of the death camp'.

* * *

As she shopped for knickers at Lillywhites, it suddenly struck Ann Todd that the abandoned evening performance during the air-raid warning when war had been declared in 1939 seemed a lifetime ago. Her acting career had continued successfully and she still took to the stage despite the bombs and made films that allowed people to forget the pain and fear of war. She had gone from having a baby during the Blitz, to sheltering during an air raid while her Spitfire pilot husband Nigel Tangye was flying in a bomber above London.

On 8 May 1945 she was in the underwear department of Lillywhites in Piccadilly Circus when the sirens sounded over London, signalling the war's end. 'We all went mad. People were crying and laughing. Customers in different forms of undress rushed to the windows and flung pants, petticoats, bras and stockings out into Piccadilly. They fluttered down onto the crowd below, who had also gone mad, like pink and white coloured petals proclaiming our victory over Hitler. They turned darkness into light.' It was VE Day, the war was over, and life could begin again. 'From now on we were able to sleep at night in our beds without fear; the most wonderful feeling in the world.'

* * *

For a week, Ken French's Spitfire unit had been stood down as it became clear from 30 April that Germany was beaten. On 8 May, 66 Squadron was told to assemble on the airfield to be informed that active operations had ceased. After a year of near-constant offensive operations, the sudden end felt strange. 'We were the survivors but we spared a thought for our many friends who had fallen by the way. The announcement was received with a sense of relief on one hand but on the other was almost an anticlimax. The war had become a way of life, our only way of life. It would be difficult just to cut off and get to normal living.'

When I visited Ken, still living alone in his Leigh-on-Sea home in Essex, his daughter had told me to simply go through the unlocked front door and I would find him in his chair. It was a surreal experience to simply wander into this WWII veteran's house, calling his name to ensure I didn't startle him. Yet there he was, propped up in an armchair, surrounded by paintings and pictures of his beloved Spitfire. Still living relatively independently aged ninety-five, his recollection of those events of 1945 were still crystal clear and his eyes brightened as he talked of his days flying the Spitfire.

'Flying the Spitfire was a dream; we ruled the skies and were afraid of nothing. We were invincible. There was nothing in the air like it; it was a perfect aircraft. I enjoyed the war and wouldn't have missed it for the world. You made good friends and lost good friends; it was a happy time and a sad time. I made friends I still have seventy-five years on. Though there are only a couple of us left now, our generation who fought the war is nearly gone.' Sadly, Ken was to join his departed friends a few months after we spoke. One less Spitfire veteran to tell the story.

* * *

On 7 May 1945, Hugh Dundas, who had been one of the very few pilots in near-constant action since the early days of the war over Dunkirk, found himself at the well-equipped airfield of Treviso, just a few miles north of Venice. 324 Spitfire Wing's log recorded: 'We no longer carry out operations from this date. In other words the war has ceased.'

Dundas added: 'And I was alive.'

His early adulthood had been entirely shaped by aerial warfare. It was time to experience life. 'I had a lot of catching up to do in other directions. And I could hardly have been better placed for the purpose, with the glorious city of Venice on my doorstep and with a comfortable, fully-staffed villa for the entertainment of visiting VIPs, who were numerous. The Dolomite mountains were two hours' drive away and Rome "a mere sixty minutes" by Spitfire.

'Slowly I unwound. And from this fortunate vantage point I spent time exploring and discovering some of the pleasures of life which I had been missing.' He was able to enjoy a cheerful *intermezzo* before buckling down, in what would be the hard austerity of post-war Britain, 'to the serious business of earning a living away from the cockpit of a Spitfire'.

On VE Day, Joe Roddis suffered his worst wound of the war. 485 Squadron began celebrations in a civilised manner with a game of football at their new base, a former Luftwaffe airfield in Germany. Roddis managed to run into some barbed wire, lacerating his arms. A quick trip to the medic and a few bandages passed him fit for the celebrations proper.

'The relief that the war was over was incredible. I'd always known we would win; I'd had total faith that we could not lose. The fact that the war in Europe was really ended didn't seem to sink in immediately. But by the end of the day with all work stopped the celebrations really began. All the messes were thrown open with free booze and food and the mood was set. Old Johnny Dallas, a sergeant rigger, had been saving a bottle of Benedictine for this day and he soon polished it off, even though I had never known him to drink before. As the evening wore on things began to get a bit hectic. Bonfires were lit at the dispersal and when somebody discovered a store filled with artillery shell cases they threw them onto the fire and things got really hot.

'At one stage a crowd of us stopped some lads from pushing a Spitfire into one of the bonfires. That closed down the celebrations. After that it was little groups of men just standing around and drinking quietly, wondering what would happen to us now.'

Ray Holmes had walked into the ancient market town of Wallingford, Oxfordshire, in bright sunshine and was in a bookshop when the shop radio announced Germany's surrender. After five years of war and 2,000 hours' operational flying, he had planned in his mind a huge party. But instead of rushing back to RAF Benson, he decided that finding the right book was more important.

Back in Benson, the officers changed into their 'best blues' uniforms and went down for a beer in the mess. The atmosphere was one of forced cheerfulness. 'The truth was that we had all been at full stretch for so long we could not relax when the tension suddenly went.'

Talk turned to demobilisation, jobs on civvy street or long service commissions, and then to those not around to see the victory.

The chatter abated when the Mess Secretary announced on the Tannoy that the mess would throw open its cellars.

'This was more like it,' Holmes said. 'We waited expectantly for the champagne to put us in the right party spirit. My first drink was an inch of Spanish sherry in the bottom of my pint beer glass. I had to finish this off rather quickly to make room for the ruby port that followed. Then somebody poured me a slosh of Gordon's gin. The cellar was already feeling the strain. The Mess Secretary suggested we should tank up for a while with beer.'

The drink flowed and the party began in earnest. Not being a drinker, Holmes spent the night with the room spinning as he lay in his bed, before he was roused the next morning for a mission to photograph the French coast. 'Some humorist at Group thought up an amusing idea not to let us go to seed . . .'

Struggling with a thumping hangover, Holmes just about managed to complete the job, albeit assisted by turning his oxygen supply to the level needed for 50,000ft.

* * *

The war in Europe might have ended but the best was yet to come for Holmes.

Churchill had decided that he needed peace and breathing space in order to consider Germany's terms of surrender. With Europe liberated, where better than the pre-war holiday resort of Biarritz in the spring?

But as Prime Minister he needed good communications with London. The men of 541 Squadron were sworn in as King's Messengers to loyally carry diplomatic mail between Biarritz and Whitehall. With the swift Spitfire XIXs doing the bulk of the travel, a letter written by Churchill from a splendid villa overlooking the golden sands would arrive in London within four hours.

Two pilots were kept on constant standby at Biarritz and after a few days Holmes found himself not only in a stunning part of France, but in the company of Britain's great war leader. Initially Holmes, known for ramming the Dornier over Buckingham Palace, had thought it a leg-pull when he was told Churchill wanted to see him.

It was not and he was ushered into the Prime Minister's bedroom.

'In an enormous double bed, propped up with pillows and surrounded by newspapers and documents, sat Mr Churchill. He beamed at me over heavy horn-rimmed glasses and extended a strong hand that looked lonely without a cigar.

'"Holmes?" he said. "Battle of Britain, they tell me?"

'"Yes, sir."

'"Glad to know you. Take a seat. Make yourself comfortable. Don't worry about me, I'm not ill; I do all my correspondence in bed and get up about noon. Had any breakfast?"

'"Yes, thank you, sir."'

After years of war, Holmes was able to explore the French countryside in peace when Churchill gave him a forty-eight-hour leave pass.

* * *

For the women of the ATA there was no bright or glorious ending to the war; their jobs simply petered out after VE Day. As each female pilot left, she knew that she had achieved more than many others of her sex; but the ATA women knew too that their flying careers had come to an abrupt end.

The ferrying work for Joy Lofthouse went on until September 1945. And then it simply stopped and she was out of a job. 'For me, it was devastating. The excitement of this amazing wartime job had gone. No civilian job could possibly live up to it. I certainly didn't intend to go back to my job at the bank.

'To be perfectly honest, I wanted the war to go on as long as possible. Wartime gave many women something they'd never had: independence, earning your own money, being your own person. Once you married, everything changed dramatically. And I had no aspirations to continue flying; the men were pouring out of Bomber Command into any commercial job available. It wasn't until the 1950s that Dan-Air had the first women on the flight deck. Commercial flying came too late for most of the ATA girls.'

However, the ATA aviatrixes had proved that women were capable of doing 'men only' jobs.

'We were trailblazers for women's emancipation,' Joy said. 'It was the first time ever in Britain that women achieved equal pay with men. We weren't like the Pankhurst suffragettes, but people will always be able to look back at us and say: "Look what these women did during the war."'

Her sister Yvonne's job continued until a month after the war ended. The only silver lining for the widow was that her final delivery was in the aircraft she most loved. 'The last plane that I ever flew was a Spitfire, from Scotland down to Yorkshire. Everything was closing down by then. It really was like resigning from a job you loved, a place where there was a lot of camaraderie.

'I had known flying wouldn't lead to anything, though I would have liked to continue in aviation. But we all knew there were so many wanting to do just that. Too many people looking for too few jobs.'

Despite the end of her career, Yvonne still cherished the experiences few others would share. 'Sometimes, when you were landing a Spitfire at dusk you felt it was almost as if you could play with the whole world. I can only describe it as an otherworldly feeling.'

Mary Ellis' flying skills meant she was one of only three ATA women kept on until the organisation was wrapped up. Her last flight was something totally unexpected and a 'first' for British women.

Shortly after Victory over Japan Day in August 1945, she was flown down to Moreton Valence near Gloucester, where the RAF's brand-new Meteor jets had been tested in great secrecy. Mary had picked up a few snippets about the British jet fighter. That its twin turbojet engines were capable of an incredible 600mph, it had four 20mm cannons and had shot down a handful of V1s. It was certainly a lot faster than the Spitfire but also a lot less agile. Still, she was left speechless when the Station Commander at Moreton Valence told her she'd be ferrying a Meteor.

'I'd never even seen one before, it was an entirely different type of plane,' she said. 'The Meteor was large and so different, with no propellers. I asked the test pilot if he could tell me anything about the plane's flying characteristics. He said the thing to watch was the fuel consumption. "The fuel gauge goes from full to empty in thirty-five minutes," he warned. "So you had better be on the ground in thirty minutes. And when you prepare to land, the power will mean that the aircraft will drop like a stone."'

With these few words of advice, Mary set about reading the pilot notes before undertaking the 100-mile flight to Exeter to deliver 222 Squadron's first ever jet.

She was nervous but steeled herself with the thought that *this is just another aeroplane*. She had after all ferried 400 Spitfires and flown seventy-five other different aircraft types. She'd also earned the nickname the 'Fog Flier' because of her skill in delivering planes in atrocious weather conditions. It didn't dawn on her that she was about to be one of the very first women in the world to fly a jet aircraft.

Mary climbed into the cockpit then felt the plane shudder as the mighty Rolls-Royce engines thundered at the press of a starter button. Then she smiled to herself. The last time she'd delivered a 'first of type' plane to an RAF squadron it was a big Wellington bomber, back in 1943. The eager RAF pilots did not believe the diminutive woman had piloted the six-crew plane all by herself. Indeed, one airman had actually searched the entire plane, looking for the pilot.

Mary opened the Meteor's throttle and felt herself pushed back into the seat as she hurtled down the runway. 'It was exhilarating.' The Meteor raced through the air, down to Exeter. 'Then I was concentrating so hard on my landing I didn't realise until I looked down that a whole crowd of people had actually gathered around the control tower.

'I landed quite safely, taxied up to dispersal close to the control tower and got out. I was amazed to see a bunch of RAF officers standing in the crowd. They were changing over from Spitfires to Meteors and this was the first Meteor jet these RAF pilots were due to fly.

'They couldn't believe that this little girl had delivered their new plane to them.'

Mary allowed herself another smile. This time there would be no doubting that a woman had flown the new aircraft. It only had room for one.

* * *

The war's denouement presented many of its other participants with new opportunities. Ray Holmes' 541 Squadron had again been chosen by Churchill to act as King's Messengers during the Potsdam Conference in July 1945, when Germany's future was decided by the three victorious powers, Russia, Britain and America.

On his first trip to Germany since the war ended, Holmes found it unnerving simply to fly with only navigation to worry about without being attacked by jets or flak.[7]

'To land at Berlin's main airport was even stranger. One visualised guns spewing up lead on your approach and expected a swarm of jackbooted soldiers to rush out with fixed bayonets when you jumped down from your cockpit. Instead, when I landed, I was guided by RAF ground crews to the Officers' Mess where two very beautiful, flaxen-haired German girls were singing English songs to a grand piano they played in turn in the lounge.'

Holmes, with .45 revolver strapped to his waist, hitched a lift into Berlin and decided to take a look at the Reich Chancellery, scene of Hitler's last stand, with an eye for some souvenir hunting. The Russians had looted almost everything from the bunker but not quite. Holmes spotted a brass candelabra swinging from Hitler's reception lounge and cut it down, scooping it up with a load of Nazi medals. He bundled the booty, along with some black-market German cameras and Zeiss binoculars, into his Spitfire and headed back to Benson in clear blue skies. Not far out from the airbase he was astonished to be told not to land, as visibility was nil, and divert to nearby Kidlington. He suddenly remembered this was code for customs officers being present on the base, tipped off that cameras and perfume were coming in from Germany without duty being paid.

Over breakfast, Holmes was told that 'the weather over Benson had now cleared'. 'The fellows on the squadron who had entrusted me with their hoarded-up cigarette rations were anxious to see the Leicas and Contaxes (standard exchange rate 1,000 cigarettes) I had traded for them. My personal camera was a beauty, a Zeiss Ikon. This cost me 400 cigarettes and, when I took up commercial photography after the war, was one of my most successful pieces of equipment. I still treasure it for its history, with Hitler's brass candelabra which is wired up on my hall wall.'

CHAPTER FOURTEEN

The Last Salute

A generation had suffered horrors on a scale that none before or since have witnessed. The war's denouement was abrupt and everyone had to readjust to 'normal life' in a world that had changed utterly.

As it always will be, the fighting was toughest for the infantryman. But in the air, a form of modern combat emerged that allowed for a swift death almost on a daily basis. The fighter plane had evolved dramatically from the biplanes of the First World War into fast, deadly objects carrying hammer blows.

There was nowhere to hide in a dogfight – it was kill or be killed. And many pilots had to contemplate their own mortality and that of their friends not just for one day but throughout the war. The men of the RAF might return to warm, dry beds, but every morning they would wake up knowing it could be their last.

Every man comes with a finite well of courage to surmount their fear. Some cracked up, while others, like Hugh Dundas, fought it year after year.

Alan Peart was of the same mould. Luck had seen him through his first combat over Dieppe and he learned the necessary skills to succeed in North Africa and Italy. Courage, self-preservation, good fortune and ability had kept him alive. His astonishing efforts in keeping twenty Japanese fighters at bay in his lone Spitfire in Burma had been recognised with a DFC. He had survived the war but was on a difficult journey of readjustment to normal life after two years on intense combat operations and nearly four years away from home, having left in the middle of 1941.

He had returned to New Zealand in February 1945 and a crowd, including his mother and young brother, had gathered in his home town of Nelson, at the northern tip of South Island, to welcome home their returning hero. When he descended from the bus they did their best not to show their disappointment.

Dysentery and other tropical ailments had eaten away at his body, dropping his weight to eight stone. 'My family was shocked at the sight of me – they were expecting a tall handsome RAF officer but instead got a faded man in a faded, ragged uniform, thin as a rake, only eight stone and not very communicative. My younger brother John got quite tearful. The crowd waiting to greet me were shocked and simply disappeared. This was not the image of a returning war hero they expected.'

When he had headed off to war, his younger brother John had been a diminutive eight-year-old, but now he was almost twelve and growing into a man. He also had the sensitivity to see that Alan was in poor shape. 'He was in a very bad state psychologically and extremely thin,' John recalled. 'This little, decrepit, bowed person stepped off the bus and my mother burst into tears.'

John also found his oldest brother could become very aggressive if he was startled or felt threatened. 'He was very on edge.'

Alan admitted that he was in a poor condition, just dumped back home with no form of rehabilitation. 'I think my family thought I was possibly psychotic because I was withdrawn and just wanted to sleep and to rest. My parents tried to give me space and quiet but I found I couldn't relate to people for a long time – perhaps years. I found it difficult to trust people; as I had spent so much time in hostile territory I was constantly in fear of a knife in the back.

'My mother fed me my favourite meal of a wonderful roast dinner. Something I'd been dreaming about for years. But because of the terrible food we'd had for so long, crawling with insects and bugs, I'd got into the habit of pulling everything apart and sorting through pieces, inspecting every mouthful for intruders. I still did this and my mother was not best pleased. After just a couple of mouthfuls I was sick. I was smoking heavily and lit a cigarette in the middle of a church service, which didn't go down well!'

In his father, Alan found someone to talk to about the shared experiences of the fighting man. Cuthbert Peart had served as a sapper in the horrific trench warfare of WWI, surviving being gassed and blown up. Alan talked with his father for the first time about the horrors they had both seen and their shared acquaintance with near-death experiences. Despite his family's support, Alan took a long time to return to normality.

'I had left New Zealand as a boy and returned a man. But I was a man with problems. I had lived among other men facing fear and death on an almost daily basis and now I had to simply go back to normal. It took me a long time to get back to normal.' Peart had been away from home for almost four years, experiencing sights and emotions beyond the understanding of those back home. He had also had very little contact with his family as his squadron moved around the various battlefields, receiving just a dozen letters.

Shortly before the war had ended, Peart was posted back to flying duties in New Zealand. He was co-piloting a Hudson bomber over the Cook Strait to North Island when news of Germany's capitulation arrived. I thought to myself, *I've made it. I am alive. I have survived.*[1]

'Dancing, drinking and cavorting around as others were doing just didn't seem to me to fit the situation. I thought about all the chaps who had been killed and about my own very narrow escapes and just wanted to be alone. I had behind me over two years of operational activity without any but very short rests, somewhere between sixty and seventy individual combats with enemy aircraft, hundreds of sorties involving strafing of enemy positions and many episodes of being bombed and strafed, as well as surviving shocking flying and living conditions.'

Peart asked to be demobilised. 'I did my duty to the best of my ability – that's all. I have no idea why I survived and others didn't. I was blessed with superb eyesight, fast reactions, and perhaps I was a better pilot than I thought I was at the time. And I was lucky.

'I found it hard to fit into a civilian way of life, to play a normal part in day-to-day social interactions. I was absorbed with watching my back and felt uncomfortable with having anyone out of sight behind me. It took me a long time to adjust to the safer environment of my home country.'

Getting back to 'normality' was not helped by the feeling that the authorities cared little for his squadron's contribution to the war after it was disbanded in early 1945. Despite having fought in Europe, Africa and the Far East, the men of 81 Squadron were simply posted individually to different locations with little fanfare or thanks.

'There were no functions or parties,' Peart recalled. 'It was a terrific anticlimax. After years of operational service with 81 Squadron we were "given the boot".

'I was saddened by how it ended and shocked that my great mates, men I'd fought alongside and seen other friends die with, simply disappeared. It was a brutal ending to the war. We'd fought the war and now we were no longer needed – the powers that be didn't seem to be concerned about us at all. I remember that my parachute that I flew with was never checked or looked at from the time I left Britain to the time I got back to New Zealand. Nothing.

'There seemed to be no recognition of our service at all – many friends had been through the mill and given great service with huge courage but decorations were few and far between.

'We had given so much and I felt as though we'd just been kicked out.'

As many of those who had been affected by the war had to do, Peart put the sadness and trauma of the war years aside, immersing himself in a civil engineering degree. He then went on to oversee major New Zealand construction works, building dams, motorways and airports, before he retired to Hamilton with a legacy of three children and seven grandchildren. Speaking from his retirement home, he was sanguine about his experiences, telling me, 'I thank the Lord for an exciting and very fulfilling life.'

* * *

In the summer of 1945, the future looked bright for Diana Barnato Walker. After years of hardship and danger ferrying aircraft in the ATA, she could look forward with some satisfaction to enjoying her wealth and starting a family with her RAF husband Derek Walker.

They hoped to look back with mirth as they told their children of the days they flew Spitfires together over wartime Europe. Their children would learn too of their mother's love of the Spitfire, born from delivering 260 of them to airfields across Britain, and that she was one of only 166 women pilots in the ATA. Diana had had a good war.

A few months after the war's end, the Walkers had their first and last marital row. Derek had elected to remain in the RAF and been given a Wing Commander's job. He flew his Mustang to Langley aerodrome, near Slough, and went to Diana's glamorous family home, Ridgemead House in Surrey, to tell her the news, adding that they'd be living in a converted Nissen hut.

Noticing her reaction, Derek was quick to qualify his remark. 'We'll only live in the Nissen until a permanent home is available, just a few months before they find us RAF married quarters . . .'

After five years of shivering in drab Nissen huts Diana was not impressed. She had been looking forward to enjoying the luxury of Ridgemead and their comfortable River House flat in London. 'The sudden realisation came over me that I would now have to cut my roots entirely in order to live the life of a serving officer's wife, living permanently on one RAF station or another. And our first home was not going to be even a Wing Commander's married quarters but a converted *Nissen hut*!'

She shivered. *And* it was winter. Diana thought living in a Nissen hut was a *lousy* idea. Her mind went back to the thin, rounded, prefabricated steel structures with the corrugated iron roof in which she'd half-frozen to death during the war.

But it was a *converted* Nissen hut, Derek vainly explained. It would be quite comfortable.

Diana sat with her arms folded, pouting. She didn't want to live in *any* sort of Nissen hut, no matter how well it might be converted. A Nissen hut, to her mind, was still a Nissen hut and she'd had 'five stinking years of them'.

Derek went to say something in reply but remained silent. He looked extremely upset and Diana wondered if it was because he thought she didn't want to live with him any more.

Later that evening Diana listened as Derek explained that the Nissen was beautifully fixed and ready for them to move in.

By the next morning the couple had made up. And Diana agreed to move into the Nissen hut, as long as he gave her time to organise everything. Then they kissed goodbye. She treasured the look of gratitude and love Derek gave her. Then he set off for Langley to fly his Mustang back to base.

It was a crisp November day and Diana decided to clear her head with a ride out on her horse Tommy the Twin over Englefield Green, which overlooked Runnymede and, in the distance, Langley airfield.[2]

'Tommy the Twin and I stopped. I was admiring the view and he was nibbling the nearby shrubs when suddenly something frightened him, making him leap forward a few paces. I pulled him up, patting him gently. He returned to his munching. At that moment I looked towards Langley again, seeing an enormous spume of black, oily smoke coming up from where I knew the airfield lay. I was very frightened, being consumed with a terrible sense of premonition that something had happened to Derek in his Mustang.'

She found out the next day that her premonition was correct. Derek's plane had crashed.

Diana was devastated. 'My shock at the loss of my wonderful Derek was tremendous. Just the thought that he wasn't around any more, that never again would I hear his laughter, know his sureness, rely on his strength, filled me with dread. He had survived a terrible war, only to die in some senseless crash. He would have gone far in whatever postwar career he had decided upon, but now he was no more. I would never hug him again, never love him again, except in my heart.'

Wing Commander Derek Walker was buried in the churchyard of St Jude's, near Ridgemead House, where the couple had married eighteen months earlier.

* * *

Hugh Dundas had fought doggedly in virtually every theatre the Spitfire graced – Dunkirk, Battle of Britain, Rhubarbs over France, North Africa and Italy. And he had done so in glorious company – Douglas Bader, Johnnie Johnson and Wilfrid Duncan Smith were friends and mentors. He had become the youngest ever Group Captain and been awarded the DFC, and the DSO and bar.

To those who did not know his incredible war record, Dundas might have appeared a precocious upstart. Thus, when he arrived at the War Office in late 1945 to discuss his RAF future, the officer interviewing him glanced at the four bands of rank on his sleeves then said: 'Well, you needn't think you are keeping all that rank now.'[3]

Dundas knew then that his future lay elsewhere. His friend and fellow pilot Max Aitken, son of Lord Beaverbrook, the newspaper tycoon and driving force behind the Spitfire's manufacture, employed him as Air Correspondent on the *Daily Express*.

Aitken then introduced Dundas to Rosamond Lawrence, who found him 'frightfully good-looking and obviously incredibly brave'. Rosamond had done her bit in the war too, helping run double agents and deception operations in France. 'I knew all about him but wasn't that impressed,' she said of their first meeting.

Dundas' newly acquired reporter's skills of inquiry had led Rosamond to think he was trying to sniff out a story. 'I was very aware of security so when he asked all these questions my instinct kicked in and I thought he was trying to get information to put in the *Daily Express*. So when he asked me to go out again I refused.'[4]

The pair were put together again when a friend hosted a small dinner party to celebrate Princess Elizabeth's engagement to Prince Philip in July 1947. This time she was charmed and agreed to continue the celebrations at the Milroy nightclub in Mayfair.

But Dundas still had some legwork to do. In his role as commander of the part-time 601 Auxiliary Squadron he decided to use the Spitfire's elegant qualities to his advantage in wooing Rosamond. 'Hughie flew down in a Spitfire to see me near our family farm to take me out while we were courting. He climbed out of his aircraft in his pale-blue overalls. He did look very glamorous by his Spitfire.'

In Rosamond, Dundas found a soulmate in whom he could confide the grief and demons brought on by war, particularly the death of his brother John in the Battle of Britain. 'Hughie told me there was never a day of his life that passed without him thinking of his brother. He thought John's death would destroy his poor mother who had adored him. He had truly admired him and it deeply affected him. Everything in Hughie's life had been following John.'

Dundas' courting by Spitfire, coupled with his renowned charm, proved effective. The couple were married in 1950, and both Douglas Bader, who had survived as a prisoner of war in Colditz, and Johnnie Johnson were at the wedding.

* * *

Nigel Tangye similarly used an aircraft but for opposite reasons to Dundas. Like many others, he and Ann Todd had married in the midst of the war, when lives were short and happiness was seized where it could be found, no matter how ephemeral.

Nigel Tangye

With some regret, Tangye returned his personal Spitfire when he left the RAF after the war. He then followed Ann to Hollywood as her career began to bloom. She had won great acclaim for her appearance alongside James Mason in *The Seventh Veil*, playing a young pianist who attempts suicide to escape her guardian's cruelties. Hollywood offers had poured in and Ann found herself starring opposite Gregory Peck in *The Paradine Case*, directed by Alfred Hitchcock. Tangye was mildly bemused by the thin veneer of Los Angeles glitz during their seven-month stay.

On their return to England he chose to remain at his ancestral home of Glendorgal in Cornwall with their daughter and Ann's son. Todd filmed mostly up in London. A romance began to develop with the renowned director David Lean and she eventually divorced Tangye in 1949, marrying Lean within months.

The former Spitfire pilot was heartbroken. He lost himself in Paris in a haze of drink and poetry, emerging months later to make something of his life by turning Glendorgal into the West Country's finest hotel.

But he still had a score to settle. In 1950, Tangye discovered that Lean and Ann were making another film together called *Madeleine.* A scene was to be shot in Cornwall, in which Todd was to have a horse bolt from under her on the beach.

It was a sunny day and the crowds had gathered to watch the famous director-and-actress couple. It was not a scene that Todd was relishing, having spent a sleepless night mulling over the action sequence.[5]

'Trembling like a leaf, I was lifted onto my horse, riding side-saddle with my long skirt draped over my foot and stirrup. Then the focus boy took the tape to measure the distance between me and the camera and shot his arm out across the horse's nose. It immediately stood on its hind legs, pawing the air and neighing. I threw my arms around the pommel and screamed. My hat and veil fell off. David became severe. We started again. The crowd laughed and I had a nasty feeling my horse was laughing too.'

As Lean reset the scene and again shouted 'Action!', out of the skies an aircraft hurtled down, on what appeared to be a strafing run, directly towards Lean, Todd and the rest of the film crew.

'It came straight at us and we all ducked. Flying very low, it skimmed along the beach. Assistant directors clung to the horse and me, seagulls screamed and the crowd, thinking it was part of the film, gazed fascinated and clapped. David lost his temper, clenched his fist and shouted at the plane as it prepared to attack again. On the second run the pilot leaned out and waved at me – it was Nigel!'

Tangye had borrowed a friend's aircraft and, using his hard-learned skills as a wartime Spitfire pilot, had decided to make his displeasure at his wife's betrayal clear for all to see. Ann Todd did not seem overly distressed by this display of lovelorn anger. 'Having successfully stopped all filming Nigel flew off home. David never knew who it was – and I never told him.'

Revenge complete, Tangye settled down to creating a stunning hotel at Glendorgal. Surrounded by his family and new wife, Moira, he found he could leave behind memories of the war.

One summer's evening, fifteen years after the war's end, some guests arrived at the hotel as Tangye was serving drinks behind the bar.[6]

'I saw a rather smart party of five, two young couples and behind them a huge man with a beautifully proportioned body and a surprisingly narrow width of head for its depth which had the same proportion to his body as a thick book on its edge. "A book on its edge" – there was an echo in my mind – a plate on its edge.

'I greeted the new guests and turned to him. It seemed superfluous for me to ask but I said: "You were at Buchenwald, weren't you? And you're Dutch!"'

Astonishingly, it was indeed the same man he had encountered during his visit to the notorious concentration camp towards the end of the war. 'His response was swift, clear to me and surprising. It was all over in a second, a slight smile, a momentary narrowing of the eyes and a lifted index finger that for a fleeting moment touched his closed lips.'

* * *

For forty-six years, Jimmy Taylor had lived with good memories of the war. He had mourned the losses among 16 Squadron's photo reconnaissance Spitfire pilots, but he had seen no horrors and did not have to struggle with thoughts of taking another human being's life. Even his time trying to get back to friendly lines after he'd been forced to bail out over Borne, Holland, in November 1944 had more of the high-spirited adventure about it. His capture and being held as a prisoner of war had not been without risks, but it had been bearable. He'd had a good war. Five decades on that was about to change, when a phone call shattered his entire view of his war.[7]

In March 1990, a small advert appeared in the RAF Association magazine asking for a Flight Lieutenant James Taylor to get in touch with Hennie Noordhuis in Holland. Taylor sent a letter and a few days later he received a phone call.

'Congratulations on being alive!' Mr Noordhuis told Taylor, then related how flying goggles had been found near Borne with the name 'WJS Taylor' marked on them. Then he dropped the bombshell: 'But did you know that three Dutchmen were executed after you landed by parachute?'

* * *

Several pairs of eyes had followed Jimmy Taylor down as he parachuted from his stricken Spitfire over Holland on Sunday, 19 November 1944. They included German paratroopers from the 500-strong regiment based in nearby Borne, who flooded the area. Dutch civilians were roughly treated by troops determined to find the Spitfire pilot.

Few witnesses had seen Taylor slip away soon after landing, but the Germans were convinced that the Dutch were hiding something. Six men were seized at random and the people of Borne were issued with an ultimatum: if the pilot was not found, the hostages would be shot at 7am on the Monday morning.

After the mayor of Borne, Jan van den Toren, intervened, saying the town could hardly be held responsible for the airman's whereabouts, the execution was postponed to 5pm.

But now the Gestapo got involved. They told van den Toren that Borne was a 'large pigsty of terrorists and collaborators'. He argued that it would have been impossible for the hostages to know where the pilot had gone. This failed to satisfy the Gestapo chief Karl Hadler, who told him that unless progress was made on the investigation 'then the rifles will speak'.

As Hadler left, the mayor ran after him, protesting that innocent men would be executed. He succeeded in getting another postponement, this time until 3pm on the Tuesday.

The Germans then said the hostages would be released if they were told the direction the airman had taken. The mayor found three witnesses who had seen the pilot, described as 6ft, blond and wearing a flying jacket over a white jersey.

The German military police were now convinced of the hostages' innocence but Hadler would allow no more than a further twenty-four-hour stay in the executions.

By Wednesday morning a feeling of relief swept through the town as news came out that the military police were going to free the hostages.

A sister of one hostage, Hendrik Roetgerink, cycled to the police cells and, using sign language, told him the good news. Her brother put his hand through the bars and gave her the thumbs-up.

Then the days passed and still the men were held in jail. On Sunday 26 November, two of the hostages were released but Roetgerink, Piet van Dijk and Jan Boomkamp remained. However, Boomkamp managed a snatched conversation with his wife, whom he had married just six weeks earlier.

At 3.30pm the Gestapo chief Hadler and some SS troopers arrived and drove the three hostages close to the site where the pilot had landed exactly a week earlier.

Informed of the latest move, Mayor van den Toren used every connection he had to delay the impending action, but both the local area commander and military chief washed their hands of the case. However, the area's German government representative promised to phone the Gestapo.

At 3.50pm three saloon cars pulled up at the parachute landing site and the hostages were bundled out. Family and friends watched as the men were marched across the field, lined up and shot.

* * *

As Hennie Noordhuis related this story to Jimmy Taylor nearly fifty years later, Jimmy felt as though his life was crumbling around him. Barely able to believe what he'd heard, he stuttered a response of regret for the families. When he put down the phone the weight of the tragedy bore down on him. 'I felt absolutely shattered. The war had been a great adventure for me, the realisation of boyhood dreams. I had flown a most wonderful aeroplane and I had not been required to hurt anyone. I had survived an engine failure, a bail-out, and an unpleasant but short-lived captivity. I had nothing about which to reproach myself, but now I'm told I caused the death of three innocent Dutch people.'

A few days later, Taylor received from Noordhuis an article he had written about Borne during the war. Reading it, he discovered that the men had been executed two days after Taylor himself had been apprehended by the German artillerymen, some distance from Borne. As he reread the account, which described a dogfight occurring before the bail-out, he became convinced that Mr Noordhuis was mistaken, as there had been two bail-outs near Borne on 19 November 1944. Jimmy was relieved. He was determined to show he could not have been responsible for the tragic deaths of the Dutch civilians.

He composed a letter to Mr Noordhuis: 'From a comparison of these two accounts, it is clear to me, as I think it will also appear to you, that by an amazing coincidence of date, time and place, two airmen bailed out in the neighbourhood of Borne at about midday on Sunday 19th November. The evidence for this is considerable.'

Taylor, determined to exonerate himself, then set out in detail why he believed the pilot was not him. As a reconnaissance Spitfire, his fighter was unarmed, so could not have been in a dogfight. He was 5ft 10in, not 6ft as described by eyewitnesses, and his hair was dark and not blond. He outlined other evidence which absolved him from the incident, including a suggestion that goggles found in the area with 'WJS Taylor' etched on them could have been picked up and moved.

'I should also like to try to identify "Pilot X",' Taylor concluded.

Not satisfied with his own interpretation of the tragic events, Jimmy was determined to set the record straight forever – the civilian deaths were not his fault. It became a passion and he set about tracing the records of all other aircraft shot down on 19 November over occupied Europe. 'I wanted to find out the exact circumstances in the hope of showing that the downed pilot was not me and that

I was not responsible for those deaths,' Taylor said. 'I didn't want that downed airman to be me at all.'

After weeks of research he eventually tracked down the name of Flight Lieutenant E. F. Ashdown of 430 Squadron who was flying a Mustang that was shot down in a dogfight over the town of Venlo. Taylor concluded that the aerial combat must have drifted south from Venlo and finished over Borne. The eyewitnesses must have mistaken the Mustang for a Spitfire. He was also certain that his goggles were simply picked up and passed through many hands before they reached Mr Noordhuis.

Finally, in order prove the theory that would exonerate him, he travelled by train, bus and taxi from his home in Leeds to the Public Record Office at Kew just outside London to examine 430 Squadron's operational reports. He was devastated by his findings. The official record showed that Ashdown was wingman to a fellow pilot who reported he'd been hit by flak and had bailed out and landed near Venlo, a full seventy miles away from Borne.

There could be no other conclusion. Taylor was the pilot the Dutch had witnessed. 'The only realistic candidate for this unwanted role was myself,' he said. 'I was now forced to accept Hennie Noordhuis' firm conviction that I was the leading player in the tragic drama that unfolded after my landing on 19 November 1944.'

He added: 'This was a huge shock, the worst moment of my life and I couldn't really believe it at first. It was my fault – if I hadn't landed in that field they would still be alive. Of course I accept I couldn't change anything – but if I hadn't done they would be alive.

'I have never recovered from the destruction of my former peace of mind that it caused.'

With this knowledge Taylor went to Borne and met Mr Noordhuis and the families of the victims, then visited a memorial to the executed men. It became the start of an annual pilgrimage of remembrance and of a warm relationship with the people of Borne. 'My memories are stirred afresh each year for the young men cut down too soon and for no necessity, just three of thousands likewise slain.'

Speaking to me from his home in Leeds, as Jimmy described his relentless search for the truth, and exoneration, it was apparent that the death of the innocent civilians still weighed heavily on the ninety-five-year-old veteran. Reliving the story of those events, and his search for the truth, required frequent pauses from the normally precisely spoken airman. It was a burden he would carry with him until he died a few months after we spoke; another of those Spitfire heroes who would not survive to see this book published.

* * *

In the aftermath of the war, while still in RAF service, the Spitfire was not an uncommon sight, a magnificent reminder of perseverance and fortitude in the face of great odds. Classic films such as *Battle of Britain,* released in 1969, only served to enhance its reputation. But as the decades passed its unmistakable outline became less frequent in the skies, replaced by screaming fighter jets and the long contrails of airliners. Most of the Spitfires were eventually sold off or broken up for scrap. In an effort to preserve an icon, enthusiasts and entrepreneurs spent millions of pounds restoring a few, featuring them at airshows and displays.

The veterans who had flown them in battle had more pressing worries now. Building new lives, new careers in the postwar years, bringing up young families and adapting to an ever-changing world. As they grew older, their memories of the Spitfire diminished, as did their numbers as old age took its toll. Then, with most veterans in their mid-nineties, a remarkable thing happened. Those enthusiasts, and entrepreneurs wealthy enough to own a preserved Spitfire, began to offer the elderly veterans a chance to take to the skies one final time.

When Allan Scott and Joy Lofthouse were separately offered trips neither hesitated for a moment in accepting. Despite the passing of seventy years since their last Spitfire flight, their love for the aircraft had never waned. The fact they were in their nineties only made them more determined. They may have lost some of their mobility but they certainly had retained their aviation spirit.

And deep down, they understood this really would be the very last time they would fly their beloved 'Spit'.

* * *

The conviction that having lost his twin sister in the 1920s to the influenza outbreak meant that he was the one 'born to survive' proved correct for Allan Scott. After three operational tours in Spitfires from 1944 he saw out the rest of the war as a test pilot, surviving a number of accidents. And despite a miraculous near-death escape from a Tiger Moth crash in 1953, followed by months of reconstructive surgery, he had not been put off flying. So when an entrepreneur offered a Spitfire trip, Allan, by then aged ninety-four, did not waver. He found himself back at Biggin Hill, where he had started his operational career in the RAF with 124 Squadron in 1941. Dressed in an all-in-one green flight suit, the years fell away as he approached the aircraft he had not flown in seven decades. Stepping into the specially fitted rear cockpit, Allan immediately felt at home. 'It's just like riding a bicycle,' he joked as he strapped in. 'It's instinct; you fly a Spitfire by the seat of your pants.'[8]

As the Merlin roared into life, the grin on Allan's face broadened and remained fixed as the fighter bounced down the runway. His mind turned back to the first time he had raced down Biggin Hill's strip, to the first time he had experienced that thrust of power as the Spitfire dashed forward, eager to embrace the air. He remembered waiting nervously on the flight deck of HMS *Eagle*, he recalled the airstrip at Malta, scrambling to get airborne to meet the enemy coming in overwhelming numbers. Then, he was airborne again, soaring into the blue, airscrew spinning as they powered upwards.

'*You have control.*'

The words filled Allan's headphones with an indescribable thrill as his pilot handed control of the Spitfire from front to back seat.

The decades disappeared as Allan gripped the control column and felt the aircraft come alive in his hands. *To hell with it, I'm ninety-four, let's put her through her paces.* He pushed the stick over and suddenly found himself in a steep turn, laughing as the Spit reacted like a thoroughbred. The old lady responded as enthusiastically as she ever had, flying over the Kent fields that the RAF had sacrificed so much to protect over those six long years of fighting.

As his pilot looked in his rear-view mirror he could see the pleasure writ large on Allan's face, a genuine delight of memory, nostalgia and joy he had not seen in any of his other passengers.

The veteran was flying over old country, bringing back memories of his days at Biggin Hill in 1941. He found the Ashford to Redhill railway line he had used as a navigation aid, telling the pilot, 'Coming back from a raid over France with the sun at our back, we would cross the white cliffs at Dover then follow this railway line towards base.' The war films might have been in black and white, but for Allan, in 2015, the colours remained as vivid as they had back in the 1940s. Back on the ground the cockpit canopy flew open to reveal a beaming veteran pilot. 'That was marvellous!' exclaimed Allan, who had been awarded the Distinguished Flying Medal for his wartime exploits, which included five kills. 'I loved the Spitfire; it was almost a part of me. It was a pleasure to get back into the air again. It handled beautifully.' As Allan climbed down he chatted excitedly to those who had helped organise the flight. 'Allan was over the moon,' observed one onlooker. 'He was both dumbstruck and awestruck. He was like a teenager.' But the nonagenarian Spitfire pilot had also left those onlookers in awe of *him*. On countless occasions Allan had fought back the fear of death and taken to the skies in the Spitfire to protect his country from a vicious enemy. He had killed and seen his friends killed. When asked about the risks he took, he responded with the modesty of many of his generation: 'I didn't do anything, I was just doing my job.' The person who asked the question was astonished. 'We couldn't begin to imagine what he went through.'

He was right.

* * *

Joy Lofthouse came as close as any woman could to facing those dangers above the skies of Britain, ferrying aircraft for the ATA. After the war, she had married a Czech RAF pilot then had been forced to flee Czechoslovakia when the Communists took control. With three young children to bring up, then a career teaching in Portsmouth, she'd given little thought to ever flying a Spitfire again. Of course, she frequently had the chance to reminisce about her days in the ATA at the 'Spitfire Girls' reunions. 'They were such impressionable years, they never quite leave you,' Joy recalled. As the years went by, numbers at the reunions dwindled, memories of their exploits flying Spitfires faded.

Then, one day in 2015, she was given the opportunity to fly in a Spitfire again. Like Allan Scott, after getting over the initial disbelief at the offer, the thought of being behind the controls once again became an overwhelming desire.

It was a sunny day in May when she found herself surrounded by media as she walked slowly, but purposefully, towards the Spitfire at Westhampnett airfield, still in use since its wartime years but now as a civilian airstrip. Despite the ninety-two years evident in the deep wrinkles, Joy still had a spring in her step as she climbed into the rear cockpit. 'I feel excited but aware of my age, so hoping that things go OK. I'm not as confident as I was when I used to fly them alone when I was young!' she told a reporter. For Joy, flying the Spitfire during the war had been the ultimate thrill. To repeat it in peacetime was pure delight. 'It is *the* iconic plane. It's the nearest thing to having wings of your own and flying.'[9]

As she sat in the cockpit, looking at the instruments she had not seen for seventy years, the initial apprehension she had felt slipped away as the Spitfire took to the skies. It was also a poignant moment for her to reflect on the loss of her sister Yvonne MacDonald, who had passed away a year earlier, in 2014. The two girls had earned the nickname 'the Spitfire Sisters', the only female siblings to fly the aircraft during the war. They were the trailblazers for the feminist generation. For a moment Joy dwelt on her sister's passing then threw the Spitfire in a tight turn. At least they had shared the same beautiful experiences of flight.

Back on the ground, Joy beamed with happiness. 'It's incredible to be in a Spitfire again after so long. I am so lucky to be given this chance to fly it again. It's hard to describe the feeling.' Then she added something that perhaps captures the enduring essence of the Spitfire for those who had flown her and grown to love her in the war. 'It was perfect. It made me feel quite young again.'

Joy Lofthouse passed away in November 2017, another of the Spitfire veterans who died before this book was published.

* * *

For sixty years Joe Roddis had buried the memory of his first love, Betty Wood, from whom he had parted at Worthing train station just before D-Day.

'As I walked away I looked back to see her crying. But I harboured no thoughts of romance. It wouldn't have been the right thing to do. As far as I was concerned, that was the end of our relationship and I got on with my life.'

Soon after the war ended, Roddis married an Auxiliary Territorial Service lady he'd met a few months earlier while still in England. Mary Martin was a striking young woman and a searchlight plotter for the heavy AA artillery. They had met at a dance in Emsworth, Hampshire.

'I saw her and knew she was the lady for me. Both she and a friend approached me for a dance but Mary got there first and that was that. She was a great dancer but I stuck to the foxtrot as I couldn't do the tango!'

They had a daughter and son and remained married until 2000, when Mary was diagnosed with a brain tumour. She died the following year. Joe was devastated at the loss of his soulmate. He remained in their three-bedroom house in Derby feeling the loneliness of a widower as he continued with his DIY and fishing.

In 2004 he was interviewed about his wartime experiences working on the fighter for a Channel 4 documentary called *Spitfire Ace*. By chance, the grandson of Betty Wood had seen the programme advertised and, knowing that she had been involved with Spitfires, told her to watch it. Betty was also now widowed and living on her own in a flat in Selsey Bill. The moment she turned on the television, Joe's face appeared on the screen with his name below.

Eager to track down her wartime companion, she wrote to Channel 4, who passed the letter on to Joe. He was delighted to hear from his old love, but unsure how to proceed. After a fortnight of deliberation, he picked up the phone. Over the next few weeks they chatted for hours before eventually arranging to meet at Chichester railway station, just eight stops down the line from Worthing where they had parted in tears six decades previously.

'I arrived by train and there she was on the platform. Even though all those years had passed she was the same Betty I had last seen at Worthing sixty years earlier. It was a totally wonderful moment; the war and the Spitfire had come full circle and brought us together again. We relived all the places we'd danced and the things we'd done during the heat of wartime.'

The friendship blossomed and just two days later Betty asked, 'What are we doing hanging about?' It was a question many who had faced death in WWII were asking in their later years. Joe returned to Derby, sold his house, its contents and his car and moved down to finally live with Betty.

'It was the start of what were to be eight of some of the most wonderful years of my life.' The couple spent holidays in Portugal, the Isle of Wight, Devon and Wales, living life to the full. Joe was eighty-three and Betty eighty-four, so there were not too many foxtrots danced. The couple moved into a bungalow and lived blissfully together. 'I couldn't have been happier. It was the perfect ending,' Joe said.

Then one morning in February 2012 Betty complained of feeling unwell. She was rushed to Chichester hospital where it was found she'd suffered a ruptured stomach ulcer. At 8pm she underwent surgery. Before she went into the operating theatre, Joe gave her a kiss and a strong hug, saying he loved her. They never spoke again; after the operation, Betty went straight onto a life support machine but never recovered. She died a few weeks later.

Joe was heartbroken. 'Words cannot describe my feelings. She was so strong and active. Life can be so cruel.'[10] When I met Joe at Goodwood airfield in West Sussex (the old Westhampnett) the hurt and loss were still clearly visible in his eyes, which filled with tears as he remembered both the happiness and sadness of those years with Betty in war and peace. Because of his close links with Goodwood, he kept his attachment to the Spitfire. Aged ninety-one, he was asked if he could start and run up a Spitfire Mark IX in front of the Goodwood crowd during a display. There was no stopping him and, with little hesitation and no reference to the manuals, he fired up the Merlin for a final time. For a moment he looked skywards, thinking of Betty and the aircraft that had brought them together. Joe Roddis passed away in April 2017. A lone Spitfire performed a flypast at his funeral.

* * *

The Spitfire's development through the war was astonishing. The power of the final mark, the Seafire 47, was such that it was equivalent to the original Spitfire I of 1938 taking off with thirty-two airline passengers on board complete with their baggage.[11] The top speed had gone from 362mph to 452mph, the rate of climb to 20,000ft from 9.4 minutes to 4.8 minutes, the range from 575 miles to 1,475 miles.[12] The RAF found a model that worked and stuck with it, every variant proving it could at least contend with, if not outdo German developments.

Nearly 23,000 Spitfires, including the navy variant, the 'Seafire', were built between 1936 and 1946.[13] It had been used in combat in every theatre of the war: the deserts of North Africa, the snows of Russia, the jungles of Burma, in temperate Europe and scorching Australia. It rarely disappointed and almost always impressed. More than thirty countries operated the Spitfire, from Taiwan to India,

Ireland and Rhodesia. It was flown in combat by Britons, Belgians, New Zealanders, Americans, Argentinians and Norwegians, to name but a few. The Spitfire went on to fight in the 1948 Arab–Israeli war, with both the Israeli and Egyptian air forces using the fighter against each other. It was the final time the fighter was shot down in action.[14] It was used operationally in the Korean War in 1950, Malaya in 1951 and remained in service with the RAF as a meteorological aircraft until 1957.

As the years pass, the number of originals inevitably dwindles; however, some fifty Spitfires remain and many more replicas have been built. One of only four flying Spitfire Mark Is was auctioned at Christie's for £3.1 million in 2015. When Lord Beaverbrook set up the Spitfire Fund in 1940, the production cost was set at £9,000.

From its first flight in 1936, through the war and beyond to today's airshows, the Spitfire has continued to seduce both fliers and spectators alike.

William Dunn, an American ace who scored 71'Eagle' Squadron's first victory in May 1941, gave some indication why.[15]

'The Spitfire was a thing of beauty to behold, in the air or on the ground, with the graceful lines of its slim fuselage, its elliptical wing and tailplane. It *looked* like a fighter and it certainly proved to be just that in the fullest meaning of the term. It was an aircraft with a personality all of its own – docile at times, swift and deadly at others – a fighting machine *par excellence*. One must really have known the Spitfire in flight to fully understand and appreciate its thoroughbred flying characteristics. Once you've flown a Spitfire it spoils you for all other fighters. Every other aircraft seems imperfect in one way or another.'

Hugh Dundas reflected similar feelings. 'There is something Wagnerian about the Spitfire story, the more so since it is certainly true that there never was a plane so loved by pilots, combining as it did sensitive yet docile handling with the deadly qualities of a fighting machine. Lovely to look at, delightful to fly, the Spitfire became the pride and joy of thousands of young men from practically every country in what then constituted the free world. Americans raved about her and wanted to have her; Poles were seduced by her; men from the old Dominions crossed the world and the oceans to be with her; the Free French undoubtedly wrote love songs about her. And the Germans were envious of her.'

Jeffrey Quill, one of the first men to fly the Spitfire, was fulsome in his praise. 'It is impossible to look back on the Spitfire without recognising it as something unique in aviation history. By the efforts of the many thousands of people who were in some way involved with it, the Spitfire threaded its way through the historical tapestry not only of Britain but of the continent of Europe and of a great overseas Empire. They helped to design it, build it, maintain it, administer it and fly it – and in all too many cases to die in it . . .

'The little Spitfires, so easily recognisable in the air, captured the imagination of the British people and became a symbol of hope and of victory. In the three subsequent years the sound of Spitfires sweeping daily over northern France, Belgium and the Netherlands, challenging the enemy to come up and fight, brought the hope of victory and liberation to the people of those occupied countries.

'The Spitfire was very much a pilot's aeroplane. It had an indefinable quality of excitement about it, an unmistakable charisma, which greatly appealed to young and eager pilots. It is to the eternal credit of a generation that to be a Spitfire pilot became the dream and pride of so many of its young men.'

* * *

Air Marshal Cliff Spink was the RAF fighter pilot who took ninety-year-old Spitfire veteran Brian Bird flying at the beginning of this book; the event which sparked my own interest in the aircraft. Cliff was my Station Commander at RAF Coningsby in 1992 and is a highly regarded aviator with many years of flying experience. So perhaps the last word on the venerable Spitfire should go to this former RAF fast jet and current Spitfire pilot:[16]

'It is difficult to capture in just a few words why the Spitfire became so iconic. It was a massive leap forward in design; it performed so incredibly well for its day. It came at a time in our nation's history when we needed "heroes" – machines as well as men and women. It had the name; what a name! It was a true pilots' aeroplane and anyone who has flown the aircraft will attest to its outstanding handling qualities. It looks just stunning; a sweeping series of compound curves and that amazing ellipsoidal wing. Finally, the deep growl of the Merlin was the perfect complement to the machine.

'I have been incredibly lucky in my flying career to have flown around sixty-five different types and marks of aircraft. The beautiful Hunter, the mind-blowing Lightning, the mighty Phantom and the very capable Tornado. I've been privileged to fly countless Second World War and vintage aircraft from many nations, including the Hurricane, the Mustang, the Kittyhawk and, of course, ten different marks of the Spitfire.

'I am often asked which is my favourite aircraft. It is a very difficult question to answer. Who couldn't be impressed with the gut-wrenching climb performance of the Lightning, almost touching the lower reaches of space, or of howling along in a Hawker Sea Fury? So I answer the question this way: if God said that I could have just one more flight, my last flight before I die, in any aircraft I have ever flown, I would choose to get airborne in a Spitfire.'

REFERENCES AND NOTES

Prologue

1 John Nichol correspondence with Ken Farlow's daughter, Helen Nock
2 This Spitfire was from the RAF's Battle Of Britain Memorial Flight. When the aircrew and ground crew realised Ken was a veteran, they invited him on to the airfield to chat and take pictures

Introduction

1 John Nichol correspondence with Brian Bird and interview for *Plane Crazy* (TVT Productions)
2 The Spitfire is operated by the Aircraft Restoration Company based at Duxford – the author is grateful to the ARC team for making this flight happen
3 There is no definitive number for Spitfires/Seafires built and figures vary depending on the source consulted; an approximate figure is 20,334 Spitfires and 2,558 Seafires

Chapter One: Birth of a Fighter

1 Allan Scott, *Born to Survive*, and John Nichol interview
2 Jeffrey Quill, *Spitfire: A Test Pilot's Story*, and John Nichol interview with Sarah Quill
3 Alfred Price, *Spitfire: A Documentary History*
4 Ibid.
5 There are a number of versions of this story. Another account has the Air Ministry giving the name 'Spitfire', to which R.J. Mitchell is said to have responded, 'Well, that's just the sort of bloody silly name they would give it'
6 Tom Moulson, *The Millionaires' Squadron*
7 Ibid.
8 Quill, op. cit.
9 Price, op. cit.
10 The prototype was also referred to as a Bf109
11 Quill, op. cit.
12 Jimmy Taylor, *One Flight Too Many*, and interview with John Nichol
13 Leo McKinstry, *Spitfire: Portrait of a Legend*
14 Taylor, op. cit.
15 Quill, op. cit.
16 Moulson, op. cit.
17 Quill, op. cit.
18 Ken Delve, *The Story of the Spitfire: An Operational and Combat History*
19 Ken French, *My Early Life*, and interview with John Nichol
20 Hugh Dundas, *Flying Start: A*

Fighter Pilot's War Years, and John Nichol interview with Lady Dundas

21 Taylor, op. cit.
22 Brian Bird, *That Was my Life* (personal memoir) and John Nichol interview
23 Ann Todd, *The Eighth Veil*
24 McKinstry, op. cit.
25 Ibid.
26 Tom Docherty, *Swift to Battle: No 72 Fighter Squadron RAF in Action*
27 Ibid.
28 Ibid.
29 Diana Barnato Walker, *Spreading My Wings*, and John Nichol interview
30 Joe Roddis with Mark Hillier, *An Airman Under Fire!*, and John Nichol interview
31 Ibid.

Chapter Two: The Fall of France

1 Jon E. Lewis, *Spitfire: The Autobiography*
2 McKinstry, op. cit.
3 Lewis, op. cit.
4 Dundas, op. cit.
5 Lewis, op. cit.
6 Ibid.
7 Richard Hough and Denis Richards, *Battle of Britain*
8 McKinstry, op. cit.
9 Moulson, op. cit.
10 McKinstry, op. cit.
11 Alan Deere, *Nine Lives*
12 David Owen, *Dogfight: The Supermarine Spitfire and the Messerschmitt BF 109*
13 Deere, op. cit.
14 Lewis, op. cit.
15 Brian Lane, *Spitfire! The Experiences of a Battle of Britain Fighter Pilot*
16 Tim Vigors, *Life's Too Short to Cry*
17 Dr Richard Campbell-Begg and Dr Peter Liddle, *For Five Shillings a Day: Personal Histories of World War II*, and Bernard Brown's interviews with Dave Homewood, Ricard Carstens and John Nichol
18 Lewis, op. cit.
19 Price, op. cit.
20 Delve, op. cit.
21 Ibid.
22 McKinstry, op. cit.
23 John Blyth's private papers and John Nichol interview
24 Hough and Richards, op. cit.
25 *Hansard*

Chapter Three: The Battle for Britain

1 Campbell-Begg and Liddle, op. cit., and Bernard Brown's interviews with Dave Homewood, Ricard Carstens and John Nichol
2 Dundas, op. cit.
3 Delve, op. cit.
4 Lewis, op. cit.
5 Roddis, op. cit.
6 Delve, op. cit.
7 Ibid.
8 Roddis, op. cit.
9 Ibid.
10 Modern historians believe Crook actually shot down a Ju87. This is Crook's own version of events
11 David Crook, *Spitfire Pilot*
12 Lewis, op. cit.
13 'Custodians of Air Power: Securing the Skies 1940–2015' produced by MOD
14 Crook, op. cit.
15 Geoffrey Wellum, *First Light*
16 Bird, op. cit.

17 Taylor, op. cit.
18 McKinstry, op. cit.
19 Dundas, op. cit.
20 McKinstry, op. cit.
21 Roddis, op. cit.
22 Ibid.
23 Lewis, op. cit.
24 Moulson, op. cit.
25 Ibid.
26 John Wilkinson, *The Lord Is my Shepherd: An Extraordinary Account of Aerial Combat over Europe During WWII*, and John Nichol interview
27 Quill, op. cit.
28 Ibid.
29 Derek Wood, *The Battle of Britain*
30 Vigors, op. cit.
31 *Britain at War* magazine, issue 92, December 2014
32 Ray Holmes, *Sky Spy: From Six Miles High to Hitler's Bunker*
33 Ralph Barker, *Sunday Express*
34 There have been some arguments and discussions about this incident over the years but this is Ray Holmes' own account
35 McKinstry, op. cit.
36 Lewis, op. cit.
37 Todd, op. cit.
38 *Britain at War* magazine, op. cit.

Chapter Four: Rhubarbs, Ramrods and Circuses

1 Robbie Robertson, *Memories: For Connie – Wife and Spitfire*, provided by Erik Mannings, 72 Squadron historian
2 Dundas, op. cit.
3 Mark Hillier, Dieter Sinanan and Gregory Percival, *Westhampnett at War*
4 Ray Wagner and Heinz Nowarra, *German Combat Planes*
5 Lewis, op. cit.
6 Paul Beaver, *Spitfire Evolution*
7 The MkV came in a number of different versions with both wing type and armaments changing. The single term 'MkV' is used throughout the text rather than specify which version
8 Joshua Levine, *Forgotten Voices of the Blitz and Battle for Britain*
9 Wilfrid Duncan Smith, *Spitfire into Battle*
10 Dundas, op. cit.
11 Ibid.
12 Hillier et al, op. cit.
13 Dundas, op. cit.
14 Lewis, op. cit.
15 Robertson, op. cit.
16 Ibid.
17 Ibid.
18 Scott, op. cit.
19 Robertson, op. cit.
20 Harry Strawn, in *To War in a Spitfire: The Diary of an American Spitfire Pilot* by Mark Hillier, Dieter Sinanan and Gregory Percival
21 Ibid.
22 Blyth, op. cit.

Chapter Five: Spitfire Women

1 Lettice Curtis, *The Forgotten Pilots*
2 Jacky Hyams, *The Female Few*
3 Beaver, op. cit.
4 Barnato Walker, op. cit.
5 Hyams, op. cit, and John Nichol interview with Joy Lofthouse
6 E. C. Cheesman, *Brief Glory*
7 Holmes, op. cit.
8 Hyams, op. cit.
9 Ibid.

Chapter Six: Malta

1 Price, op. cit.
2 McKinstry, op. cit.
3 Price, op. cit.
4 Lewis, op. cit.
5 Lord James Douglas-Hamilton, *The Air Battle for Malta*
6 Moulson, op. cit.
7 Price, op. cit.
8 Ibid.
9 Douglas-Hamilton, op. cit.
10 Price, op. cit.
11 Douglas-Hamilton, op. cit.
12 McKinstry, op. cit.
13 Christopher Shores and Clive Williams, *Aces High*
14 Lewis, op. cit.
15 Douglas-Hamilton, op. cit.
16 Ibid.
17 Ibid.
18 Ibid.
19 Price, op. cit.
20 Douglas-Hamilton, op. cit.
21 Ibid.
22 McKinstry, op. cit.
23 Scott, op. cit.
24 Ibid.
25 Laddie Lucas, *Five Up*
26 Douglas-Hamilton, op. cit.
27 Scott, op. cit.
28 McKinstry, op. cit.
29 Lucas, op. cit.

Chapter Seven: Dieppe, August 1942

1 Alan Peart, *From North Africa to the Arakan: The Engrossing Memoir of a WWII Spitfire Ace*, and John Nichol interview
2 Quill, op. cit.
3 Lewis, op. cit.
4 Quill, op. cit.
5 Delve, op. cit.
6 Brian Kingcome, *A Willingness to Die: Memories from Fighter Command*
7 Quill, op. cit.
8 Norman Franks, *The Greatest Air Battle: Dieppe, 19th August 1942*
9 Combined Operations website – www.combinedops.com/Dieppe.htm Operation Jubilee
10 Franks, op. cit.
11 Peart, op. cit.
12 Strawn, op. cit.
13 Ibid.
14 Ibid.
15 Peart, op. cit.
16 Johnnie Johnson, *Wing Leader*
17 Franks, op. cit.
18 Ibid.
19 Ibid.
20 Ibid.
21 Ibid.
22 Ibid.
23 Ibid.

Chapter Eight: North Africa

1 Strawn, op. cit.
2 Peart, op. cit.
3 Robertson, op. cit.
4 Greggs Farish and Michael McCaul, *Algiers to Anzio with 72 and 111 Squadrons*
5 Ibid.
6 Robertson, op. cit.
7 Peart, op. cit.
8 Farish, op. cit.
9 Modern Spitfire pilots think it unlikely the wartime aircrew would have used emergency boost on the ground. But Strawn's own recollections are used here
10 Beaver, op. cit.
11 Farish, op. cit.
12 Dundas, op. cit.

13 Strawn, op. cit.
14 Dundas, op. cit.
15 Ibid.

Chapter Nine: The Relentless Fight in Europe

1 Price, op. cit.
2 Ibid.
3 Ibid.
4 Barnato Walker, op. cit.
5 Alan Paisey, *Duty Hails the Sunrise – An Evader's War: The Story of Terry Kearins – Fighter-Bomber Pilot, Evader, Farmer*
6 Ibid.
7 Beaver, op. cit.
8 Todd, op. cit.
9 There is no mention of Todd's daughter in this account
10 Nigel Tangye's private papers
11 Todd, op. cit.
12 Tangye, op. cit.

Chapter Ten: Italy

1 Tom Hughes, *My Valley, the Clouds!*, provided by Erik Mannings, 72 Squadron historian
2 Farish, op. cit.
3 Hughes, op. cit.
4 Peart, op. cit.
5 Lewis, op. cit.
6 Farish, op. cit.
7 Ibid.
8 Peart, op. cit.
9 Chester Nimitz,and E. B. Potter, *Sea Power*
10 Dundas, op. cit.
11 Charles H. Bogart, *German Remotely Piloted Bombs*
12 Farish, op. cit.
13 Hughes, op. cit.
14 Farish, op. cit.

Chapter Eleven: Spitfires out East

1 Delve, op. cit.
2 Ibid.
3 Peart, op. cit.
4 Ibid.
5 Igor Zlobin, *Spitfires over the Kuban*
6 David Isby, *The Decisive Duel: Spitfire vs 109*

Chapter Twelve: A Foothold in France

1 Barnato Walker, op. cit
2 Hyams, op. cit.
3 French, op. cit.
4 Tony Cooper's account from BBMF Yearbook 2014, provided by Clive Rowley
5 Tangye, op. cit.
6 D-Day Museum, Portsmouth
7 Roddis, op. cit. (John Nichol interview)
8 French, op. cit.
9 McKinstry, op. cit.
10 Delve, op. cit.
11 Lewis, op. cit.
12 Tangye, op. cit.
13 French, op. cit.
14 Barnato Walker, op. cit.

Chapter Thirteen: The Beginning of the End

1 Taylor, op. cit.
2 Wilkinson, op. cit.
3 Dundas, op. cit.
4 Holmes, op. cit.
5 Bird, op. cit.
6 Roddis, op. cit (John Nichol interview)
7 Holmes, op. cit.

Chapter Fourteen: The Last Salute

1 Peart, op. cit.
2 Barnato Walker, op. cit.
3 John Nichol interview with Lady Dundas
4 Ibid.
5 Todd, op. cit.
6 Nigel Tangye, *Facing the Sea*
7 Taylor, op. cit.
8 John Nichol interview and 'Shropshire fighter ace Allan, 94, in Spitfire heaven', *Shropshire Star*, 10 October 2015
9 John Nichol interview and BBC News, 7 May 2015
10 Hillier et al, op. cit.
11 Quill, op. cit.
12 Figures vary from source to source; these are taken from 'Supermarine Spitfire – 40 Years On', published in 1976 as part of a symposium celebrating the fortieth anniversary of the first flight
13 There is no definitive number of Spitfires and Seafires built; numbers vary between 22,000 and 23,000 depending on the source consulted
14 Delve, op. cit.
15 Price, op. cit.
16 Air Marshal Cliff Spink CB CBE FCMI FRAeS, correspondence with John Nichol

BIBLIOGRAPHY

Barnato Walker, Diana, *Spreading my Wings* (Grub Street, 2003)
Beaver, Paul, *Spitfire People* (Evro, 2015)
Beaver, Paul, *Spitfire Evolution* (Beaver Westminster, 2016)
Bird, Brian, *That Was my Life* (Personal Memoir)
Bogart, Charles H., *German Remotely Piloted Bombs* (US Naval Institute Proceedings, 1976)
Brew, Steve, *Blood, Sweat and Valour* (Fonthill, 2012)
Campbell-Begg, Richard and Liddle, Peter, *For Five Shillings a Day: Personal Histories of World War II* (Collins, 2000)
Carter, Eric, *Force Benedict* (Hodder & Stoughton, 2014)
Cawthorne, Nigel, *The Complete Illustrated Encyclopedia of the Spitfire* (Anness Publishing, 2012)
Cheesman, E. C., *Brief Glory* (Air Transport Auxiliary Association, 2011)
Collett, Max, Personal War Diary
Crook, David, *Spitfire Pilot* (Grub Street, 2008)
Curtis, Lettice, *The Forgotten Pilots* (Self-published, 1998)
Deere, Al, *Nine Lives* (Goodall Publications, 2009)
Delve, Ken, *The Story of the Spitfire: An Operational and Combat History* (Greenhill Books, 2007)
Docherty, Tom, *Swift to Battle: No 72 Fighter Squadron RAF in Action* (Pen & Sword, 2009)
Douglas-Hamilton, Lord James, *The Air Battle for Malta* (Mainstream, 1981)
Duncan Smith, Wilfrid, *Spitfire into Battle* (John Murray, 2004)
Dundas, Hugh, *Flying Start: A Fighter Pilot's War Years* (Penguin, 1988)

Farish, Greggs and McCaul, Michael, *Algiers to Anzio with 72 and 111 Squadrons* (Woodfield, 2002)

Franks, Norman, *The Greatest Air Battle: Dieppe, 19th August 1942* (William Kimber, 1979)

French, Ken 'Paddy', *My Early Life* (Eburon Academic, 2013)

Furniss-Roe, Bill, *Believed Safe* (William Kimber, 1987)

Glancey, Jonathan, *Spitfire: The Biography* (Atlantic Books, 2006)

Hillier, Mark, Sinanan, Dieter and Percival, Gregory, *Westhampnett at War* (Yellowman, 2010)

Hillier, Mark, Sinanan, Dieter and Percival, Gregory, *To War in a Spitfire: The Diary of an American Spitfire Pilot* (Yellowman, 2011)

Holmes, Ray, *Sky Spy: From Six Miles High to Hitler's Bunker* (Airlife, 1989)

Hough, Richard and Richards, Denis, *Battle of Britain* (Pen & Sword, 2007)

Hughes, Tom, *My Valley, the Clouds!* (Personal Memoir, 2005)

Hyams, Jacky, *The Female Few* (History Press, 2012)

Isby, David, *The Decisive Duel: Spitfire vs 109* (Little, Brown, 2012)

Johnson, Johnnie, *Wing Leader* (Goodall Publications Ltd, 1990)

Kingcome, Brian, *A Willingness to Die: Memories from Fighter Command* (The History Press, 2006)

Lane, Brian, *Spitfire! The Experiences of a Battle of Britain Fighter Pilot* (Amberley, 2009)

Levine, Joshua, *Forgotten Voices of the Blitz and Battle for Britain* (Ebury, 2007)

Lewis, Jon E., *Spitfire: The Autobiography* (Constable & Robinson, 2010)

Lucas, Laddie, *Five Up* (Wingham, 1991)

McKinstry, Leo, *Spitfire: Portrait of a Legend* (John Murray, 2007)

March, Peter, *The Spitfire Story* (Sutton Publishing, 2006)

Marsden, Barry, *Portraits of Heroes* (Amberley Publishing, 2011)

Moulson, Tom, *The Millionaires' Squadron* (Pen & Sword, 2014)

Myers, Jay (compiled and edited), *Securing the Skies 1940–2015* (RAF Museum, 2015)

Neil, Tom, *The Silver Spitfire* (Weidenfeld & Nicolson, 2013)

Nimitz, Chester and Potter, E. B., *Sea Power* (Prentice Hall, 1960)

Owen, David, *Dogfight: The Supermarine Spitfire and the Messerschmitt BF109* (Pen & Sword, 2015)

Paisey, Alan, *Duty Hails the Sunrise – An Evader's War: The Story of Terry Kearins – Fighter-Bomber Pilot, Evader, Farmer* (Hatherley, 2014)

Peart, Alan, *From North Africa to the Arakan: The Engrossing Memoir of a WWII Spitfire Ace* (Grub Street, 2012)

Price, Alfred, *Spitfire: A Documentary History* (Macdonald and Jane's, 1977)

Quill, Jeffrey, *Spitfire: A Test Pilot's Story* (Arrow Books/Crecy, 1985/1996)

Robertson, Robbie, *Memories: For Connie – Wife and Spitfire* (Personal Memoir, 2007)

Roddis, Joe and Hillier, Mark, *In Support of the Few* (Yellowman, 2013)

Schrader, Helena, *Sisters in Arms* (Pen & Sword, 2006)

Scott, Allan, *Born to Survive* (Ellingham, 2013)

Shores, Christopher and Williams, Clive, *Aces High* (Grub Street, 1994)

Tangye, Nigel, *Teach Yourself to Fly* (Hodder Education, 1938)

Tangye, Nigel, *Facing the Sea* (William Kimber, 1974)

Taylor, Jimmy, *One Flight Too Many* (Greystones, 2012)

Todd, Ann, *The Eighth Veil* (William Kimber, 1980)

Vigors, Tim, *Life's Too Short to Cry* (Grub Street, 2006)

Wagner, Ray and Nowarra, Heinz, *German Combat Planes* (Doubleday, 1971)

Wellum, Geoffrey, *First Light* (Penguin, 2009)

Wilkinson, John, *The Lord Is my Shepherd: An Extraordinary Account of Aerial Combat over Europe During WWII* (Two Geez Co, 2016)

Wood, Derek, *The Battle of Britain* (Bracken, 1990)

Zlobin, Igor, *Spitfires over the Kuban* (Lend-lease.airforce.ru/english/index.htm)

PICTURE CREDITS

Endpapers © Geoff Nutkins, www.aviartnutkins.com

Integrated

p. 3 © Helen Nock
p. 15 © Sarah Quill
p. 35 © Diana Barnato Walker
pp. 38, 94 © Dundas Family Archive
p. 48 © Bernard Brown
p. 58 © Key Publishing
pp. 74, 115, 168 © Mark Hillier
pp. 89, 136 © 1940 Media Ltd
pp. 109, 217, 272, 296 © Erik Mannings
p. 121 © Mary Ellis
p. 127 © Joy Lofthouse
p. 153 © Allan Scott
pp. 163, 189, 307 © Alan Peart
p. 234 © HistoryNetArchives
p. 239 © 41 Squadron Association
p. 251 © Alan Paisey
p. 263 © Getty Images
p. 323 © Jane French
pp. 333, 391 © Tangye Family Archives
p. 335 © Scott Blyth
p. 345 © Barry Perks
p. 354 © C Rosscow Family
p. 360 © Ann Holmes
p. 366 © Chris Bird

Plate Section

1, 2, 17 © Craig Sluman
3, 5, 6 © 1940 Media Ltd
4, 21, 23, 24 © John Nichol
7, 8 © Helen Nock
9 © Claire Hartley
10 © Harald Joergens Photography
11, 18 © Mark Hillier
12, 13, 14 © Scott Blyth
15 © John Dibbs
16 © Barry Perks
19 © Alan Peart
20 © Andy Perkins
22 © Chris Bird
25 © Ann Holmes

See quote by John Nichol
in obituary of Harry Irons, DFC
RAF rear gunner on Halifax & Lancaster
Bombers, who survived 90 bombing missions
The Times. Sat Nov 24 2018

INDEX

Page numbers in italic type refer to photographs.

SH B
BL SH J
GURGAON II PUNJAB